A

RYUKYU ISLANDS

Formosa Strait

■Taipei

TAIWAN

owloon

G KONG

MW01079349

LUZON

PHILIPPINES

■Manila

MINDORO

PANAY

CEBU LEYTE

PALAWAN   NEGROS

Sulu

Sea

MINDANAO

■Kota Kinabalu

SABAH

Celebes Sea

P A C I F I C

O C E A N

Molucca Sea

HALMAHERA

Straits of Makassar

SULAWESI

BURU

SERAM

Banda

Sea

IRIAN JAYA

PAPUA
NEW
GUINEA

UMBAWA FLORES

Arafura

SUMBA   EAST TIMOR   *Sea*

| 0 | 200 | 400 | 600 | 800 | 1000 km |

SOUTHEAST ASIAN AFFAIRS 2000

The **Institute of Southeast Asian Studies** was established as an autonomous organization in 1968. It is a regional research centre for scholars and other specialists concerned with modern Southeast Asia, particularly the many-faceted problems of stability and security, economic development, and political and social change.

The Institute's research programmes are the Regional Economic Studies (RES, including ASEAN and APEC), Regional Strategic and Political Studies (RSPS), and Regional Social and Cultural Studies (RSCS).

The Institute is governed by a twenty-two-member Board of Trustees comprising nominees from the Singapore Government, the National University of Singapore, the various Chambers of Commerce, and professional and civic organizations. A ten-man Executive Committee oversees day-to-day operations; it is chaired by the Director, the Institute's chief academic and administrative officer.

SOUTHEAST ASIAN AFFAIRS 2000
EDITORIAL COMMITTEE

Chairperson	*Chia Siow Yue*
Editor	*Daljit Singh*
Production Editor	*Tan Kim Keow*

SOUTHEAST ASIAN AFFAIRS 2000

 INSTITUTE OF SOUTHEAST ASIAN STUDIES

Cataloguing in Publication Data

Southeast Asian affairs.
1974–
Annual
1.   Asia, Southeastern.
I.   Institute of Southeast Asian Studies.
DS501 S72A

ISSN 0377-5437
ISBN 981-230-095-3 (softcover)
ISBN 981-230-096-1 (hardcover)

Published by
Institute of Southeast Asian Studies
30 Heng Mui Keng Terrace
Pasir Panjang
Singapore 119614

Internet e-mail: publish@iseas.edu.sg
Website: http://www.iseas.edu.sg/pub.html

Typeset by International Typesetters Pte Ltd.

Printed in Singapore by Prime Packaging Industries Pte Ltd

FOREWORD

We are pleased to present the twenty-seventh issue of *Southeast Asian Affairs*, a comprehensive annual review of political and economic trends and developments in Southeast Asia.

Designed to be easily readable yet in-depth, informative and analytical, the annual has come to be a standard reference for scholars, policy-makers, private sector executives, and journalists, who seek to understand and keep up-to-date on the dynamics of Southeast Asian developments.

The year 1999 saw the economies of Southeast Asia recovering from the regional crisis and the focus of attention shifting to the sustainability of the recoveries. However, Indonesia still faced serious challenges.

I take this opportunity to thank the authors who have contributed to this publication. While the Institute encourages the statement of all points of view in the publication, the authors alone are responsible for the facts and opinions expressed in their articles. Their contributions and interpretations do not necessarily reflect the views of the Institute.

Chia Siow Yue
Director
Institute of Southeast Asian Studies

April 2000

CONTENTS

INTRODUCTION

The big story in Southeast Asia in 1999 was the economic recovery, the speed and strength of which, like the severity of the 1998 downturn, caught many by surprise. Malaysia and Thailand, two of the three countries most affected by the crisis saw gross domestic product (GDP) growth rates of 5.4 and 4.1 per cent, respectively. Thailand recovered while following prescriptions of the International Monetary Fund (IMF), Malaysia behind the shelter of capital controls. The sustainability of these two recoveries and the merits and pitfalls of resort to capital controls were matters of considerable debate during the year.

However, equally significant were developments in Indonesia. The country's economy barely grew in 1999 after declining 13.7 per cent in 1998, though growth for 2000 was projected at 3–4 per cent. The new government of President Abdurrahman Wahid was making a start in tackling the huge challenges facing the country. The restructuring of the battered financial sector still had a long way to go, and total public debt could rise to 145 per cent of the GDP.

1999 saw East Timor deciding to break away from Indonesia in a referendum. The violence perpetrated by Indonesia-backed militias drew much adverse publicity in the world's media. When Indonesia agreed to international humanitarian intervention, Philippines, Thailand, Singapore, and Malaysia made contributions.

With the formal admission of Cambodia as the tenth member, ASEAN finally attained its goal of being a ten-nation Association. But there were also unprecedented doubts about the credibility of the Association, a problem that it has sought to address, starting with the Hanoi summit of December 1998. Bilateral relations between some member countries, though better than in 1998, remained problematic.

Apart from the developments in East Timor and the uncertainties posed by Indonesia, the regional security environment remained relatively benign. Tensions in the Spratly Islands increased somewhat, though there was no danger of any major conflict. In the broader East Asian region, Sino-U.S. relations were volatile, but ended the year on a better note. Developments relating to Taiwan continued to be a potential danger to the U.S.-China relationship.

Southeast Asian Affairs 2000 addresses these issues from a regional perspective in the first four chapters. The rest of the volume consists of ten country surveys and five special theme articles, of which three deal with the economies of the three countries most affected by the regional crisis, namely, Indonesia, Malaysia, and Thailand.

Daljit Singh
Editor
Southeast Asian Affairs 2000

THE REGION

SOUTHEAST ASIA IN 1999
A False Dawn?

Daljit Singh

If 1998 was the year of economic crisis, 1999 was the year of recovery. The pervasive gloom of 1998 receded somewhat, but Southeast Asia still, at best, presented a mixed picture. Economic recovery among the older members of the Association of Southeast Asian Nations (ASEAN) generated a palpable sense of optimism. Even Indonesia, with its battered economy, could inspire some hope after it held a relatively peaceful and fair parliamentary election, followed by a presidential election which resulted in the establishment of a democratic government with the moral and political legitimacy to govern. But there was also tragedy, followed by humanitarian intervention in East Timor and, for Indonesia, enormous uncertainties remained. Elsewhere, the reforms needed to deal with the weaknesses in state and corporate governance which the crisis had highlighted were only partially addressed, raising doubts about the sustainability of the recoveries. Conditions in Laos, Myanmar, and Vietnam were worse than in 1998. The durability of the new democracy in Indonesia was not assured, while in the rest of Southeast Asia, progress towards more tolerant, enlightened, and democratic societies was patchy, mixed with stassis, even regression.

ASEAN sought to overcome a crisis of credibility. The broader Asia-Pacific strategic environment remained relatively benign. There were, however, more signs of Sino-American competition. China's claims and posture in the South China Sea remained a troubling long-term strategic lever against Southeast Asia.

The Association of Southeast Asian Nations

A Question of Credibility

> ASEAN has become a feeble managing vehicle [of the Southeast Asian regional order] ... ASEAN has been diminished in international standing and, in important respects, is not the same entity that was set up in 1967 based on a set of common understandings about reconciliation among governments of convergent political outlooks. (Michael Leifer)[1]

DALJIT SINGH is a Senior Research Fellow at the Institute of Southeast Asian Studies, Singapore.

> ASEAN has overextended itself — with members so vastly different as Myanmar and Singapore it has lost credibility, and its ability to provide any semblance of security across maritime Southeast Asia has been undermined. (Paul Dibb)[2]

> ASEAN's inability to deal with the challenges posed by intransigent regimes in Myanmar and Cambodia was mirrored by its ineffectiveness in dealing with transnational issues ... ASEAN disarray throughout the year was the product of many factors ... (Carlyle A. Thayer)[3]

The above are but three examples of sceptical assessments of ASEAN. Regional governments, or at least some of them, did acknowledge that the Association had a credibility problem. At the ASEAN Ministerial Meeting (AMM) in Singapore in July, Prime Minister Goh Chok Tong stated:

> ... whether or not criticisms that have been levelled at ASEAN are deserved, they exist. This is a fact we must deal with, because perceptions, even inaccurate perceptions, can define political reality.

Foreign Minister Jayakumar said: "... the essential challenge that ASEAN faces is one of credibility. But I can state with confidence that we have taken a firm step forward in beginning a process of renewal." Earlier, at the Hanoi summit in December 1998, Thai Prime Minister Chuan Leekpai had observed that the crisis had "raised doubts and questions about whether ASEAN can regain its vibrancy and vitality. Some have gone so far as to write us off", while Malaysian Prime Minister Mahathir had noted that the crisis had "created the impression of an ASEAN in disarray".

Critics have pointed to a number of events or ASEAN's response to them which diminished ASEAN's credibility. They include the admission of Myanmar into the Association in 1996; the haze over Indonesia, Malaysia, Brunei, and Singapore in 1997 caused by fires in Indonesia; Hun Sen's coup in Cambodia in 1997 which overturned the power-sharing arrangements in the coalition government sanctioned earlier by the United Nations Transitional Authority in Cambodia (UNTAC); the regional economic crisis; the deterioration of bilateral relations between some ASEAN member countries in 1998; and developments in East Timor in 1999.

However, a blanket censure of ASEAN's behaviour in relation to these developments would be unfair because ASEAN's performance was in fact a mixed one. It would have been unrealistic, for instance, to expect ASEAN to prevent or resolve the regional economic crisis. It was caused by a combination of external factors like massive short-term capital flows and domestic weaknesses in individual ASEAN countries, in relation to both of which there was little that ASEAN as an organization could do. As ASEAN Secretary-General Rudolfo Severino has said, blaming ASEAN for failure to deal with the crisis is "something akin to blaming the OAS [Organization of American States] for the financial crisis in Mexico some years ago, or for the forest fires in Brazil, or the OAU [Organization of African Unity] for Africa's recent sorrows".[4] Yet, just as in the past the economic success of its members had boosted ASEAN's credibility, now the economic crisis, by exposing the many shortcomings in state and corporate governance, hurt the Association's image. It also weakened ASEAN by weakening its member countries, especially Indonesia which had been regarded as "the first among equals" in the Association.

On the haze and on Cambodia, ASEAN did more than what it is credited for. The solution to the regional haze problem depended very much on Indonesia's capacity and willingness to stop the clearance of plantation and forest land by burning. Still, ASEAN had a Co-operation Plan on Transboundary Pollution since 1995. The 1997 haze led to much more frequent consultations on measures to address the problem. In frank discussions, officials have touched on sensitive areas like Indonesia's land and forestry use policies.

In response to the 1997 coup in Cambodia engineered by Hun Sen, ASEAN postponed Cambodia's admission into the Association, originally scheduled for July 1997, and established a task force of three ASEAN foreign ministers to help achieve a settlement of the problem. ASEAN urged Hun Sen to return to the power-sharing arrangements stipulated under the 1991 Paris Accords and the ASEAN Post-Ministerial Conference (PMC) supported ASEAN's position. Thus, although Japan played an important role, ASEAN was pro-active in seeking a solution.

ASEAN's credibility in the West and among civil society groups in ASEAN countries was undoubtedly affected by the admission of Myanmar into the Association in 1996. ASEAN may have underestimated how this event would affect perceptions of the Association, especially when it was followed in quick order by the economic crisis and its political fall-out, both of which weakened ASEAN. By 1999, ASEAN's policy of "constructive engagement" with Yangon had not produced any significant result. The coming of the economic crisis seemed to make the prospect of change even more remote. It made the generals in Myanmar feel more insecure because of the significant indirect economic impact of the crisis on Myanmar and the dark political lessons they would have likely drawn from the fate of the Soeharto regime.

The importance of bilateral relations between ASEAN members for the Association's strength and credibility tended to be obscured by bigger and more dramatic events like the regional crisis. Yet in 1998 their deterioration between several states was as important a factor as any other in weakening ASEAN and contributing to an impression of disarray. The difficulties in bilateral relations were brought about partly by the political aftershocks of the Asian crisis. Indonesian President Habibie's and Philippine President Estrada's support for former Deputy Prime Minister Anwar Ibrahim soured these two countries' relations with Malaysia. A number of issues in Singapore-Malaysia relations in 1998 brought the relationship to a low point not seen for many years. They included the relocation of Malaysian CIQ (Customs, Immigration, and Quarantine) facilities in Singapore for railway services, alleged violations of Malaysian airspace by Singapore military aircraft and the publication of

Senior Minister Lee's memoirs. Relations between Singapore and the Habibie administration in Jakarta were also testy.

In 1999, bilateral relations between the older members improved from the lows of 1998, but they remained problematic. The CLOB (Central Limit Order Book) International issue continued to contribute to Singapore-Malaysia tensions while other outstanding issues like the relocation of Malaysian CIQ facilities remained unresolved. Relations between Malaysia and the Philippines were adversely affected again by Malaysia's occupation of Investigator Shoal in the Spratlys, also claimed by the Philippines. Myanmar-Thailand relations deteriorated seriously over the hostage crisis involving the Myanmar embassy in Bangkok.

Finally, ASEAN could not have wagered for a more difficult test for its principle of non-intervention in the internal affairs of a member state than the unleashing of death and destruction in East Timor by Indonesia-backed militias.[5] Indonesia's actions in East Timor had always been a sensitive matter in ASEAN, and whatever each country privately felt about the events of 1999, it proved difficult, if not impossible, at least initially, for ASEAN as an organization or for individual members to express public outrage or to urge humanitarian intervention (though some civil society groups did). After Indonesia yielded to international pressure for humanitarian intervention, Philippines, Thailand, Singapore, and Malaysia contributed to the Australian-led International Force for East Timor (INTERFET) and later to the U.N. Transitional Authority in East Timor (UNTAET). ASEAN's image was not helped by Dr Mahathir's public remarks questioning the validity of the referendum in East Timor well after its outcome.

"Enhanced Interraction"
The principle of non-intervention became a focus of some attention when Thai Foreign Minister Surin Pitsuwan said in an address in June 1998 that ASEAN countries should be prepared to "intervene" in domestic affairs "in the form of peer pressure or friendly advice, when a matter of domestic concern poses a threat to regional stability".[6] He dubbed this "constructive intervention". However, a month later, at the AMM in Singapore, to remove the impression that he was suggesting a modification of the principle of non-intervention, he renamed the idea "flexible engagement". In the same speech he made it clear that ASEAN must adhere to the principle of non-intervention but at the same time find a way to deal with new problems and challenges which damage ASEAN's credibility if left unaddressed: "The principle of non-intervention is not the real issue ... the real issue is how we can work together in dealing with the new challenges of a new millennium." "Flexible engagement" was discussed at the 1998 AMM in Manila. It met opposition from most members, with only the Philippines siding Thailand. The international media publicity to this division added to the impression of an ASEAN in disarray.

However, the Meeting decided, as a compromise, to have "enhanced interaction" in the future. "Enhanced interaction" was not defined, but presumably it meant more frank and frequent exchanges of views in private. It was tried at the next Ministerial Meeting in Singapore in July 1999, at the "Sentosa Retreat", out of sight of the media. The Joint Communiqué at the end of the AMM stated that at the Retreat the foreign ministers held "frank and wide-ranging discussions" and described the Retreat as "part of a continuous process of serious re-examination of the longer term issues facing ASEAN". The chairman of the meeting, Singapore Foreign Minister S. Jayakumar, described the session as "heart-to-heart brainstorming". He added:

> I have never come across discussions with such candour. The Foreign Ministers spoke of views which they told me they would not have expressed, if not for the retreat.[7]

Subjects discussed ranged from civil society, human rights, democracy, to the future of ASEAN and of the ARF. A frank exchange of views in private at annual retreats on domestic issues which can have adverse impact on neighbours or on the credibility of ASEAN would constitute progress in the quality of ASEAN discussions, but critics doubted it would have any effect on policies.

All members regard the retention of the principle of non-intervention as essential. What is at issue is the need for some adjustments to take account of changed circumstances. Non-intervention has after all been a governing principle in relations between states since Westphalia in the seventeenth century. However, it has been under review internationally in recent years so that it can be made relevant to changes in international society.

Yet it would be wrong to assume that ASEAN countries have never at all "interfered" in each other's affairs. Various instances can be cited of such "intervention" in the past — leaders, usually in private, took up domestic issues in other member countries, especially when such issues could have adverse effects on neighbours or on the region, and there have also been attempts to mediate or mitigate strained bilateral relations between members.[8] Such "interventions", made in the "ASEAN Way" have sometimes been successful. On the other hand, there is no way of compelling a country to change its behaviour if it does not want to. There is no prior political price for membership of the Association nor political or economic sanctions for unacceptable behaviour.

AFTA, and Engaging the Outside World

ASEAN's problems of the past few years have not necessarily impacted adversely upon the Association's economic co-operation schemes. Indeed, the targets for the implementation of the ASEAN Free Trade Area (AFTA) have been brought forward — to 2002 for the six older members, 2003 for Vietnam, 2005 for Laos and Myanmar, and 2010 for Cambodia. This means that by these dates member countries will have tariff lines of only 0–5 per cent on their manufactured products. In fact, by the beginning of the year 2000, 90 per cent of goods traded in ASEAN would have tariffs of less than 5 per cent and some would have no tariffs at all. Further, the original six members agreed to bring tariffs for all products down to zero by 2010, ten years ahead of the APEC (Asia-Pacific Economic Co-operation) developing country target of 2020. Agreements were also reached to begin liberalization of trade in unprocessed agriculture products and in services such as finance, transport, telecommunications, and tourism. Member countries were also working towards an ASEAN Investment Area.

ASEAN also continued to expand its engagement with the outside world, though the admission of Myanmar still affected dialogue with the European Union (EU). The Association was more actively engaged with its northeast Asian neighbours through the ASEAN+3 arrangement (see below). It was working on free trade with Australia and New Zealand — the two sides agreed in 1999 to do a study on the feasibility of establishing a free trade area by the year 2010. ASEAN continued to have economic and other discussions with the EU in the Asia-Europe Meeting (ASEM) process, and, together with Australia and New Zealand, was embarking upon dialogue with Latin America. And the ASEAN Regional Forum (ARF) in which ASEAN plays the leading role, maintained its security dialogue and confidence-building activities, though consensus was still not forthcoming on a proposal to embark on preventive diplomacy.

However, critics have argued that reductions of tariffs on goods is not enough. ASEAN has made a start but still has a long way to go to remove non-tariff barriers on goods, services, and investments. They also point to the exceptions lists for tariff reductions for almost every country, and Malaysia's moves in 1999 to protect its automobile industry. As for ASEAN's engagement with the outside world, the role and effectiveness of the ARF remained a subject of debate while, to the outside observer, the prospects of East Asian regionalism were at best uncertain.

ASEAN's Dependence on Outside Support

ASEAN has claimed that the primary responsibility for the regional order in Southeast Asia rests with the Association and its members rather than with outside powers. Professor Jayakumar was only echoing what has been stated many times before when he said, welcoming Cambodia's formal admission to the Association: "... we want a Southeast Asia whose future will be determined by Southeast Asians not by others in faraway capitals." Yet, in reality the region has relied on the United States, Japan, and the EU for its economic and security well-being. It was, therefore, no surprise that the economic crisis required bailout by the International Monetary Fund (IMF) for two of the ASEAN member countries, and major aid and assistance from outside, especially Japan.

Although ASEAN member countries have a combined population of over 500 million, their combined economic and military power and potential is small in relation to the major powers. In 1996, before the regional economic crisis, the combined gross domestic product (GDP) of the ten countries that now constitute ASEAN was no more than the combined GDP of South Korea (with a population of 45 million) and Taiwan (21 million people). Further, ASEAN's combined economic or military power cannot be harnessed for a common objective because it is not a supranational organization, nor a military alliance but rather a loose co-operative endeavour of ten independent states that jealously guard their sovereignty.

To compensate for these limitations, ASEAN has had to rely on outside support. During the Cold War it was able to achieve its external successes, for instance, on Cambodia and the Vietnamese boat people, not only because a common fear of communism enabled the then five or six countries to get their act together, but, equally important, because of support of the West, and in the case of the Cambodian issue, also of China. Generally, the West and Japan supported ASEAN in the context of their Cold War strategy because of the pro-Western and anti-communist orientation of ASEAN member governments. After the Cold War the very rapid growth of the ASEAN economies during the 1990s and ASEAN's initiatives to establish AFTA and the ARF added to the Association's credibility, so much so that it almost began to believe that its successes were achieved all on its own steam.

ASEAN has been both substance and smoke and mirrors, each reinforcing the other. In certain respects it achieved more than what its own power endowments would have led one to suspect, making it appear larger than itself. The whole superstructure of dialogue partnerships and post-ministerial conferences, and later the ARF and ASEM contributed to the sense of political largeness, even clout, which was in part an exercise in skilful political guile. It worked well during the Cold War because of a mixture of adroit diplomacy and external support, and because the geographical territory of the then members of the Association was not subjected to the test of a major external military attack (it escaped this mainly because others, most notably the United States, maintained the balance of power in the region).

After the Cold War, the political and strategic concerns of the United States and the West generally, in relation to Southeast Asia, changed. Relatively higher priority was accorded to economic issues and to human rights and democratization. It was against this backdrop that ASEAN's complexion changed to one of greater political conservatism and less cohesiveness with its expansion to ASEAN-10, making it more difficult for it to move the region in the direction of more political openness and greater respect for human rights. The ASEAN-6 of Sultan Bolkiah, Soeharto, Mahathir, Ramos, Goh Chok Tong, and Chuan Leekpai was qualitatively different from the ASEAN-10 which saw the addition of Hun Sen, the politburo chiefs of Vietnam and Laos, and the head of the Myanmar junta. Further, in so far as the West's and Japan's strategic interests began gradually to focus more on China, the expanded ASEAN, with widely different political and security priorities of members, was not seen as an effective vehicle for a common approach to the People's Republic of China (PRC).

One effect of the economic crisis was a keener appreciation among policy

élites of ASEAN member states, or at least of those member states that have
been the principal drivers of the Association, of ASEAN's limitations. The
crisis had also demonstrated that the IMF, based in Washington, did not react
as fast in dealing with the Asian crisis as it did with the Mexican crisis in 1994.
One reason for this was that the latter impinged much more directly and
urgently on the national interests of the United States than the Thai crisis of
July 1997 did. Yet a Japanese-ASEAN proposal made in September 1999 for an
Asian Monetary Fund which could respond more speedily, and with more
capital, to Asian crises was torpedoed by the United States. Furthermore, any
reform of the international financial system, including some monitoring of
the activities of hedge funds, a topic which aroused much favourable interest
in Southeast Asia in the wake of the crisis, was seen to be unlikely to be
implemented because it was not in the interests of the leading Western powers, especially the United States, to do so.

ASEAN+3

It was such realities that gave push to the idea of an East Asian regionalism
based upon the ASEAN+3 forum which first met at the second ASEAN Informal Summit in Kuala Lumpur in 1997 soon after the financial cyclone hit the
region, although it had already constituted the Asian half (but without Cambodia, Myanmar, and Laos) of the ASEM process from a few years earlier.

If ASEAN by itself was not seen as having the necessary critical mass to
achieve better financial and economic security in a world of huge daily trans-
continental flows of speculative funds, why not team up with the larger economies of Northeast Asia? East Asian regionalism, if one went by the actions and
rhetoric of its proponents, was more than just an idea by 1999. ASEAN Secretary-
General Rudolf C. Severino described the third ASEAN+3 summit in Manila
in late November 1999 as "part of a general convergence of purpose in East
Asia, a process that has been building up". He went on to say:

> ... the developing forum may serve to diffuse any potential rivalries
> among the stronger countries of East Asia ... synergies in the economies
> may strengthen the economic muscle of the region. Closer financial
> cooperation ... could give the region a greater voice in international
> financial decisions that is not possible for ASEAN alone.[9]

There was talk of expanding AFTA to an East Asian Free Trade Area to be
established through a bilateral building block approach, for example, a Japan–
South Korea free trade area, a Japan-Singapore one, and so forth.[10]

The finance ministers of the thirteen countries met for the first time in
Manila in April 1999. Their deputies and heads of central banks had already
been meeting to discuss co-operation in relation to economic recovery and
prevention of future crises and develop Asia's thinking on the reform of the
international financial system. Just before the summit in Manila, senior officials of the thirteen countries met for the first time, and this was expected to

be repeated at future summits. Foreign ministers were to met in the margins of the ASEAN-PMC meetings in Bangkok in the year 2000 to review progress in the implementation of the Joint Statement on East Asia Co-operation issued at the end of the ASEAN+3 meeting in Manila. And trade ministers of the ten East Asian countries were to meet for consultations in May 2000 in Myanmar, immediately following the annual retreat of the ASEAN economic ministers. An East Asian Vision Group, headed by former South Korean Foreign Minister Han Sung Joo, will present its recommendations on East Asian co-operation at the 7th ASEAN Summit in Brunei in 2001.

A joint statement on East Asia Co-operation issued at the Manila Summit mentions co-operation not just in economic and social fields but also in "the political-security area" in relation to which the heads of state/government agreed to "continuing dialogue, coordination, and cooperation to increase mutual understanding and trust towards forging lasting peace and stability in East Asia". The leaders also agreed to "intensify coordination and coopera- tion" in various international and regional fora such as the United Nations, the World Trade Organization (WTO), APEC, ASEM, and the ARF as well as in regional and international financial institutions.

Thus the much-maligned East Asian Economic Caucus (EAEC) of the early 1990s was making a comeback, in reality if not in name, and with the addition of an openly articulated political and security dimension. Yet, strangely, the world hardly seemed to notice. Any significant jelling of an East Asian commu- nity could have major implications for U.S. interests and role in the western Pacific. But there has hardly been a protest, at least not in public, from Wash- ington, which had thundered against the EAEC in the early 1990s for seeking to divide the Pacific and exclude the United States. The reasons for this were not clear. Perhaps the United States felt assured that the motives behind the enterprise were not anti-American, especially since most East Asian countries want to see a continuation of the forward American military presence, or perhaps, also, the United States did not think the scheme would go far be- cause of differences between China and Japan.

Nor were there concerns in Southeast Asia that movement towards East Asian regionalism could affect security ties with the United States. For one thing, unlike the early 1990s, there was now greater confidence that the United States would stay in East Asia and the western Pacific for its own interests. If in the early 1990s the United States seemed like a policeman tired of his beat after the collapse of its principal menace and with severe domestic budgetary and social problems to attend to, by 1999 it looked like a revitalized colossus straddling the globe, and not always sensitive to the interests of others. Ironi- cally, different elements in the perception of the United States — that it was indispensable, perhaps too powerful, and that its forward military deployments in East Asia could more or less be taken for granted — seemed to be making it easier to think in terms of an East Asian community in the wake of the humbling regional economic crisis.

Yet any assumption that a robust forward U.S. presence could now be taken for granted may prove to be misplaced in the longer term. The degree of importance accorded to Asia in Washington and how best to secure U.S. interests there, are likely to continue to be a dynamic, not a static, process subject to debate in the context of changes in East Asia, changes in the potential military and political costs of forward deployments, and the vagaries of congressional and domestic opinion. How East Asians engage the United States, how they relate to China, and what they say and do in these contexts will be important.

Loose East Asian co-operation would not subject ASEAN to difficult choices, if it can leverage on the larger economies while retaining a credible U.S. military presence for maintaining the balance of power. However, an East Asian regionalism which promises to be really effective could. It may then prove difficult to keep the United States militarily engaged as a hedge against an eventual dominant Chinese role, because, unlike the situation in western Europe, the U.S. presence would not be welcome to a major East Asian player, namely, China.

It Is the Only One That There Is

ASEAN will live on because it is the only vehicle that gives Southeast Asia a collective voice and some bargaining power *vis-à-vis* the great powers. With the formal admission of Cambodia, 1999 finally saw all countries of Southeast Asia as members of the Association. There was also, for the first time, the prospect of a eleventh member, East Timor, in the near future.

The Association was taking some steps to deal with the credibility problem. A Plan of Action was adopted at the ASEAN Summit in Hanoi in December 1998 stipulating a broad range of actions, particularly in the economic and financial areas, for implementation in six years (1999–2004). In the domain of peace and security, the Hanoi Action Plan calls for the formulation of draft rules of procedure for the operation of the High Council as envisioned in the Treaty of Amity and Co-operation and draws attention to the importance of resolving border disputes between members. At the 1999 Manila Informal Summit an agreement in principle was reached to set up a permanent ministerial troika to address issues of peace and stability. These two moves — in relation to the High Council and the troika — suggest renewed attention to bilateral and other intra-regional problems. These are moves in the right direction, provided they can be implemented in a meaningful way. If, for instance, the High Council is given powers to resolve disputes, ASEAN would have taken a significant step forward. Inter-state peace between members, maintained so far, cannot be taken for granted. It will have to be continually worked at, in view of the disputes which remain unresolved and the incomplete socialization of some new members in the habit of non-use of force.

However, ASEAN faces a variety of challenges, including dealing with China and the United States. The challenges call for greater unity of purpose. If this cannot be achieved with the present ten-member ASEAN, some other way may have to be explored to move ahead, for example, through *ad hoc* "coalitions of the willing" prepared to move forward on specific issues even if some members are reluctant to do so. On 20 October 1999, meeting in Vientiane a month before the ASEAN Informal Summit in Manila, the leaders of Vietnam, Laos, and Cambodia "stressed the need to further strengthen and develop their friendly cooperation and traditional solidarity".[11] It was a reminder of the political diversity within the Association which could make unity of purpose difficult on some important issues.

Strategic and Security Developments
Indonesia continued to pose the single biggest uncertainty to the politics and security of Southeast Asia, especially to its maritime part with its strategically important sealanes. A fragmentation of the country would have far-reaching consequences, but there was no immediate danger of this happening as 1999 drew to a close. In the absence of international support, the separatist forces in Acheh were unlikely to succeed so long as there was a functioning government at the centre, in Jakarta, which continued to have the support of the main political groups in the country. But if the centre does not hold, fragmentation will become more likely.

The broader East Asian security environment was relatively benign in 1999, despite continuing uncertainties about the Korean peninsula (although Pyongyang agreed not to test-fire another ballistic missile), Taiwan, and the implications of the pending U.S. decisions on Theater Missile Defense in northeast Asia. The deteriorating relationship over Kashmir between nuclear-armed India and Pakistan, while not impacting directly on Southeast Asia, was nevertheless a source of unease in view of Southeast Asia's growing links with an emerging Indian economy, and the geopolitical connections between the two regions.

U.S.-China Relations
The East Asian security environment is determined principally by the triangular U.S.-China-Japan relationship, and especially the key U.S.-China one. The latter relationship is a source of much longer term uncertainty for East Asia, given the strategic rivalry between the two powers and their different visions of a stable East Asia, for the Americans one based on the existing bilateral U.S. alliances with five regional countries, for China without those alliances.[12]

The year 1999 saw U.S.-China relations on a roller coaster ride from the lows in the aftermath of the American bombing of the Chinese embassy in Belgrade in April to a more accommodating mutual stance later in the year, as highlighted in the agreement on China's entry into the WTO and the decision to resume military-to-military contacts. The WTO agreement was a historic one, reflecting a recognition on the part of China that further reform was critical for China's longer-term economic health and stability, and hence for becoming a more complete great power, notwithstanding the risks to Communist Party rule that it might entail.[13] On the American side, the agreement reflected not just the importance of the Chinese market for American goods and services, but more important, an American decision to continue to engage China and bind it to a rule-based international regime. The agreement elicited favourable reactions in Southeast Asia both for the promise of better business opportunities from China's WTO membership and for its broader strategic import.

In the interest of this crucial bilateral relationship, the U.S. was trying, through quiet diplomacy, to manage the Taiwan issue in the run-up to the presidential election there following President Lee Teng Hui's controversial statement to a German radio station that Taiwan-China relations should be viewed as state-to-state relations, which infuriated China. Given the high priority China accords to its economic development and modernization programme, it was unlikely to want war with Taiwan or confrontation with the United States. So, while a military crisis in the Taiwan Straits looked unlikely as 1999 drew to a close, provocative acts by Taiwan or miscalculation by China, which could bring about such a crisis, with incalculable consequences, could not be entirely ruled out.

U.S. Presence

The robust U.S. military presence in the western Pacific remained in place, welcomed by most countries. During 1999 the Japanese Diet endorsed the new operational guidelines under the U.S.-Japan Mutual Security Treaty, which have strengthened the alliance, notwithstanding Japan's decision to acquire its own military intelligence satellites after North Korea's launch of a ballistic missile over Japan in August 1998. Earlier, the United States and South Korea had publicly agreed that U.S. forces would remain in Korea even after reunification.[14] A joint U.S.-Australia task force was to be set up to review the U.S.-Australia security alliance to optimize its ability to meet the new challenges for the Asia-Pacific region.[15] A Visiting Forces Agreement with the Philippines was concluded, paving the way for the first military exercise, scheduled for 2000, between the two countries for some years. Manila's anxieties over China and its actions in the South China Sea were clearly a factor behind this development. Meanwhile the "places not bases" arrangements with non-alliance countries assisted the U.S. presence. In this context, it had been announced in 1998 by the Singapore Defence Minister that U.S. aircraft carriers would have access to berths at Singapore's new Changi naval base.

The United States did not acquit itself well in the early phases of the regional economic crisis. When the IMF rescue package for Thailand was being prepared in 1997, the State Department view that the United States should contribute to the package was ignored by the administration, causing Thailand, an ally of long standing, to feel that the United States did not care about its severe financial plight. Subsequently, in 1998, the United States sought to make amends through high-level visits to regional countries and contributed US$8 billion to the rescue packages for Indonesia and South Korea. Its open markets and booming economy also helped Asian recovery.

On the whole, so far there has been surprisingly little negative political fall-out for the United States from the regional crisis. The fears in some quarters that the political and social upheavals from the crisis would see a surge in anti-Americanism did not materialize. In the Southeast Asian countries most affected by the crisis — Indonesia, Malaysia, and Thailand — the public was aware enough of domestic failings not to be swayed by the argument that the crisis was caused mostly by forces originating from the United States. On the other hand, the crisis and its political consequences probably increased fears of globalization among the ruling circles in Vietnam, Laos, and Myanmar.

One casualty of the fall-out from the Asian crisis was the Australia-Indonesia Security Agreement dating from 1995. The Habibie government cancelled the agreement in 1999 because of unhappiness about Australia's conduct in relation to East Timor. In the region as a whole, Australia came out as being rather insensitive and high-handed, arousing ambivalent feelings — appreciation for its timely humanitarian intervention in East Timor and regret about its perceived arrogance.

Whither Co-operative Security?

As U.S. alliances were being strengthened and China was modernizing its military forces, where was co-operative security heading? Not very far if one assesses it by the yardstick of ability to resolve security problems. The twenty-two-member ARF, the main multilateral co-operative security mechanism in the region, would not be in a position for a long time, if ever, to undertake effective conflict resolution in the region, given the position of some members that this should be attempted only by the countries directly involved in a conflict, and preferably bilaterally.

Yet, if assessed by softer criteria, the ARF was serving a useful purpose in building political and security dialogue and confidence between the states of the Asia-Pacific. It was noted in the chairman's statement issued at the end of the sixth meeting of the ARF in Singapore in July 1999 that discussions had become more frank over the years. There has also been increasing involvement of senior defence and military officials in the ARF process. Senior defence officials have met by themselves over lunch on the side of the ARF meeting and had useful exchanges, a practice that would be continued at future ARF meetings. The Support Group on Confidence-Building Measures (CBMs) and the other inter-sessional groups have continued with their work. However, the ARF in 1999 still had not been able to move to the second stage of its agreed road map, that is, preventive diplomacy, because of China's opposition. ASEAN was tasked to prepare a paper on the concept and principles of preventive diplomacy for discussion among ARF members at the next meeting in the 2000.

It is easy to be dismissive of the value of co-operative security in the Asia-Pacific. After all, it is unable, at least at present, to prevent or resolve conflict. Critics also contend that progress has been held up by China. One analyst, for example, has said: "... the important proviso that dialogue would 'move at a pace comfortable to all participants' has given China a virtual right of veto over progress from stage to stage."[16] However, the importance of dialogue, confidence-building, and security institution building in a region conspicuous by the paucity of such features should not be underestimated. While China has not so far been prepared to move to the stage of preventive diplomacy, it has readily embraced the ARF's confidence-building agenda, which is a success for the ARF, given China's suspicions about the organization when it was first set up.

It is also easy to exaggerate the importance of co-operative security as liberals are sometimes wont to do. When the ARF was set up in 1993/94 most countries regarded the bilateral treaties of the United States with five regional countries, and especially that with Japan, as the fundamental bedrock of security in the Asia-Pacific. The ARF was only to supplement them. If one purpose of the ARF was to engage China, it was also to keep the U.S. engaged as an indispensable component of the East Asian balance. These realities have not changed since. Multilateral co-operative security is still in its infancy in the Asia-Pacific. Its capacity to manage the crucial Sino-American relationship is feeble. And, it will make no headway if Sino-American rivalry intensifies.

The central strategic issue in the Asia-Pacific during the first half of the twenty-first century would be the peaceful management of the rise of China, and to a lesser extent of the rise of a more "normal" Japan, so that both of them, burdened in different ways with baggages of the past, can take their rightful places as prosperous and peaceful great powers. The chances of this long and complex transition being managed peacefully would be much lower if co-operative security is not backed by credible forward-deployed U.S. power.

The South China Sea Disputes
The Spratlys Islands did not present a pretty picture in 1999. While there was little or no danger of a major conflict, a combination of factors increased the prospects of the occurrence of unpleasant military incidents. Some of these factors were not new: the overlapping claims, and the presence in the area of military forces of all claimants, except Brunei. But in 1999 there was also increased assertiveness on the part of some countries, in violation of an implicit understanding not to occupy or build on hitherto unoccupied shoals and reefs. Given the often close proximity of military forces, it may not always be easy for military commanders operating in disputed areas to assert or defend national claims without the use of force if such assertiveness continues.

Early in 1999 the Philippines discovered that structures on Mischief Reef which China claimed were fishermen's shelters had been significantly enlarged. In June, Malaysia was found to have constructed a two-storey structure with a helipad on Investigator Shoal, also claimed by the Philippines. In August the Philippines lodged a formal protest with Kuala Lumpur, which Malaysia ignored, merely stating that the two reefs were occupied because they were "part of our territory" and that Malaysia had "not taken any action that will contribute to tension".[17] Subsequently, Philippine and Malaysian planes engaged in a standoff over Investigator Shoal and Vietnamese gunners on Tennent Reef fired on a Philippine reconnaissance plane. In early November a Philippine naval ship ran aground at Scarborough Shoal, claimed by both the Philippines and China. It was not clear if it had been removed by the end of the year. During the same month, the Philippines Defence Secretary announced that his country planned to hold a joint military exercise with the United States on Palawan Island, facing the Spratlys, which drew a prompt protest from the Chinese embassy in Manila.

Such incidents highlighted the sorry state of ASEAN co-operation in relation to the South China Sea. ASEAN countries had not only not attempted to arrive at a common position or understanding among themselves on their respective claims in the Spratlys, but in 1999 seemed increasingly at odds with each other through unilateral actions on the ground.[18]

Meanwhile China has never explicitly disavowed its extensive claims to the South China Sea which go beyond the Spratly Islands and are manifested in its well-known broken line which extends to near Natuna Islands. In May 1992 it had passed a national law defining its territorial sea and contiguous zone and in the process reiterating its claim to the South China Sea.[19] In 1996 it ratified the 1982 United Nations Conference on Law of the Sea (UNCLOS) but claimed an exclusive economic zone (EEZ) by drawing straight baselines along much of its coast and by applying archipelago principles to the Paracel Islands when a strict interpretation of UNCLOS would not allow it. Chinese fishermen have been fishing in areas claimed by Manila, despite arrests and warnings by the Philippines. In May 1999 the Philippine Navy in fact sank a Chinese fishing vessel. At the same time China has continued to oppose the involvement of multilateral forums like the ARF or outside third parties in the South China Sea disputes.

It may be argued that China is no more a sinner than the other claimants, given the fact that all the claims have little validity under UNCLOS.[20] However, China stands out by the extent of its claims — virtually to the whole of the South China Sea and as the only great power claimant. It is also interesting that China expressed opposition to the military exercise between the United States and the Philippines, scheduled for 2000,[21] showing how the strategic kaleidoscope has been turning in the South China Sea since the American withdrawal from bases in the Philippines almost a decade ago.

China's South China Sea claims raise a longer-term strategic spectre for ASEAN, given the Association's long-standing desire not to be dominated by any major power and to try to ensure a balance in the influence of the major powers in Southeast Asia. How will such a balance be maintained, say twenty years down the road, when a major power, which is a potential superpower, is not only located on ASEAN's borders but has extensive territorial claims in the maritime heartland of Southeast Asia? How do you ensure a measure of independence and breathing space *vis-à-vis* the major powers when a potential superpower becomes a geographic bedfellow?

But in 1999, recovering from a painful economic crisis, ASEAN had more immediate and pressing worries. The economic crisis, the need for China's co-operation in the ASEAN+3 framework, China's growing economic linkages with the region and its cultivation of ASEAN countries seemed to relegate regional strategic concerns in relation to the South China Sea to a relatively lower priority. There was also a tendency among some in Southeast Asia to believe that China's longer-term intentions were probably not malign, because, going by its past history, it was unlikely to be an expansionist power. Perhaps — if expansion means territorial conquest. However, unpleasant possibilities cannot be ruled out. China's policies will be shaped also by contemporary geopolitical dynamics, domestic factors, and the possession (at some point) of power projection capabilities into Southeast Asia. A coercive policy need not necessarily entail the actual use of force, though in recent years China has not shied away from the use of force where it was deemed necessary to advance its interests.[22]

Elections and Political Change

There was a sense of *déjà vu* in some of the developments in Indonesia in 1998 and 1999, like the replay of a bad movie from the 1950s and 1960s: the destruction of properties and rapes of ethnic Chinese; religious clashes in Ambon, leaving thousands dead; massacres in East Timor; and separatist demands from Acheh and West Irian.

They were an indictment not just of Indonesia but also of Southeast Asia because Indonesia is the region's largest country and has been the leading member of ASEAN. Also, after all, Southeast Asian leaders have increasingly invoked a regional identity (for example, "ASEAN-10", "One Southeast Asia") and, as the contagion effect of the Asian economic crisis showed, foreign investors have also tended to take an undifferentiated regional approach (though they should know better). They were a stark reminder that economic growth rates alone do not make for modern and mature states and societies. The quality of institutions and governance is crucial. Further, Southeast Asia cannot afford to ignore human rights and the environment, which are also issues of increasing importance for the international community.

The instability arising from a failure to manage societal change could potentially be among the most important security problems facing Southeast Asia. The region is undergoing historic economic and social transformation, in common with much of East Asia, as it industrializes its economies and educates its peoples. The new forces of globalization only accelerate the pace of change. Structures, institutions, and relationships are likely to come under great stress unless they adapt to the times.

If assessed by the quality of governance, institution-building, and management of political change, Southeast Asia presented at best a mixed picture in 1999. And all the states were under challenge to varying degrees by forces unleashed by the economic crisis, the dynamics of globalization, or because of failure to carry out domestic reforms.

The Older ASEAN Members

Political change came to Indonesia in 1998–99, almost with a vengeance, after over thirty years of the authoritarian Soeharto regime. In 1999 the country at last had a democratically elected government which enjoyed the support of the main political groups. However, the durability of Southeast Asia's newest democracy remained a question mark.

The new government under President Abdurrahman Wahid faced enormous economic and political problems, including the challenge of bringing a wayward military under civilian control. And, given the fact that the President had had two strokes before, his health was a matter of serious concern. His passage from the political scene is likely to bring to power his vice-president who may not enjoy the confidence of the major forces across the country's political and religious divide.

If 1999 showed a fragile democracy in Indonesia struggling painfully to build the institutions for better governance, in Malaysia, which had been blessed with sounder institutional moorings and capacity, there was a less dramatic but unmistakeable deterioration of some important institutions,[23] though the economy did show a strong turn around. There was a sense of coming political change, but the confrontations spawning it still had to run their course. That a historical transformation of the political landscape could be taking place seemed confirmed by the general elections of November 1999 in which the United Malay National Organisation (UMNO), the core political force of the Barisan Nasional ruling coaliton, saw significant erosion of its support among ethnic Malays, an increasing numbers of whom voted for the opposition Barisan Alternatif (BA), particularly Islamic party PAS (Parti Islam SeMalaysia). It was not clear at the end of 1999 whether the final denouement would lead to greater Islamicization, a healthy two-(coalition) party system, or a return to status quo ante under a revitalized UMNO and National Front.

In the general election, the Barisan Nasional still won a comfortable two-thirds majority in parliament. Yet the desertion by Malay voters of the party which has symbolized Malay political power since independence in 1957 was highly significant, because it could threaten the legitmacy of UMNO as the guardian of Malay political power. The causes of UMNO's decline and PAS' resurgence were not difficult to divine: a perception among many Malays that Anwar Ibrahim's treatment at the hands of the authorities has been unfair and cruel, and the effectiveness of the Islamic party's message in the northern states that in contrast to UMNO it stood for a clean, non-corrupt government.

A suitable *political* response was needed from the top UMNO leaders to these challenges. Yet it was difficult to see it coming, given the way Malaysia Inc. has been constructed over the past two decades and given the sad spectacle of Dr Mahathir and Anwar Ibrahim each finding himself in a political box after burning all bridges with the other. Rather, the indications at the end of 1999 were that administrative and repressive means would be used to thwart the BA and PAS. These carry the risk of being counterproductive in the long run.

Across the Johor Straits, Singapore Inc. was also under challenge, though for different reasons. Singapore has justly been proud of its clean administration and effective governance. But the government's role has been pervasive, on the tacit assumption that with the best and the brightest in the land, and motivated by noble design, the government is best equipped to shape Singapore in the desired direction. This role has been exercised with cleverness and sophistication, for instance, the private sector remains the engine of growth and government-linked companies operate largely on commercial principles. Yet 1999 showed further awareness on the part of Singapore's leaders that while this model worked well in lifting Singapore out of developing country status, it may be ill-suited for competition in the developed league and in the New Economy. The New Economy in particular would require creativity and risk-taking that Singapore's system may have discouraged in the past. Hence, the changes in the education system in recent years to encourage creative thinking and the calls in 1999 for more entrepreneurship and risk-taking.

But it may not prove easy to realize these changes without also bringing about deeper changes in society, even politics. As a Singaporean Internet entrepreneur said: "We have been founded as a nation based on order ... but going forward that could become our liability. We need to learn how to have a bit of disorder".[24] Perhaps more than a bit of it, which would be against a deeply ingrained ethos of the Singapore system. Whether the disorder can be arranged and managed by the state and yet produce the desired results is left to be seen. There is little likelihood that the political controls will be significantly relaxed any time soon. Senior Minister Lee Kuan Yew said that the political out-of-bound markers will change as society changes. "What we must avoid", he was reported as saying "is the wholesale onslaught of our way of doing things, our methods of dialogue and intercourse and to bring about change that can make the system collapse".[25] Yet there are also signs that the government realizes that it has to be seen to be moving towards more openness, for example, its decision to allow Speakers Corners, like in Hyde Park, though with certain restrictions.

Emerging slowly from the economic crisis, Thailand was struggling to put in place the necessary reforms that would improve state and corporate governance whose weaknesses had been shown up by the economic crisis. Economic and political reforms have moved in tandem. New economic legislation to address economic problems — passed or under debate — covered areas such as bankruptcy, competition policy, money laundering, reform of financial institutions, privatization, and educational reform. On the political side implementation of the new (1997) reform constitution and acts such as the Official Information Act (1997) led to greater transparency and more public political participation. Entrenched vested interests were sometimes able to resist change, but overall the Chuan government and an increasingly strong civil society were able to maintain the reform momentum.

In the Philippines, the Estrada administration compared increasingly unfavourably with its predecessor, the Ramos administration, because of poor judgement in the selection of people to key advisory positions to the President, and ill-considered snap decisions springing more from emotion than reason. The consequential decline in credibility weakened the political clout to push ahead with the reforms started by his predecessor, contributing to a sense of stagnation, if not backsliding. Although the Philippines was not seriously affected by the Asian crisis, post-crisis growth is not as robust as that of its neighbours. The economy grew by 3.2 per cent in 1999 after declining 0.5 per cent in 1998. The Asian Development Bank projects a growth of 3.8 per cent for 2000.

Indochina and Myanmar
Vietnam, Myanmar, and Laos, fearful of change, were either marking time or sliding back. In Vietnam the regime continued to be in a survivalist mode. Growth rates were down to less than half of what they were a few years ago. A new phase of bold reforms, a *doi moi* II, was overdue in order to galvanize the economy to faster growth and more efficiency but was unlikely to be coming any time soon. A lack of consensus within the party, the fear of the political consequences of change, and genuine confusion over how and which way to move after seeing the effects of the Asian crisis on the more open economies, seem to have sapped the desire for reforms of the order needed. It is left to be seen if the Ninth Party Congress, presently scheduled for 2001, will result in any bold decisions.

The economic recovery in the older ASEAN member states may not help Vietnam as much as it hopes. It will not be status quo ante. For one thing, the other regional countries, more directly affected by the Asian crisis, have undertaken reforms and are likely to be more attractive destinations for foreign investments at a time when there has been increasing disenchantment with Vietnam for its bureaucratic obstacle course and other disincentives. Also, the significant slowdown in growth rates in Vietnam has not been due wholly to the indirect effects of the Asian crisis; it has also been the result of diminishing returns from the first phase of reforms in the late 1980s and early 1990s.

There are about 2 million new entrants to the work-force each year and a population growth rate of about 2 per cent. In terms of average national per capita income growth, Vietnam needs an economic growth rate of 2 per cent to just stand still. Given the World Bank's estimates of GDP growth of 3.5 per cent for 2000 and 3 per cent for 2001, it will do only slightly better. (It receives over US$2 billion in external aid and about US$3 billion in remittances from Vietnamese living or working abroad). But this would be a far cry from the optimism the country inspired in the early 1990s as the next Asian tiger.

In Myanmar the political stassis seemed set to continue. Three years after admission into ASEAN, there was no sign of political evolution. The continuing deterioration of the economy is likely to make the regime more insecure and repressive. An indication of how far Myanmar continues to fall behind the rest of the region is the condition of higher education. Universities are closed down if and when there is student unrest. They were closed in 1996 and were beginning to be slowly reopened only in 1999. About 100,000 students who did not take their final examinations in 1996 were still waiting to do so. Another 300,00 to 400,000 who had passed their entrance examinations are waiting to enter the universities.

In Laos a combination of mismanagement and severe effects of the Asian crisis has sent the economy reeling. Inflation is 140 per cent a year and over the two years 1998 and 1999 its currency, the kip, has fallen 900 per cent against the U.S. dollar.[26] The economic meltdown has produced inevitable strains on the small urban population in an otherwise rural country with the majority of people living on subsistence agriculture. On 26 October 1999 there was a small demonstration of students and teachers calling for freedom of expression, multi-party democracy, and release of political prisoners, which was quickly squelched by the security police and many of those involved arrested. There has been increased militarization of the regime, with seven of the eight politburo members now military men.

Out of the four new members of ASEAN, Cambodia was the only one where the situation was better in 1999, compared with 1998 and the years before. This was due to the achievement, at last, of relative political stability because of the accommodation between the Hun Sen and Prince Ranariddh (and the consequent emergence of Hun Sen as the undisputed leader) and the end of the long-drawn Khmer Rouge insurgency. With political stability and pursuit of economic reforms, the economy was set to stabilize and improve. However, the country was starting from a very low base and still faces massive problems of poverty, environmental degradation, and an HIV (human immunodeficiency virus) epidemic.

NOTES

1. Michael Leifer, *Political and Security Outlook for Southeast Asia*, Trends in Southeast Asia series no. 2 (Singapore: Institute of Southeast Asian Studies, January 2000).
2. Paul Dibb, "Asia's Insecurity", *Survival*, Autumn 1999.
3. Carlyle Thayer, "Southeast Asia: Challenge to Unity and Regime Legitimacy", in *Southeast Asian Affairs 1999* (Singapore: Institute of Southeast Asian Studies, 1999).
4. Rudolfo Severino, Secretary-General of ASEAN, "Asia Policy Lecture: What ASEAN

Is and What It Stands For" (Speech given at the Research Institute for Asia and the Pacific, University of Sydney, Australia, 22 October 1998).

5. Any assessment of ASEAN must of course take into account the limitations which the Association originally set for itself. These were that ASEAN would not be a supranational organization and that members would refrain from interference in each other's internal affairs. Were it not for these preconditions, ASEAN would not have been set up in the first place nor achieved the progress it subsequently made, given the history of conflict and suspicion among the original five members. Thirty years on, the four new members on the mainland of Southeast Asia found it easy to join the organization precisely because of these principles. The critics of ASEAN, however, would contend that whatever its built-in limitations, the international community would expect a regional organization, especially one like ASEAN which has been touted as the most successful example of regionalism in the Third World, to do more to manage or mitigate crises in its own backyard.

6. Surin Pitsuwan, "Thailand's Foreign Policy during the Economic and Social Crisis" (Paper presented at a seminar in the Faculty of Political Science, Thammasat University, 12 June 1998).

7. *Sunday Times* (Singapore), 25 July 1999.

8. For a more detailed examination, see John Funston, *ASEAN and the Principle of Non-Intervention — Practice and Prospects*, Trends in Southeast Asia no. 5 (Singapore: Institute of Southeast Asian Studies, 2000).

9. *Far Eastern Economic Review*, 23 December 1999, p. 27.

10. Tommy Koh, Executive Director of the Asia-Europe Foundation in Singapore, "Progress toward an East Asian Free Trade Area", *International Herald Tribune*, 14 December 1999, p. 8.

11. *Voice of Vietnam* (Hanoi), 1430 Greenwich Mean Time, 20 October 1999.

12. China has recently been open in its condemnation of America's alliances in Asia. See, for instance, the defence statement, *China's National Defence* (Beijing: State Council, 1998).

13. Some have argued that membership in the WTO, by helping dismantle China's wasteful industrial policy, is crucial for China's financial stability. See Yasheng Huang, "WTO Entry Is Critical to China's Stability", *Asian Wall Street Journal*, 28 September 1999, p. 10.

14. It is stated in *United States Security Strategy for the Asia-Pacific Region 1998* that "The US welcomes the public statements of ROK President Kim Dae-Jung affirming the value of the bilateral alliance and the US military presence even after reunification of the Korean peninsula".

15. *Straits Times* (Singapore), 31 August 1999, p. 7.

16. Jeannie Henderson, *Reassessing ASEAN*, Adelphi Paper 328 (London: Oxford University Press, 1999).

17. *Straits Times* (Singapore), 25 August 1999, p. 20.

18. However, ASEAN countries did prepare and try to get China committed to a draft Code of Conduct on the South China. It was presented to China at the ASEAN+3 meeting in Manila in November 1999. China said that it would study the document. Even if China were to accept the document without revision, which seemed unlikely, the Code will probably not materially affect the situation in the South China Sea.

19. Also in 1992, it gave a concession to an American oil exploration company, Crestone Energy Corporation, in a disputed area around Van Guard Reef, which was clearly on Vietnamese continental shelf. In 1995, in a carefully planned move, it installed a pre-constructed structure on Mischief Reef and claimed it was meant to be a shelter for its fishermen.

20. For an analysis of the validity of the claims under UNCLOS, see Chapter 3 in this volume.

21. Chinese Foreign Ministry spokesman Zhang Qiyue said in Beijing on 2 November 1999 that China was against the Philippines and the United States holding joint exercises which were aimed at China. The Philippines denied they were aimed at China. *Straits Times* (Singapore), 4 November 1999, p. 34.
22. China used force to seize the Paracel Islands from South Vietnam in 1974 when Saigon no longer enjoyed U.S. protection. In 1988, when it was clear that the Soviet Union would not come to Vietnam's assistance, it used force to capture some Vietnamese-held positions in the Spratly Islands.
23. See Khoo Boo Teik, "Unfinished Crises: Malaysian Politics in 1999", in this volume.
24. *Sunday Times*, 12 March 2000, Singapore.
25. *Sunday Times*, 19 September 1999, Singapore.
26. *Asiaweek*, 24 December 1999.

SOUTHEAST ASIA
Towards a Sustained Recovery?

Anne Booth

"Asia's astonishing bounce-back" was the cover story of the *Economist* at the end of August 1999. In the latter part of 1999, other daily and weekly journals covering Asian affairs also proclaimed the economic crisis to be over; some declared the patients not just to be out of intensive care but ready to be discharged from the convalescent home. But while there appears to be convincing evidence of a remarkable turnaround in South Korea, was this really the case for the worst affected Southeast Asian economies? The Indonesian economy, which had suffered the largest decline in gross domestic product (GDP) in 1998 was buffeted by two severe shocks in August and September 1999, which made predictions of a rapid return to positive growth look distinctly dubious. On the one hand, the Bank Bali scandal seemed to demonstrate that officials close to President Habibie were apparently just as corruption-prone as were those around former President Soeharto, while the post-election turmoil in East Timor severely damaged the reputation, at home and abroad, of both the army and the civilian administration. Both events led to a fall in the value of the rupiah and fears that investor confidence, still very fragile, would be further undermined. In October 1999, the People's Consultative Assembly refused to accept President's Habibie's account of his brief term in office, whereupon he withdrew from the presidential election. The subsequent ballot led to the election of the well-known Islamic leader and democracy activist, Abdurrahman Wahid, as president. Megawati Soekarnoputri, the daughter of Indonesia's first president, whose party had garnered the largest number of votes in the June elections, became the vice-president. But the honeymoon period for the new team was brief, and by early December the increasingly strident calls for a referendum in Aceh, and continued religious violence in the province of Maluku, were causing widespread fears that the Indonesian state was teetering on the verge of disintegration.

If we judge the severity of the crisis by the decline in real GDP in 1998, then both Thailand (–9.4 per cent) and Malaysia (–7.5 per cent) were only slightly less badly affected than Indonesia (–13.7 per cent). Although by the

---

ANNE BOOTH is Professor of Economics with reference to Asia at the School of Oriental and African Studies, Univesity of London.

end of 1999 it was clear that the pace of recovery was faster in these two economies, many observers were still stressing the painful legacy of the crisis, especially in the financial sectors, and expressing doubts that the lessons had really been learnt. In Thailand, disputes over economic policy were by the end of 1999 making the coalition led by Chuan Leepkai look increasingly fragile. In Malaysia, Dr Mahathir's election victory was interpreted as an endorsement of his policies by the business community, but the erosion of support for the United Malays National Organisation (UMNO) in the northern states indicated that the endorsement was less than whole-hearted in those parts of the country to which the benefits of growth have been slower to spread, or where support for the former deputy prime minister was strongest. In other parts of the ASEAN region, the signals were also mixed. While the Philippines had been less severely affected in terms of GDP decline, projections prepared by the International Monetary Fund (IMF) for 1999 and 2000 indicate that it will experience a slower recovery than either Malaysia or Thailand. The economies of Vietnam, the Lao People's Democratic Republic (PRD), Cambodia, and Myanmar, sometimes called the ASEAN transitional economies, had the highest growth rates in 1998, and in the case of Vietnam, the government is making quite optimistic projections for 1999–2000. But in all these economies, there is cause for concern about the medium-term economic outlook.

This chapter is divided into four parts. The first part gives a very brief summary of the huge literature that has emerged on the Asian crisis since mid-1997, and discusses the policy implications of this literature. The second part assesses the current state of the four worst affected economies where GDP growth contracted in 1998: Indonesia, Thailand, Malaysia, and the Philippines, and looks at the legacy of the crisis. The third part examines the transitional economies: Vietnam, the Lao PDR, Cambodia, and Myanmar, and suggests reasons for their being apparently unscathed by the economic hurricane which devastated their neighbours in 1997–98. The final part of the survey will examine the economic future of the region as a whole over the next few years. It explores what the longer-term implications of the crisis are for economic management throughout the ASEAN region, and examines the extent to which the crisis has affected the ability of the ASEAN countries to deal with such long-term development challenges as human resource development, infrastructural improvements, and higher standards of probity and accountability in both the public and the private sectors.

The Explosion of Literature on the Asian Crisis

Professor Kindleberger began his well-known book, *Manias, Panics and Crashes,* with the observation that "there is hardly a more conventional subject in economic literature than financial crises".[1] He went on to point out that few books appeared on the subject in the decades following 1945 because at least until the mid-1970s, recessions were mild in the major Western economies, and major depressions were thought to be a thing of the past. Kindleberger pointed out that the study of financial crises receives a tremendous boost when crises erupt, but tends to wane in periods of sustained economic growth. Such a boost was given in many parts of the world in the 1930s, and indeed that decade's rich lode of data continues to be mined by scholars in many parts of the world, and shows little sign of exhaustion. The "Great Depression" literature continues to expand, not just with reference to the North Atlantic economies, but also in the context of Asia, Africa, and Latin America.[2] The advent of two serious recessions in the Western economies in the early 1980s and the early 1990s, together with the spectacular stock market crash of October 1987, and the "Third World" (mainly Latin American) debt crisis which rumbled on through much of the 1980s, together gave rise to a new spate of crisis literature. Kindleberger in the preface to the revised edition of his book pointed out that "the contemporary world is very much on my mind as I work on my revision in the summer of 1988; news about failing banks and insolvent institutions breaks almost daily".

But by and large, the crisis literature of the 1980s, and the early part of the 1990s ignored Asia for the rather obvious reason that the major Asian economies, from the 1960s right through to July 1997, seemed quite untouched by economic fluctuations in other parts of the world. Certainly in Japan, the bursting of the asset bubble in the early 1990s ushered in a period of economic stagnation from which the economy has yet to emerge. But in Hong Kong, Taiwan, and China, in South Korea, and in the main economies of the Association of Southeast Asian Nations (ASEAN), the engine of economic growth appeared to be beating faster than ever in the decade from 1985 to 1995. Taken as a group, the developing economies of East and Southeast Asia grew at over 7 per cent per annum in per capita terms over the 1985–95 decade, a much faster growth rate than any other major region in the world, as the 1997 *World Development Report* pointed out. In 1996 some warning signals emerged, especially in Thailand, but few observers expected that economy to experience anything more than a slowdown in the frenetic pace of economic growth that had occurred in the decade up to 1995. Virtually no one, as far as I know, predicted that a slowdown in Thailand would have a serious impact on growth in other parts of the region.

In early July 1997, the Thai authorities were forced to bow to the inevitable and allow the baht to float against the dollar and other currencies. The rest, of course, is already history. The impact of the Great Asian Crisis on the literature of financial crises has already been prodigious, as Kindleberger's dictum would have predicted. The full gamut of late twentieth century communication technologies has been enlisted by pundits of all persuasions to put forward their views on the origins of the crisis, and the lessons it offers. Most of us cannot keep up with the literature now pouring out in the conventional formats of journal article and scholarly monograph, let alone what is emerging on the Internet. Truly, this crisis seems to have had something for everyone. Those economists who made their reputations analysing financial crises in Latin America and elsewhere now have some fascinating new case studies on which to further hone their theoretical and econometric tools. Those who made reputations criticizing "mainstream" explanations of the Asian miracle now have some powerful new ammunition which they can aim at their more conventional colleagues at the Bretton Woods institutions, and indeed at global capitalism itself. The workshops, conferences, monographs, and of course the web pages seem likely to go on proliferating for some years to come.

But to those economists whose main interest is the study of long-term economic development in the ASEAN economies, much of this work is rather disappointing. One of the reasons, it has to be admitted, is that many of the international pundits who have been speaking or writing on the Southeast Asian crisis since late 1997 have only a slender grasp of Southeast Asian economic history, and indeed in many cases have had no previous engagement with the region. Often they appear to have been using the events in Thailand, Indonesia, or Malaysia simply to prove their own theories of economic crises or disprove rival theories. While there may be little harm in this kind of academic activity, much of it is of dubious benefit to those policy-makers now struggling to deal with the aftermath of the crisis, or to improve economic institutions so that similar cataclysms cannot occur again. It would be beyond the scope of this survey to examine in depth the reasons for the severity of the crisis in Indonesia, Malaysia, and Thailand, but perhaps it is worth pointing out that, even after two years, there still appears to be important differences of opinion among both the foreign observers, and among experts within ASEAN as to why the crisis occurred.

The quotations in the boxed section (see pages 30–34) are intended to give a summary of the views of a range of individuals and institutions, including the major international financial institutions (the IMF and the Bank for International Settlements [BIS]), the Washington policy establishment, well-known financial newspapers and journals, and academic commentators from the United States. In addition, views from Malaysia, Singapore, and Thailand are included. These views are hardly exhaustive but they do give a reasonable overview of the main strands in the debate as it emerged in 1998 and 1999. It is obvious that there is considerable common ground among many (although not all) of these various explanations. Most see the crisis as the result of easy global liquidity conditions and weaknesses in the domestic financial systems in the affected countries. All agree that "Latin American" fiscal recklessness, exemplified by large budget deficits, was not a problem in Asia in the 1990s, although Pasuk and Baker, and Siamwalla, both stress the weakening of macroeconomic management that occurred in Thailand in the early 1990s.[3] Among American commentators there is a clear difference between those who see the root cause of the crisis in weak domestic institutions (leading to crony capitalism in all its manifestations) and those who view the crisis as the result of panic, which in turn was induced by inadequate or badly implemented international rescue packages. Broadly speaking, most Washington-based commentators fall in the first camp, while the main spokesman for the second camp is Professor Jeffrey Sachs and his colleagues at the Harvard Institute for International Development.[4] But critics of the IMF are also to be found in high places in Asia, as the quote from Lee Kuan Yew (quotation 19 in the boxed section) makes clear. And as the second quote from Professor Paul Krugman (quotation 15) demonstrates, the views of Jeffrey Sachs and others that market panic aggravated the crisis, had become widely accepted by mid-1998. Professor Krugman's policy conclusion that a "curfew" on capital flight would be necessary to restore confidence had of course already been implemented in Malaysia in early September 1998.

The views of Prime Minister Mahathir are important because they reveal the sense of disillusionment, even betrayal, that many Asian politicians, civil servants, business people, academics, and journalists feel about their treatment at the hands of global capital markets. Why did the markets turn so savagely against a group of economies who had been their darlings, praised by international development agencies, major financial institutions, the rating agencies, and many other experts for doing practically everything right? True, there may have been policy mistakes, and some corruption in government decision-making, but surely these problems were not sufficiently serious to provoke the ferocious onslaught of late 1997 and early 1998? There must have been other malign forces at work, whose main aim was to destroy the "Asian miracle" and discredit the politicians who had done so much to bring it about.

Whatever the verdict of history will be on Prime Minister Mahathir, or indeed on the role of currency speculators, one trend emerged very clearly in the first part of 1998. Several eminent American academic economists with impeccable scholarly credentials, including Professors Stiglitz, Bhagwati, and Krugman began to question the benefits for developing countries of unrestricted access to global capital markets. Indeed, the idea that some "sand in the wheels" of international financial markets was needed to curb huge speculative movements in capital had been around at least since the late 1970s when Professor Tobin had suggested a tax on international financial transactions.[5] The currency crises which erupted in Latin America and the Western Europe in the early 1990s all provoked further discussion of the costs and benefits of free and unregulated global capital markets. By early 1998 the then chief economist at the World Bank, Joseph Stiglitz, was arguing that there may be a case for government interventions to control capital flows; he suggested that the Chilean imposition of a reserve requirement on all short-term capital inflows could be emulated in other parts of the world.[6] On the day the *Financial Times* carried Professor Stiglitz's article, the paper editorialized:

> The case for early and complete freedom for international capital flows has, unquestionably, been damaged. The world's leaders must now ask themselves how to maximize the benefits of capital flows to developing countries, while minimizing both the number of panics and the damage they do.

This view can be compared with that of the Malaysian government (see quotation 11). While Dr Mahathir's views were considered extreme when they were first expressed in the latter part of 1997, the subsequent policy of pegging the ringgit and implementing controls on capital flows has won cautious approval from several commentators, including of course Professor Krugman. I will examine the Malaysian experience in more detail in the next section. But I think it is clear from the quotes in the boxed section below that many — probably the majority — commentators, however sympathetic they may be to arguments in favour of greater controls on international capital flows, see domestic policy failings as the root cause of the crisis in Thailand, Indonesia, and Malaysia. The key question then becomes: to what extent have the lessons of the crisis been learnt? Could the policy mistakes of the past be repeated in the future, as economic recovery gets under way and the grim events of 1997–99 retreat into history?

DIFFERENT VIEWS ON CAUSES OF THE CRISIS

International financial institutions

(1) "That this region might become embroiled in one of the worst financial crises in the post-war period was hardly ever considered — within or outside the region — a realistic possibility. What went wrong? Part of the answer seems to be that these countries became victims of their own success. This success has led domestic and foreign investors to underestimate the countries' economic weaknesses. It had also, partly because of the large-scale financial inflows that it encouraged, increased the demands on policies and institutions, especially but not only in the financial sector; and policies and institutions had not kept pace. The fundamental policy shortcomings and their ramifications were fully revealed only as the crisis deepened. Past success may also have contributed to a tendency by policymakers to deny the need for action when problems first became apparent." (IMF, *World Economic Outlook*, May 1998, p. 3)

(2) "A fragile financial sector, weak supervision and prudential regulation, and a corporate sector burdened with high levels of short-term debt were at the heart of a series of crises in Asia in the second half of 1997. In particular they greatly increased the complexity of managing in a sound and productive manner the foreign funds that surged into Asia in the mid-1990s." (Bank for International Settlements, *68th Annual Report*, p. 33)

(3) "In most of Asia, relatively strong fiscal positions allowed governments to pursue counter-cyclical policies in the wake of the crises, and to commit large public funds to recapitalize banking systems and speed up financial sector restructuring. The strength of economic fundamentals nevertheless varied widely across the region. In Singapore, a long tradition of prudent fiscal management had been accompanied by a strong external position and a well capitalized and regulated banking system. ... By contrast, in Indonesia and Thailand, combinations of large current account deficits and poorly regulated banking sectors contributed both to the greater severity of the 1998 downturns and to more subdued recoveries." (IMF, *World Economic Outlook*, October 1999, p. 55)

The international financial press

(4) "It's been a crisis of microeconomics. This is not a crisis of budget deficits and wasteful government spending, which happened in Latin America, say, in the 1970s. This is a crisis really centered on the private sector, with different components. First, you had a tremendous amount of liquidity in the region in the 1990s. Second, you had a crisis in how capital was allocated in countries like Thailand, which does not have very good banking supervision ... Third, in the case of Korea, the problem is government industrial policy. You've had policy-driven lending to finance a massive expansion of industrial capacity." (David Hale, Zurich Group economist, *Fortune*, 12 January 1998, p. 10)

(5) "... all the tiger economies suffered from too much cheap money, combined with a financial system that failed to allocate it efficiently. Banks did not assess credit risks properly, lending largely on the basis of personal relationships, and taking on risks in the belief that the government would always bail them out. Bank supervisors were at best incompetent, at worst corrupt." ("East Asian Economies Survey", *Economist*, 7 March 1998, p. 7)

(6) "The vulnerability of the Asian economies was partly explained by the nature of domestic government intervention and by the fact that banks were often officially influenced conduits for loans rather than financially secure loans on their own behalf. Explicit and implicit guarantees help explain the scale and nature of domestic and international lending. So did the apparent elimination of foreign exchange risk. Finally a financial panic has caused — and is causing — greater damage than the underlying weaknesses of these economies could justify." (Martin Wolf, "Ins and Outs of Capital Flow", *Financial Times*, 16 June 1998)

The Washington policy establishment

(7) "The main problem in East Asia was not macroeconomic, but structural. Deep flaws afflicted the financial system. They include excessive leverage, and a banking system based excessively on directed lending, connected lending, and other collusive personal relationships. Ten years ago, finance experts called it relationship banking, and thought it might help to minimize 'problems of asymmetric information and incentive incompatibility'; today we call it crony capitalism." (Jeffrey A. Frankel, "The Asian Model, the Miracle, the Crisis and the Fund", speech delivered at the U.S. International Trade Commission, 16 April 1998)

(8) "If ... the fundamental trigger of crisis in each case was a decline in investors' confidence in the soundness of the long-term investments backing up their short-term deposits, then there would be no necessary reason to expect the same macroeconomic precursors in each case. Instead, in a financial system organised around relationships rather than information, the confidence of investors in the soundness of relationship lending itself is an absolute fundamental. And the potential for contagion from one country to another may depend more on the extent to which investors perceive similarities between the two countries' financial systems than on the extent of actual similarity." (Janet Yellen, "Lessons from the Asian Crisis", Council on Foreign Relations, New York, 15 April 1998)

(9) "Like other financial crises of years past, the Asian crisis can be traced to a set of interrelated problems. In this case, three factors predominated; financial-sector weaknesses cum easy global liquidity conditions; problems in the external sector; and con-

tagion running from Thailand to other economies." (Morris Goldstein and Dennis Weatherstone, "The Asian Financial Crisis", *International Economics Policy Briefs, 98-1*, Washington: Institute for International Economics, March 1998)

(10) "If we are to piece together the lessons of the recent crises and devise an effective approach to these issues it will be important to start from the right place. Some conjure a specter haunting the world's governments; the global capital markets whose advances they cannot resist, whose sudden rejections they cannot survive. The facts of the most recent financial crises tell a different story.

The truth is that the crises that have occurred have disproportionately involved the judgements of countries' own citizens. Careful studies by the G-10 and the IMF of the crises in the European exchange rate mechanism and the Mexican peso crisis were able to attribute only a small fraction of the capital flows involved to speculative trade by foreigners ... I understand that these studies have been echoed in the very recent IMF study into the behaviour of hedge funds in Asia.

Where foreign capital has been involved it has most often been foreign capital that governments have sought actively to attract ... we saw it in Thailand, in the tax breaks on off-shore foreign borrowing and other domestic incentives for Thai banks to take on unsustainable amounts of foreign debt; we saw it in Korea, where discriminatory controls kept long-term capital out, and ushered short-term capital in."

("Deputy Secretary Summers' Remarks before the International Monetary Fund", U.S. Treasury, from the Office of Public Affairs, Washington, 9 March 1998)

The Malaysian reaction

(11) "The crisis that affected the East Asian region was triggered by speculative activities of hedge funds, which made huge profits through massive short-term capital flows, and in the process, seriously destabilised these East Asian currencies." (Mid-Term Review of the Seventh Malaysia Plan, 1999)

(12) "We in Malaysia laughed at the suggestion that our country would follow the fate of Mexico. How could that happen when our economy was so sound? We had practically no foreign debt. Our growth was high. ... Quite a few people in the media and in control of the big money seem to want to see ... Southeast Asian countries, and in particular, Malaysia, stop trying to catch up with their superiors ... There may be no conspiracy as such, but it is quite obvious that a few at least ... have their own agenda which they are determined to carry out. We have always welcomed foreign investments, including speculation ... But when big funds use their massive weight in order to move ... shares up and down at will and make huge profits by their manipulations, then it is too much to expect us to welcome them, especially when their profits result in massive losses for ourselves." (Prime Minister Mahathir interview, *Far Eastern Economic Review*, October 1997, p. 32)

American academic views

(13) "... while there were significant underlying problems and weak fundamentals besetting the Asian economies at both a macroeconomic and microeconomic level, the imbalances were not severe enough to warrant a financial crisis of the magnitude that took place in the latter half of 1997. A combination of panic on the part of the international investment community, policy mistakes at the onset of the crisis by Asian governments, and poorly designed international rescue programs turned the withdrawal of foreign capital into a full-fledged financial panic, and deepened the crisis more than

was either necessary or inevitable." (Steven Radelet and Jeffrey Sachs, "The Onset of the East Asian Financial Crisis", Harvard Institute for International Development, 30 March 1998)

(14) "I will argue that in order to make sense of what happened to Asia, it is necessary to adopt an approach quite different from that of traditional currency crisis theory. Of course Asian economies did experience currency crises, and the usual channels of speculation were operative here as always. However, the currency crises were only part of a broader financial crisis, which had very little to do with currencies or even monetary issues per se. Nor did the crisis have much to do with traditional fiscal issues. Instead, to make sense of what went wrong we need to focus on two issues normally neglected in currency crisis analysis: the role of financial intermediaries (and of moral hazard associated with such intermediaries when they are poorly regulated) and the prices of real assets such as capital and land." (Paul Krugman, "What Happened to Asia?", mimeographed, January 1998)

(15) "In the summer of 1998, I began to reconsider my own views about the crisis. The scope of global 'contagion' — the rapid spread of the crisis to countries with no real economic links to the original victim — convinced me that IMF critics such as Jeffrey Sachs were right in insisting that this was less a matter of economic fundamentals than it was a case of self-fulfilling prophecy, of market panic that, by causing a collapse of the real economy ends up validating itself. But I also concluded that the threat of further capital flight would prevent Asian economies from simply reflating, that is, increasing public spending and cutting interest rates to get their economies growing again. And so I found myself advocating temporary restrictions on the ability of investors to pull money out of crisis economies — a curfew, if you like, on capital flight — as part of a recovery strategy." (Paul Krugman, "Capital Control Freaks: How Malaysia got away with Economic Heresy", <www.slate.com/Dismal/99-09-27/Dismal.asp>)

(16) "The crisis in Mexico taught us about the role of external imbalances and problematic macroeconomic fundamentals in leading to speculative attacks on currencies. Many of these factors were present in Southeast Asia. The real appreciation of many of the currencies in the region slowed export growth in some countries and even led to falling exports. ... At the same time imports continued to soar. The result was substantial current account deficits ...

These macroeconomic factors are not sufficient to explain the Southeast Asian experience. What matters is not the size of the current account deficit but what is being used to finance and the form that the financing takes. Recently the evidence suggests that much of that investment has been directed towards excess (misguided) real estate investment. Furthermore financial institutions exposed themselves to greater risk by relying too heavily on short-term borrowing in foreign currency combined with long-term assets denominated in local currency. The crisis could not have happened without these failures in the oversight of the domestic banking system."

(Joseph Stiglitz, "More Instruments and Broader Goals: Moving towards the Post-Washington Consensus", *1998 WIDER Annual Lecture*, Helsinki, 7 January 1998)

(17) "... the Asian crisis cannot be separated from the excessive borrowings of foreign short-term capital as Asian economies loosened up their capital account controls and enabled their banks and firms to borrow abroad. In 1996, total private capital inflows to Indonesia, Malaysia, South Korea, Thailand, and the Philippines were $93 billion, up from $41 billion in 1994. In 1997, that suddenly changed to an outflow of $12 billion. Hence it has become apparent that crises attendant on capital mobility cannot be ignored." (Jagdish Bhagwati, "The Capital Myth", *Foreign Affairs* 77, no. 3 (May/June 1998)

Lee Kuan Yew

(18)   "The Crisis got dangerous when the IMF wanted to reform not just the Indonesian economy, but also Soeharto's governance of Indonesia … The IMF of course had to cater to the needs of the U.S. Congress. Congress would not give out more money to the IMF unless corruption and nepotism were stopped. Soeharto became a litmus test of IMF resolve. Had it not been linked in that way, had it just remained a question of the economy being put right, Soeharto would have gone along with the IMF. But he refused to change. When he restored projects which were scrapped because his family were involved, that was a direct challenge to the authority of the IMF and the markets sold out Indonesia. The rest is history." (Lee Kuan Yew, "Interview", *Asiaweek*, 21 May 1999)

The decline of technocratic influence: views from Thailand

(19)   "Partly the macro-managers had tried to have the best of both worlds — the pegged exchange rate which facilitated trade, and the liberalization of finance which stimulated investment. Partly the macro-managers had come to believe the praise accorded them. They refused to heed the advice that this combination would not work.

Partly they seemed dazzled by the glamorous financial world which developed in Bangkok in the early 1990s. The regulators seemed reluctant to impose the constraints which would slow it down.

But partly this reluctance has a murkier side. Powerful people could make easy money because of lax control. The two heads of the economic technocracy, the finance minister and the central bank governor, came under intense political pressure. From 1995 onwards, these posts offered only temporary employment. Many good candidates were not keen to apply. Politicians and other powerful people resisted closer supervision of the finance industry, argued against unpegging the currency and undermined the tradition of fiscal discipline. Up to and beyond the IMF bailout, policies were delayed or distorted at the behest of particular interests."

(Pasuk Phongpaichit and Chris Baker, *Thailand's Boom and Bust* [Chiang Mai: Silkworm Books, 1998])

(20)   "I conclude that it is a dispirited and demoralised technocracy that confronted the economic crisis. Indeed it is doubtful whether an autonomous technocracy exists any more. True, the Bank of Thailand is still very much in charge of monetary policy (including exchange rate policy) and of the supervision of financial institutions, but it has been so badly wounded … that it no longer has much authority with the public to obtain adequate support for its actions. The fiscal-policy side of the technocracy has clearly disintegrated. The degree of cooperation between the four key agencies is now minimal." (Ammar Siamwalla, "Can a Developing Democracy Manage Its Macroeconomy? The Case of Thailand", in *Thailand's Boom and Bust: Collected Papers* [Bangkok: Thailand Development Research Institute, 1997])

The Worst-Affected Economies:
Facing a New Set of Macroeconomic Challenges
The Turnaround in Macroeconomic Indicators

Before the crisis hit, Indonesia, the Philippines, Thailand, Malaysia, and South Korea together were running modest budget surpluses, and very large current account deficits, reflecting the large gap between private investment expendi-

TABLE 1
Net Capital Inflows to the Five Asian Crisis Economies, 1994–99[a]

	1994	1995	1996	1997	1998	1999
Net private capital inflow[b]	36.1	60.6	62.9	–22.1	–29.6	–18.1
Net direct investment	8.8	7.5	8.4	10.3	9.7	9.4
Net portfolio flows	9.9	17.4	20.3	12.9	–7.3	4.5
Other net investment	17.4	35.7	34.2	–45.3	–32.0	–32.0
Net official flows	0.3	0.7	–4.6	30.4	20.2	–4.5
Change in reserves[c]	–6.1	–18.3	–5.4	30.5	–52.1	–39.9
Current account	–23.2	–40.5	–53.4	–24.3	68.8	49.3

[a] Thailand, Indonesia, Malaysia, the Philippines, South Korea.
[b] Because of data limitations, other net investment may include some official inflows.
[c] A minus sign indicates an increase.
SOURCE: International Monetary Fund, *World Economic Outlook* (October 1999), table 2.2.

tures and private savings. In 1996, according to IMF data (Table 1), the combined current account deficit of the five countries was US$53.4 billion dollars which was well over half the total current account deficits of all developing and transitional economies. In some countries, much of this deficit was funded by inflows of long-term investment capital, but especially in Thailand by 1996 much of the deficit was covered by short-term, more speculative capital inflows.[7] By 1998 the five countries were running a combined balance of payments surplus of US$68.8 billion. This massive turnaround in two years was achieved in spite of the fact that budget deficits in all these economies had increased. The reason for the magnitude of the change lay mainly in private sector investment expenditures, which declined precipitously as the crisis deepened. In all the worst affected ASEAN economies, total investment expenditures as a percentage of GDP dropped between 1997 and 1998; the magnitude of the decline was most marked in Malaysia and Indonesia. As most investment goods in these economies are imported, the decline in investment expenditure was reflected in a very sharp decline in imports. Exports increased relative to GDP everywhere in the region (Table 2).

As can be seen in Table 1, in the pre-crisis years (1994–96) net inflows of portfolio and "other" investment far exceeded inflows of direct investment. But in 1997–99, inflows of direct investment stayed remarkably constant. It was the "other" investment flows which turned negative in 1997–99; these would have been partly foreign speculators pulling money out of time deposits, but they also reflected decisions of local residents to place their liquid reserves in foreign bank accounts as the crisis deepened and confidence in currencies such as the baht and the rupiah collapsed. It is difficult to know how much money left Indonesia, for example, in 1997/98 but it is rumoured that Indonesian residents sent billions of dollars offshore at the height of the crisis. It is, of course, well-known in the international finance literature that very dif-

TABLE 2
Private Consumption, Investment, and Exports, 1997–98
(Percentage of GDP)

Country	Consumption		Investment		Exports	
	1997	1998	1997	1998	1997	1998
Singapore	40.7	40.3	41.4	39.3	n.a.	n.a.
Malaysia	46.4	44.7	49.1	30.3	94.6	102.0
Thailand	53.6	53.2	32.3	26.7	48.4	58.9
Philippines	72.7	74.4	24.5	21.3	49.0	55.7
Indonesia	63.1	71.0	32.2	22.1	27.9	35.8
Myanmar	88.4	86.2	14.9	12.8	0.7	0.5
Vietnam	n.a.	n.a.	28.3	25.1	n.a.	n.a.

SOURCES: Singapore, Malaysia, and Indonesia: data from national statistical offices at constant prices; Thailand, Philippines, and Myanmar: data from *International Financial Statistics*, vol. 52, no. 10 (Washington: International Monetary Fund, October 1999) at current prices; Vietnam: *Vietnam Economy in 1998* (Hanoi: Central Institute for Economic Management, March 1999), table 9.

ferent motivations drive flows of direct investment from those which drive other, more speculative capital flows; the experience of the Asian crisis economies simply confirms this.[8] But it is unlikely that direct investment flows will increase substantially over the next few years in any ASEAN economy, so even if portfolio inflows increase in the year 2000, it seems likely that total private capital flows will stay negative.

This will inevitably have far-reaching macroeconomic consequences for the four most severely affected ASEAN economies. As is clear from Table 1, in 1997–98 net official capital inflows increased dramatically as private capital inflows turned negative. But this mainly reflected the emergency IMF assistance which will not continue; the IMF in fact predicts that official flows will be negative in 1999–2000 as these loans are paid back. While some longer-term official development assistance will be available to Indonesia and the Philippines, and perhaps to Thailand as well, it seems clear that all four economies will have to adjust to a regime of much lower imports and capital inflows, which will mean that the current account of the balance of payments is likely to stay in surplus for the foreseeable future. This in turn implies that, with increasing budget deficits, private investment expenditures will be well below private savings. This may not necessarily be a bad thing; a significant part of the private investment boom in Malaysia, Indonesia, and Thailand in the decade 1986–96 was in non-traded goods, especially in the real estate sector, where there is now massive over-supply. For the next few years private investment will likely favour the traded goods sectors where returns should be high, especially if the very large nominal devaluations of the baht, the rupiah, the ringgit, and the peso which occurred in 1997/98 are not eroded by accelerating inflation. The challenge for governments will be to create an appropriate climate of incentives for a recovery led by the traded goods sectors, while at the same time resisting calls for "de-linking" from the global economy. Here it is essential the right lessons be drawn especially from the Malaysian experiment with capital controls.

Problems in the Financial Sectors and Their Budgetary Implications
One of the most publicized consequences of the crisis, especially in Thailand and Indonesia, are the massive problems in the banking system, which in the latter part of 1999 had hardly begun to be addressed in either country. In Thailand it has been estimated that in late 1999, non-performing loans amounted to over 40 per cent of outstanding loans; in Indonesia the figure was certainly higher.[9] In both countries most local banks have stopped lending, even to their best clients. While some "quality customers" have been able to secure loans at reasonable interest rates from local branches of foreign banks, many small and medium-sized companies have only been able to survive by tapping the underground lending market where interest rates are very high.[10] Thai policy has been to encourage banks to create their own asset management companies to take bad loans off their books, although for this plan to work, banks will have to raise new capital to absorb the losses they will have to take as the bad loans are sold off at a heavy discount.

The Thai government came under criticism in the latter part of 1999 for not setting up a government-managed asset management company to sell off the bad debts of the banking system. While the Malaysian asset management company (Danaharta) appears to have functioned reasonably well, the Indonesian agency (Indonesian Bank Restructuring Agency, or IBRA) has been the target of growing criticism during the year 1999. This was partly because of slowness in announcing details of its restructuring plans for the banking system, but in the latter part of the year, as details of the Bank Bali affair became widely discussed in the media, it was clear that at least one senior official was involved in highly dubious practices. (Although the head of IBRA, Glenn Yusuf, was not directly implicated in the Bank Bali scandal, he was replaced in January 2000.) It also became clear during 1999 that the total cost of recapitalizing both the state and the nationalized private banks under IBRA's care would be massive and a high proportion of this cost would be a charge on the government budget. This was because the main instrument of bank recapitalization was treasury bonds, which were to be placed directly in the portfolios of the banks in question. In an address to a Jakarta business audience in January 2000, the Economics Co-ordinating Minister, Kwik Kian Gie, stated that in the coming fiscal year (April to December 2000) it was estimated that net interest payments on the bank restructuring bonds would amount to 4 per cent of GDP, and would absorb more than 10 per cent of the central government budget.[11] Interest payments on these bonds will continue to be a substantial, if declining, extra burden on the budget in coming years, making projections of continuing deficits and mounting public debt look all too plausible. Public debt was estimated to be around 100 per cent of GDP in Indonesia in 1999 (compared with 48 per cent in Thailand). Most observers argued that, with budgetary deficits set to grow in 2000 and 2001, the debt to GDP ratio would rise further.[12]

It is clear that the problem of mounting budget deficits would severely constrain the capacity of the Indonesian government to spend more on infrastructure and education, expenditures which in turn are considered to be essential if the economic recovery is to be sustained in the longer term. In Thailand, officials were more optimistic that infrastructure and educational expenditures could be sustained, even if that meant budgetary deficits of between 4 and 6 per cent of GDP over the next few years. Certainly given the much lower stock of public debt outstanding in Thailand relative to GDP, projections of continuing budgetary deficits give less cause for concern, although they do run counter to Thailand's long-standing tradition of fiscal conservatism. In Malaysia there is less concern about a projected budget deficit of around 5 per cent of GDP in 2000; the Malaysian government has run similar deficits in the past and funded them through domestic borrowing. The Malaysian government argues that its controversial policy of imposing capital controls and pegging the ringgit to the dollar has permitted it to run a more expansionary fiscal policy without having to worry about the implications for the balance of payments. In the short run there may be some truth in this argument, although if the deficit is funded through borrowing from the central bank, there will inevitably be an increase in domestic inflation.

Should the ASEAN Economies Control Capital Flows?
As several of the quotes in the boxed section make clear, it is now being suggested that some aspects of the "Washington consensus" policy package may not be optimal for relatively small, open, low- and middle-income economies struggling to achieve the twin objectives of rapid growth and domestic price stability in a world where cross-border capital flows are growing rapidly. This applies especially to complete convertibility in the capital account, where as we have seen there is now some support for the views of Professors Stiglitz and Bhagwati in the financial press and elsewhere. As Carlos Diaz-Alejandro pointed out with reference to the Latin American crisis of the early 1980s, unrestrained convertibility was not the expectation of the architects of the Bretton Woods system; it has only become part of the dogma of the IMF and the World Bank more recently.[13] It is a dogma that many developing countries, in Southeast Asia and elsewhere, are now being advised to ignore.

Does this mean that the ASEAN economies should return to the regimes of pegged exchange rates and strict controls on capital movements, which were after all quite widely followed in the early post-independence era? Most economists who have studied this period in, for example, Indonesia or the

Philippines would probably counsel against a return to such policies. Usually they resulted in black markets for foreign exchange, widespread smuggling of exports and imports, and the emergence of a number of devices that permitted both private business people and government officials to send funds offshore. Indeed, some commentators argued that this is what would happen in Malaysia after Dr Mahathir's government imposed capital controls and pegged the ringgit in early September 1998. In fact, these dire consequences did not result from the Malaysian action, which has led to arguments in other parts of the ASEAN region that the Malaysian alternative to IMF orthodoxy should be emulated. But in assessing these arguments, two points should be borne in mind.

First, the ringgit was pegged not at its pre-crisis level, but at the massively devalued point which it had reached in August 1998. It is highly probable that the ringgit would have appreciated in the last months of 1998 and into 1999, as the baht and even the rupiah did. Thus the policy of pegging the ringgit in fact has led to its undervaluation relative to other currencies in the region; this in turn has given a boost to both export and import-competing industries in Malaysia. Whatever the original claims for the policies of imposing capital controls and pegging the currency, in fact they have facilitated an export-led recovery. Second, there can be little doubt that these policies were imposed in early September 1998 to prevent panic on the financial markets in the wake of the arrest of Anwar Ibrahim, which took place a few days after the package was announced. No doubt it was successful in this aim; the political uncertainty following the arrest would certainly have precipitated further capital flight and probably a further temporary decline in the value of the ringgit. These effects might well have been short-lived but the imposition of a currency peg and capital controls did prevent them from occurring.

The Malaysian capital controls were eased in March 1999, although this does not appear to have led to a significant return of either long-term direct investment or portfolio investment. The IMF has argued that flows of foreign direct investment into Malaysia have declined relative to both Thailand and South Korea since the imposition of the capital controls, although it is not clear how much this decline is due to the remaining controls and how much to the continuing climate of political uncertainty as the Anwar trial drags on.[14] The results of the 1999 election may assuage some investor fears (both domestic and foreign) although the increased support for the Islamic party may encourage some potential foreign investors to look elsewhere. So while the Malaysian experiment certainly allowed Dr Mahathir to proceed with the arrest and imprisonment of his most important political rival with little fear of dire economic consequences, it is not in my view plausible to argue that it represented a significant challenge to IMF "orthodoxy". Indeed, given that the policies were imposed a full year after the crisis erupted, when the ringgit had already undergone a substantial devaluation, and significant capital flight had already occurred, it is very difficult to assess what their impact on economic recovery has been. Certainly the Malaysian economy appears to have returned to positive growth in 1999, but so has Thailand and (especially) South Korea where IMF "orthodoxy" has been the order of the day, although both countries ran budget deficits in 1999 and are projected to do so again in 2000.

If the Malaysian experiment is at best ambiguous in its lessons regarding capital controls and a pegged exchange rate, neither in my view is anything to be gained from other policies of "self-reliance", including a return to extensive trade protection, and a trade, taxation, and exchange rate regime that penalizes exporters and subsidizes import-substituting industry. There is plenty of evidence that such a regime has been responsible for a good part of the inequitable distribution of income between urban and rural areas in many parts of Southeast Asia for the last four decades, and indeed longer. The policy reforms in Thailand, Indonesia, and Malaysia over the 1980s which reduced or abolished export taxes, and removed at least some of the disincentives to export have together been hugely beneficial to the working poor in these countries. Much more could be done to level up the playing field for different categories of producer and worker but to return to the kind of regime that prevailed in (to take the extreme case) Indonesia in the early 1960s would be a tragedy.

The Ones That Got Away:
Why Have Some ASEAN Economies Not Been Affected?

The economies of Laos, Myanmar, and Vietnam all grew quite strongly in 1998 (4 per cent, 5.8 per cent, and 5.7 per cent respectively), at least according to official data. In Vietnam the government has published quite optimistic projections for further growth in 1999–2000. Even in Cambodia, where reliable data are still difficult to come by, economic growth is expected to be quite robust over the next few years, albeit from a very low base. In one sense it is easy to explain the fact that these economies have apparently been little affected by the turmoil around them; in all cases they have very undeveloped domestic financial systems and thus did not attract the predatory attentions of international fund managers. Inward flows of portfolio capital, and other forms of speculative capital were minimal. In the case of Myanmar in particular, the non-convertibility of its currency further isolated the domestic economy from the currency turmoil in Thailand and elsewhere, although in 1998 the unofficial (black market) rate of the kyat fell sharply.

There are, however, several reasons why the claim that the ASEAN transitional economies largely escaped the crisis has to be treated with caution. First, the national income and other data for all four economies are not reliable. In Myanmar in particular, it is argued that the government's projections for economic growth in the fiscal year ending March 1999 are greatly exaggerated. In fact the official estimates of economic growth for the preceding year have been scaled down.[15] Second, it seems clear that the impact of the crisis on the foreign trade and inward flows of foreign direct investment has been serious, especially in those economies where earlier in the 1990s direct investment from Singapore, Malaysia, and Thailand was a significant proportion of total inflows. In Myanmar, where almost half of approved inward investment flows were from other ASEAN economies, approvals dropped sharply in 1998, and some large projects which had already been approved were unlikely to be implemented.[16] On the trade side, the Thai government has revised downwards its projections of electricity consumption and it appears likely that it will have to revise its agreement to purchase electricity from Laos. The Laotian currency in fact has experienced a very rapid depreciation since June 1997 (from around 960 kip to the U.S. dollar to 7,700 in January 2000). But this probably had little to do with "contagion" from Thailand and was much more the result of the very large budget deficits, which the government apparently is unable to bring under control.[17] Although the Vietnamese dong and the Cambodian riel also depreciated after June 1997, by late 1998 both currencies had stabilized, and were little changed in value through 1999.

Possibly the most severe medium-term effect of the crisis in the more mature ASEAN market economies on the transitional economies will be that it will strengthen the position of those senior politicians who advocate slowing down the pace of economic reform. There can be no doubt that the crisis has made policies of economic liberalization and greater linkages with the regional and global economy look more perilous that they did three or four years ago. Thus it is hardly surprising that in Vietnam, for example, the government has declared that it can proceed only cautiously with state enterprise reform, because too rapid implementation could lead to "social chaos". A planned stock market, on which equity of state enterprises could be traded, has been indefinitely postponed.[18]

Looking to the Future: Are More Financial Crises Inevitable and How Can Their Effects Be Mitigated?

Drawing on the work of economic historians such as Kindleberger, there seems a strong case for arguing that financial crashes are the inevitable consequence of booms in immature capitalist economic systems. To quote Raymond Goldsmith, they are a "childhood disease of capitalism" rather than a disease characteristic of old age.[19] The analogy could be taken further by pointing out that once children have succumbed to illnesses such as measles or chicken pox, they are almost always immunized from further attacks. Can the ASEAN countries, including those which remained relatively unscathed by the crisis of 1997–99, expect to be immune from further crises in the future? The answer to this question will depend on how well the lessons of the crisis of 1997/98 have been learnt, and to what extent the economies of the regions are able to reform their audit, regulatory, and judicial institutions. Given the severity of the contraction in GDP in 1998, and the protracted nature of the recovery process especially in Indonesia, it is likely that, as in Latin America in the 1980s, as much as a decade's economic growth could be lost. In order to at least mitigate the impact of future crises on economic growth, it is imperative that lessons be learnt. All disasters bring with them the opportunity for a fresh start, and the economic crisis in ASEAN should be no exception.

What then are the key lessons? First of all, it seems to me essential that all ASEAN governments must recognize that (with the exception of Singapore) they are still immature capitalist economies, with weak financial institutions, open to global influences, and thus prone to financial crises. They must respond more aggressively to warning signs. There can be little doubt that the sustained growth of the last three decades in the worst-affected economies led many policy-makers and businesspeople to believe that they were impervious to the kinds of economic fluctuations that have buffeted Latin America, and indeed the economies of the Organization for Economic Co-operation and Development (OECD). In particular, the fact that East Asia was largely unaffected by the severe downturn of the early 1990s created a climate of false optimism, both in the international financial community and in the domestic economies. This in turn encouraged speculative investment in several sectors, and aggravated the cronyism and corruption in ruling circles that had already become a serious problem in the 1980s. The over-hyping of the fast-growing Southeast Asian economies by the World Bank, and indeed by many other institutions, both government and private, as well as individual commentators, added to the conviction that Asian economies were somehow immune to the diseases which had afflicted other capitalist economies at various stages in their economic development.

I have already argued that policies involving the imposition of a currency peg, together with exchange controls, should be resisted everywhere in ASEAN. It is true that the currency peg in Malaysia has prevented an appreciation of the ringgit from the low point reached in mid-1998, and this has facilitated an export-led recovery. But in the longer term, attempts to maintain a fixed peg will almost certainly lead to an overvaluation of the currency, and thus amount to a tax on producers of traded goods, the very people who must be relied on to spearhead an economic recovery. The re-imposition of exchange controls, abandoned in most economies in the region by the late 1960s, would also lead to a resurgence of black markets and smuggling. This in turn would create new opportunities for corruption and rent-seeking even as governments in Thailand, the Philippines, and Indonesia try to cope with the bitter legacy of the past. In addition, to maintain a currency peg with capital controls, high domestic interest rates would be essential and this would deter productive long-term investment.

Direct controls on foreign direct investment inflows or indeed on other forms of long-term investment flows should be avoided; the policy challenge is surely to develop policy tools to prevent destabilizing speculative flows. Controls on the inward flow of long-term investment capital could only damage economic recovery by deterring new investments and encouraging established investors, domestic as well as foreign, to leave. There are various mechanisms available for deterring short-term speculative inflows, and the ASEAN economies most at risk from such inflows may wish to utilize them.[20] But a key lesson of the crisis should not be overlooked; much of the outflow of funds that took place in 1997/98 was not the work of foreign speculators but of local people who, for whatever reason, had lost confidence in the ability of their governments to manage the economy. Restoring the confidence of these savers, and encouraging them to repatriate their funds will be a crucial part of the recovery process.

Governments must continue in their efforts to level the playing field between different producers in different parts of the economy. Policies that "target" particular producers whether to promote home production or exports, are unlikely in my view to be successful anywhere in Southeast Asia. They are more likely to lead to a resurgence of cronyism and corruption. Interventions that worked (or are supposed to have worked) in South Korea in the 1960s and 1970s are unlikely to have the same effect in Thailand or Indonesia in the first decade of the new century. As Professor Fabella has argued in the context of the Philippines, the crisis has given the government an opportunity to restructure incentives in favour of efficient producers in both agriculture and manufacturing industry. In the Philippines, where the banking sector was not severely damaged and the corporate sector not burdened by massive foreign debts, such a policy should be able to proceed smoothly, especially if the Central Bank concentrates on keeping interest rates low and permits the peso to find its market value.[21]

In Thailand and Indonesia, the implementation of such an incentive restructuring policy is hampered by problems in the banking system, and their resolution is clearly of paramount importance. It is clear that such a resolution will take time, and in the Indonesian case will impose a very considerable burden on the budget. This in turn will limit the capacity of the government to increase expenditures on, for example, infrastructure rehabilitation, education and healthcare, civil service reform, and improving the quality of the law enforcement agencies. Few observers doubt the importance of establishing strong independent regulatory and audit agencies in Indonesia, and indeed in other parts of the region, which can regulate not just the financial sector but also government departments and state enterprises. In the past the weakness of government audit agencies has been blamed for many of the problems in the state enterprise sector as well as in line ministries in Indonesia, while in Thailand, the political contamination of the central bank which occurred in the early 1990s meant that it was no longer able to function as an independent watchdog for a rapidly expanding financial sector.

Empowering independent government regulatory and audit agencies will inevitably offend powerful vested interests not just in Thailand, Indonesia, and Malaysia but in other parts of the region as well. It will not, however, demand huge budgetary resources. On the other hand, improving education and healthcare, extending physical infrastructure, and reforming the civil service and the police force will take both time and very substantial financial resources. Contrary to popular myth, most ASEAN governments have not invested heavily in education and healthcare over the past three decades; in Indonesia, for example, education expenditures have seldom exceeded 2 per cent of GDP.[22] In Vietnam, the educational sector is widely believed to have suffered from the process of economic restructuring pursued since the latter part of the 1980s. In Myanmar a report compiled by a United Nations Working Group in 1998 emphasized that real per capita expenditures on education and health have fallen steadily over the 1990s and that by the mid-1990s, military expenditures were more than 220 per cent of combined health and education expenditures, a far higher ratio than in other parts of ASEAN.[23] Although the available evidence suggests that the impact of the economic crisis on educational enrolments and access to healthcare in Indonesia and Thailand were not as catastrophic as some early forecasts had predicted, there can be little doubt that drop-outs from the educational system have increased, especially at the post-primary levels.[24]

Thus it is quite possible that the economic recovery in Thailand and Indonesia will be constrained by skill shortages. In addition, there can be little doubt that demands for more efficient and honest bureaucracies will intensify as recovery proceeds, both in these countries and elsewhere in the ASEAN region. In Indonesia in particular, the government has already made substantial concessions towards administrative decentralization. The changes embodied in the two laws passed in May 1999 will together transform governmental and financial links between Jakarta and the regions over coming years. Whether these changes will be sufficient to keep some of the resource-rich outer island provinces inside Indonesia in coming years remains to be seen. What does seem clear is that the demands for greater regional autonomy which the Indonesian government is facing will also be made with increasing force in other ASEAN countries in coming years. How Indonesia copes with its regional discontents may thus offer important lessons, both positive and negative, to other countries in the region.

NOTES

1. Charles Kindleberger, *Manias, Panics and Crashes: A History of Financial Crises*, 2nd edition (London: Macmillan, 1989).
2. A forthcoming volume edited by Peter Boomgaard and Ian Brown looks specifically at the impact of the 1930s world crisis on Southeast Asia.
3. Other commentators have made the same point in the Indonesian context. See, for example, Hal Hill, *The Indonesian Economy in Crisis: Causes, Consequences, and Lessons* (Singapore: Institute of Southeast Asian Studies, 1999), table 15. Several commentators have pointed out that technocrats in the Indonesian Ministry of Finance actually encouraged the IMF to include a number of conditions regarding the abolition of monopolies and so forth in the first IMF standby loan to Indonesia in late 1997. For a discussion of this point by an influential Japanese

commentator, see the article by Eisuke Sakakibara in *Yomiuri Shimbun,* 10 December 1999.

4. Apart from the article by Eisuke Sakakibara quoted in the previous note, see, for example, Ross H. McLeod, "Some Comments on the Rupiah 'Crisis'", in *Indonesia's Technological Challenge,* edited by Hal Hill and Thee Kian Wie (Canberra and Singapore: Australian National University and Institute of Southeast Asian Studies, 1998), and the chapter on Indonesia by the same author in *East Asia in Crisis: From Being a Miracle to Needing One?* edited by Ross H. McLeod and Ross Garnaut (London: Routledge, 1998).

5. For an overview of the issues, see in particular Barry Eichengreen, James Tobin, and Charles Wyplosz, "Two Cases for Sand in the Wheels of International Finance", *Economic Journal* 105 (1995): 162–72.

6. Joseph E. Stiglitz, "Boats, Planes and Capital Flows", *Financial Times,* 25 March 1998.

7. *Economist,* 24 August 1996, pp. 67–68.

8. For a classic account, see J.E. Meade, *The Theory of International Economic Policy, Vol 1: The Balance of Payments* (London: Oxford University Press, 1951), chap. XXII.

9. Total non-performing loans of Thai banks are estimated to be around 2.26 billion baht; of this total, 1.1 billion are in state banks. See *Financial Times,* 20 January 2000. A detailed discussion of the non-performing loans of the Indonesian banking system is given by Raden Pardede, "Survey of Recent Developments", *Bulletin of Indonesian Economic Studies* 35, no. 2 (August 1999). Pardede points out that the revealed losses in the state banks in Indonesia are much larger than in the private banks, although the latter had a much larger share of the market by the time of the crisis.

10. *Far Eastern Economic Review,* 4 November 1999, p. 11.

11. Speech by Kwik Kian Gie to the U.S.-Indonesian Roundtable, Jakarta, 8 January 2000

12. *Far Eastern Economic Review,* 23 December 1999, pp. 40–41.

13. Diaz-Alejandro, Carlos F., "Good-Bye Financial Repression, Hello Financial Crash", *Journal of Development Economics* 19, no. 1 (1985), as reprinted in Andres Velasco, ed., *Trade, Development and the World Economy* (Oxford: Basil Blackwell, 1988), p. 383.

14. *Far Eastern Economic Review,* 28 October 1999, p. 81.

15. Tin Maung Maung Than, "Myanmar's Golden Anniversary: Economic and Political Uncertainty", *Southeast Asian Affairs 1999* (Singapore: Institute of Southeast Asian Studies, 1999), p. 224.

16. Ibid., p. 229. See also Nick J. Freeman, "Greater Mekong Sub-Region and the 'Asian Crisis': Caught between Scylla and Charybdis", *Southeast Asian Affairs 1999* (Singapore: Institute of Southeast Asian Studies, 1999), pp. 36–38.

17. Andreas Schneider, "Laos: A Million Elephants, A Million Tourists?" *Southeast Asian Affairs 1999* (Singapore: Institute of Southeast Asian Studies, 1999).

18. Melina Nathan, "Vietnam: Is Globilazation a Friend or a Foe", *Southeast Asian Affairs 1999* (Singapore: Institute of Southeast Asian Studies, 1999), p. 343.

19. Raymond Goldsmith, "Comment on Hyman Minsky, The Financial-Instability Hypothesis: Capitalist Processes and the Behaviour of the Economy", in *Financial Crises: Theory, History, and Policy,* edited by Charles P. Kindleberger and Jean-Pierre Laffargue (New York: Cambridge University Press, 1982), p. 42.

20. *Economist,* 14 March 1998, p. 116.

21. R.V. Fabella, *The Economic Choices We Face,* Discussion Paper 98-03 (Quezon City: University of the Philippines School of Economics, 1998).

22. For an extended discussion of progress in education in the ASEAN economies since the 1960s, see Anne Booth, "Education in Southeast Asia: Myths and Reali-

ties", *ASEAN Economic Bulletin* 16, no. 3 (December 1999).

23. *Human Development in Myanmar: An Internal Report* (Report prepared by the United Nations Working Group, Yangon, July 1998).

24. For a discussion of recent data on education, see Anne Booth, "Survey of Recent Developments", *Bulletin of Indonesian Economic Studies* 35, no. 3 (December 1999). A recent report by UNICEF also draws attention to higher school drop-outs in Thailand (*Economist*, 22–28 January 2000, p. 70).

HOW VALID ARE THE SOUTH CHINA SEA CLAIMS UNDER THE LAW OF THE SEA CONVENTION?

Jon M. Van Dyke and Mark J. Valencia

The South China Sea disputes continue to plague policy-makers and defy solution. Six governments — China, Taiwan, Vietnam, Malaysia, the Philippines, and Brunei — claim all or some of the islands and rocks in the south central South China Sea, known as the Spratly Islands, as well as all or some of the surrounding sea, seafloor, and associated resources. And all except Brunei have military forces on their claimed features. This article reviews the conflicting claims and recent developments in the context of regional politics and international law, including the law of the sea.

China's 1995 occupation of Mischief Reef on the Philippine-claimed continental shelf and its 1999 construction of fort-like structures there considerably raised tension in the area. Further exacerbating the situation, just before the June 1999 ASEAN Regional Forum (ARF) meeting in Singapore, a Philippine navy vessel rammed and sunk a Chinese fishing vessel in the area.

Going into the ARF meeting, some countries hoped that a code of conduct drafted by the Philippines might be accepted by the other claimants, particularly China. But it was not to be. China opposed even discussing such a code at the ARF because it insists that the South China Sea issues should only be discussed by the parties directly concerned — and then only on a bilateral basis. More fundamentally, from its perspective China is the rightful "owner" of the South China Sea and thus feels that any such code should emanate from its own initiative.

In the end, after considerable pressure from other ARF members, including the United States, China agreed to "consider" a revised code — but only if it is informal and not binding. Thus the draft was simply referred to a working group. And China's past record of adherence to such agreements as the ASEAN Declaration on the South China Sea and the Indonesian Workshops' Bandung Statement — both of which barred unilateral actions that would increase tension in the area — does not instil confidence that China will approve such a code, or abide by it even if it does approve it.

Making matters far worse, China is not the only claimant singing a discordant note. Shortly before the June ASEAN and ARF meetings, Malaysia com-

---

JON M. VAN DYKE is Professor at the William S. Richardson School of Law, University of Hawaii. MARK J. VALENCIA is Senior Fellow at the East-West Center, Honolulu.

pleted construction of a two-storey concrete building and a helipad on Investigator Shoal, which is also claimed by the Philippines, China, Taiwan, and possibly Vietnam.

This surprise unilateral action by a founding member of the Association of Southeast Asian Nations (ASEAN) has several implications. First, it clearly splits ASEAN solidarity on this issue *vis-à-vis* China. Some diplomats even suspect that Malaysia cut a side deal with China at the expense of ASEAN. Second, it violates and perhaps fatally undermines the ASEAN Declaration on the South China Sea and the Bandung Statement. And third, it may open the floodgates to a new wave of occupations by other claimants, particularly the Philippines. Clearly anticipating a negative reaction by fellow ASEAN members, Malaysia refused to discuss the issue at the ASEAN Foreign Ministers' Meeting and joined China in arguing that the South China Sea should not be on the ARF agenda. Malaysia opposed the draft code on the ground that it was more like a "treaty" and that each article needed to be carefully studied.

The United States then weighed in, saying basically "enough is enough". The United States fears that these disputes could "drift into crisis" and wants ASEAN to consider concrete proposals to relieve tensions. Secretary of State Madeline Albright, speaking at the ARF meeting, warned: "The stakes are too high to permit a cycle to emerge in which each incident leads to another with potentially greater crisis and graver consequences. … We cannot simply sit on the sidelines and watch." Another senior U.S. official, worried that time is running out for a peaceful solution, said: "There is a need not simply to have a policy of benign neglect waiting for something bad to happen, but rather to talk about the issue." These statements were made despite China's insistence that "outsiders butt out" and firmly juxtaposed the United States and China on yet another issue. Thus the tenor of the U.S.-China relationship may affect the South China Sea process. Moreover, with tension rising between China and Taiwan, incidents between the two in the Spratly area can be anticipated.

Although ASEAN officials agreed on a Philippines-proposed draft code of conduct for the South China Sea at ASEAN's late November 1999 Informal Summit, China refused to accept it, in part because it included the Paracels, which are occupied by China but claimed by Vietnam. The draft code reaffirms the applicability of international law and Law of the Sea to the South China Sea disputes, including freedom of navigation and overflight; eschews the use or threat of force; emphasizes self-restraint; and encourages intensified efforts to find a "fundamental and durable" solution to the disputes and to build trust and confidence. In particular, it calls on all parties to "refrain from taking actions that establish a presence on unoccupied island reefs, shoals, cays, and other features in the "Area".[1]

China did say that the draft could be the basis for further "positive" discussions. And it reiterated its offer to jointly develop the area. But Malaysia and Vietnam also have reservations, particularly regarding the area to be covered by the code[2] or, for that matter, by any joint development arrangement. Moreover, the Philippine proposal had already been watered down after it failed to achieve agreement at the ASEAN Foreign Ministers Meeting in Singapore in July. A key provision of that draft called for a moratorium on construction or expansion of structures in the Spratlys — exactly what Vietnam and Taiwan were reportedly doing at that very moment. The need for such a code is underscored by recent near clashes between China and the Philippines, Malaysia and the Philippines, and Vietnam and the Philippines.

The South China Sea Claims under International Laws[3]

The claims of the neighbouring nations include claims to the islets in the Spratly group, and thus one set of questions can be classified as "sovereignty" issues. How does a nation gain sovereignty over an isolated and essentially uninhabitable outcropping of land? How strong are the various nations' claims to these features? One commentator has observed that "it is certainly insufficient in international law to deduce title from evidence of geographic knowledge and records of navigation routes".[4]

The "sovereignty" issues are complex enough, but they become particularly important because the "sovereign owner" of a land area may — in some circumstances — be entitled to the adjacent ocean and seabed resources. The principles governing these entitlements can be characterized as "boundary delimitation" issues, and they require a separate — and also complex — analysis.

Sovereignty Issues: Who Owns the Spratlys?

The *Clipperton, Palmas, Minquiers and Ecrehos* and *Gulf of Fonseca* precedents[5] focus on "discovery" and — in particular — on "occupation" of small islets. Although they do not require too much activity when the islet is uninhabitable, they do demand some formal acts and a sufficient presence to let others know of the claim. In the Spratlys, no nation's claim appears to have been sufficiently strong or unchallengeable to persuade others to keep out of the region. Although China has argued that Western requirements of formal declarations of sovereignty should not apply in Asia, their suggested substitute — long contact with a region — does not appear to be sufficient because it does not put others on notice that a claim of exclusion has been made. Besides, China has stated several times that it will resolve the South China Sea issues according to international law and the principles in the 1982 United Nations Law of the Sea Convention.

If the historic claims do not resolve the question of ownership, then do the recent occupations of the islets lend weight to any of the claims? France made some minimal attempts to exert physical control over seven of the islets in the 1930s, but it was not until Japan entered the region in August 1938 that anything akin to "effective control" occurred. Japan used Itu Aba, the largest Spratly islet, as a submarine base to intercept shipping in the area. Their installations were abandoned in 1945, and more recently the islets have been occupied by others. In the Peace Treaty signed by Japan on 8 September 1951,

Japan renounced its rights to the Spratlys, but no recipient was named. Taiwan has effectively controlled Itu Aba from 1946 to 1950 and from 1956 to the present. Vietnam has controlled many Spratly features since 1973. The Philippines has controlled some islets since 1978. Malaysia began controlling features in the southern portion of the area in 1983, and China began its efforts to occupy islets in 1988. In each case, other nations have challenged the occupations. The result has been a crazy-quilt pattern of occupation and an uneasy stalemate. Nevertheless, some of these occupations may at some point ripen into a legitimate entitlement of sovereignty.

Is "contiguity" or geographical proximity relevant here? Malaysia, the Philippines, and even Vietnam argue that they are entitled to some or all of the Spratlys because these islands are near their main land territories. Contiguity was rejected in both the *Clipperton* and *Palmas* decisions, and was not a factor in the *Minquiers and Ecrehos* case, but the argument has a persistent practical appeal. China, of course, thoroughly rejects it.[6]

In summary, international legal principles will not unambiguously resolve the competing sovereignty claims to the Spratlys. All the claims are weak, because the claimants are not able to demonstrate continuous and effective occupation, administration, and control, as well as acquiescence by other claimants. Each claimant undoubtedly realizes that if the dispute were presented to a tribunal or arbitrator, it may not ultimately or completely prevail. An independent decision-maker is likely to allocate these tiny islets according to the common legal principles of equity and fairness. In the long run, each claimant might be better served by putting aside the issue of sovereignty over the islets and working with the other claimants to multilaterally develop the resources of the disputed area. Such an approach would not formally reject any of the claims, would allow each nation to maintain its legal position, and would also allow the resources to be developed for the benefit of the people of the region.

Boundary Delimitation Issues under the Law of the Sea Convention

China, Vietnam, the Philippines, Malaysia, Brunei, Indonesia, and Singapore are parties to the Law of the Sea Convention. Thailand, Laos, and Cambodia have signed, but have not yet ratified it. Taiwan is not eligible to be a party. Countries that are awaiting formal ratification are obliged to act in a manner that does not defeat the basic objects and purposes of the treaty.[7] Many countries have said that they view the Convention as expressing the customary international law that applies to ocean issues, and the International Court of Justice (I.C.J.) has also ruled that at least certain parts of the Convention are now customary international law. It seems justified, therefore, to apply the provisions of the Convention to this dispute, but it is also necessary to remember that certain parts of the Convention may not be universally accepted, or accepted by the South China claimants, and that regional practices can sometimes alter norms that are accepted elsewhere.

Do Any of the Spratly Islets Have the Capacity under Article 121 to Generate Exclusive Economic Zones or Continental Shelves?

Features That Are Submerged at High Tide Cannot Generate Maritime Zones

This traditional principle of customary international law is confirmed in Article 121 of the Law of the Sea Convention. Claims to maritime zones based on reefs that are submerged at high tide, even if artificial structures have been built on them, are not valid.[8]

The central question that must be addressed before the maritime boundary issues can be unravelled is whether any of the Spratly islets have the capacity to generate an exclusive economic zone (EEZ) or continental shelf. Between twenty-five and thirty-five of the eighty to ninety distinct features in the Spratly region are above water at high tide, and these outcroppings qualify as "islands" under Article 121 of the Law of the Sea Convention and appear to be entitled to territorial seas. Article 121(3) says, however, that "[r]ocks which cannot sustain human habitation or an economic life of their own" do not generate EEZs or continental shelves.

The Spratlys were not inhabited except by occasional wandering fishermen until recent times. Although they were occasionally visited, they had no independent economic life *of their own*. The language in Article 121(3) appears to require that the relevant "economic life" of features must be "of their own". Thus an artificial economic life supported by a distant population in order to gain control over an extended maritime zone is not sufficient.

The largest islet, Itu Aba, is 0.43 square kilometres in area. Spratly Island is 0.15 square kilometres and only five others are larger than 0.1 square kilometres — Thitu Island, West York Island, Northeast Cay, Southwest Cay, and Sand Cay. The others are truly tiny. The highest feature is Namyit Island, at 6.2 metres.[9] Only ten of the islets appear to sustain trees naturally — Itu Aba, Loaita Island, Namyit, Nanshan Island, Northeast Cay, Sand Cay, Southwest Cay, Thitu Island, West York Island, and Sin Cowe.[10] Only a few of the islets have been used for guano exploitation — Spratly Island and Amboyna and Southwest Cays. Itu Aba and Thitu have been used historically as regional bases for fishermen from Hainan island and elsewhere.

In an earlier writing, one of the present authors suggested that only islands that have shown the ability to sustain stable human populations of at least fifty persons should be allowed to generate maritime zones, and that the Spratlys do not meet this requirement.[11] Other authors have reached similar conclusions regarding the inability of these islets to sustain human habitation and thus to generate EEZs or continental shelves.[12] More important is state practice. Vietnamese officials now appear to have adopted the view that the Spratly islets *cannot* generate EEZs or continental shelves. For instance, Ho Si Thoang, Chair of Petro Vietnam, has been quoted as saying that "by international law a chain of atolls like the Spratlys are not entitled to a 200-nautical mile economic zone".[13] And at the First Meeting of the Technical Working

Group on Legal Matters in the Indonesian-Canadian workshops on the South China Sea, held in Phuket, Thailand, 2–5 July 1995, the Vietnamese Legal Adviser, Nguyen Qui Binh, said that Vietnam did not think the Spratly islets had the capacity to generate EEZs or continental shelves.[14] Ambassador Hasjim Djalal of Indonesia — who is now President of the Assembly of the International Sea-Bed Authority and the co-ordinator of the Indonesian-sponsored workshops on the South China Sea conflicts — has also expressed that view. Although the arguments against allowing any of the Spratlys to generate extended maritime zones seem strong, occasional authors continue to suggest that at least some of the islands can generate such zones.[15] And China frequently acts as if it assumes the islets can generate extended zones.

How should this issue ultimately be resolved? Can the claimant-nations agree that none of these islets should be deemed capable of generating extended maritime zones? Alternatively, can the countries of the region agree that the islets should generate a "regional zone" that would be jointly managed by a Spratly Management Authority?

We think the best approach, in terms of international law, logic, and practicality would be to deny extended maritime zones to any of the Spratlys. The concept of extended maritime zones was accepted in the 1982 Law of the Sea Convention because it seemed appropriate to allow coastal populations to have primary responsibility to manage and exploit adjacent resources. Where there is no indigenous population, however, this logic does not apply, and the extended zone should not be permitted. Article 121(3) is based on this perception and should be interpreted in this light.

But if agreement cannot be reached on this approach, a fall-back position might be to allow the islets to generate a "regional" zone, that would be shared and jointly managed. This position would recognize that the Spratlys have been visited and, to some minimal extent, used by the people of the region for centuries, and that it should continue to be viewed as a shared resource. This conclusion has a precedent in the *Gulf of Fonseca* case, where Honduras, Nicaragua, and El Salvador were recognized as having a "condominium" ownership over the waters and resources of the Gulf of Fonseca, which were characterized as jointly owned historic waters.

Should Some of the Spratly Features Now Be Characterized as "Artificial Islands", and, If So, What Is Their Legal Status?

Article 60(8) of the Law of the Sea Convention states clearly that artificial islands do not have the capacity to generate EEZs or continental shelves. Some of the current structures built on reefs can only be characterized as "artificial islands". The Chinese occupations of Subi Reef, Johnson South Reef, and Mischief Reef; the Malaysian occupation of Dallas Reef and Investigator Shoal; and the Vietnamese occupations of Vanguard and Prince of Wales Banks, all seem to fit this description.

Article 60(8) was designed to discourage nations from building up submerged reefs and low-tide elevations in order to generate extended maritime zones. If it is not interpreted according to its clear language, then we would foresee continued efforts to reclaim submerged features in order to lay claim to open ocean areas.

Are the Spratly Islets That Are Above Water at High Tide Entitled to Generate 12-Nautical-Mile Territorial Seas?

Article 3 of the U.N. Law of the Sea Convention allows "Every State" to establish territorial seas around its land areas "to a limit not exceeding 12 nautical miles", and Article 121 allows every feature that is above water at high tide to generate such a zone. Vietnam declared a twelve-nautical-mile territorial sea around the Spratlys in 1977[16] and China did so in its 1992 Territorial Sea Law. One commentator reports that Malaysia has claimed a twelve-nautical-mile territorial sea around Swallow Reef and Amboyna Cay but not around its other claimed features (Holler-Trost, as cited above).

Even though the Law of the Sea Convention allows countries to declare twelve-nautical-mile territorial seas around coasts and islands, it does not necessarily follow that a territorial sea of this size is legitimate in all locations and for all purposes. Article 300, entitled "Good faith and abuse of rights", reminds countries that they must not invoke rights under the Convention in a manner that imposes an unacceptable burden on other nations. Examples can be found where states have agreed to establish territorial seas of less than 12 nautical miles around islands that are on the "wrong" side of a median boundary line. The Venezuelan island of Isla Patos, between Venezuela and Trinidad and Tobago, the Abu Dhabi island of Dayyinah, between Abu Dhabi and Qatar, and the Australian islands in the Torres Strait, between Australia and Papua New Guinea, all have territorial seas of only three nautical miles. These examples provide a logical precedent for the South China Sea, because these islands — like the Spratlys — are all small and have no permanent civilian population. The islands in the crowded Aegean Sea generate only six-nautical-mile territorial seas. Hasjim Djalal has observed that the Spratly islets are not entitled to any territorial seas at all, and instead should simply be protected by small "safety zones".[17] Certainly the claimant parties could agree that the islets that are above water at high tide generate territorial seas of less than twelve nautical miles, and such an agreement would be consistent with the view that the resources of the region should be shared by the peoples of the region, or possibly by the international community as a whole.

What Continental Shelf Claims Can Be Made by the Claimant States?

The geography of the South China Sea presents an interesting challenge in interpreting and applying Article 76 of the Law of the Sea Convention on the "Definition of the Continental Shelf". If one concludes that the Spratly islets do not have the capacity to generate EEZs or continental shelves, then the maritime boundaries of these zones must be determined by reference to the continental land masses and the larger bordering islands. The continental shelf southeast of Vietnam and northwest of the Sarawak (Malaysia)/Brunei border extends substantially beyond 200 nautical miles from their irrespective coasts. Under Article 76(5), Vietnam and Malaysia would each apparently be allowed to claim the resources on this shelf out to 350 nautical miles, in the absence of competing claims. Malaysia's extended continental shelf claim to the north and east and Brunei's extended continental shelf claim do not appear to be justified, however, because of the East Palawan Trough near the coast. A Philippine claim based on an extended continental shelf also would not be justified because of the deep indentation on the sea floor just west of the main Philippine islands.

What Is the Role of the Continental Shelf Commission?
Article 76 and Annex II of the Law of the Sea Convention establishes a twenty-one-member Continental Shelf Commission, which has the responsibility to evaluate claims by coastal nations for shelves extending beyond 200 nautical miles. Because of the complex formula found in Article 76, it is necessary to have some neutral body evaluate the claims made by nations seeking additional resources. It is not clear, however, what this Commission should do in a situation where the extended claims overlap. Although phrased as "recommendations", the Commission's decisions must be respected by the nations concerned. If any of the South China Sea nations were to submit a claim to the Commission, the Commission's ruling could have an important impact on the ultimate delimitation of boundaries in this region.

What Principles Govern the Delimitation of Maritime Boundaries?
Once the difficult and complex issues identified above are addressed and resolved, it then becomes appropriate to determine how the maritime boundaries in the region should be drawn. Article 6 of the 1958 Convention on the Continental Shelf and Article 12 of the 1958 Convention on the Territorial Sea and Contiguous Zone adopted the "equidistance principle" as the method for resolving competing claims to surrounding waters. Under this principle, a disputed area is divided along a line equidistant between the countries involved. But the 1982 Law of the Sea Convention carefully avoids referring to "equidistance" as the proper approach, and instead provides in Articles 74(1) and 83(1) a carefully crafted formula that gives only subtle hints regarding how disputes should be resolved.

> The delimitation of the exclusive economic zone [and continental shelf] between States with opposite or adjacent coasts shall be effected by agreement on the basis of international law, as referred to in Article 38 of the Statute of the International Court of Justice, in order to achieve an equitable solution.

The goal is thus to achieve an "equitable" resolution to boundary disputes, and a variety of principles have been developed to achieve this goal.

The "equitable principle" with the most direct relevance to the South China Sea maritime boundary dispute is that islands do not have an equal capacity with land masses to generate maritime zones. Because of this principle, even if one or more of the tiny Spratly islets were deemed to be capable of generating extended maritime zones, they would not command equal strength with an opposing continental area or larger island. The focus on control of the Spratlys may, therefore, be misdirected. To put the process of the boundary delimitation in perspective, it is useful to survey the methods that have been used in recent years by the I.C.J. and arbitral tribunals.

The I.C.J. and arbitral tribunals adjudicating maritime boundary disputes now follow a standard sequence in approaching a controversy. Professor Jonathan Charney has recently described this common approach as follows:

> First, they define the relevant geographical area and the area in dispute. Second, they identify the relevant areas and coastlines. Third, they spell out all the relevant considerations. Fourth, they develop a provisional line based upon an analysis of the relevant considerations. Fifth, they check that line against some of the considerations to determine whether the line is "radically inequitable" and if so, they adjust it accordingly.[18]

The "equitable principles" that have been used in recent years to resolve boundary disputes include the following:

- *The equidistance approach can be used as an aid to analysis, but it is not to be used as a binding or mandatory principle.* In the 1985 *Libya/Malta* case, the 1984 *Gulf of Maine* case, and most recently the 1993 *Jan Mayen* case, the I.C.J. examined the equidistance line as an aid to its preliminary analysis, but then adjusted the line in light of the differences in the length of the coastlines of the contending parties. This preliminary equidistance line is drawn from the coastlines themselves, not from any straight baselines. The Court has made it clear in all these cases that the equidistance line is not mandatory or binding.

- *The proportionality of coasts must be examined to determine if a maritime boundary delimitation is "equitable".* It has now become well established that an essential element of a boundary delimitation is the calculation of the relative lengths of the relevant coastlines. If this ratio is not roughly comparable to the ratio of the provisionally delimited relevant water area, then the tribunal will make an adjustment to bring the ratios into line with each other. In the *Jan Mayen* case, the I.C.J. determined that the ratio of the relevant coasts of Jan Mayen (Norway) to Greenland (Denmark) was 1:9, and ruled that this dramatic difference required a departure from reliance on the equidistance line. The final result was perhaps a compromise between an equidistance approach and a proportionality-of-the-coasts approach, with Denmark (Greenland) receiving three times as much maritime space as Norway (Jan Mayen).

Similarly, in the *Libya/Malta Continental Shelf* case, the I.C.J. started with the median lines between the countries, but then adjusted the line northward through 18′ of latitude to take account of the "very marked difference in coastal lengths"[19] between the two countries. The court then confirmed the appropriateness of this solution by examining the "proportionality" of the length of the coastlines of the two countries and the "equitableness of the result".

The proportionality-of-the-coastlines is thus not a mathematically mandatory requirement, but rather provides a rough sense of justice which the tribunal uses, along with other factors, to achieve a result that it deems to be "equitable".

- *Geographic considerations will govern maritime boundary delimitations and non-geographic considerations will only rarely have any relevance.* The *Gulf of Maine* case was perhaps the most dramatic example of the Court rejecting submissions made by the parties regarding non-geographic considerations, such as the economic dependence of coastal communities on a fishery, fisheries management issues, and ecological data.

  The concept of the continental shelf as a "natural prolongation" of the adjacent continent is a geographical notion, but it has not received prominence in recent decisions. Nevertheless, this term does appear in Article 76 of the 1982 Law of the Sea Convention, and thus may continue to be of some relevance in the South China Sea dispute. To some extent, the principle of non-encroachment has taken the place of the natural-prolongation idea.

- *The principle of non-encroachment.* This principle is explicitly articulated in Article 7(6) of the 1982 U.N. Law of the Sea Convention, which says that no state can use a system of straight baselines "in such a manner as to cut off the territorial sea of another State from the high seas or an exclusive economic zone". It has recently been relied upon more expansively in the *Jan Mayen* case, where the Court emphasized the importance of avoiding cutting-off the extension of a coastal state's entry into the sea. Even though Norway's Jan Mayen Island is minuscule in comparison with Denmark's Greenland, Norway was allocated a maritime zone sufficient to give it equitable access to the important capelin fishery that lies between the two land features. The unusual sixteen-nautical-mile wide and 200-nautical-mile long corridor drawn in Canada and France's *St. Pierre and Miquelon* case also appears to have been based on a desire to avoid blocking access to the open ocean for Canada's Newfoundland coast.

- *The principle of maximum reach.* This principle first emerged in the *North Sea Continental Shelf* cases, the Federal Republic of Germany (FRG) versus Denmark and FRG versus Netherlands[20] where Germany received a pie-shaped wedge to the equidistant point even though this allocation cut into the claimed zones of Denmark and the Netherlands. Professor

Charney reports that this approach has been followed in all later cases: "No subsequent award or judgment has had the effect of fully cutting off a disputant's access to the seaward limit of any zone.[21] In the *Gulf of Fonseca* case, the Court recognized the existence of an undivided condominium regime in order to give all parties access to the maritime zone and its resources, and in the *St. Pierre and Miquelon* case France was given a narrow corridor connecting its territorial sea with the outlying high seas. The geographical configuration in the *Jan Mayen* case presented different issues. But even in this situation the Court gave Norway more than it "deserved" considering the small coastline and geographical size of Jan Mayen island. The motive apparently was to enable Norway to have at least "limited geographical access to the middle of the disputed area", which contained a valuable fishery.

Professor Charney identifies several interests that are served by the maximum reach principle —"status" (by recognizing that even geographically disadvantaged countries have rights to maritime resources, the right "to participate in international arrangements as an equal", navigational freedoms, and "security interests in transportation and mobility".[22] Among the South China Sea claimants, the non-encroachment and maximum reach principles may be especially helpful to Brunei because its limited coastal frontage would otherwise be in danger of being dominated by the longer coasts and larger claims of Malaysia.

- *Each competing country is allocated some maritime area.* This principle is similar to the non-encroachment and maximum reach principles, but it is worth restating in this form to emphasize how the I.C.J. has reasoned in recent years. Although it has attempted to articulate consistent governing principles, its approach to each dispute submitted to it has, in fact, been more akin to the approach of an arbitrator than that of a judge. Instead, of applying principles uniformly without regard to the result they produce, the Court has tried to find an "equitable solution" that gives each competing country some of what it has sought, and thus to reach an "equitable solution".

- *Islands have a limited role in resolving maritime boundary disputes.* Islands can generate maritime zones, but they do not generate full zones when they are competing directly against continental land areas. This conclusion has been reached consistently by the Court and arbitral tribunals. Although we believe that the Spratly islets should not be allowed to generate any extended maritime zones, even if they are allowed to do so, their capacity to generate such a zone would be very weak in relation to competing claims from continental or large-island land masses. Because the features in the Spratly group are extremely tiny outcroppings, it is virtually certain that a tribunal would give these features only limited relevance in delimiting maritime boundaries.

- *The vital security interests of each nation must be protected.* This principle was also recognized in the *Jan Mayen* case, where the I.C.J. refused to allow the maritime boundary to be drawn too close to *Jan Mayen* island, and it can be found in the background of all recent I.C.J. decisions. Even as early as the 1917 decision of the Central American Court of Justice on the *Gulf of Fonseca*, it was emphasized that the waters of the Gulf had to be viewed as jointly owned by the three adjoining states because of the "primordial interests" of "the economic, commercial, agricultural and industrial life of the riparian States" as well as "the interest of national defense".[23] The refusal of tribunals to adopt an "all-or-nothing" solution in any of these cases illustrates their sensitivity to the need to protect the vital security interests of each nation.

Will High Sea Areas Remain after the Maritime Boundaries Are Delimited, and, If So, How Will This Area Be Governed?

If the Spratly islets are not permitted to generate extended maritime zones, and if the principles laid out in the Law of the Sea Convention are applied, then an area beyond national jurisdiction will remain in the centre of the South China Sea. Under the Law of the Sea Convention, the fishery resources in this zone would be governed by the freedom of the seas principle found in Article 87, as modified by the 1995 Agreement on Straddling and Migratory Stocks.

Of more importance to the South China Sea disputes, the seabed mineral and hydrocarbon resources in areas beyond national jurisdiction, if any, would be governed by the International Sea-Bed Authority. It is unclear how that body would operate in a semi-enclosed sea such as the South China Sea. Outside powers would certainly need the approval of the International Sea-Bed Authority to explore and exploit sea-bed resources there. But it might also be appropriate to have a regional advisory board to ensure regional involvement in decision-making.

A Shared Regional "Common Heritage"?

Although the Convention does not explicitly authorize this approach, it may be appropriate for the nations of this region to assert a regional claim of ownership over the resources of the South China Sea beyond areas of national jurisdiction. This result may be appropriate in light of the unique problem created by the ambiguity over whether the Spratly islets can generate extended maritime zones.

The unusual 1992 decision of the I.C.J. Chamber in the *Gulf of Fonseca* case concluding that El Salvador, Honduras, and Nicaragua hold undivided interests in the maritime zones both landward and seaward of the closing line across the Gulf of Fonseca may provide a useful precedent for a solution to the South China Sea disputes.

If one accepts the early Chinese contacts with the Spratlys, one has to also recognize that China was in some sense a colonial power over Vietnam and other areas of this region. Once this colonial domination ended, Vietnam and the other areas would logically have inherited the sovereign claims made by the colonial master, just as the Central American republics inherited the claims made by their colonial master, Spain. But the islets and the maritime space cannot be easily divided, because China still exists and still claims this region. It may therefore be appropriate to see the jurisdiction over the islets and the surrounding marine space as shared between China and Vietnam as well as the other nations that were dominated by China in earlier periods.

It has also become increasingly common for countries to establish joint development areas in disputed maritime regions, and this approach may be a logical solution in the Spratly area. Jose de Venecia, a close confidant of then-president Fidel Ramos and a leading member of the Philippine Congress introduced a resolution proposing a "condominium system" for the whole South China Sea. In August 1995, Taiwan's President Lee Teng-hui proposed that the twelve nations and territories with interests in the region give up their claims to the disputed islets and invest US$10 billion to establish a South China Sea Development Co. to develop the natural resources co-operatively.[24]

The Claimant States Have a Duty to Co-operate in Managing
the Resources and Protecting the Environment of a Semi-Enclosed Sea
Articles 122 and 123 of the Law of the Sea Convention establish the concept of a "semi-enclosed sea" and require the nations bordering such seas to co-operate with regard to a number of issues. The South China Sea meets the definition of a "semi-enclosed sea" under Article 122, because it consists "entirely or primarily of the territorial seas and exclusive economic zones of two or more coastal States". Article 123 provides that the coastal states "shall endeavor, directly or through an appropriate regional organization" to co-ordinate (a) management, conservation, and exploitation of the living resources, (b) protection and preservation of the marine environment, and (c) scientific research.

Each Claimant's Position Is Weak under International Law
and Thus Each Should Consider a Shared Management Approach
The preceding analysis applying the relevant international law principles to the claims and disputes in the South China Sea indicates that although some results can be predicted, ambiguities remain, and it is impossible to be certain how an international tribunal would allocate the islets, resources, and maritime space of this region. Each of the claims has significant weaknesses under international law, and it is highly unlikely that any of the claimants would receive all of its claimed areas in an adjudication by the I.C.J. or an arbitral tribunal. A better result for all the claimants would be to establish a joint development authority through direct negotiations.

Who Owns Mischief Reef?

Mischief Reef is well within the Philippine-claimed 200-nautical-mile EEZ and sits on the Philippine-claimed legal continental shelf. But China sees the feature as part of its claim to the entire Spratly area based on discovery and usage. Although a few rocks may be exposed at low tide, the reef is covered at high tide and is thus not an "island" under Article 121 of the Law of the Sea Convention. But the construction of facilities and its occupation by China catapulted this obscure feature into the international limelight. The 1995 dispute over the reef cooled when, in the face of a stinging international outcry and ASEAN solidarity, China backed off. It offered bilateral use and development of the reef area and agreed with the Philippines on a "code of conduct" that rejected the use of force to settle disputes. At that time, China said it would resolve its Mischief Reef and other South China Sea disputes according to the Law of the Sea Convention, which it has ratified, and international law.

But the dispute erupted anew. In October 1998, the Philippines discovered that China was building fort-like structures on Mischief Reef. The Philippines countered by detaining twenty Chinese fishermen and impounding their boats for illegal fishing in the area. After a series of acrimonious exchanges, the two sides met on 22–23 March 1999 in Manila to discuss the issue. But little was accomplished. China rejected the Philippine demand that it dismantle the structures. It also denied it had ever offered joint use of the structures to the Philippines, and demanded that Manila cease all reconnaissance flights over the disputed reef. The talks nearly collapsed when China refused to put in writing a verbal commitment not to build any new structures on any Philippine-claimed feature and only reluctantly agreed to state that the Mischief Reef structures would remain for civilian use.

Most international observers believe China's claim to Mischief Reef is weak in international law. First, the Law of the Sea Convention does not authorize claims for submerged features, particularly those that sit on another country's continental shelf. And even if China could successfully argue that the original natural reef did in places rise above high tide and thus that these rocks could generate a territorial sea, it must be able to demonstrate continuous, effective occupation and exercise of authority, as well as acquiescence by other nations, not just discovery. As explained earlier, China bases its claims on historical usage, not on any recent exercise of authority over the Spratlys, and other nations have certainly not acquiesced to China's assertions of sovereignty.

The Philippines' claims based on historical exercise of authority is also weak, but in the case of Mischief Reef, its claim that the feature is within its EEZ and on its legal continental shelf is reasonable. Under the Law of the Sea Convention, no country can build on another's continental shelf without permission. And, as explained above, features that are submerged at high tide cannot generate maritime zones, whether or not they have artificial structures built on them.

The case of Malaysia's occupation of and construction on Investigator Shoal is similar, in that Investigator Shoal apparently does not clear water at high tide and therefore cannot generate extended maritime zones by itself. But it does sit on Malaysia's claimed continental shelf.

Obstacles to Be Overcome

At a press conference in Singapore on 13 August 1990, the visiting Chinese Premier Li Peng said:

> China is ready to join efforts with Southeast Asian countries to develop the [Spratly] Islands, while putting aside for the time being the question of sovereignty ... Under the proposal, Vietnam, China and the Philippines would withdraw their military units from the islands in favour of joint development of the area's seabed and marine resources.

Ever since this proposal that the question of sovereignty be set aside and the resources of the area be jointly developed,[25] commentators have discussed the possibilities of implementing joint development to alleviate tension and avoid conflict. But focused proposals on implementation remain elusive, because the claimants have not agreed on the desired resolution of the Spratlys dispute.

Is the goal a final solution that would allocate maritime space and island ownership, and delimit maritime boundaries, with or without joint development? Is the goal an interim solution such as joint development, or an agreed "commons" area? Or is the goal simply confidence-building and a *modus operandi* or *vivendi* such as a code of conduct and an agreement to continue "discussing" joint development?

Different perspectives among the claimants on these goals are an impediment to progress. Thus the first step forward should be discussion and agreement on the desired goal. *If* the goal is joint development as an interim solution, several obstacles will need to be addressed. One of the worst fears of some of the claimants is that China's vision of joint development is development of resources on their legal continental shelves. Until China clarifies exactly what it claims and why, and dispels this worst fear, other claimants are unlikely to enter into serious discussions of joint development.

The claimants should begin the process of examining the options and developing institutions appropriate to the region. The current fragile standoff among the claimants could result in military strife and the involvement of outside powers. It is in the interest of all the people of this region to explore and develop the resources in the Spratly region co-operatively, but such efforts are now blocked by the stalemate over the competing claims.

NOTES
1. "Estrada Sees Protracted Row in Spratlys", *Philippine Star*, 25 November 1999.
2. See, for instance, Dario Agnote, "Membership of ASEAN Split on Pact", *Washington Times*, 22 October 1999.

3. The following material is adapted from Mark J. Valencia, Jon M. Van Dyke, and Noel A. Ludwig, *Sharing the Resources of the South China Sea* (The Hague and Boston: Martinus Nijhoff, 1997), chap. 3, pp. 39–60.

4. R. Haller-Trost, "International Law and the History of Claims to the Spratly Islands" (Paper presented at South China Sea Conference, Australia Enterprise Institute, 7–9 September 1994).

5. Arbitral Award of His Majesty the King of Italy on the subject of the Difference Relative to the Sovereignty over Clipperton Island (France versus Mexico), 28 January 1931, *American Journal of International Law* 26 (1932): 390 [hereafter cited as *Cipperton* arbitration]; Arbitral Award Rendered in Conformity with the Special Agreement Concluded on 23 January 1925, between the United States of America and the Netherlands Relating to the Arbitration of Differences Respecting Sovereignty over the Island of Palmas (Miangas), 4 April 1928, reprinted in *American Journal of International Law (AJIL)* 22 (1928): 909 [hereafter cited as *Palmas* arbitration]; The Minquiers and Ecrehos Case (France/United Kingdom), International Court of Justice (I.C.J.), 1953, p. 47 [hereafter cited as *Minquiers and Ecrehos* case]; Land, Island and Maritime Frontier Dispute (El Salvador/Honduras; Nicaragua intervening), I.C.J., 1992, p. 351 [hereafter cited as *Gulf of Fonseca* case].

6. See, for example, Ji Guoxing, *The Spratlys Dispute and Prospects for Settlement* (Malaysia: Institute of Strategic and International Studies), 1992.

7. Article 18, Vienna Convention on the Law of Treaties, 22 May 1969.

8. Article 47(1) of the Law of the Sea Convention does allow dying reefs to be used as archipelagic basepoints and Article 7(4) allows baselines to be drawn from low-tide elevations if they have lighthouse on them or have received "general international recognition".

9. Two authors have listed Namyit's elevation as 19 metres: J.R.V. Prescott, *Maritime Jurisdiction in Southeast Asia: Commentary and Map* (Honolulu: East-West Center, 1981), p. 32; Ying Cheng Kiang, *China's Boundaries* (Chicago: Northeastern Illinois University Institute of China Studies, 1984), p. 43.

10. 1 & 2 Office of the Hydrographer (United Kingdom), *South China Sea Pilot*, 1965, pp. 107–13, 271–75.

11. Jon M. Van Dyke and Dale L. Bennett, "Islands and the Delimitation of Ocean Space in the South China Sea", *Ocean Yearbook* 10 (1993): 75–80, 89.

12. See, for example, Lee G. Cordner, "The Spratly Islands Dispute and the Law of the Sea", *Ocean Development & International Law* 25 (1994): 64, 69; see also Gerardo M.C. Valero, "Spratly Archipelago Disputes", *Marine Policy* 18 (1994): 314, 315. Quite significant is the statement made by the Legal Adviser for the Philippine Department of Foreign Affairs, who wrote that the "disputed Spratly Islands are mostly coral reefs which allow only sparse growth of mangroves, shrubs, and stunted trees. This area can hardly support human habitation". Jorge R. Coquia, "Maritime Boundary Problems in the South China Sea", *University of British Columbia Law Review* 24 (1990): 117, 120. A consultant for the Crestone Oil Company has characterized the islets as "tiny" and "of virtually no economic value". Daniel Dzurek says in "Southeast Asian Offshore Oil Disputes", *Ocean Yearbook* 11 (1994): 157, 171, that the "reefs and islands in the Spratly Islands are miniscule and had no economic importance until the development of the new Law of the Sea" (Nonetheless Dzurek asserts that Spratly Island is entitled to generate a continental shelf, because the garrisoning of troops there establishes that it "can sustain human habitation").

13. See Daniel Dzurek, "Southeast Asian Offshore Oil Disputes in the South China Sea" — citing "Petro Vietnam Official on Spratlys Exploration", *Bangkok Post, Inside Indochina* (supplement), 2 November 1993, as transcribed in *Foreign Broadcast Information Service Daily Report: East Asia*, 3 November 1993, p. 54.

14. This was said to Van Dyke. But in its 12 May 1977 Statement Declaring a Territo-

rial Sea, a contiguous Zone, a Continental Shelf, and an Exclusive Economic Zone (para. 5), Vietnam made a broad claim for all such zones which one commentator has interpreted to include the Spratlys and Paracels as well as its mainland coasts.

15. See, for example, Dzurek, "Offshore Oil Disputes", op. cit.; Prescott, *Commentary and Map*, op. cit.; Victor Prescott, "Sharpening the Geographical and Legal Focus on the Potential Regional Conflict in the Spratly Islands" (Paper presented at the Workshop on the Spratly Islands: A Potential Regional Conflict, Institute of Southeast Asian Studies, Singapore, 8–9 December 1993).

16. Statement of 12 May 1977.

17. "Project on Managing Potential Conflicts in the South China Sea", *Summary of Proceedings of First Technical Working Group Meeting on Legal Matters in the South China Sea* (Phuket, Thailand, 2–5 July 1995), p. 10.

18. Jonathan I. Charney, "Progress in International Maritime Boundary Delimitations Law", *American Journal of International Law* 88 (1994): 227, 234 [hereafter cited as Charney, "Progress"].

19. Libya-Malta Continental Shelf Case, I.C.J., 1985, pp. 13, 49 para. 66.

20. I.C.J., 1969, pp. 1, 45 para. 81.

21. Charney, "Progress".

22. Charney, "Progress".

23. *Gulf of Fonseca* case, note 5 above, I.C.J., 1992, p. 596, para. 397.

24. "Lee Urges Joint Venture Plan for South China Sea Works", *Japan Times*, 22 August 1995.

25. However, see also Shen Changjin, "Nanhai Zhanbei Xingshi Yu Gongtong Kaifa Yanjiu" [Strategic situation in the South China Sea and joint development], quoted in Sheng Lijun, "China's Policy towards the Spratly Islands in the 1990s", Working Paper no. 287 (Canberra: Australian National University, June 1995), pp. 20–21: "We think that we may hold negotiations with countries concerned on such issues as areas of joint development, the principles for conducting this joint development and joint investment. After paying an administration fee or rent to our country, foreign investors can be invited into the areas of joint development, with the purpose of exploiting the rich resources of the Nansha Islands for our country's 'four modernisations'. Countries involved can also have certain economic benefits. This is beneficial both to our country's 'four modernisations', and also to local stability and the development of friendly relations with neighbouring countries."

THE EAST TIMOR CRISIS
A Test Case for Humanitarian Intervention

Leonard C. Sebastian and Anthony L. Smith

On 11 June 1999, the United Nations Mission in East Timor (UNAMET) was established through the Security Council Resolution 1246 to implement the 5 May Agreement between Indonesia and Portugal which granted East Timor a referendum or "consultation" on its future. The term "consultation" was used for two reasons. First, to placate a Habibie administration concerned that an outright referendum would open up deep divisions within East Timor and lead to civil war. Second, apprehension that letting East Timor go would open the Pandora's box by encouraging separatist tendencies elsewhere in Indonesia's vast archipelago. The 5 May Agreement concluded that if the East Timorese voted to reject autonomy, then Indonesia would have to undertake the legal procedures necessary to restore East Timor's status prior to 17 July 1976 in order to begin the transition to independence. The U.N. Consultation, originally scheduled for 8 August 1999, was initially delayed until 30 August due to the deteriorating security circumstances created by Jakarta-backed militia violence.

What made this particular U.N. operation unique was the character of the U.N. intervention. Under the terms of the organization's charter, this was not a "Chapter 7" intervention. The Indonesian police (Polri) remained responsible for security in East Timor for the duration of the U.N. Consultation. In this regard, the U.N. presence was by invitation, and the authority it could exercise was limited by its mandate. Significantly, U.N. police personnel would be confined to their role as advisers. Under such circumstances, the United Nations was operating under the provisions of "Chapter 6", that is, through acceptance by all the parties concerned.

The U.N. Consultation set in motion a painful process of self-determination for the Timorese people which reached its conclusion through a People's Consultative Assembly (MPR) decree on 28 October 1999 to officially recognize East Timor's historic vote for independence and declare null and void a 1978 decree annexing the territory. The MPR vote on the decree recognized the result of the 30 August ballot, where of 98.6 per cent of eligible voters who cast their votes, 78.5 per cent voted for independence. Voters defied threats

LEONARD C. SEBASTIAN and ANTHONY L. SMITH are Fellows at the Institute of Southeast Asian Studies, Singapore.

and intimidation by pro-Jakarta militia, who had the backing of 20,000 Indonesian police and troops in the territory.

The MPR decision effectively meant the birth of one of the world's smallest nations, and signified the end of Indonesia's claim to the former Portuguese colony. Jakarta effectively ceased *de facto* control when the International Force for East Timor (INTERFET) arrived in the wake of post-ballot violence which saw tens of thousands of people forced to flee from the territory or to the mountains in an attempt to escape Indonesian military-sponsored terror. Many have yet to return to their villages. East Timor's population was estimated at 850,000 before the 30 August self-determination ballot. Some 260,000 fled East Timor and sought refuge in the neighbouring Indonesian province of East Nusa Tenggara. Only half of these refugees have returned to the territory under U.N. High Commission for Refugees (UNHCR) auspices since early November. A combination of logistical shortcomings and security problems related to access to militia-controlled refugee camps had slowed down repatriation of refugees. At present, the United Nations and its humanitarian agencies are seeking to raise US$199 million in emergency funds for the East Timorese both in the territory and in refugee centres in neighbouring East Nusa Tenggara.

Humanitarian Intervention

Military intervention has been initiated during the course of history by the great powers and their allies in order to solidify their respective spheres of influence. In the 1990s a new type of intervention took place, usually sanctioned by the United Nations and often justified in terms of protecting the human rights of others. East Timor is a striking example, which illustrates graphically how the norms have changed to some extent in the post–Cold War era. In 1975, under an intervention paradigm that was commonplace during the Cold War, the world acquiesced to Indonesia's *invasion* of East Timor and the brutal suppression of its independence movement. Contrast that situation with the approach adopted for East Timor in 1999 where in the course of its intervention, the international community used every diplomatic tactic at its disposal short of war to defend *human rights*.

The new norms regarding humanitarian intervention were reinforced by U.N. Secretary-General Kofi Annan's pointed reminder in September 1999 that "massive and systematic violations of human rights — wherever they may take place — should not be allowed to stand". This placed on notice countries that believe that sovereignty allows them to get away with genocide, ethnic cleansing, and other atrocities. He also announced the arrival of a new era of U.N. interventionism in which an activist Security Council would play a crucial role. He spoke about the possible repercussions to any state embarking on "criminal behaviour" on the assumption that the sacrosanct nature of frontiers and sovereignty would deter the Security Council from taking action to halt crimes against humanity. In this regard, intervention refers to the willingness on the part of sovereign states to act collectively to enforce the standards of civilized conduct established by the international community. While there is nothing new in a U.N. secretary-general promoting the rule of law in international relations, what makes Annan's remarks salient is that humanitarian intervention seems to be an "idea whose time has come". While humanitarian intervention cannot be seen as replacing the traditional pursuit of power interests, it has added a new important dimension — albeit unevenly applied — to international politics.

Humanitarian intervention has occurred in a number of instances in the post–Cold War world. Some of the more significant interventions, of quite varying natures are: the establishment of no-fly zones in northern and southern Iraq in 1991 to protect, respectively, the Kurdish refugees and the Marsh Arabs; Bosnia-Herzegovina (1992–95); Somalia (1992); Cambodia (1994); Rwanda (1994); Haiti (1994) by a U.S. intervention force; Albania (1997) by an Italian intervention force; Kosovo (1998-99); Sierra Leone (1999); and finally East Timor (1999). Impressive as this list may sound, humanitarian intervention is a contested notion. It should also be noted that of the "humanitarian interventions" listed above, national self-interest played a major role for some participating nation-states. However, this does not undermine the essential point, that increasingly humanitarian disasters are viewed as subjects of international concern in a globalized world.

The growth of human rights/international humanitarian law and the impressive growth of international institutions have made humanitarian intervention possible. Yet, traditionalists would argue that international law reiterates the importance of non-intervention as a principle of international relations and the avoidance of war. It is this ambiguity that surrounds the concept with two bodies of law seemingly pulling in opposite directions. There does not exist any treaty or international agreement that codifies the right for intervention. The U.N. Charter itself contains a contradiction. Article 2 (7) guarantees state sovereignty: "Nothing contained in the present Charter shall authorize the United Nations to intervene in matters which are essentially within the domestic jurisdiction of any state". At the same time Article 1 (2) reaffirms the principle of equal rights and the "self-determination of peoples". Sometimes these two principles are at odds. Chapter 7 of the Charter also gives the Security Council the right to determine breaches to "peace and security", and *ipso facto*, issues that fall outside the sole domain of domestic jurisdiction. Increasingly, substantial human rights abuses are considered as beyond the exclusive realm of a strict interpretation of state sovereignty by a large section of the international community — perhaps the most important test was South Africa's apartheid regime in response to which the international community, including the United Nations, shunned South Africa on the grounds that its policies were so offensive that the matter could not be considered solely a domestic one.

It has been pointed out that more states oppose the right of humanitarian intervention than support it. Most countries with a colonial experience remember how external intervention was used under various pretexts in the cause of colonialism. On the Security Council, both China and Russia oppose intervention in another state's affairs regardless of the circumstances. Furthermore, the record for humanitarian intervention is patchy and inconsistent. The U.S. intervention in Haiti was an attempt to reassert democracy, but has failed to fully achieve this objective. Similarly, ethnic tensions have resurfaced in Kosovo. In Somalia, even though hundreds of thousands of lives were saved through the introduction of food aid, the resulting chaos surrounding an attempt to put a clan leader on trial ended in a debacle and consequently an undignified retreat ensued. It would be a mistake to declare that the international community will act to prevent humanitarian crises whenever and wherever they occur. There are some important limitations on intervention, including: (1) the finite political, economic, and military resources to tackle global problems; (2) the need for support from both the home and the host populations; (3) the need to avoid a wider regional or global war which would lead, at best, to a pyrrhic victory; (4) the importance of a speedy victory; and (5) the support of the permanent members (P-5) of the Security Council who have the authority to thwart any intervention.

Nevertheless, emotional support among the populations of most open societies does exist for need for humanitarian intervention. The need for principles for humanitarian intervention was emphasized strongly in a 1999 U.N. report on the safe areas in Bosnia and Rwanda where the international community was criticized for being unable to protect unarmed civilians from being terrorized. Ultimately, these contrasting responses suggest that intervention in the post–Cold War era remains problematic. For the agenda on humanitarian intervention to become viable may require significant assessments in three areas. First, developing a doctrine of intervention that will allow the United Nations greater freedom of action. Second, the need to work out practical considerations, namely, the objectives or strategy troops should undertake once they arrive in an operational environment. Finally, there is the question of consent. Who gives authority to a particular mission and what would be the nature of the authorizing body?

East Timor may be a useful case study as it meets certain criteria. The international community had a stake in East Timor when it accepted the right of the East Timorese for self-determination. The United Nations played a significant role in brokering the process with Indonesia and Portugal and organized the referendum. Attempts by the pro-autonomy groups backed by the Indonesian military to thwart the process made it a special case. The inability of the Indonesian civilian authorities to prevent the violence meant that their *de facto* sovereignty over East Timor was null and void. The United Nations was also forced to act because of its own involvement in the process. Having managed the referendum, it had a direct interest to ensure that its authority would not be transgressed, particularly in the context of the ensuing humanitarian disaster that accompanied the post-ballot phase. Faced by a community of like-minded states led by Australia, given a robust mandate by the Security Council, cajoled by other governments, and embarrassed by the international media, even a state as powerful as Indonesia had to succumb to the inevitable. Perhaps the U.N. response to the East Timor emergency could point the way forward to an approach to intervention that may find resonance in the international community.

Historical Background

East Timor will have to build from scratch after pro-Jakarta militia, under the protective role of local military leaders, destroyed almost all its buildings and infrastructure after the results of the U.N.-supervised ballot were announced on 4 September. However, the real issue for East Timor to resolve before any form of rebuilding begins would be the need for reconciliation between the country's two warring factions — the pro-autonomy and pro-independence groups. Bridging this gap will require an end to the culture of violence that has been endemic to a population seemingly trapped in a state of permanent civil war since the collapse of the Caetano regime in Lisbon in April 1974 precipitated the decolonization of Portugal's colonial empire.

Though the declaration of independence on the part of the Fretilin government on 28 November 1975 attracted support only among Portugal's former colonies in Africa, the pretext for the 7 December 1975 invasion by Indonesia, an invitation from elements of the defeated Timorese Democratic Union (UDT) Party in refuge in West Timor, lacked credibility. It is noteworthy that in all the years prior to 1975, Indonesia never laid claim to the territory, and refrained (when a more plausible excuse might have been found) from overt intervention during the conflict between the UDT and Fretilin parties in August–September 1975. It is, of course, a matter of record that from 14 October 1974 Indonesia, fearing the emergence of a Marxist regime in East Timor, was active in destabilizing the situation there through a clandestine intelligence operation called Operasi Komodo.

For a short period of time (from 19 August to 7 December 1975), prior to the incorporation of East Timor into Indonesia, Fretilin seems to have been successful in governing the territory and defending its borders. Though its power derived partly from its defeat of political rivals after the UDT coup attempt on 11 August, the Fretilin did enjoy popular support. In elections for local councils held under Portuguese auspices prior to the UDT coup, Fretilin candidates gained 55 per cent of the popular vote. Having witnessed the marginalization of the pro-Indonesia UDT and Apodeti forces, Indonesia, concerned about the possibility of an emergent Marxist regime in East Timor becoming a veritable "Cuba" on its doorstep, stepped up its clandestine operations to destabilize East Timor. On 6 June 1975 Indonesian troops entered the enclave of Oecusse Ambeno — a part of East Timor territory surrounded by Indonesian territory — and followed up those actions by attacking the border town of Batugate on 6 October 1975. Although the main invasion of East Timor by Indonesian troops took place on 7 December 1975, the annexation of East Timor did not occur formally until 17 July 1976. Indeed, the Fretilin administration seems to have survived in many parts of East Timor until the second half of 1978.

With the advantage of a larger military force, by the mid-1980s, the Indonesian military were able to control most of the territory of East Timor. The early battles were not well conducted, and there are numerous eyewitness accounts of widespread civilian killings. Terror and famine, as much as military action, were used to destroy opposition to military rule. Against such odds, the Falintil (Fretilin's military arm) were reduced to waging mobile warfare in small bands.

The counter-insurgency war conducted by the Indonesian military has been costly in human terms. Estimates vary, but it is generally accepted that there were fatalities numbering in the region of 120,000 to 200,000 people from the pre-1975 population of 650,000.[1] Confronted by overwhelming military force, and thereby forced to conduct their guerrilla campaigns in remote areas, Fretilin changed tactics in the 1980s, forging a common front with other groups and shifting the focus of the struggle to the urban areas by adopting Intifada-style tactics. The CNRM (National Council of Maubere Resistance) became the political common front of the anti-Indonesia movement.

During the Cold War, East Timor as an international issue ceased to have much relevance despite periodic U.N. resolutions starting with the Security Council resolution of 22 December 1975 which "deplored" Indonesia's seizure of the territory and called for a withdrawal of the Indonesian military. Since 1975, the U.N. position has been that the Indonesian annexation was not lawful and amounted to a denial of the right of the population to exercise self-determination. General Assembly resolutions between 1976 and 1982 reiterated these sentiments, as did deliberations in the U.N. Decolonization Committee. In 1983 further voting on the issue was suspended, and the General Assembly charged the secretary-general with the responsibility of negotiating an end to the dispute. From that time, successive secretaries-general have convened negotiations in a variety of settings in order to attempt some compromise between the parties.

The United Nation's early role in resolving the East Timor issue had been relatively muted. The visit of the secretary-general's envoy to East Timor in 1976 did not kindle any significant support. Similarly, Portugal, despite its responsibility as the former colonial power, was lethargic in pursuing the issue. In contrast, the early 1990s saw a flurry of activity. The November 1991 Santa Cruz massacre heightened international exposure on East Timor. Subsequently, a series of meetings under U.N. auspices, especially one convened in Austria in 1995, brought the various Timorese groups together to discuss protecting human rights and promoting development. And with a change in political administration in Lisbon, Portugal took a renewed interest in events in the territory.

Indonesia's invasion and brutal rule over East Timor had blighted its foreign policy and put its leaders on the defensive at international forums. Consequently, the province had become such a burden to Indonesia that Foreign Minister Ali Alatas described it as a "pebble in its shoe". The forced resignation of Soeharto in May 1998 reopened the policy debate over East Timor. For Soeharto's successor, Dr B.J. Habibie, the territory seemed more trouble than it was worth. The issue began to hot up in January 1999, not long after Australia's Prime Minister John Howard sent a letter in December 1998 to President Habibie suggesting that the East Timorese be given a greater say in their future. The Australian policy switch elicited a strong knee-jerk reaction from the élite within President Habibie's inner circle.

UNAMET

On 27 January, calculating that pro-autonomy forces would win in any referendum ballot, an Indonesian cabinet decision was made to initiate a process that would conceivably lead to referendum, settling once and for all the thorny question of East Timor's status. However, elements of the Indonesian Armed Forces (TNI), perhaps less confident of victory in a ballot, chose another means of trying to keep East Timor within Indonesia. By February, pro-Jakarta militia began intimidating the Timorese ahead of the 30 August vote as Indonesian government officials portrayed the violence as clashes between rival groups while accusing the international media of exaggerating the facts. In hindsight, this militia tactic of violence and wholesale intimidation backfired as it shored up significant support for independence as many East Timorese came to see independence as the only option to ensure their security in the long term.[2] The timing of the referendum for either autonomy or independence was rushed partly because those involved in the talks did not know if the offer would survive President Habibie's administration. The United Nations and the wider international community may have also gambled on Habibie's ability to control the TNI. Armed Forces Chief General Wiranto initially went along with this plan, with operational control for East Timor overseen by the Armed Forces Intelligence Agency (Bais).

After a lengthy series of negotiations between Indonesia, Portugal, and the United Nations, a further agreement, dated 5 May 1999, was signed. This agreement noted the different positions of Indonesia and Portugal on the issue of East Timor's future, but both signed a statement saying that in order to further the peace process, the secretary-general "should consult the East Timorese people on the constitutional framework for autonomy". It was also decided that this would involve a U.N.-administered referendum to decide if the East Timorese accepted or rejected the proposed autonomy. The United Nations Mission in East Timor (UNAMET) was established to organize the entirety of the voting process. The 5 May Agreement concludes that if the East Timorese voted to reject autonomy then Indonesia would have to undertake the legal steps necessary to restore East Timor's status prior to 17 July 1976 (the date of East Timor's official annexation by Indonesia) in order to begin the transition to independence.

The vote in East Timor was in fact the second such major operation by the United Nations to run a free and fair poll in its entirety. The first was the 1993 Cambodian elections under the auspices of the United Nations Transitional Authority in Cambodia (UNTAC), in which the United Nations wrote the electoral law, registered voters, and supervised the polls. What made UNAMET unique was that it gave the sole responsibility for security to the Indonesian police (Polri), as stipulated in the 5 May Agreement. In other words, UNAMET went into East Timor without the protection of armed U.N. peacekeeping troops. The agreement also prescribed the absolute neutrality of Polri and the TNI in the referendum process. The duties of the Indonesian police included protection of U.N. staff, disarmament of armed groups, and the supervision of ballot papers and boxes while in transit.

The mission included 240 international staff, 270 civilian police (CivPol), 50 military liaison officers (MLO), 425 U.N. volunteers (UNV), and 668 local East Timorese staff for translation and driving (plus 3,600 East Timorese who were hired for five days to run the actual referendum). More than 400 four-wheel drive vehicles were especially flown into East Timor by the United Nations in order to cope with local conditions. All vehicles were fitted with radios which, together with 500 hand-held radios, were essential for communication in the field. The total cost of the operation was estimated at US\$52.5 million, relying, as U.N. missions tend to, on pledged contributions from U.N. member states. Australia contributed nearly one-third of the amount, while contributions also came from, *inter alia*, Finland, Japan, New Zealand, Norway, and Portugal.

The 5 May Agreement contained strict criteria on who could vote in the referendum. Those eligible to vote were defined as "persons born in East Timor", "persons born outside East Timor but with at least one parent having been born in East Timor", and "persons whose spouses fall under either of the two categories above". East Timorese living in exile overseas could also vote if they could get to polling centres in Portugal and Australia. There were also polling centres in some large cities in Indonesia as well. The criteria for registration effectively disenfranchised transmigrant groups, even those who had been in East Timor for more than two decades. However, it was deemed necessary by the United Nations to avoid an even greater problem of outsiders coming in to take part — particularly from West Timor.

In total, 200 registration centres were established in order to allow the East Timorese people to decide between the two options, which were either "Do you accept the proposed special autonomy for East Timor within the Unitary State of the Republic of Indonesia?" or "Do you reject the proposed special autonomy for East Timor, leading to East Timor's separation from Indonesia?". The special autonomy that was proposed would have given the local administration control over most aspects of governance except foreign affairs, external defence, court of appeal, symbols of state, and monetary and fiscal polices. The original proposal that East Timor manage its own resources was amended in the final agreement to state that while natural resources were to be under East Timorese control, an exception would be made in the case that a resource was "strategic or vital" to the central government in Indonesia. This clearly raised a question over the future exploitation of the oil reserves in the Timor Gap. Under this proposal, Jakarta would continue to fund the administration of East Timor, while the provincial authorities would be able to seek external aid. In fact, the funding of East Timor, claimed to be 90 per cent of East Timor's total expenditure, was one of the main campaign planks of the pro-autonomy movement within East Timor.

In any event, discussion about special autonomy for East Timor is purely academic as the people overwhelmingly overturned this option on 30 August 1999 by rejecting special autonomy, "leading to separation from Indonesia". Noteworthy is that there was no option for those who favoured the retention of full integration with Indonesia, autonomy being the next best option for such individuals.

An extensive voter education programme was carried out. Great emphasis was placed on persuading the local people of their unique chance to decide on their future in an election that was freer and fairer than any they had experienced in the past. Much use was made of verbal communication to counter the problem of low literacy levels amongst the East Timorese people in rural areas. 30 August 1999, the polling day for the Popular Consultation for East Timor, was a remarkable success in that more than 98 per cent of registered voters cast a vote in the referendum. In order to keep the voting patterns secret, all ballot boxes, once checked in at the counting centre in Dili, were then randomly mixed prior to the final count. Therefore the final result, 78.5 per cent rejecting autonomy and opting for independence, is a nation-wide result. The breakdown of results by region will never be known.

However, these careful procedures did not placate the militia, the pro-autonomy supporters, and some of the official Indonesian observers. Alleging "collusion" between UNAMET and the National Council for East Timorese Resistance (CNRT), the militia renewed their attacks towards the end of polling day itself. Most polling centres reported breaches of the voting rules and regulations including intimidation, roadblocks, the burning of homes, carrying weapons too close to the polling stations, and the firing of shots into the air.

This intimidation was to foreshadow events just a few days later when hundreds, or possibly thousands, died at the hands of the pro-Indonesian militia groups and forced the majority of the UNAMET teams to abandon East Timor. Prior to the actual vote, there was strong international pressure on the Habibie administration to allow the process to go ahead, including a strongly worded letter from the U.S. President, Bill Clinton, which warned that violence and intimidation in East Timor would hold "consequences" for the U.S.-Indonesian relationship.

What had become evident by voting day was that the Indonesian police, charged with protecting the U.N. mission, failed to stem militia actions. Despite protestations from military officials that the violence in East Timor was perpetrated by rogue elements within the military, the fact remains that the deep ties many military figures have in East Timor gave it a vested interest in implicitly supporting a campaign of terror against those who favoured independence.

Many militiamen were armed with automatic weapons and hand grenades, to supplement a plethora of home-made weapons, despite a cantonization agreement, which was supposed to include disarmament. They appear to have known exactly who the leading supporters of independence were and where they lived. The militiamen went about their killing in a terrifyingly organized way. They had also singled out people in refugee camps in West Timor, and in convoys and boatloads of refugees trying to escape. The violence was particularly bad for those districts near the West Timorese border, for example, the enclave of Oecussi-Ambeno was especially vulnerable where 1,000 men, women, and children were reportedly murdered immediately after the referendum. The *International Commission of Inquiry on East Timor*, released by the U.N. Office of the High Commissioner for Human Rights in January 2000, established clear complicity between the TNI and the militia based on the testimonies of East Timorese and U.N. personnel. It concluded that the post-referendum violence "took the form of vengeance" and included executions, gender violence ("women were targeted for sexual assault in a cruel and systematic way"), destruction of 60 to 80 per cent of both public and private property, disruption to 70 per cent of the health services, destruction of educational institutions, and the displacement and forcible relocation of thousands of people to West Timor. The report thus confirms that the militia violence was designed to create the illusion of a civil conflict. It also draws the obvious conclusion that the Indonesian army was "responsible for the intimidation, terror, killings and other acts of violence" committed in East Timor throughout 1999.

A second report, the Indonesian government-sanctioned *Inquiry into Human Rights Abuses* (known as KPP HAM), commissioned by Indonesia's Attorney-General, Marzuki Darusman, drew similar conclusions. However, KPP HAM actually cited thirty-three people who deserve further investigation, including the then TNI chief of staff, General Wiranto. The chairman of the report body, Djoko Soegianto, verbally summarized the accusation in this way:

> The crimes against humanity committed in East Timor occurred entirely, directly or indirectly, because of the failure of the (former) TNI chief to ensure security in the implementation of the government's two options.

This report caused President Abdurrahman Wahid to insist on General Wiranto's resignation from his ministerial portfolio leading to a crisis situation whereby the general initially refused his president's wish to step down.

While Jakarta's political leaders may have agreed to the referendum in the first place, it appears in the end they could not control elements of their own military. The suggestion has been made that the violence was the result of a civil conflict between rival East Timorese political factions, but this simplistic explanation obscures the fact that the militia enjoyed little legitimacy amongst the East Timorese population and had relied on substantial external support. The violence abated considerably with the arrival on 20 September of the first wave of Australian, New Zealand, and British troops, which constituted the core of U.N. mandated force in East Timor operating under the U.N. Charter's Chapter 7 and under Security Council Resolution 1264.

INTERFET

The securing of East Timor by INTERFET troops under Operation Stabilize was considered a dangerous venture with nationalism on the rise in Jakarta. The Security Council approved the INTERFET operation both to restore peace and security, and support the UNAMET mission, which had seriously floundered under the circumstances. The Security Council also gave the multinational force some fairly robust rules of engagement, in particular, INTERFET did not have to wait to be fired on to return the engagement, unlike U.N. peacekeeping operations. The INTERFET forces were not ostensibly U.N. forces, and constituted a "coalition of the willing" with U.N. approval. Fears that the multinational force could face high-level aggression from pro-Jakarta militia have proved unfounded. The appropriately 8,000-strong force, led by Australia (contributing around 4,500 troops, thus forming the bulk of the operation), has met only isolated incidents. Slowly, the INTERFET forces were able to enter into the main regional towns in East Timor, mostly without incidents.

The militia groups simply melted away and posed no serious threat. The only high-profile engagement occurred on 10 October 1999 when INTERFET troops clashed with a group of Indonesian security personnel along East Timor's border with East Nusa Tenggara resulting in the death of an Indonesian policeman. This incident resulted from a misunderstanding over the poorly mapped border. The most serious challenge from the militia occurred on 18 October when twenty militiamen attacked a five-man Australian patrol that left three militia dead and three wounded. Apart from a handful of other incidents, including some spear-throwing near the border area and a token "attack" over the border to commemorate Indonesia's initial invasion on 7 December, the multinational force has had a free hand to secure East Timor. Understandably, fear of militia penetration still permeates the villages and towns near to the border with West Timor.

INTERFET was able to secure the countryside, organize the distribution of relief supplies, and help resettle the hundreds of thousands of East Timorese that had been uprooted. The United Nations estimates that 500,000 East Timorese were displaced from their homes. The main challenge to INTERFET was not from the militia in East Timor, but the retrieval of as many as 260,000 East Timorese forcibly transported to West Timor, and still under the thumb of pro-Indonesian forces. Many were able to return either by special flights out of Kupang or on their own accord, slipping back through the border. The withdrawal of Indonesian troops and the handover of full-military command in East Timor to the force commander Major-General Peter Cosgrove (who left East Timor on 23 February 2000) had provided the multinational force with the unfettered authority it required to undertake its tasks. Kofi Annan, U.N. Secretary-General, on the departure of Cosgrove, used the opportunity to single out Australia for praise over its speed in committing troops to East Timor just weeks after the UNAMET-organized referendum. Annan remarked that the United Nations would have taken months to act, by which time the violence would have carried on unabated and it would have been "too late to pick up the pieces".

The intervention of the Australian-led multinational force allowed the United Nations, through its UNAMET mission to begin large-scale humanitarian relief to a country which was left without infrastructure and enough sources of food and drinkable water. This was coupled with a Consolidated Inter-Agency Appeal for US$199 million, announced on 27 October 1999. INTERFET itself was versatile. It repaired roads, ran medical clinics, re-roofed government buildings, built sewage treatment ponds and bridges, distributed food, removed garbage, renovated churches, airports, and at least one city market.

The establishment of security played a major role in convincing Indonesia of the futility of attempting to hang on to East Timor, in part or in full. On 28 September, at a meeting between Indonesia and Portugal, Indonesia agreed in principle to transfer all authority over East Timor to the United Nations. On 28 October 1999, the last formal link between Indonesia and its claim to East Timor as its "27th province" was severed when the MPR formally recognized, by a unanimous vote, the result of the Popular Consultation in East Timor. The waning support by elements of the TNI with regard to the militia groups is most likely a direct result of the realization of INTERFET's overwhelming military strength in dealing with lightly armed bandits.

UNTAET

By 25 October, the Security Council passed Resolution 1272 to empower Secretary-General Kofi Annan to set up the U.N. Transitional Authority in East Timor (UNTAET) in order to "to exercise all legislative and executive authority including the administration of justice" until formal independence. The mission is to be placed under the authority of the Special Representative of the Secretary-General, Sergio Vieira de Mello of Brazil. A U.N. peacekeeping force will formally replace INTERFET under the command of Lieutenant-General Jaime de los Santos of the Philippines. The United Nations authorized a force of 8,950 troops, 200 military observers, and a 1,640-strong contingent of civilian police. UNTAET is empowered to "take all necessary measures" to fulfil its mandate, which includes the delivery of assistance, reconstruction of infrastructure, and the creation of democratic institutions. At the time of writing, the budget and method of financing the operation had not been determined.

The biggest initial problem towards resolving the current conflict is the status of the pro-autonomy East Timorese. In the wake of the post-ballot violence, the pro-autonomy camp came up with a proposal which would divide East Timor into eight regencies. The three eastern regencies would be allowed to have independence while the remaining five would have autonomy within Indonesia. Such a stance was worrying if accounts reporting several thousand militiamen undergoing training in West Timor with tacit support from the Indonesian military to conduct a hit-and-run guerrilla war across the East Timor border were to be believed. General Wiranto had refuted these allegations. However, if true, such covert activities could undermine international efforts to stabilize the humanitarian situation and establish basic security within the territory. Having said that, in the face of *force majeure*, it is unlikely that the militia will be a force to destabilize East Timor without the significant backing of the Indonesian military. Furthermore, the realization that the pro-autonomy militias enjoy no backing from any significant portion of the East Timorese population has seen the decline of this idea as a realistic one. Elements of the TNI, who previously supported the militia groups, seem to have stopped giving assistance to these groups at this time. The major task for the United Nations and the East Timorese leaders, in lieu of the demise of the militia threat, is the long-term economic future of the territory.

Development Prospects
The creation of a newly independent society and economy in East Timor, however, does present a harsh study in development from the ground up. Unemployment is rife, while expectations for the newly independent state are too high to be met. Facilities on East Timor were 70 per cent damaged. Apart from roads, ports, airfields, and power plants, East Timor has almost none of the basic elements of a functioning nation: no budget or banking system, no judiciary or law enforcement or government institutions. Its healthcare, trade, and agriculture systems are a shambles. Most of its people are subsistence farmers; most are illiterate. There is no manufacturing to speak of, with the private services sector thin — including hotels and retailing — now that its Indonesian and Chinese owners have left. All this means that there is little in the way of industry that can pay for the services of government. The traditional livelihoods of the populations, revolving around primary production, have been disrupted by the militia violence which resulted in the death of farm animals, and the destruction of tools and vehicles. This has seriously hampered the current crop cycle.

Previously, the Indonesian government had picked up the bill for the administration of East Timor, providing the annual US$110 million needed for the administrative budget (although much of this money subsequently returned to Java through a network of Indonesian civil servants and contracts). This is the first vacuum the Indonesian withdrawal creates. But another will be harder to fill: the departure of most of the country's professionals and public servants. Indonesians ran electricity, water, banks, hospitals, transport companies, and the airport. Their exodus began early last year and is complete.

East Timor was a poor territory even prior to the events of 1999, with 90 per cent of the 884,000 population living in rural areas and 70 per cent with subsistence life-styles (1998 figures). The gross domestic product (GDP) was US$168 (half the Indonesian average), with 50 per cent of households on the poverty line, while life expectancy was measured at fifty-six years (nine years lower than the Indonesian average). The short-term problems facing East Timor are immense. Four months after arriving as a liberating force in East Timor, the United Nations is struggling to mend the social fabric. In a land where U.N. Secretary-General Kofi Annan says 80 per cent of the population is "without visible means of support" and where frustration is increasing at the slow pace of reconstruction, some are turning to violence and crime to vent their anger or to satisfy their hunger. In the short term, the biggest challenge facing UNTAET is the maintenance of law and order as the depth of the social malaise and rising petty crime could potentially threaten the political unity forged during East Timor's long fight against Indonesian occupation. The cohesion of East Timor's political factions within the context of national reconciliation is at best fragile. The U.N.-chaired National Consultative Commission (NCC), comprising the pro-independence umbrella group, CNRT, the church, and representatives of the pro-integration side debates policy issues and currently serves as the nearest thing to a government-in-waiting.

On a brighter note, the World Bank mission to East Timor had concluded on 9 November 1999 that the country should be an economically self-sufficient country in the medium term. For at least the next decade or two, East Timor will be dependent on foreign aid. The potential for growth identified by the World Bank team focused mainly on agriculture, particularly coffee, as central to the country's economy. East Timorese arabica coffee, grown organically primarily due to a lack of funds to buy fertilizer and pesticide, sells at a premium on the American market. In 1998 the U.S. market took US$20 million worth of East Timorese coffee, which meant that many East Timorese coffee growers earned vastly more in that year than when coffee had been regulated under monopoly control, which characterized primary production in Soeharto's Indonesia. Previously, coffee production was controlled by front companies belonging to the TNI.[3]

There are reserves of gold, manganese, and other minerals. Huge reserves of high-quality marble exist. There is also oil potential in the Timor Gap, although this particular reserve is difficult to tap and would be costly to exploit. Nevertheless, a renegotiated Timor Gap treaty should in time bring in some petro-dollars. Tourism has been touted as another possibility for the future given the pristine nature of the landscape, the beaches, and the sea. But again this remains a long-term prospect given the devastation of infrastructure; East Timor will only attract those interested in educational or adventure tourism in the short term, which is not the most lucrative tourist market. Foreign investment seems unlikely until political stability is deemed to have returned, although Portugal has tried to drum up investors for infrastructural development.

A donor's meeting was held on 17 December 1999 with delegates from over fifty countries pledging US$520 million for the reconstruction of East Timor over the next three years. This amount will adequately cover the recurrent budget and go some way towards development and construction efforts. The CNRT leader Xanana Gusmao was reportedly very happy with the amount, which may have exceeded the CNRT's expectations of what they could realistically expect from the international community. With limited time before international attention moves elsewhere, it is imperative that funds be raised soon. The money will be spent by the United Nations who will administer the province for at least a year under Sergio Vieira de Mello, UNTAET's Chief of Mission, with the strong possibility of renewal of U.N. terms as with many other missions. Despite growing "aid fatigue" in the developed world, East Timor should remain a popular aid cause in the considerations of some nations. At the very least, its former colonial master, Portugal, can be expected to maintain an active aid relationship, while Australia and New Zealand will also contribute in the long term due to geographical proximity (and, some would suggest, because of guilt over their earlier acquiescence to Indonesia). There is no doubt others, such as the European Union, the United States, and Japan, will also make contributions. Nevertheless, aid distribution entails great problems for a society like East Timor, where there is a danger of the development of dependency on foreign handouts. Gusmao has been quoted as saying that U.N. development agencies and non-governmental organizations (NGOs) are "neo-colonialists" — meaning it is better for the East Timorese leaders to direct development assistance as best suits their needs.

East Timor's economic prospects are at least as good as an independent state as they were under Indonesia's rule, without the tangled web of Indonesia's "toll-gate" enterprises regulating the productive sector. With the emergence of economic globalization, few nation-states can claim to be entirely self-sufficient economically, and trade and investment remain important components of economic development. Globalization means that smaller units have a greater chance of survival because of their access to global markets as global trade is freed over time. East Timor will do just as well, or better, to participate in the global market-place under its own auspices.

East Timor and the Wider Region

The quiescence of the Association of Southeast Asian Nations (ASEAN) over the East Timor crisis further battered its international image. Though Indonesia was castigated for the bloodletting when pro-Jakarta militias ran amok in East Timor after the independence vote, East Timor became ASEAN's millstone when the Association failed to speak up and stop the rampage. ASEAN's inaction at the start of the crisis surrendered the moral and political high ground to Australia — though whether Australia's initiative was borne out of altruism or national interest in its quest to be a serious regional power will be an issue that will be hotly debated. Touted as a regional organization that keeps the peace, ASEAN's effectiveness was seriously questioned.

However, what ASEAN's moral ambivalence has created is a situation where the Association's voice may no longer be credible whenever it calls for Asian solutions to Asian problems. This is not to say that ASEAN is irrelevant, but it is in grave danger of becoming irrelevant. In that sense, ASEAN's reticence did not serve it well at a time when the traditional concept of national sovereignty was being challenged world-wide and human rights were considered an important dimension in foreign policy. Such an approach to foreign policy had become evident in the policies of many states in the West following the conflict in Somalia, Bosnia, and Kosovo. Furthermore, an agenda stressing the concept of humanitarian intervention to alleviate human suffering was also promoted vigorously by U.N. Secretary-General Kofi Annan. Confronted by such pressures, ASEAN's mindset about strict non-interference in the internal affairs of member states had undermined its clout as a regional organization.

Having said that, there were mitigating political circumstances behind ASEAN's timid response to the East Timor crises. ASEAN was trapped in the conventional view that East Timor was an internal matter for Indonesia to solve by itself. To compound that perception, there was a sense that because the Indonesian military was involved, no ASEAN state wanted to displease an institution that in the minds of most ASEAN élites would outlive any presidency in Indonesia. Furthermore, a strained relationship with Indonesia, ASEAN's largest country, was troublesome, especially for smaller ASEAN states, and it could be a source of tension and instability in the region. Possibly, from ASEAN's perspective, saving ASEAN and keeping it intact was the more significant objective than saving the people of East Timor. ASEAN's founder members — Singapore, Malaysia, Thailand, and the Philippines saw a stable Indonesia as the essence of ASEAN. Compounding this situation is that the newer entrants to ASEAN — Vietnam, Myanmar, Laos, and Cambodia — are vehemently opposed to humanitarian intervention and maintain an absolutist view of state sovereignty. Hence, with Indonesia as the cornerstone of regional stability, ASEAN leaders were reluctant to speak out strongly against Indonesia and saw the protection of ASEAN solidarity as a competing morality. There would have been consequences whichever side ASEAN took in East Timor's case. For ASEAN élites, the possible isolation and the hostility of Indonesia — seen as the price to be paid for speaking out strongly against Indonesia — was justifiable and as politically correct as Australia's interventionist approach. While individual member states, notably the Philippines and Thailand and to a lesser extent Singapore, gave support to the referendum's outcome (both in public statements and in significant contributions to INTERFET), ASEAN as an organization was unable to deal with this issue.

Australia intervened in the way that it did, and its relations with Indonesia have hit rock-bottom. Nothing captured this situation more vividly than the unilateral decision by Indonesia on 16 September 1999 to cancel the 1995 Australia-Indonesia Agreement on Maintaining Security. The significance of the treaty was not so much its security content, which was insubstantial, but its political dimension. The abrogation of the treaty was a formal warning that relations were rapidly approaching hostility and was a sobering reminder of the gravity of the crisis. Under the administration of the new president, Abdurrahman Wahid, there has been some warming of the bilateral relationship with Australia, but accusations continue to surface from cabinet ministers and generals about Australia's supposed role in inciting the East Timorese to independence. The relationship is still not what it was prior to the crisis.

Rather than intervene and thereby throw up a plethora of issues they could not deal with, ASEAN countries did the next best thing: some contributed to the INTERFET and U.N. peacekeeping forces. On this matter, ASEAN unity was never at risk because Indonesia relented under Western pressure, and each member state made its own decision to opt in or out of peacekeeping missions. Thailand, a proponent of "flexible engagement" to enable ASEAN countries to comment critically on each other's policies, readily became Australia's deputy in East Timor to play a bigger role in the region. Playing second fiddle to Australia served ASEAN's interest. In any case, no ASEAN country had the logistical and financial resources to mobilize thousands of troops at short notice for the United Nations. It was a huge and costly operation that only Australia was capable of, with considerable assistance from its traditional ally, New Zealand, as the second largest contributor. Except for Indonesia and Malaysia, no other ASEAN state opposed Australia's leading role in East Timor.

East Timor's transition to independence will introduce a new player in the region, and poses an interesting proposition for ASEAN. Independence will mean that East Timor will conduct a separate foreign policy. Indonesia will undoubtedly expect East Timor to "toe the line" in broad foreign policy terms and "Finlandization" could well be the model for an independent East Timor. The reality is that East Timor will have to come to terms with living cheek by jowl with the largest nation in Southeast Asia. East Timor will at least be expected to follow ASEAN's Zone of Peace, Freedom, and Neutrality (ZOPFAN) and not become a "trojan horse" by aligning closely with extra-regional powers, such as China or the United States. Furthermore, East Timor could well be the eleventh member of ASEAN — at least the previous Habibie administration made some indications along these lines.

It is in East Timor's interest to join ASEAN as quickly as it is able following formal independence. This concession would be a small one when gaining recognition and ultimately protection of its new statehood: one ASEAN member surely will not invade another. To protect the sovereignty of its new nation, East Timor could do no better than join ASEAN, which firmly established the principle in 1967 of not interfering in the affairs of fellow members. The leadership of the pro-independence movement in East Timor may not necessarily accord with Jakarta's views. Jose Ramos-Horta has made statements opposed to participating in Southeast Asian regionalism, stating that an independent East Timor should join the South Pacific Forum instead of ASEAN. Xanana Gusmao is more inclusive; he stated that East Timor could serve as a bridge between Southeast Asia and the South Pacific. Gusmao's tour of Southeast Asia at the beginning of February 2000 seemed to indicate that he was interested in some kind of role within the ASEAN grouping. The media speculated that Gusmao had asked Malaysia to sponsor East Timor's membership. Other existing members may be reluctant following recent inclusions of poorer members into the ASEAN fold who are not really ready to engage in greater intra-regional trade and investment facilitation through the ASEAN Free Trade Agreement (AFTA). Therefore, opinion within ASEAN is not divided on "if" but "when" East Timor might be admitted. There is also a range of half-way measures that could be afforded to East Timor in the mean time, such as "dialogue status", or a more participatory "observer status", which is currently held by Papua New Guinea.

Conclusion

For the long term, there are three main challenges. One is keeping East Timor from becoming a ward of the international community and allowing the eventual withdrawal of peacekeepers. The second is maintaining Indonesia's acceptance of East Timor's independence. As a small state, East Timor may want to adopt the strategy of seeking some form of "free association" with certain larger countries. Some island states in the Pacific already have such an association such as Palau, Niue (with Australia), the Cook Islands (New Zealand), or American Samoa and the Marshall Islands (United States). A further example can found in the Commonwealth of Independent States (CIS), whereby a number of central Asian republics have opted to link themselves to Russia's economy, forming the "rouble zone". While it is too early to surmise East Timor's future status, "free association" could resolve economic and security issues. Obvious candidates are Australia and Portugal, while Indonesia would seem a non-starter in the eyes of the bulk of the East Timorese population. Such a status could help overcome the third challenge, namely, the broader strategic issue of preventing future crises in East Timor.

The year 1999 has been a defining year for East Timor. At the beginning of the year there was a general acknowledgement by the Indonesian leadership that the status of East Timor may need to be reconsidered. By the end of 1999 East Timor had gained its independence after twenty-four years of Indonesian rule. This process was, in the end, a traumatic one. The East Timorese paid a heavy price, not only in terms of a terrorized population, but also in terms of destroyed infrastructure. The question that must be posited is, did the United Nations make a crucial error of judgement in allowing the consultation to go ahead given the uncertainly of the security environment? It is easy to cast judgement in hindsight, and reprimand the United Nations for its failure to predict events. The United Nations will have to provide its own security in future operations to avoid the fiasco of relying on a host nation — in the East Timorese context, Indonesian "security".

However, there are some important reasons why the United Nations may, in hindsight, feel some vindication in seizing the opportunity to hold a consultation on the future of East Timor. First of all, President Habibie offered a crucial "window of opportunity" to hold the historic ballot. It was certainly a well-founded fear that the offer would not survive Habibie's short-lived transitional administration. Leading contenders for the presidency and vice-presidency, Abdurrahman Wahid and Megawati Soekarnoputri, had oscillated on the issue of whether or not they would support the outcome of the referendum, or even the holding of a referendum in the first instance. Immediately prior to the referendum, Megawati had expressed her opposition to East Timorese independence, and large numbers of pro-Indonesian supporters in East Timor publicly supported her and her party's image. Second, the growing unpopularity of the TNI following the fall of Soeharto, and their publicly stated disengagement from domestic politics, may have convinced the international community that the civilian authorities had control over them. The then commander of the TNI, General Wiranto, was regarded, prior to the chaos in East Timor, as a democratic soldier intent on reversing the tarnished image of the military. The opposite turned out to be the case. Reports differ on whether or not Wiranto initially supported the East Timor referendum, but whatever the case, he appears to have turned against the process when the military realized it was not going to go Indonesia's way and the Acehnese resistance stiffened as a result of events in East Timor. Third, and of greatest import, would Indonesia have accepted the presence of foreign troops on territory it regarded as its own soil? The answer is that this was never acceptable to either the Indonesian military or the civilian authorities. Only after the disaster of September 1999, which generated enormous pressure from the international community, and convinced Habibie that his own forces were out of control, did Indonesia reluctantly offer an invitation for INTERFET to enter East Timor.

The Australian-led INTERFET operation played a crucial role in bringing a modicum of stability back to East Timor. INTERFET acted within two weeks of the most extreme violence, while it would have taken the United Nations months to organize the same response — by which time far greater destruction and loss of human life would have occurred. The arrival of 8,000 troops with robust rules of engagement, who did not hesitate to confront the militia, convinced the militia groups and their sponsors that the game was lost. In this sense INTERFET played a crucial deterrence role; a role that will need to be maintained by the U.N. forces over the next few years. The arrival of INTERFET forces also played a crucial role in convincing the Indonesian élite that the East Timorese ballot box would have to be respected, leading to Indonesia's MPR approving the result of the Popular Consultation on the Future of East Timor on 25 October 1999. Earlier claims by Indonesian authorities that UNAMET had conspired to achieve a victory for independence were, in the end, not upheld.

But 1999 was not just a defining year for East Timor. It has also been an important test of the emerging nature of humanitarian intervention in the post–Cold War environment. Furthermore, it has been an important test for the Asia-Pacific. Every case of intervention is rather different, but there is an important trend occurring in international relations where much of the international community is paying far closer attention to issues of human security. Far from being able to intervene to right every wrong around the world, the timing was, however, right for intervention in East Timor. The Habibie administration was vulnerable to international pressure, which was applied to good effect. In the absence of traditional balance of power arrangements that characterized Europe in the last century and the entire world until the end of the Cold War in 1989, new patterns of security are emerging in the Pacific. East Timor, a problem ignored from 1975, finally had the support of the majority of the world's governments after the 30 August referendum. And the resulting carnage in East Timor saw the reaction of many states in the region, and a few outside it, to assist the INTERFET operation. Surrounding the East Timor crisis were a group of like-minded states in the Asia-Pacific who were in general agreement on the course of action to take in the event of a humanitarian crisis. Essentially, the consensus held by the contributors to the INTERFET operation, which was by no means shared by all states in Asia, revolved around recognition that the people of East Timor were sovereign, and that their overwhelming decision to opt for independence was worthy of support.

NOTES

1. William Frederick and Robert Worden, eds., *Indonesia: A Country Study*, 5th ed. (Washington, D.C.: Library of Congress, 1993), p. 65.
2. For details for the extent of militia intimidation, see United Nations Office of the High Commissioner for Human Rights, "Report of the International Commission of Inquiry on East Timor to the Secretary-General", January 2000; U.S. Department of State, "1999 Country Reports on Human Rights Practices: Indonesia", 25 February 2000 <www.state.gov/www/global/human_rights/1999_hrp_report/indonesi.html>; and the Carter Center weekly reports on East Timor <www.cartercenter.org/reports.html>. All of these reports also document collusion between elements of the TNI and the militia.
3. *Time* magazine, quoting diplomatic sources, estimated that leading Indonesian generals in East Timor pocketed US$20 million per annum from coffee production. See Eric Ellis, "Being Free Is Not the Same Thing as Being Prosperous", *Time*, 20 September 1999.

BRUNEI
DARUSSALAM

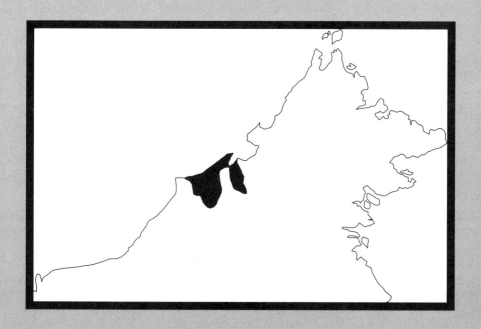

BRUNEI DARUSSALAM
Weathering the Storm

Mohamad Yusop bin Awang Damit

Nineteen-ninety-nine turned out to be an eventful year in the politics and economics of Southeast Asia, with countries slowly emerging from a nightmare of economic reversal that had bottomed the previous year. The monarchic state of Brunei Darussalam was not unaffected by the crisis, and, even more important, by the fall in oil prices. However, despite obvious signs of economic dislocation, unheard of in the sultanate's history since oil revenues started filling its coffers, the larger society remained undisturbed. Political stability aside, there were other factors that helped buttress society and prevent the fall-out from the economic slowdown from reaching crisis proportions. This article will delineate how the government and the state machinery coped with the critical issues of economy and society in 1999.

Economic Development

The year saw the heightening of government efforts to bring the country out of recession. The economy performed sluggishly, with the estimated gross domestic product (GDP) growth for the year dropping to 0.6 per cent. Like other countries in the region, Brunei was not insulated from the regional financial crisis. Yet it was not too adversely affected by the crisis partly because of the fact that the Brunei dollar, which was pegged at one-to-one to the Singapore dollar, had fallen by only 15–20 per cent against the U.S. dollar. What cushioned Brunei from more exchange rate depreciation was Brunei's earnings in U.S. dollars for its oil and gas exports, which constituted 90 per cent of its exports.[1]

Indirectly, however, the crisis had caused many of Brunei's trading partners, particularly the countries of the Association of Southeast Asian Nations (ASEAN) and Japan, to reduce their demand for oil, thus affecting Brunei's exports. This was aggravated by the slump in oil prices, which dropped to a low of US$9 a barrel at the beginning of 1999. As oil remains the mainstay of the economy, the drop in oil prices drastically slashed Brunei's revenues. Government revenue from investment, which is mainly controlled by the Brunei

Mohamad Yusop bin Awang Damit is Dean of the Faculty of Arts and Social Sciences, Universiti Brunei Darussalam.

Investment Agency (BIA), was affected by the unfavourable investment climate. In addition, the collapse in early 1998 of the Amedeo Development Corporation, owned by His Royal Highness (HRH) Prince Jefri, also the chairman of the BIA, had some effect on government investment. The government task force set up in September 1998 to investigate alleged irregularities in Amedeo had yet to make its findings public.

However, in July 1999 the Brunei High Court ordered Amedeo to be wound up, leaving a debt of B$6 billion owing to more than twenty-five creditors. Two other Amedeo-sponsored companies, Jerudong Park Hotel (B) Sdn. Bhd. and Amedeo Fishing Sdn. Bhd., were also ordered to be wound up.[2] A Singapore firm of accountants, Foo, Kon & Tan, was appointed to oversee the liquidation process. Many creditors, expressing their concern over the executive managers' declaration that a number of Amedeo's assets and project values both within and outside Brunei were listed as unknown, lodged claims ranging from B$1 billion to B$5.1 billion. The big surprise during the liquidators' meeting was that HRH Prince Jefri too put in a claim, for B$5.1 billion, the exact amount the BIA was bidding.[3]

Meanwhile, the government worked out different strategies to pull Brunei out of its economic problems. The Brunei Economic Council, set up in September 1998 to steer the sluggish economy through the crisis, met several times. In early March 1999, the chairman of the Council, HRH Prince Mohamed Bolkiah, the Minister of Foreign Affairs, announced that he had received seven reports from various committees which included reports on Finance and Banking, Facilitation of Economic Policies, and Diversifying from Oil and Gas. The reports identified the reasons behind the economic problems faced by the country and offered short- and long-term remedial measures. The council later considered each of the reports in detail.[4] However, by the end of 1999 the council had yet to make its recommendations on how to overcome the sluggish economy.

Nevertheless, it was reported at the beginning of 1999 that the government had considered increasing oil production to give a boost to the ailing economy.[5] Since 1981, Brunei has adopted a conservation policy by reducing its oil production so that future generations can continue to enjoy the wealth of the nation. Oil production was reduced gradually to a level of 150,000 barrels a day. This target was achieved in 1988. In view of the economic slowdown, the government planned to increase oil production by at least 50,000 barrels a day. Brunei sold about 90 per cent of its crude oil under term agreement, while the rest was sold on the spot market. Under term agreement, 28 per cent was exported to ASEAN countries, 18 per cent to Japan, 27 per cent to Korea, 6 per cent to Taiwan, 18 per cent to the United States, 1 per cent to Europe, and 1 per cent to other countries. Owing to a fall in demand for oil from the region, Brunei's oil for the first time entered European markets in 1999.[6]

As a result of the drop in revenue, due to falling oil prices and poor investment returns, in 1998 Brunei was estimated to have spent more than what it earned by around B$600 million, with the deficit projected to rise to B$1 billion in 1999. Hence, the authorities were planning to increase production from oil reserves to reduce the deficit and bankroll the nation's development expenditure, which in turn would facilitate growth of the business sector.

Although experiencing a sharp decline in oil exports, Brunei was enjoying a steady growth in demand for its liquefied natural gas (LNG). In 1998 the sultanate delivered over 5 million tonnes of LNG to Japan and South Korea, two important customers; it is contracted to deliver 6.71 million tonnes a year to the two East Asian countries from 1999 until 2013. In an effort to cope with these increasing shipments of gas to Japan and South Korea, Brunei is building a bigger LNG carrier, with a capacity of 135,000 cubic metres. For this purpose a contract was signed in March between Brunei Gas Carriers Sdn. Bhd., which is 80 per cent owned by the government of Brunei, and Mitsubishi Heavy Industries of Japan.

The government announced a development budget of almost B$1 billion for 1999, similar in size to the development budget allocated the previous year. A large part of the budget was for vital infrastructure projects such as electrical power, road construction, and building projects, with a large sum under building projects going to national housing development. The 1999 budget was designed not only to further develop the infrastructure of the country but also to boost the languishing economy.

Brunei's economy is predominantly government-driven. However, lately the government has begun to loosen its grip by commercializing some of its development projects and activities, and even some of its public services, on an *ad hoc* basis. One such venture was the commercialization of the development and operation of the Muara Container Terminal through a strategic partnership with the PSA (Port of Singapore Authority) Corporation, a leading world port operator. An agreement was reached between the PSA Corporation and a local company, Archipelago Development Corporation, to develop, operate and manage Muara Port's container terminal. The two organizations have set up a joint-venture company known as PSA Muara Container Terminal Sdn. Bhd.[7]

The economic downturn has led the government to venture further in this direction of commercialization, corporatization, and privatization of government development projects and services. The aim is to procure external financing and reduce the budget deficit. At the same time, Brunei was also considering a plan to develop its capital market. Although the finance, banking, and insurance sectors have played their part in supporting the growth and development of the economy, the authorities plan to exploit their potential further and venture into new areas to develop a full-fledged domestic capital market. The relevant authorities were also considering a plan to renew efforts to develop the country as a financial centre.[8] The idea of turning Brunei into a global financial centre had been in the offing for some years and it was only in 1999 that concrete plans were prepared. It was reported that Brunei was engaging legal and financial experts in London to prepare the laws to trans-form Brunei into a tax haven for foreign companies. Brunei was confident that it could become a financial centre because it had the advantages of a good position and good communication facilities, together with political and financial stability.[9]

Relentless efforts are under way to make Brunei a Service Hub for Trade and Tourism (ShuTT) for the Brunei-Indonesia-Malaysia-Philippines East ASEAN Growth Area (BIMP-EAGA) by 2003. The commercialization of Muara Port's container terminal was part of this effort. The country's telecommuni-cation system was upgraded with the completion of a multi-million-dollar project of high-capacity info-communication infrastructure, dubbed "RAGAM 21", which integrated Brunei into the world's advanced multimedia infrastructures. It was expedited to bring two major events, the 20th Southeast Asian (SEA) Games held in Brunei in August 1998 and the APEC 2000, to be held in November 2000, to people in all corners of the world. But more importantly, the project would pave the way for the transformation of Brunei society into a fully fledged information society.[10] A Tourism Master Plan has been prepared. It contains short-to-medium and long-term plans of action to develop and expand the tourism industry. Pehin Dato Abdul Rahman, the Minister of Industry and Primary Resources, stated:

> While focusing on the economic and social benefits to be gained from tourism, the master plan also at the same time puts emphasis on pre-venting any erosion of the socio-cultural and religious values of the Bruneian society as well as conserving the natural environment of Bru-nei Darussalam.

To promote Brunei internationally as a tourist destination and to accelerate the growth of the tourism industry locally, the year 2001 has been designated Visit Brunei Year. The minister emphasized that the tourism industry was to be led by the private sector and that it could create more than 11,000 employ-ment opportunities as well as generate a quarter of a billion Brunei dollars in revenue.[11]

The economic slowdown caused the government to scale down its spend-ing for 1999. All government agencies were advised to review their spending, which resulted in substantial cuts in their budget allocations.[12] This austerity measure dealt a hard blow to the construction sector, which depended largely on government contracts. While major government projects slowed down, prices too dropped by as much as 50 per cent, causing major contractors with large financial commitments to go out of business.[13] Contractors were also affected by long delays in payment by the government for completed projects because these delays resulted in their incurring heavy interest costs. A senior govern-ment official explained that the problems, which had been there for some time, were "caused by administrative delays in the department concerned".

The result was a situation where only companies with very strong reserves could participate in large local projects. This eliminated home-grown contractors, who were unable to cope with inordinate payment delays. These delays also tarnished Brunei's image. To alleviate the plight of businessmen, the government at the beginning of the year worked out a more expeditious method to release payments by co-ordinating with the banks. It brought about a marked improvement in the construction sector, and also helped to counter widespread allegations that the government had run out of funds to settle its bills.[14]

The recession in construction, the second largest industry, was evident from abandoned projects and empty blocks of properties around Bandar Seri Begawan. In order to salvage the collapsing construction industry, the authorities were considering a move to allow foreign investors to own property in Brunei. Currently, foreigners cannot legally own property because the country's existing land code does not permit a foreigner to buy and own land and buildings on it.[15]

The knock-on effects of the sluggish construction sector could be seen in other sectors, particularly the retail sector. The continued repatriation of foreign workers, who had numbered more than 60,000 before the economic downturn, caused suffering to the retailers. This was exacerbated by a rush to neighbouring countries by Bruneians in search of cheaper goods. Shops in Miri and Labuan experienced a boom, while in Bandar Seri Begawan an increasing number of shops, even in the posh Yayasan complex, closed down because of vanishing customers.

Despite the economic problems, the government pressed on with its long-term programme to diversify from oil. A state-owned company, Semaun Holdings, had been formed to spearhead the growth of local industries. Another state-run agency, the Brunei Industrial Development Authority (BINA), was formed to co-ordinate government industrialization programmes.[16] In August, the government announced that it had set aside over B$20 million for the development of small and medium enterprises. The government was optimistic about the success of the diversification programmes based on trends for the period 1991–97, which saw the non-oil sector's contribution to GDP rise to 60 per cent. By playing a prominent role in the BIMP-EAGA, Brunei hoped to transform its small market of only around 300,000 people into a community to service a market of over 50 million consumers.[17]

Brunei is also keen to develop into a prime *halal* meat exporter. A modern abattoir, the Australian-designed PDS Abattoir Sdn. Bhd., was set up in March 1999 to import young healthy two-to-three-year-old Australian cattle of European origin. The company planned to export Brunei *halal* slaughtered prime beef. In addition, it planned to work out a joint venture with a Malaysian firm to produce processed *halal* beef products such as beef burgers, beef frankfurters, beef breakfasts, and cold cuts. The main aim of the company was to meet the country's growing demand for high-quality imported beef of assured *halal* standard.

By mid-1999 there was a new optimism in the air because oil prices had begun to rise again. This encouraging development gave confidence to business circles because it meant that government development and other public spending would also rise. It also spelt a brighter future for a new offshore oil field jointly developed by the government of Brunei, a French company, Elf Petroleum, and a New Zealand company, Fletcher Challenger. This partnership is a milestone in the history of oil production in Brunei because hitherto Brunei Shell Petroleum Company had been the sole producer of oil and gas in the sultanate. The oil field had been discovered in 1990 and started producing oil and gas in March 1999. Another cause for optimism was that the steps taken by the government to revitalize its economy had put in place measures for stronger economic recovery and for sustainable growth.

With the encouraging signs of improvement in the economy, Brunei was looking forward to hosting the APEC (Asia-Pacific Economic Co-operation) meeting in November 2000. This would be the second biggest international event ever hosted by Brunei, after the SEA Games in early August 1998. In February 1999 Brunei hosted the APEC Business Advisory Council (ABAC), attended by nearly one hundred business leaders from the APEC economies.[18]

Socio-Political Development

The economic downturn affecting the country did not bring about social and political unrest. The welfare system insulated the population from the impact of economic problems. Moreover the local people, who were employed mainly in the public sector, were not affected by the sizeable retrenchment of foreign workers in the construction industry. It would have been a different story, however, had a significant number of locals been affected by such retrenchments. In fact, when Standard Chartered Bank, the second biggest employer in the country's banking industry, decided to lay off forty-two mostly local staff in its restructuring process, it shocked the small close-knit Bruneian society and brought sharp criticism from the Labour Department.[19] Such developments did not encourage Bruneians in search of better job security and benefits to feel confident about taking up jobs in the private sector, something the government had been encouraging them to do in view of its inability to absorb large numbers of school leavers into the public sector.

This may be one of the reasons why the government had not carried out any public sector salary revision exercise since independence in 1984. Salary increases in the public sector would work against efforts by the government to encourage job seekers to take up jobs in the private sector. However, in February 1999 the government decided to abolish the salary bar of civil servants, including the armed forces and daily-rated staff, across the board from Division One to the lowest staff level.[20] This move, coming on top of the subsistence allowances given to all civil servants at the end of 1998, was seen as an attempt to mollify public opinion at a time when many were feeling the pinch from the economic crisis. On the other hand, the government decided to reduce perks such as housing allowances for ministers, deputy ministers, and permanent secretaries, a move which reportedly enabled it to save more than B$3 million a year.

Official statistics released in February 1999 showed a drop in the crime rate, to 2,750 cases in 1998 compared with 3,269 in 1997 and 3,152 in 1996.[21] This was a significant social indicator that the economic problems had not adversely affected the population at large. However, social problems of drug abuse, vandalism, and theft among youths were reported to have risen. It was reported that the trend was caused mainly by "a breakdown in the social fabric where people seem to have lost their way in [the] midst of a changing society". The report added that many of the victims came from broken families where divorce, especially among young married couples, was relatively high. The authorities tackled the problem at the national level by involving parents in forming the Youth Parent Movement (Gerakan Ibu Bapa Belia, or GIBB), to steer young people away from self-destructive behaviour. The movement was a platform to launch various youth development programmes and activities to distract them from involvement in anti-social activities.[22]

The most important event of 1999 involving mostly young people had been the prestigious 20th SEA Games, which Brunei had hosted for the first time. It was held in early August but the main preparations had started several months before. About 17,000 people, mainly students, had been directly in-volved in field presentations, the choir and flip card shows during the opening and closing ceremonies. The Games were a success, making Bruneians proud and giving them the confidence to hold such big events in the future. Another prestigious but less grand sports event hosted by Brunei was the World Grand Prix Badminton Finals held in February 1999. This global sporting event, which was beamed throughout Asia by Star Television, put Brunei on the world map. The APEC Summit meeting, to be held in November 2000, will add to its growing international profile.

On the political front, there was no significant change other than several reshuffles of top bureaucrats in 1999. The exercise was significant in that several young civil servants were promoted to the top position of permanent secretary. Apart from injecting new blood into the administration to make it more effective and efficient, it was also seen as an exercise to train and groom younger bureaucrats for future responsibilities in the top echelon. HRH Prince Mohamed declared that Brunei could not be left out but must move with its neighbours. The committee established some years ago to review the 1959 Constitution, currently a dormant one since the abortive rebellion of 1962, submitted its report for a final decision. The prince revealed that the report recommended the introduction of elections.[23] Another significant change that took place in 1999 was the appointment of Professor Dato Mahmud Saedon bin Awang Othman, an Al-Azhar-trained Islamic scholar, as the new vice-chancellor of Universiti Brunei Darussalam. He had had a long career in Malaysia as an academic at the Malaysian National University and the International Islamic University before returning to Brunei three years ago to take up duties as head of the Shariah Department at the Ministry of Religious Affairs and as the Government Islamic Legal Expert. The new vice-chancellor swiftly announced his aim to speed up the localization of academic administration at the university, the main contention among local staff at the thirteen-year-old university. He initiated a ten-year strategic plan for the university with an eye towards localization, with emphasis on Islamic input in all its programmes.

A scrutiny of reports and discussions in the local media in 1999 would suggest a greater openness and tolerance in Brunei society than in previous years. For instance, the collapse of Amedeo and its effects on government finances, the *reformasi* protests in Indonesia and similar events in other parts of the world were given unrestricted coverage in the local press and media. The advent of modern technology, the widespread penetration of the electronic media and access to the Internet, and cable and satellite television would have made futile any government attempts to be restrictive. In a related development a second English newspaper, *News Express*, made its debut in July 1999. The daily paper was privately owned and its appearance represented competition to the *Borneo Bulletin* and its sister Malay paper, *Media Permata*, for the small readership in a population of just over 300,000.

It was also interesting to see the increasing number and variety of issues raised in the letters column of the local press, which became a channel for expressing opinions on certain issues, including dissatisfaction and grievances against the administration. From such letters and opinions expressed in public forums, such as regular meetings of the "Thursday Club" at Universiti Brunei Darussalam, it was noticeable that a growing number of people were prepared to come forward to express their views and opinions. Following these developments, the government set up the Management Services Department (MSD) as a channel for people to voice their views on the performance of government departments and ministries. The MSD launched a weekly programme on local television to explain government and administrative policies and procedures to make them clear and comprehensible to the people.[24]

Besides making their views heard through these avenues, people were urged to channel their views to the village heads, the *ketua kampong*, and *penghulu*, who in turn would pass them on to the relevant authorities. These grassroots leaders are elected through popular vote by secret ballot. In 1992, the government had formed the Consultative Council of Mukim and Village with the main objective of advising the government on matters affecting the population at the local level. However, the Council had been less effective partly because the members behaved like public servants rather than as representatives of the people and partly because the leaders themselves were frustrated by the system, which is too bureaucratic and cumbersome. The Council held a convention once, chaired by the Minister of Home Affairs. During 1999 the government tried to reorganize the Council to enable it to operate more effectively.

In order to ensure that the government was functioning efficiently and effectively, His Majesty (HM) the Sultan continued his visits to various government departments and ministries to see for himself the running of government agencies and to have a dialogue with their members. During the visits, he often asked the relevant ministers and their subordinates questions regarding policies and their implementation. These visits, often made at short notice, served to keep them on their toes. HM the Sultan also visited villages in various parts of the state to observe the welfare of the people and the development being brought to the area. During such visits, the monarch often handed his subjects house keys and land grant certificates under the national housing and land schemes. He often called at the residence of the village heads and a few of the villagers. He also participated regularly in Friday prayers with the local population at different mosques throughout the country. Throughout these visits it was noticeable that the popularity of the monarch was undiminished, and in fact such visits strengthened the bond between the monarch and his subjects.

In early August 1999, the government announced the release of Muhammed Yassin Affendy bin Abdul Rahman, the secretary-general of the defunct Partai Rakyat Brunei (PRB, or Brunei People's Party) from detention. Yassin Affendy had been detained after his involvement in the abortive rebellion of 1962. In the early 1970s he and several top PRB leaders broke out from the detention centre where they were being held and escaped to Malaysia, where they were given political asylum. Some years ago, some of those leaders, including Yassin, returned of their own accord. However, before they could regain their freedom they had to undergo a rehabilitation programme at the Jerudong Detention and Rehabilitation Centre to determine that they were no longer a threat to the nation. The release of Yassin Affendy was a significant development in Brunei's attempts to reconcile with its past.

Foreign Affairs
Brunei continued to play a quietly active role in the efforts of ASEAN to contain the regional economic crisis. Its financial strength gave Brunei a role in helping neighbouring countries, either by pledging funds to support their currencies or by investing in infrastructural projects. At the Third ASEAN Informal Summit, HM the Sultan emphasized the importance of ASEAN countries working closely together in the face of the economic crisis.[25] As a small country, Brunei was anxious not to see the regional economic downturn result in political and social turmoil in the region, particularly to immediate neighbours Malaysia, Indonesia, and the Philippines. Problems in these countries might result in Brunei having to cope with illegal immigrants and currency smuggling activities among those attracted by the Brunei dollar's strength. Anticipating such a scenario, Brunei at the beginning of the year strengthened its border controls, particularly at the main entry points. One of the methods used was the introduction of a drive-through immigration clearance system at

Kuala Lurah near Limbang and Sungai Tujuh near Miri. There were bad traffic jams at both points because the new system was unable to cope with the volume of traffic passing through the checkpoints. The introduction of the new system and public frustration resulted in some issues related to the revival of the long-standing problem of Brunei's claim to Limbang being mentioned in the local press. It forced the authorities to clarify that the checkpoints at Kuala Lurah and Sungai Tujuh should not be considered as the borders between the two countries.[26] The dispute over the borders, particularly with Limbang district, remains a thorny issue in Brunei-Malaysia relations.

In September 1999, an allegedly negative remark made by a deputy Malaysian minister concerning HM the Sultan's contribution to Islam and Islamic countries caused a public stir in Brunei. The remark, considered by Bruneians as an insult to their monarch, was published by *Harakah,* a weekly political paper of an opposition party in Malaysia. Both the Brunei Youth Council and the Brunei Solidarity National Party, the only political party existing in Brunei, protested and submitted their petitions to the Malaysian ambassador in Brunei and demanded an apology from the deputy minister. The Malaysian government, however, disassociated itself from the matter. HM the Sultan made a subtle response to the matter in a *titah* in conjunction with an annual Quran reading competition. The matter ended abruptly when the deputy minister sent a personal letter and apologized to him and his people, although he maintained that his speech had been twisted by an opposition party in Malaysia.[27]

In 1999, HM the Sultan made high-profile appearances on the international stage when he attended the APEC leaders meeting in New Zealand in September, the Commonwealth Heads of Government Meeting (CHOGM) in South Africa, and the Third ASEAN Informal Summit in the Philippines in November. The November 2000 APEC meeting in Brunei would not only be an honour but also a recognition of Brunei's standing internationally. Preparations for the big event carried out in 1999 included regular promotions in the local media to inform the public about APEC.

Another significant development in Brunei's foreign affairs was the appointment of the first woman ambassador to France, an important development in equal rights for women in a country that is considered conservative.[28] It must be said, however, that several Bruneian women already hold important positions as heads of government departments, including two who hold permanent secretary positions.

An equally significant development was the exposure of HRH Prince Al-Mutadee Billah, the Crown Prince, to foreign affairs. Since his appointment as the Crown Prince in 1998, the prince had been meeting foreign leaders and ambassadors, including Prime Minister Goh Chok Tong of Singapore. His first official trip overseas was to Malaysia and Singapore. Such exposure was important for the Oxford-trained prince in adjusting and preparing for his position as the future ruler of Brunei.

Conclusion

The economic problems that shook Brunei's financial foundations shocked most Bruneians and gave them a rude wake-up call. The problems exposed the fundamental weaknesses of the country's economic system and triggered debates and a reappraisal of economic policies. The strategies and reforms adopted to bring the country out of the slowdown contained some positive elements for sustainable economic growth and development in the country. The plan for economic diversification, including commercialization, corporatization, and privatization, is now being taken more seriously to avoid the limitations of relying on oil and gas only. In a sense the economic crisis that Brunei went through was a blessing in disguise.

Socially and politically, Brunei is a stable country. The economic problems of the past two years were an important test of national strength and cohesion. There is no doubt that the popularity of the monarch is an important unifying factor politically and socially.

NOTES

1. *Borneo Bulletin*, 17–18 July 1999.
2. *Borneo Bulletin*, 22 and 27 July 1999.
3. *Borneo Bulletin*, 22 and 23–24 October 1999.
4. *Borneo Bulletin*, 3 March, 16 and 17 June, and 14 July 1999.
5. *Borneo Bulletin*, 13 January 1999.
6. *Perjalanan Negara Brunei Memasuki Alaf Baru* (Jawatankuasa Tertinggi Penerbitan Buku Perjalanan Negara Brunei Darussalam Menuju Alaf Baru, 1999), pp. 25–27.
7. *Borneo Bulletin*, 4 March 1999.
8. *Borneo Bulletin*, 26 January 1999.
9. *Borneo Bulletin*, 26 January 1999.
10. *Borneo Bulletin*, 19 March 1999
11. *Borneo Bulletin*, 14 July 1999.
12. *Borneo Bulletin*, 23 February 1999.
13. *Borneo Bulletin*, 7 April 1999.
14. *Borneo Bulletin*, 27 January and 10 May 1999.
15. *Borneo Bulletin*, 17–18 July 1999.
16. *Borneo Bulletin*, 17–18 July 1999.
17. *Borneo Bulletin*, 1 April 1999.
18. *Borneo Bulletin*, 8 February 1999.
19. *News Express*, 2 October 1999.
20. *Borneo Bulletin*, 31 February 1999.
21. *Borneo Bulletin*, 10 February 1999.
22. *Borneo Bulletin*, 26 March 1999.
23. *Borneo Bulletin*, 6 August 1999.
24. *Borneo Bulletin*, 8 September 1999.
25. *News Express*, 29 November 1999.
26. *Borneo Bulletin*, 18 February and 2 March 1999.
27. *Borneo Bulletin*, 1, 3, 4, 7, and 8 September 1999; *News Express*, 3 and 4 September 1999.
28. *Borneo Bulletin*, 12 October 1999.

CAMBODIA

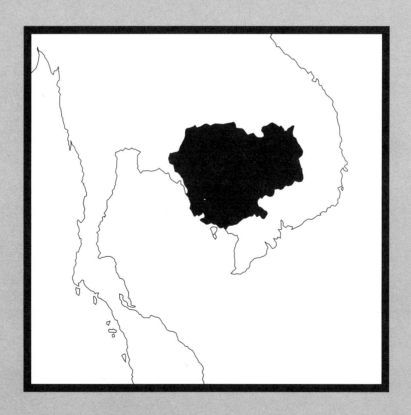

CAMBODIA
Hun Sen Consolidates Power

Milton Osborne

After the turmoil of 1997, marked by the bloody clashes in July of that year, and the political standoff that followed the elections of July 1998, Cambodia in 1999 experienced a year of remarkable stability. The extent to which this political stability was matched by an improvement in the lot of the general population continues to be a matter for debate, but there is no argument against the proposition that, at the level of national politics, Prime Minister Hun Sen's dominance has been clearly established. Given the long catalogue of Cambodia's past and present problems, it is unsurprising that this combination of stability and prime ministerial dominance has not meant that all difficulties have been overcome as the country still struggles to emerge from its mendicant economic status. At the time of writing (December 1999), there is still uncertainty about how, if ever, trials of former Khmer Rouge leaders might be held. And, far too often neglected as having a bearing on politics, environmental issues continue to pose a present and future challenge to the government in Phnom Penh. This is a far from exhaustive list and to it should be added the problems of endemic criminality and the grave public health challenge flowing from an unchecked epidemic of human immunodeficiency virus (HIV) and acquired immune deficiency syndrome (AIDS).

The Political Equation

The starting point for any discussion of politics in Cambodia during 1999 was the emergence of a coalition government in November of the previous year. When the elections of July 1998 left no party with the constitutionally required two-thirds majority of the 122 seats in the National Assembly to form government (the Cambodian People's Party [CPP] gained sixty-four seats; FUNCINPEC, forty-three; and the Sam Rainsy Party, fifteen), a period of tense stalemate ensued. As the CPP's most prominent member and effective *de facto* political leader of the country, Hun Sen made clear his unreadiness to contemplate any solution that did not ensure that he must be at the head of any government that was formed. At the same time, FUNCINPEC and Sam Rainsy

---

MILTON OSBORNE is a former Australian public servant and academic. He is the author of eight books on the history and politics of Southeast Asia.

Party supporters in Phnom Penh sought to overturn the election results, both through appeals to the National Election Committee claiming fraud, and through street protests in the capital. Neither of these tactics proved successful, nor did the initial intervention of King Norodom Sihanouk, in September, lead to a solution. It was not until November, and this time with Sihanouk able to play an effective part in bringing Hun Sen and Prince Ranariddh, the FUNCINPEC leader, together that a solution was finally found. This involved the CPP and FUNCINPEC agreeing to work together in coalition with Hun Sen appointed as Prime Minister and with Ranariddh filling the role of President of the National Assembly. Although not involved in the talks that led to the constitution of the coalition, Sam Rainsy gave it his approval to the arrangement.

The significance of this agreement cannot be overestimated. Ever since the U.N.-supervised elections of 1993, Cambodia's domestic politics had been characterized by tension between the CPP and FUNCINPEC, as each party and its leaders sought to assert a position of dominance in the uneasy coalition that had been formed in that year. While it was clear that Hun Sen and the CPP established themselves as the dominant partners in the post-1993 period, FUNCINPEC continued to look forward to the possibility of reversing this situation. Only when Ranariddh and his followers abandoned this increasingly vain hope at the end of 1998 was the path to stability at the domestic level open.[1]

Travel down this path has meant that Ranariddh has ceased to play any major part in Cambodia's politics during 1999 and his FUNCINPEC colleagues have either accepted that co-operation with the CPP is preferable to confrontation or, in a number of cases, have simply left Cambodia to live abroad. Sam Rainsy continues to act as Cambodia's most active critic of the Hun Sen administration, but his effectiveness has been limited by the small number of his supporters in the National Assembly and by his tendency to spend much of his time out of the country. Many of his criticisms are well-founded as they focus on the corruption that still characterizes Cambodian life at every level of government. Yet they are criticisms that have little effect as the CPP retains its grip over the key organs of government, both civil and military. Moreover, there is considerable doubt in Phnom Penh political circles about the extent to which Sam Rainsy actually wants to exercise any executive power. Said to have expressed the wish to be "Cambodia's Aung San Suu Kyi", there is a sense that he has recognized he has no chance of gaining a place in government. In short, nothing that has occurred during 1999 leads to a conclusion that there is likely to be any sudden change to the dominance that Hun Sen has now achieved. Rather, observers are now asking if that dominance can be translated into the eventual emergence of a more equitable and less corrupt society.

A "New Hun Sen"?
Whatever is the case, foreign observers are in general agreement that Hun Sen

has both neutered his opposition and in doing so developed a modified political persona that contrasts considerably with the aggressive, and even truculent image that he was quite ready to display in previous years. Some attribute this development to the period of mourning he went through following the death of his mother which, it is suggested, caused him to reflect on the spiritual side of life. A more likely explanation is he recognized that, for a country as dependent on aid as Cambodia is, the image of a ruthless and combative politician as its leader was likely to be counterproductive. Certainly, the less confrontational image that he has cultivated played a part in ensuring that Cambodia's economic needs received sympathetic consideration when the country's leading donors met in Tokyo in February 1999. Actively working to promote his position within Cambodia, he has played particular attention to sponsoring the construction of schools and health clinics, activities that have distinct echoes of Sihanouk's policies in earlier decades. He has displayed a consistent interest in Cambodia's agricultural sector and taken some limited steps towards regulating the logging industry. In February, in an effort to show that the army should be regarded as neutral politically, Hun Sen tendered his resignation as military commander-in-chief. At the same time he has become more accessible to foreign journalists, with resultant coverage that is in general much more positive than has previously been the case.[2]

Yet there should be no mistaken judgment that Hun Sen's own view of the nature of politics in Cambodia has changed. He remains in the long tradition of Cambodian rulers for whom politics is a zero-sum game. Neither is it clear that he has genuinely put aside a personality that can readily lapse into rage if his policies are called into question. If anything fundamental has changed since the turbulent recent past it is the acceptance by Hun Sen's main rivals, Ranariddh and his FUNCINPEC colleagues, that there is no longer any point in trying to oppose Hun Sen's paramountcy.

Khmer Rouge Trials

No single issue has been of greater interest to the international community during 1999 than the question of when, or if, the Cambodian government would bring to trial former Khmer Rouge leaders who are now living in the Pailin region of western Cambodia, most notably Khieu Samphan and Nuon Chea, who surrendered to the Phnom Penh government at the end of December 1998 and who were initially given a red carpet welcome by Hun Sen.

This issue is seen as of great importance for two reasons. First, because of the revulsion felt by so many observers that men who were at the top of the Pol Pot regime should not be brought to account for the horrors which that regime perpetrated. Secondly, the fact that men such as Khieu Samphan should be allowed to live unpunished is seen as a reflection of a broader "culture of impunity" which permeates the whole of Cambodia society and allows wrongdoers at every level to escape the consequences of their criminal actions. Complicating matters even further is the fact that while Khieu Samphan and

Nuon Chea remain at large, as does Ieng Sary who defected to Phnom Penh much earlier, the government now has two other prominent Khmer Rouge figures in custody. These are Ta Mok, widely regarded as one of the most brutal of the Khmer Rouge leaders, and Duch, the former director of the infamous Tuol Sleng extermination centre. In September, Ta Mok was brought before a military court and charged with genocide, but no date was set for his trial.

At the end of 1999 the issue of Khmer Rouge trials remained unresolved, though a draft law to establish a special tribunal to try the former Khmer Rouge leaders was introduced into parliament in late December. (It was subsequently given parliamentary approval in January 2000.) It remains unclear whether the tribunal to be established under the new law will meet the concerns of the international community and the United Nations. Previously, various proposals had been put to the Cambodian government by the United Nations which would have established a special tribunal composed of both Cambodian and foreign judges. Under the new law, there is provision for the presence of foreign judges on a tribunal, but Cambodian judges will be in the majority. Such an arrangement would seem to go some way towards overcoming the problems that have clearly been in Hun Sen's mind as he contemplates the question of how any trials should take place. The first concern relates to issues of sovereignty. While the international community, through the United Nations, but with the notable exception of China, has argued that the Cambodian justice system does not have the necessary expertise to conduct a proper trial of the former Khmer Rouge leaders, the Cambodian government questions the right of outsiders to dictate how it should conduct its affairs. Just as importantly to Hun Sen's government, though this is not a position espoused publicly, is the consideration that any trial would open up the question of what should be done with the large number of other former Khmer Rouge members who occupy positions of importance in both the civil and military administrations.

There are also fundamental jurisprudential questions that remain to be resolved, particularly if Cambodia is to emerge as a country in which there is adherence to the rule of law. While it is clear that there is a widespread feeling in the Cambodian population that the former Khmer Rouge leaders deserve punishment, there is some concern, particularly among foreign observers, that no current legal provisions exist for the punishment of "auto-genocide", although legislation has been passed that provides for detention without trial for up to three years for persons charged with genocide. These observers are concerned that there is a risk that an unsatisfactory precedent could be set by convicting someone such as Khieu Samphan as the result of retroactive legislation. Although apparently highly "academic" in character, arguments over this issue gain weight in the light of problems that have emerged in failed cases of prosecution in the case of the Rwanda genocide.[3]

The issue is further confused by the fact that a conviction has been brought down in the case of the murder of the three foreign backpackers who were kidnapped in July 1994 and subsequently murdered by a remnant Khmer Rouge band led by Nuon Paet. Yet while a conviction was achieved in Nuon Paet's case, his former Khmer Rouge comrades, Chhouk Rin and Sam Bith, the latter now a senior officer in the Cambodian army, remained free until December 1999. In that month it was reported that Hun Sen had ordered the arrest of Chhouk Rin, but not of Sam Bit. The delays and apparent inconsistencies associated with this case appear to exemplify the government's uncertainties of how to deal with the fact that there are thousands of former Khmer Rouge members who continue to hold senior positions throughout the civil and military administration.[4]

Corruption, Scandals and the Rule of Law

The year 1999 began with a scandal already the cause for heated accusations and counter-accusations and continued with an apparently endless succession of allegations of corrupt practices. At the end of 1998 a consignment of highly toxic waste from Taiwan was dumped on a site near the deep water port of Sihanoukville. Just who was responsible for giving authority for the dumping to take place has never been satisfactorily established, though it is clear that there had to have been involvement of officials at both the local and central government level. Once it became clear that the material involved was highly toxic there was an initial reaction of buck-passing before, finally, procedures were put in place to remove the dumped material. With officials anxious to put the matter behind them, there has been a lack of detailed investigation of the event and its consequences, which appear to include serious effects on the health of those who were exposed to the toxic material.

Another long-running issue involving corruption was the diversion of funds associated with mine-clearing operations which depend on the injection of substantial funds from foreign donors. With Cambodia still one of the most dangerous countries in the world as the result of uncleared land mines, and as a consequence a country still plagued by mine injuries, a continuing program of mine-clearing is essential both to minimize danger to humans and to stock and to bring potentially productive agricultural areas back into use. Although there is no question that mismanagement and fraud has taken place, efforts to apportion blame, including through an audit by a foreign accounting firm, have left many questions unanswered and the whole programme under a cloud.

To add to the almost daily diet of revelations concerned with corruption and scandal, the death through assassination of actress Piseth Pelika in July added more grist to the rumour mill. With the publication, first in the French magazine *L'Express*, and subsequently in Phnom Penh newspapers, of what has been alleged to be Pelika's diary, there appeared to be evidence that the late actress had a close relationship of some kind with Prime Minister Hun Sen.[5]

The suggestion that this had led to an aggrieved party engineering Pelika's death was widely accepted in Phnom Penh and taken as yet another instance of the way in which those with links to the élite could disregard the law. This said, and in a fashion that reinforces the view that Hun Sen is currently unchallengable, there is no reason to believe that the alleged personal scandal in any way undermined his strong position.

Yet issues relating to the rule of law have frequently emerged at a much less prominent level of society. Allegations are regularly made that members of the armed forces and the police are ready to resort to force, including fatally, to enforce their will, with or without the justification of orders from the authorities in Phnom Penh. Instances of such action include the killing of thirteen Jarai hill people in July and the alleged terrorizing of civilians by members of the army in Sihanoukville in October. Allegations of mistreatment of prisoners in custody and in the prison system are made regularly, and there seem to be no sanctions against police frequently shooting alleged criminals in the street rather than going through arrest procedures.

A further long-running and unresolved issue relates to the restructuring of Cambodia's armed forces. Foreign donors have been divided over the terms and procedures to be followed in order to reduce sharply the size of Cambodia's army (under the government's own projections, 55,000 soldiers are to be demobilized over a five-year period). In the past, the Phnom Penh administration had come under sharp criticism for accepting the existence of a top heavy officer corps and the payment of wages to "ghost soldiers". While some reduction in personnel numbers has taken place, there is a clear need for further reductions and the introduction of an effective scheme that will ensure widespread corruption associated with the military is reduced if not eliminated.

External Relations

At the end of 1998 ASEAN signalled that it was ready to have Cambodia join the organization and issued an invitation for it to do so, without at the time setting a date for its entry. Formal accession finally took place at a small ceremony held in Hanoi on 30 April 1999. With this goal accomplished, Cambodia's foreign relations throughout 1999 focused principally on ensuring that it gained the best possible deal in terms of economic assistance from various foreign donors. In pursuing this goal it was aided by a general inclination among Western nations and in Japan to move from concern with the recent past to what it was hoped would be a more fruitful future. Sanctions applied after July 1997 were quietly dropped and Hun Sen's government succeeded in gaining economic aid to the tune of US$470 million following a February 1999 donors' meeting in Tokyo. A donors' review meeting held in Phnom Penh in June gave strong approval to the policies the government was implementing.

Despite the active and continuing criticism of a range of non-governmental organizations (NGOs), both domestic and foreign, and the vocal opposition of a small number of American members of congress, the United States has shown little interest in criticizing the government in Phnom Penh. Washington showed its general acceptance of the status quo by placing no barriers in the way of Hun Sen's visit to the United States at the time of his son's graduation from West Point in May. Japan has continued to be a major donor as has France, which continues to try and rebuild the special position it once enjoyed in the immediate post-colonial years. Within ASEAN, Vietnam has continued as a consistent supporter of Cambodia. Its backing had been important in overcoming reservations held by other ASEAN governments about Cambodia's accession to membership, and good relations between Hanoi and Phnom Penh remain as a pivotal feature of Cambodian foreign policy. When Vietnamese Communist Party chief, Le Kha Phieu visited Phnom Penh in June, the two countries reached an agreement designed to resolve all remaining border disputes by 2001. Meanwhile, and after having its membership of the United Nations suspended following the events of July 1997, Cambodia was readmitted to the United Nations, a development marked by Hun Sen's attending and addressing the 54th General Assembly in New York.

While not, for the most part, playing a prominent public role — defending Hun Sen's reluctance to have the United Nations dominate any trial of Khmer Rouge leaders was a notable exception to this general picture — China continued to be an important supporter of the status quo in Cambodia. In this, which is a major reversal of the policies it pursued in the 1980s, China has shown itself content with a situation that means no foreign state has an unchallenged position of influence within Cambodia, as Vietnam once did. From Hun Sen's point of view, China's current benign attitude is important at a time when Chinese businessmen remain of major importance to Cambodia's slowly developing commercial sector.

The Economy

Discussion of Cambodia's economy is hindered by the questionable nature of many of the statistics on which judgment of developments must rely. Nevertheless, there is broad agreement among foreign observers that after the turbulent period that followed the events of July 1997 the return to relative calm has provided the circumstances that allow for the possibility of a more positive outlook. On the basis of government estimates, gross domestic product is predicted to rise by 4 per cent in contrast to the meagre figure of 1 per cent for the previous year. Concurrently, inflation is predicted to decline sharply, falling from more than 12 per cent in 1998 to an estimated 6 per cent.

Whether Cambodia actually does achieve the results just cited, it will continue to depend heavily on foreign aid and investment. Yet foreign investment has declined quite sharply over the past three years. From a figure of US$239.9 million in 1996, the figure for 1998 was around US$120 million, with the same amount expected for the whole of 1999. The decline reflects several factors. Investment was sharply reduced after the violence of July 1997, but equally important was the shift in Cambodia's position as a low-cost manufacturing centre. Following the Asian economic crisis, other regional countries devalued their currencies making themselves attractive for foreign investors who had previously taken advantage of the low cost of labour in Cambodia.

The Phnom Penh government has hopes that it will be able to increase its earnings of foreign exchange as tourists return to visit the Angkor temple complex. Tourist visits were sharply down during 1998 and continued to be disappointing during the first half of 1999. Although hard figures are not available for the second half of 1999, anecdotal evidence suggests that there has been a substantial increase in the number of foreign tourists coming to Cambodia. From Phnom Penh's point of view these numbers can seem misleadingly large since many are a reflection of one-day visits made by tourists flying direct from Bangkok to Siemreap and then returning to Bangkok, so contributing little to Cambodia's revenues.

Conscious of widespread criticism of the extent of illegal logging, of its environmental dangers, and of the revenue lost to the government as a result of this activity, Phnom Penh has moved to introduce a more effective control of the logging industry. It is too early to judge how effective this control will be, and the logging industry has been one of the most blatant examples of corruption permeating the highest ranks of the administration. Realization of the extent of the loss to state revenues — some US$90 million in 1997 alone according to World Bank figures — and pressure from both international agencies and NGOs appear to have brought a new sense of realism to the administration of this vital feature of the economy.

The Environment and Health

The environment is often neglected in discussion of Cambodian politics, yet the future of the environment and its links to politics make it a topic of the greatest importance. Through most of the 1990s Cambodia's environment suffered as the result of massive illegal logging, a situation condoned by authorities at the highest level for the revenue that this produced. Damagingly, timber has been extracted in the most wasteful fashion, with large areas subjected to clear felling techniques that leave nothing but barren ground behind after lumber has been extracted. Matters had reached such a serious point that in two major studies on logging carried out by the World Bank and the Asian Development Bank during 1997 the conclusion was reached that the rate of logging taking place was unsustainable, that the loss of legitimate revenue to the state was enormous, running in tens of millions of dollars, and that unless a stop was put to the rate of logging the country's timber reserves would be exhausted in five years time. In addition, the reports made clear that unchecked logging, both legal and illegal, was having serious environmental effects, in particular leading to increased runoff that was washing vast quantities of topsoil into Cambodia's rivers and the Great Lake.

Since the reports were issued, the government has moved to impose some form of order on the logging industry, although illegal logging still continues because of the attractive returns that are to be gained from the sale of tropical hardwoods. But little has been done to combat other activities that are destructive of the environment. Pollution from the large number of factories that have been established in Phnom Penh in recent years is poured into the Tonle Sap and Mekong Rivers with little regard for the consequences downstream. This activity is one of the causes for decreased fish catches in the Phnom Penh region. Of greater concern are the problems that are now arising in relation to the Great Lake, which is the breeding ground for the bulk of the fish so vital as a protein supply for the Cambodian population. Indeed, an agreed statistic is that no less than 60 per cent of the Cambodian population's annual protein intake comes from the fish that breed in the Great Lake and are harvested there or in the Tonle Sap River at the end of the wet season.

The largest fresh-water lake in Southeast Asia, Cambodia's Great Lake is now endangered by a range of factors. The clear felling of timber to which reference has just been made has resulted in increased runoff of soil into the lake leading to an accelerated rate of sedimentation. At the same time, settlement on the fringes of the lake has increased sharply in recent years as Cambodia's growing population has looked for new and readily exploitable regions for agriculture. Areas that previously were uncultivated during the dry season are now being farmed and as a result vegetation that provided spawning grounds for fish during flood time has been removed. Because of inadequate statistics there is only anecdotal evidence on which to rely, but there appears no doubt that fish catches in the Great Lake have declined significantly, as they have also further downstream.

Problems associated with fish catches are not confined to the Great Lake. There is disquiet over the granting of fishing licences to individuals that permit them to erect netting barriers on some of the key fish-spawning grounds on tributaries running into the Mekong. More broadly, management of the Mekong and its tributaries is an issue that deserves attention as Cambodian authorities must contend with developments both within and outside the country. Whether the government in Phnom Penh can exert any influence over developments in Thailand (with, for instance the potential Kok-Ing-Nan Rivers water diversion proposal) or in relation to the hydroelectric works projected for tributaries of the Mekong in Laos, is at best uncertain. But much more potentially worrying in the long term are the dams on the Mekong itself that have been built or planned for the future by the Chinese government. With one dam already completed and another due to be completed shortly, China has plans for a further two dams to be constructed by 2010. These dams, and possibly a further three to be constructed at a later date, will radically alter the flow of the Mekong by "evening out" the current differences between the river's flow during the wet and dry seasons. Since the current breeding cycle for fish in Cambodia's Great Lake appears to be directly related to the massive rise and fall of the lake each year, the suggestion that there should be a major change in this existing pattern can only be matter of great concern. For whatever changes might take place in Cambodia's economy over the next several decades the need to rely on the protein provided by fish will remain.

As a country still with only the most rudimentary public health infrastructure and a population suffering from a wide range of endemic diseases, Cambodia now faces a major new problem with the spread of HIV/AIDS. Once again statistics are unreliable, but it is probable that on a pro-rata basis more people are infected with HIV/AIDS in Cambodia than in any other Southeast Asian country. With one hundred persons contracting the HIV virus each day, the ultimate economic and social costs of this epidemic, which shows no sign of slowing, will be enormous.

A Limited Role for King Sihanouk

Despite continuing fragile health, King Norodom Sihanouk has survived to celebrate his seventy-seventh birthday in October 1999. Marginalized for many years as Cambodia's warring factions struggled for supremacy, he has shown himself still capable of playing a role as a moral authority who is generally above politics but ready to insert himself into the political process when he believes he can do so effectively. The most notable instance of such an action was his success in brokering the arrangements that led to the coalition formed in November 1998. More recently, in October 1999, he made clear his disagreement with Hun Sen's view that the creation of an international tribunal to try Khmer Rouge leaders would violate Cambodian sovereignty — as noted earlier, this is an issue that remains unresolved.

To the extent that he is able to play the role of moral arbiter, there are concerns in Phnom Penh political circles that his eventual passing from the scene could remove a limited but important factor that acts as balance against the unlimited authority of the present leadership. Certainly, there is no clear picture of what would happen to the monarchy when Sihanouk has gone, despite provisions in the constitution which provide for the appointment of a new monarch. Various scenarios have been proposed, including the end to the monarchy, though this is a proposition that is not usually discussed other than in private. Of Sihanouk's surviving children who might be considered as a successor, the most frequently mentioned is Prince Norodom Sihamoni, Sihanouk's son by the present queen. Yet both Sihanouk and Sihamoni himself have stated that the prince has no interest in occupying the throne in the future. Hun Sen's views on the issue are unclear, but many well-informed observers in Phnom Penh argue that it would be wrong to assume that the present prime minister is anxious to see the elimination of the monarchy, always providing that a successor to Sihanouk does not seek to take an active role in politics.

More of the Same?

Only a bold commentator would suggest that there will be no political surprises as Cambodia prepares to enter a new millennium. The difficulty at the moment is to identify what those surprises might be. Although, from time to time, there are suggestions that Hun Sen faces challenges from within his own party — the name of Chea Sim (CPP leader) is sometimes mentioned — no convincing evidence has emerged to justify a judgement that Hun Sen's position is in any way under threat. So if Cambodia is to move beyond stability to a genuine improvement in political, economic, and social terms its population must rely on Hun Sen for leadership. At the very least, he faces an awesome task.

NOTES

1. Pierre P. Lizée, "Testing the Limits of Change: Cambodia after the July Elections", in *Southeast Asian Affairs*, edited by Daljit Singh and John Funston (Singapore: Institute of Southeast Asian Studies, 1999).
2. As an example, see Barry Wain, "A Complex Pragmatist, His Beliefs Remain Elusive", *Asian Wall Street Journal*, 6 July 1999.
3. For some detailed discussion of these issues, see articles in *Phnom Penh Post*, 29 October–11 November 1999 and 12–25 November 1999.
4. *Australian*, 9 and 10 June 1999; *Phnom Penh Post*, 10–23 December 1999.
5. For details, see *Phnom Penh Post*, 15–28 October 1999 and 29 October–11 November 1999.

INDONESIA

INDONESIA
Democratization and the Threat of Disintegration

Harold Crouch[1]

Indonesia's political transformation continued during 1999 and culminated in the October election of Abdurrahman Wahid — usually known as Gus Dur — as the country's fourth president. In contrast to Indonesia's first two presidents who were always "elected" unanimously and the third who, as vice-president, acceded to the presidency on the resignation of his predecessor, President Abdurrahman won office in a competitive and constitutional process, the outcome of which was in doubt until the last votes were counted. Indonesia's political system still fell short of ideal democratic standards but its progress towards democratization had been enormous.

Indonesia's democratic transformation proceeded in extraordinarily difficult circumstances. The economy, which had been devastated by the Asian financial crisis in 1997, remained in deep recession as investors waited for political uncertainties to be resolved. Economic disruption brought great suffering to much of the population and contributed to regular outbreaks of social conflict, including severe ethnic and religious clashes, in various parts of the country. Long-standing separatist demands in Aceh and Irian Jaya gained increasing popular support and East Timor won its independence following a U.N.-supervised referendum. By the end of the year the prospect of further disintegration of the country could not be dismissed.

During the year much thought was devoted to fundamental change in the political system. The 1945 Constitution was no longer considered sacred and immutable. Several constitutional amendments were adopted by the People's Consultative Assembly (MPR) and more were planned for its next session in the year 2000. New legislation on regional autonomy was adopted but the debate continued between those who advocated the introduction of a federal system and those who defended the existing unitary state. Meanwhile, the influence of the Armed Forces continued to decline and military personnel faced the prospect of charges for human-rights offences.

HAROLD CROUCH is Senior Fellow, Department of Political and Social Change, Research School of Pacific and Asian Studies, Australian National University.

The Election Laws and the General Election

The Habibie government was widely seen as a carry-over from Soeharto's discredited New Order but without the previous regime's repressive power. In the face of international pressure and widespread domestic demands for democratic reform, the government released political prisoners, removed restrictions on the press, and held competitive national and regional elections.

The package of new electoral laws adopted in January was the result of a compromise that produced an extraordinarily complex, and indeed virtually unworkable, system under which the distribution of seats in each province was based on proportional representation but individuals would be elected to represent particular districts within the province. The composition of the parliament (DPR) was biased against Java — where almost 60 per cent of the population lives — with only 234 of its 462 elected members representing constituencies in Java. One of the most controversial aspects of the legislation was the continued appointment of members of the Armed Forces (TNI, Indonesian National Military) to legislative bodies although their numbers were halved from seventy-five to thirty-eight in the 500-member DPR and from 20 to 10 per cent in the regional assemblies (DPRD). The legislation also provided for a 700-member MPR consisting of 500 members of the DPR, 135 regional representatives (elected by the provincial DPRDs), and sixty-five appointed "group" representatives (proposed by organizations representing religion, economic groups, ethnic minorities, veterans, women, and others). The MPR is the supreme body with the power to elect the president, establish the broad direction of policy and change the constitution. In contrast to the Soeharto-era MPR in which half the members were directly appointed by the president, the new MPR promised to be a much more representative body. Finally, a new law on political parties removed earlier restrictions and allowed forty-eight parties to contest the election instead of the three permitted under the New Order.

The election was held on 7 June when 105,720,661 valid votes were cast after an unexpectedly peaceful campaign. A crucial difference with previous elections was the relative neutrality of the state apparatus. The military had cut its formal ties with the Golkar Party the previous year and its commander, General Wiranto, pledged that it would remain neutral during the election campaign. Although defeated parties raised many complaints, no one seriously accused the military of interfering with the ballot. The most important complaint involved civil servants actively supporting Golkar in some regions — especially outside Java and in remote rural areas. Golkar's control of the central and regional administration meant that its supporters in the bureaucracy could put pressure on voters even though civil servants were supposed to be neutral. However, it seems that many civil servants were not prepared to put all their eggs into the Golkar basket and did not want to be identified as Golkar supporters when there was a strong chance that Golkar would be defeated in the election.

As had been widely anticipated before the election, five parties emerged as the main victors. The Partai Demokrasi Indonesia — Perjuangan (PDI-P, Indonesian Democracy Party — Struggle) won 33.76 per cent of the national vote, followed by Golkar with 22.46 per cent, Partai Kebangkitan Bangsa (PKB, National Awakening Party) with 12.62 per cent, Partai Persatuan Pembangunan (PPP, Unity and Development Party) with 10.72 per cent, and Partai Amanat Nasional (PAN, National Mandate Party) with 7.12 per cent. The distribution of seats in the DPR, however, did not directly reflect the national vote because the constituencies were provinces rather than the nation as a whole. The PDI-P won 153 of the 462 elected seats (33 per cent) but the regional bias in the system favoured Golkar, which won 120 seats (26 per cent). The regional bias also favoured the PPP which, despite winning fewer votes than the PKB, took fifty-eight seats (12.5 per cent) while the PKB, which was based in East Java, won only fifty-one (11 per cent). PAN's thirty-four seats were more or less in line with its share of votes. Of the rest, two small Muslim parties, Partai Bulan Bintang (PBB, or Crescent and Star Party) with thirteen and Partai Keadilan (PK, or Justice Party) with seven, were most successful while another fourteen parties won between one and five seats each. In regional terms, ninety-two (60 per cent) of the PDI-P's 153 seats were won in Java and Bali while seventy-nine (66 per cent) of Golkar's seats were won outside Java and Bali. The PPP's support was more evenly spread with thirty-three (57 per cent) of its fifty-eight seats outside Java while PAN was evenly divided with seventeen seats in Java and another seventeen outside. Finally, the PKB was heavily based in Java where it won forty-two (82 per cent) of its fifty-one seats.

The election also produced provincial DPRDs, which each elected five regional representatives to sit in the MPR. (As a result of the decision of the people of East Timor to separate from Indonesia and the chaotic conditions that followed in that province, regional representatives were elected from only twenty-six provinces and the total number of members of the MPR was reduced to 695.) Because of the bias in favour of the Outer Islands, almost half (sixty-two) of the 130 regional representatives were Golkar supporters. When the MPR convened in October, the Golkar bloc had grown to 182, almost equal to the PDI-P bloc which, with the addition of thirty-two regional representatives, had now reached 185. The PPP's bloc grew to seventy, the PKB bloc to fifty-seven while PAN and the PK amalgamated to form the "Reform" bloc consisting of forty-nine members. And, of course, the TNI and the Police Force formed their own bloc of thirty-eight members. The remaining seats were held by twenty-two members representing small Islamic parties, nineteen representing small nationalist-oriented or Christian parties, and seventy-three apparently unaffiliated regional and "group" representatives.

The Presidential Election and the New Government

President Habibie's strategy required that his party, Golkar, form an alliance with the PPP and the small Muslim parties. As the leader of the Indonesian

Muslim Intellectuals' Association (ICMI) during the Soeharto era, Habibie had developed ties with Muslim organizations and hoped to attract the support of the modernist Muslim parties which were inclined to doubt the Islamic credentials of his main rival, Megawati Soekarnoputri. Habibie also hoped to win the support of the TNI by offering the vice-presidency to General Wiranto. Further, it was widely believed that Golkar's superior financial strength would give it the means to persuade wavering MPR members to support its candidate. On the other hand, Habibie could not rely on the full support of his own party where a strong faction — led by the party's chairman, Akbar Tanjung — was by no means committed to supporting him. Habibie's prospects were also hurt by the public perception of his government as merely a continuation of the discredited Soeharto regime, and particularly his obvious reluctance to conduct a serious investigation of corruption allegations against the former president. The involvement of some Golkar officials in a huge banking scandal that broke in late July further undermined public confidence in the president and he was hurt by a nationalist reaction to his handling of policy on East Timor which resulted in a humiliating vote against integration.

Habibie's main challenger was Megawati Soekarnoputri, the daughter of Indonesia's first president who had been overthrown by Soeharto in the mid-1960s. Although Megawati herself never displayed outstanding political skills and appeared to have only a limited grasp of policy issues, she was widely perceived as a "victim" of the Soeharto regime which had deposed her as leader of the Indonesian Democracy Party (PDI) in 1996. She was nevertheless able in effect to take over that party when an overwhelming majority of its supporters flocked to her new party, PDI-P. The PDI-P stood for secular nationalism and resisted moves to strengthen Islamic influence on the state. Although Megawati seemed to think that as "winner" of the general election, she was more or less automatically entitled to be elected as president, she, like Habibie, could not in fact hope to win the presidency without seeking the support of other parties in the MPR.

Megawati's most important early ally was the PKB, which had been formed on the initiative of the Nahdlatul Ulama (NU), the traditionalist Islamic organization based in rural Java which claimed 30 million adherents. Although he did not hold any formal position in the PKB, its dominant figure was the NU chairman, Abdurrahman Wahid (Gus Dur). Gus Dur rejected the goal of "Islamizing" the state and had been associated with non-Muslims in founding the Democracy Forum during the last years of Soeharto's rule. He insisted that the PKB became an "open" party willing to co-operate closely with non-religious parties. While the party's leaders, including Gus Dur, publicly expressed support for Megawati, Gus Dur also sometimes seemed to be distancing himself from her. The PKB's relatively low vote in the general election, however, seemed to rule out the possibility of Gus Dur emerging as a presidential candidate and, in any case, his near blindness and the effects of two strokes in 1998 were widely seen as making him ineligible.

PAN was another potential participant in a reformist alliance supporting Megawati. The party's reformist outlook and "open" image had attracted prominent Muslim and non-Muslim intellectuals, who favoured an alliance with other "anti-status-quo" parties but its main base lay in the large modernist Muslim organization, the Muhammadiyah, which had little sympathy for Megawati. PAN's leader, Amien Rais, had previously been the Muhammadiyah's general chairman but he aimed to appeal to a broad reformist constituency not limited to modernist Muslims. The party's poor performance in the general election, however, dashed Amien's own presidential hopes and forced him to revise his initial strategy. When, after the election, Megawati made no approach to him, Amien took the initiative to establish a loose coalition between PAN and several Muslim parties — including the PPP, PBB, and PK — which were totally opposed to Megawati but only lukewarm in favour of Habibie. Initially, the Poros Tengah (Central Axis), as it called itself, seemed able to muster only about 120 members of the MPR. Amien aimed, however, to form a larger Muslim bloc by attracting the traditionalist PKB, which was still committed to supporting Megawati. In order to wean its members away from Megawati, Amien surprised virtually all observers by nominating Gus Dur for the presidency. The Muhammadiyah, the second largest Muslim organization in Indonesia which represented Islamic modernism in contrast to the NU's traditionalism, had been in rivalry with the NU for most of the twentieth century and Amien and Gus Dur had long been in the habit of making derogatory remarks about each other. Although Gus Dur accepted the nomination, he, in his usual ambiguous way, continued to proclaim his own support for Megawati. Meanwhile PAN in effect abandoned its earlier image as an "open" non-religious party.

President Habibie's expectation was that, whatever commitment Amien had made to Gus Dur, in the final analysis most of the Poros Tengah would give their support to him rather than the physically infirm Gus Dur. When the MPR convened in October, however, Habibie was abandoned by his own party chairman, Akbar Tanjung, who was apparently offered the vice-presidency by Megawati with the result that, late in the evening, Habibie's "accountability report" to the MPR was rejected by 355 votes to 322 and he decided to withdraw from the presidential race. The next twelve hours were filled with ceaseless manoeuvring by various possible candidates (except the confident Megawati, who had gone to bed) and by the next morning, 20 October, Gus Dur — despite his earlier expression of support for Megawati — had secured the support of the Poros Tengah and the Habibie faction in Golkar, which by then was ready to support anyone but Megawati. And it seemed that most of the TNI/police bloc — perhaps suspicious of Megawati's populism — were also converted to Gus Dur's side, while most of the PKB group voted for him. In the end Abdurrahman Wahid won with 373 votes against Megawati's 313. The "betrayal" of Megawati triggered rioting by her enraged supporters not only in Jakarta but in far-away Solo, Denpasar, and Medan. Sensing that the rioting might continue unless Megawati's supporters were assuaged, Gus Dur persuaded her to accept his support for the vice-presidency, which she won comfortably the next day.

Gus Dur's cabinet was formed in consultation with Megawati, Amien Rais, Akbar Tanjung, and General Wiranto and was quickly dubbed a cabinet of national unity. It included representatives not only of all five major political parties but also some smaller ones. Of the thirty-five members of the cabinet (including the Commander of the TNI, the Attorney-General, and the State Secretary who each has cabinet status), five were linked to the PKB; four each to the PDI-P, Golkar, and PAN; two to the PPP; and one each to the small Muslim parties, the PK and PBB. Another six, including the military commander, were either active or retired military officers while eight had no obvious party affiliation. The "rainbow" quality of the cabinet was also apparent in its ethnic and regional makeup.

In contrast to the cabinets of much of the Soeharto era, economic policy was not entrusted to "technocrats". The key position of Co-ordinating Minister for the Economy, Finance, and Industry was given to Kwik Kian Gie, a PDI-P politician of Chinese descent, well-known for his newspaper columns on economic and business issues. A PAN leader with an academic background in management was appointed as Minister of Finance, and a Golkar-affiliated businessman took the Industry and Trade portfolio. A PDI-P leader with a background in banking was appointed as Minister of State for Investment and Public Enterprises. The new Foreign Minister, Alwi Shihab, was a close confidant of Gus Dur and a leader of the PKB.

The "Loss" of East Timor

Apart from the presidential election, the MPR made another historic decision when it finally endorsed the results of the referendum in East Timor and thus recognized East Timor's withdrawal from the republic. The future of East Timor had been put on the national agenda when President Habibie suddenly announced in a media interview on 9 June 1998 that he was prepared to grant special autonomy to East Timor in return for international recognition of the province as part of Indonesia. Habibie's offer gave new impetus to ongoing U.N.-sponsored talks between the Indonesian and Portuguese Foreign Ministers but no agreement seemed in sight at the end of the year. It was at this point that a letter sent to Habibie in December 1998 by the Australian Prime Minister, John Howard, triggered a drastic change in Indonesia's position. Howard proposed that some form of self-determination be held after a lengthy period of autonomy — a proposal which essentially endorsed the position of Portugal and the Timorese resistance in contrast to Indonesia, which saw wide autonomy as the final solution. The significance of the Australian proposal lay in the fact that Australian was the only "Western" country that had explicitly recognized Indonesian sovereignty over East Timor. Although Habibie angrily rejected Howard's proposal, the changed Australian stance seems to have set in motion a re-thinking of Indonesia's position and, following a cabinet meeting on 27 January 1999, the Indonesian government announced that it would give the people of East Timor the opportunity to accept or reject its autonomy proposal later in the year. If they rejected the proposal, the government would recommend to the forthcoming session of the MPR that East Timor be permitted to withdraw from the Republic of Indonesia.

The TNI, which had always been strongly committed to retaining East Timor, did not indicate public opposition to the new approach. General Wiranto had participated in the discussions that led to the announcement of the new policy and had apparently not protested. Did this mean that the military leadership supported the holding of the referendum? Although many officers were dismayed at the prospect of a referendum, it seems that the top leadership saw it as an opportunity to settle the East Timor issue once and for all by making sure that the vote would be in favour of continued integration with Indonesia. The stipulation of the 5 May agreement between the governments of Indonesia and Portugal and the Secretary-General of the United Nations that "the absolute neutrality of the TNI and the Indonesian Police is essential" was to be totally disregarded.

It was standard practice for the TNI to recruit and train local civilians in units known as *wanra* (Perlawanan Rakyat — People's Resistance) to take part in military operations in regions faced with rebellion. In East Timor, in addition to *wanra*, new paramilitary groups were sponsored by the military outside the formal military structure and used to terrorize and intimidate supporters of independence. In early 1999 so-called militias were operating in all thirteen of East Timor's *kabupaten* and were soon brought together loosely in the Fighters for Integration Force (Pasukan Pejuang Integrasi — PPI) under the leadership of the former *bupati* of Bobonaro, Joao Taveres. The PPI itself claimed that the total militia strength was over 50,000 but most observers believed the numbers to be less than 10,000. That the militias worked closely with the TNI and the regional administration was obvious to all.

President Habibie's new approach to East Timor raised both the hopes of pro-independence groups and the fears of the pro-integration camp. Conflict between the two sides had been rising and during 1999 clashes became everyday occurrences. In May the U.N. Secretary-General stated that "credible reports continue to be received of political violence, including intimidation and killings, by armed militas against unarmed pro-independence civilians" and he noted that the militias seemed "to be operating with the acquiescence of elements of the army".[2] Estimates of the death toll during the first six months of 1999 ranged from several dozen to 200. Meanwhile, as the date for the registration of voters approached, the number of internal refugees increased and aid organizations estimated that 59,000 were no longer living in their home villages where they might be expected to register.

The agreement between Indonesia and Portugal on 5 May had entrusted the organization of the referendum to the United Nations Assistance Mission in East Timor (UNAMET). Continuing violence forced the postponement of voter registration twice but finally 438,513 voters were enrolled in East Timor itself and another 13,279 in Indonesia and overseas. Although clashes continued to take place throughout August, the referendum was finally held in a remarkably peaceful atmosphere on 30 August when 99 per cent of registered votes actually voted. The result, announced on 4 September, showed that 344,589 (78.5 per cent) of the valid votes rejected the autonomy proposal and only 94,388 (21.5 per cent) supported it. The people of East Timor had overwhelmingly opted for independence.

Conditions deteriorated very quickly as militia members launched a campaign of destruction and killing which left Dili, other towns, and much of the countryside in ruins. Within a few days, thousands of people had fled to the hills around Dili while others were taken in military trucks to West Timor. Foreign observers, such as those of the Carter Center, reported that their members "have on numerous occasions witnessed militia members perpetrating acts of violence in full view of heavily-armed police and military personnel who either stand by and watch or actively assist the militias".[3] But it was not only foreigners who were shocked by what they saw. The Jakarta newspaper, *Kompas*, reported that "The Indonesian security forces often seemed to do nothing when violence broke out"[4] and the Indonesian Human Rights Commission noted that terrorist activities took place "directly witnessed and permitted by members of the security forces".[5] General Wiranto, however, adamantly denied that his troops were supporting the militias and explained the destruction as a natural response to electoral violations perpetrated by UNAMET. As he put it, "This dissatisfaction is proper (*wajar*), and has been expressed in the form of spontaneous actions".[6] On another occasion he told a journalist:

> You can see and feel yourself how a disappointed person, who has been treated unjustly in front of his eyes, whose complaints have been ignored, in the end will be disappointed and angry. Then they express their disappointment. Must we confront them with force?[7]

The massive destruction was a huge blow to Indonesia's international reputation. Martial law in East Timor was declared at midnight on 6 September and military reinforcements were sent but the violence continued. The leader of a U.N. Security Council mission said: "I don't think anybody here has any doubt that there has been complicity between elements of the defence forces and the militias. In some areas, there is no difference between them in terms of action and motivation." The mission therefore recommended that an international force be sent to East Timor "without delay" and that "apparent abuses of international humanitarian law" be investigated.[8] Meanwhile, U.S. President Bill Clinton declared bluntly that the Indonesian military was backing the militias and announced the suspension of military co-operation while the Chairman of the U.S. Joint Chiefs of Staff, General Henry Shelton, was speaking daily by telephone with Wiranto. Ominously, the International Monetary Fund suspended the visit of an aid team to Indonesia.

On the evening of 12 September, the Indonesian cabinet finally agreed to accept the deployment of an international force in East Timor. The International Force East Timor (INTERFET), under Australian command, began to land on 20 September. Although the 5 May agreement provided for Indonesian forces to retain responsibility for security in East Timor until the MPR had made a final decision on East Timor's future, the Indonesian presence declined rapidly and all had left by early October. With the MPR preoccupied with its vote on President Habibie's "accountability report" and the presidential election the next day, the reversal of the 1976 MPR decision incorporating East Timor into Indonesia was passed unanimously without debate by the weary MPR members shortly before midnight on 19 October.

National Disintegration?

Developments in East Timor were watched closely in other regions that had grievances against rule from Jakarta. At both ends of the archipelago — in Aceh and Irian Jaya — long-standing separatist movements drew inspiration from East Timor's struggle and concluded that Jakarta's inability to prevent East Timor's independence augured well for their own prospects. On the other hand, nationalists were committed to maintaining the unity of Indonesia while the TNI, which had been deeply humiliated by the loss of East Timor, made it clear that it would not tolerate separatism in other regions. Separatism, however, was not the only problem. In several regions, most seriously in Maluku and West Kalimantan, fighting between ethnic and religious communities resulted in heavy casualties.

The most serious challenge was in Aceh where it was widely acknowledged that a referendum would result in a vote for independence. The grievances of Aceh's 4.1 million people are multiple. Although the province's natural resources make a big contribution to the national budget, the level of poverty in Aceh itself remains high. Many Acehnese also resent the influx of people from other parts of Indonesia while their Islamic identity is expressed in the demand for the implementation of Islamic law. Perhaps the most fundamental grievance was a consequence of the often brutal behaviour of the military during the decade after 1989 when around 1,500 to 2,000 people were killed and many wounded or tortured during military operations against the separatist Free Aceh Movement (GAM). Military atrocities were widely publicized in the months after Soeharto's fall and General Wiranto personally apologized for the behaviour of "individual" soldiers. Although Aceh's status as a "military operations region" (DOM) was lifted, the military responded to rising GAM activity with increased repression, including several mass killings of civilians in 1999. During the seventeen months from the lifting of DOM in August 1998 to the end of 1999, 447 civilians and eighty-seven members of the security forces had been killed and another 144 were missing.[9]

President Habibie's offer of a referendum on independence to East Timor stimulated the demand for a similar referendum in Aceh and several huge strikes and demonstrations took place in the latter part of the year. Popular support was such that the security forces made no effort to prevent a massive commemoration of the founding of GAM on 4 December 1999 and even permitted the leader of GAM's military wing, Teuku Abdullah Syafei, to appear three times on television to appeal to his followers to remain calm. The election of Gus Dur, who indicated ambiguous support for a referendum, raised hopes which were quickly disappointed when the new president later restricted the scope of any referendum to issues other than independence. Whatever his personal inclinations, Abdurrahman Wahid knew that the DPR would not support a referendum on independence while the TNI was totally opposed to it.

Pro-independence sentiment was also very strong in Irian Jaya. Since the post-Soeharto liberalization, the leadership of the independence cause had passed from guerrillas in the jungle to prominent public figures in Jayapura and other cities. Like the Acehnese, the Papuans — as they prefer to call themselves — complained that their mineral wealth was being exploited by Jakarta while their own people were left in poverty. They also felt threatened by the influx of people from other parts of Indonesia, including nearly 300,000 people from Java and Bali over the previous thirty years under the central government's official transmigration scheme and several hundred thousand "spontaneous" transmigrants from nearby islands. By the 1990s about one-third of Irian Jaya's population of 2.5 million was not indigenous. Like the Acehnese, the Papuans, too, had suffered severely from heavy-handed military operations.

The fall of Soeharto was followed almost immediately by renewed agitation for independence. In sharp contrast to the approach of his predecessor, President Habibie invited 100 leaders from Irian Jaya to participate in a "National Dialogue" at the presidential place in Jakarta on 26 February. To Habibie's dismay, however, they issued a statement calling for independence. Agitation continued during the year and culminated on 1 December 1999 in a flag-raising commemoration in Jayapura. Like the similar commemoration in Aceh on 4 December, the government authorities adopted a benign approach, which was reciprocated by the Papuan leaders who agreed to raise the Indonesian national flag together with the Papuan flag and to sing the Indonesian national anthem along with their own Papuan anthem. President Abdurrahman responded by ordering the release of all Papuan political prisoners and spending the last evening of the 1900s in Jayapura where he announced the change in the name of the province to Papua but rejected the demand for independence.

In contrast to both Aceh and Irian Jaya, the conflict in Ambon and other parts of Maluku province was not a result of a regional demand for independence but arose from antagonisms within local society itself. Among the two million inhabitants of the province, Muslims make up 57 per cent, Protestants 37 per cent, and Catholics 6 per cent, but on the island of Ambon itself Protestants constituted 52 per cent, Catholics 4 per cent, and Muslims 43 per cent. Christian-Muslim tensions have been exacerbated in recent decades by a steady influx of Bugis, Butonese, and Makasarese migrants from Sulawesi who gradually dominated local markets and transport businesses. Although ethnically distinct from Ambonese Muslims, these migrants were Muslims and strengthened the Muslim side of the balance. Rivalry between the communities was further aggravated in the 1990s where Muslim governors increasingly appointed Muslims to senior positions, although Christians were by no means excluded. The immediate cause of the conflict that tore the province apart in 1999 was a minor altercation between an Ambonese Christian public-transport driver and two Bugis Muslim youths which exploded in widespread fighting in the city of Ambon on 19 January 1999, the eve of Lebaran, marking the end of the Muslim fasting month. Intermittent fighting continued until 27 July when another large clash in Ambon triggered a renewal of conflict in other parts of the province. By mid-December 775 people had been killed during the year and 115 churches and mosques destroyed.[10] But the worst was yet to come. In the final week of the year as Christians celebrated Christmas and Muslims fasted during the month of Ramadan, several hundreds were killed, and by the end of the year the death toll far exceeded 1,000. In mid-December the number of refugees in Maluku was 83,000 while over 80,000 had fled to South Sulawesi.

Mass killings also took place in February and March 1999 in the Sambas *kabupaten* in the north of West Kalimantan. In West Kalimantan, the indigenous Malay and Dayak communities each make up about 40 per cent of the population, the rest consisting of various migrant minorities. Large-scale ethnic conflict has broken out quite regularly in West Kalimantan, most recently in 1996–97 when several hundred people were killed in Dayak-Madurese clashes. Like the spark that started the ethnic fire in Ambon at about the same time, a quarrel involving a public-transport driver quickly developed into a clash between the Malay and Madurese communities. Unlike Ambon, however, where Muslim Ambonese were allied with Muslim migrants, in Sambas indigenous Christian Dayaks supported indigenous Muslim Malays against the immigrant Muslim Madurese. At the end of March, the official death toll was 186 but it is likely that many deaths were not reported to the authorities. More than 2,000 houses were burnt and virtually the entire Madurese community, which previously made up about 8 per cent of the Sambas population, had fled to Pontianak and other towns where they remained as refugees.

In the post-Soeharto era the sense of having been exploited and neglected was felt not only in Aceh and Irian Jaya but also in other resource-rich provinces such as East Kalimantan and Riau where voices were also raised calling

for independence. But in these provinces there were no long-established separatist movements with guerrilla armies. Their calls for independence, therefore, seemed designed more to strengthen their bargaining position in demanding more powers and money from the centre. In South Sulawesi, too,
students took to the streets in October 1999 to demand independence but
their movement, which seemed to be more a protest against the failure of
President Habibie — a native son of South Sulawesi — to retain the presidency, soon faded away.

Nevertheless, discontent with the centralized system of the New Order was
strong, especially outside Java. The Habibie government therefore included
decentralization on its reform agenda. Far-reaching regional autonomy laws
were adopted in May 1999 although not expected to be fully implemented
until the year 2001. The new Law on Regional Government (No. 22/1999) in
principle transferred authority over all fields except foreign affairs, defence
and security, justice, monetary and fiscal policy, religion, and a number of
broad economic-policy areas including macro-developmental planning, state
economic institutions, and development of human and natural resources, as
well as high technology. The new powers, however, would not devolve to the
twenty-seven provinces[11] but to over 300 districts (*kabupaten* and cities) throughout the country. The law explicitly envisaged that the districts would be responsible for such fields as public works, health, education and culture, agriculture, communications, industry and trade, investment, the environment,
land matters, co-operatives, and labour. The role of provincial governments
would be limited to the administration of central-government affairs in the
regions, cross-district matters, and functions that the district administrations
were not yet ready to handle. Another fundamental reform provided for the
election of regional heads — governors in provinces, *bupati* in *kabupaten* and
mayors in cities — in contrast to the practice of the Soeharto era when they
were in effect appointed by the centre after blatantly manipulated elections.
A second law on the distribution of finance between the central government
and the regions (No. 25/1999) allowed regional government to retain a larger
share of revenues produced in their regions.

The two laws contained substantial ambiguities and uncertainties that would
only be resolved in later regulations. An official of the National Planning
Agency calculated that if the laws were applied the following year, ten provinces would face bankruptcy while four resource-rich provinces would make
enormous gains. There was also concern that many district administrations
would lack the skilled staff necessary to carry out the functions allocated to
them. And prospective investors were worried about the problems of having to
deal with competing district governments rather than single provincial governments.

The government's move towards decentralization was not sufficient for
some of the non-Javanese regions which called for the establishment of a
federal state. The issue of federalism had received increasing attention after

the PAN leader, Amien Rais — himself a Javanese — raised it in 1998. In Indonesia, however, the concept of federalism had been discredited in the past by its association with a Dutch scheme to thwart independence in the 1940s. Nationalists regarded federalism as no more than a step towards national disintegration while pro-federalists argued that federalism is in fact needed, in the present circumstances, to prevent national disintegration. In November 1999 the East Kalimantan DPRD adopted a resolution calling for a federal state while a Congress of the People of Riau was due to be held in early 2000 for the same purpose. The federal proposal, however, was strongly opposed by the predominantly Javanese military leaders and the main political parties. A few days after his election, the wily new president, Gus Dur, confided, "Actually we would like to have a federal system", but, he added, Indonesians do not like the word "federalism". "Doing things without naming them is the Indonesian way", he explained.[12] If the new autonomy laws are indeed implemented, the distribution of power in the Indonesian political system will have undergone a fundamental change.

Democratic Consolidation and the Role of the Military

The democratization begun by President Habibie — a former senior minister in the authoritarian regime — continued under President Abdurrahman — a founder of the opposition Democracy Forum during the late Soeharto era. The atmosphere in the presidential palace was transformed first by Habibie and even more by Gus Dur. Not only did Gus Dur complete the release of political prisoners begun by Habibie but he welcomed former prisoners as visitors to the palace, as in the case of the renowned novelist Pramudya Ananta Toer, and at a Ramadan meal in the case of the youthful leader of the Partai Rakyat Demokrasi (PRD, Democratic People's Party), Budiman Sujatmiko, both of whom were anathema to the military. Not only did he end the hostility to East Timor but he welcomed as a friend the East Timorese leader, Xanana Gusmao, who had been Soeharto's and Habibie's prisoner. He maintained his old habit of chatting casually with journalists and even speculated openly on the future of some of his cabinet ministers. And when aggrieved public servants demonstrated in the square in front of the palace, he crossed the road to reason with them — something unimaginable when Soeharto was president.

The atmosphere in the MPR was also transformed. No longer did its members listen in respectful silence to the president's "accountability report" as they had in the past when Soeharto addressed its five-yearly sessions. In October 1999 some members even booed Habibie and eventually his report was rejected. To his great credit, it should be acknowledged, Habibie did not retire to his home but sat through the highly critical debate on his report. The elected MPR under the leadership of Amien Rais and the DPR under the leadership of Akbar Tanjung could no longer be expected to rubber-stamp whatever proposals were put before them by the president. At the October 1999 session the hitherto "sacred" 1945 Constitution was amended for the first time when nine paragraphs were revised mainly with the intention of limiting the president's powers and increasing the DPR's authority. The most important amendment limited the president and vice-president to two five-year terms while most of the others used stronger language to assert the DPR's authority. Ironically, one of the amendments, which obliged the president to consult the DPR before granting amnesties to prisoners, led to a delay in the release of political prisoners.

Although required constitutionally to meet only once every five years, it was decided to call the MPR into session annually and it was expected that the president would report on his achievements during the previous year — with the possibility that his report might be rejected. This change, combined with the democratically elected membership of the MPR, in effect introduced a strong parliamentary element to Indonesia's presidential system. Although the president could not be deposed if he lost the confidence of the majority of the DPR, as would be the case with a prime minister under a parliamentary system, the president could be deposed at the annual MPR session if his report were deemed unacceptable. Gus Dur may have had this possibility in mind when he included representatives of all the significant parties in his "rainbow" cabinet — in addition to considerations related to the fostering of national integration.

Democratization requires the withdrawal of the military from a direct role in politics. Following the fall of Soeharto the military had been greatly discredited. Public condemnation of the military for its role as the backbone of the Soeharto regime was reinforced by revelations of massive human-rights abuse in Aceh, Irian Jaya, and East Timor, as well as military involvement in abuses in Jakarta and elsewhere. In response to public criticism, reform-minded officers formulated what they called the "New Paradigm" in place of the old *dwifungsi* (dual function) doctrine. Although the New Paradigm — which was adopted at an Armed Forces seminar in September 1998 — did not completely abolish the military's political role, it envisaged its drastic, even if gradual, contraction.

A major reform was the abolition of *kekaryaan* — the practice of appointing active military officers to civilian positions in the government administration. In 1999 about 3,500 to 4,000 were serving in posts ranging from cabinet minister, provincial governor, and ambassador, down to junior officials in local governments. From 1 April officers had to retire from the military before they could serve in non-military positions. At that time four of twenty-one cabinet ministers, ten of twenty-seven governors and 128 *bupati* and mayors out of 306 were active military officers.[13] The new rule did not prevent retired officers being appointed to civilian positions but the general democratization of the political system, especially the election of regional heads, made it unlikely that any but the most exceptional retired officers would gain such appointments. Although the abolition of *kekaryaan* did not abolish appointed military representation in the national and regional DPRs and the MPR, their numbers were halved from 2,800 in the past.

When President Abdurrahman formed his cabinet in October 1999 five of the thirty-five ministers (including the Commander of the TNI who enjoyed cabinet status) were active officers and one was a retired officer. General Wiranto took the influential post of Co-ordinating Minister for Political and Security Affairs but the military ministers did not form a cohesive bloc. Two had served as regional governors and were apparently appointed for that reason rather than as military "representatives" while two were senior officers who made it clear that they would have preferred to continue their military careers. For the first time since the 1950s a civilian, Juwono Sudarsono, was appointed as Minister of Defence and for the first time ever a naval officer, Admiral Widodo Adisucipto, was appointed as Commander of the TNI.

The renaming of the old Department of Defence and Security as the Department of Defence symbolized the direction of reformist thinking in the military. The reformers believed that army methods were often inappropriate for maintaining domestic order. In April, therefore, the Police Force was separated from the Armed Forces (which were renamed as the TNI) and given the primary responsibility in the first instance for handling demonstrations, rioting, and other threats to domestic order. In the long run, it was planned that the TNI would concentrate on external defence while an enlarged and re-trained Police Force would deal with internal security. In the short run, however, the TNI, especially the army and marines, continued to back up the police, whose manpower was currently only 180,000 in a country of 210 million. Despite the reforms, in practice the police often continued to use the brutal methods to which they had been accustomed in the past.

Despite the reforms implemented during the last year, the TNI retained a formidable political presence through the army's territorial organization. The military is still organized primarily as an internal-security force, rather than a defence force with around two-thirds of the army's troops spread throughout the country in small units parallel to civilian government. The TNI's territorial organization is rationalized as part of the national defence doctrine but, in reality the territorial forces are primarily concerned with maintaining political stability and have considerable capacity to intervene in local politics. As long as this capacity remains in place, civilian government continues to be vulnerable to military pressure. The army's territorial structure became the focus of a surprisingly public debate among serving military officers at the end of the year. The initiator of the debate was the recently appointed Regional Commander in Sulawesi and one of the leading reformers, Major-General Agus Wirahadikusumah, who told a DPR commission in December that the territorial structure was an "instrument of power", which should be reduced and eventually abolished.[14] Agus's proposals, however, were publicly rejected by other officers and he himself admitted that only about 20 per cent of officers sympathized with his views.

Meanwhile the authority of the civilian government over the military was facing a fundamental test on the issue of what human-rights activists called the military's "culture of impunity". In November 1999 an investigative committee appointed by President Habibie presented the new government with a 484-page report on military violence in Aceh and urged that priority be given to five cases where the evidence was clear — a rape in 1996, torture, and disappearances at a military interrogation centre, and three mass shootings. Independently, a fact-finding team established by the provincial government and headed by a colonel had also concluded that one of the shootings, that of Teuku Bantaqiah and his followers in West Aceh, was not due to an "armed clash" as claimed by the military but "unilateral shooting".

The cases listed to be brought to the courts in Aceh involved only middle-ranking officers but the investigation of the post-referendum devastation in East Timor focused attention on senior officers, including the then Commander of the TNI and Minister of Defence and Security, General Wiranto. In September, President Habibie established a Fact-Finding Commission in an unsuccessful attempt to pre-empt the establishment of an international investigation of possible "crimes against humanity" by the U.N. Commission on Human Rights. In a report to the U.N. Security Council on 21 December, three U.N. investigators concluded that there were grounds to believe that the TNI was involved in "war crimes" in East Timor and made the following recommendation:

> Unless, in a matter of months, the steps taken by the government of Indonesia to investigate TNI involvement in the past year's atrocities bear fruit, both in the way of credible clarification of the facts and the bringing to justice of the perpetrators — both directly and by virtue of command responsibility, however high the level of responsibility — the Security Council should consider the establishment of an international criminal tribunal for this purpose.[15]

President Abdurrahman, however, had already taken the view that the trial of Indonesian military officers in an international court would be a violation of "national sovereignty" but he expressed his support for the trial of offenders in Indonesia if recommended by the Indonesian commission.[16]

Meanwhile, the Indonesian Fact-Finding Commission energetically continued its enquiries. In East Timor itself, it took testimony which pointed to the direct involvement of the TNI in planning and assisting the destruction that followed the referendum. In addition, members of the team witnessed the exhumation of twenty-six bodies, including those of three Catholic priests murdered at Suai, which were buried near a beach about two miles across the border in West Timor. On their return to Jakarta and armed with powers to subpoena witnesses, the Commission called senior military officers to testify, these including General Wiranto, as Commander of TNI at the time, Major-General Adam Damiri, the Bali Regional Commander with authority over East Timor, Major-General Zacky Anwar Makarim, the TNI's Liaison Officer with UNAMET, Major-General Syafrie Syamsuddin, a senior staff officer in the TNI headquarters, Brigadier-General Tono Suratman, the former East Timor military resort commander, and several former *bupati* and militia leaders from East Timor. General Wiranto denied that the TNI had ever adopted a policy "to kill, burn and force refugees to leave" East Timor. Instead, he claimed that the destruction had been due to the emotional reaction of supporters of integration to what they saw as an unfair referendum conducted by UNAMET.[17] The commission failed to submit its report by its deadline, 31 December, but was given an extra month to complete its enquiries. The evidence presented by military officers to the commission before the end of the year did little to dispel the impression that the military was deeply involved in supporting the militia and had done little to prevent the post-referendum devastation.

The prospect that some senior TNI leaders might be tried for human-rights offences during the year 2000 was a cause for concern among many military officers. The newly appointed Commander of Kostrad, Lieutenant-General Djadja Suparman, warned that the treatment of senior officers before the Fact-Finding Commission (and also the DPR) might upset ordinary soldiers who might react violently and thus harm the ordinary people. "Not just ordinary soldiers, I also feel hurt", he said, adding in the traditional military style that he detected a conspiracy involving both foreign and domestic elements who were aiming systematically to destroy the TNI.[18] Djadja's comments were answered by the reformist Agus Wirahadikusumah who indicated that he did not object to the trial of military officers when he stated that Indonesian soldiers "are not dedicated to the service of generals but to the TNI as an institution and to the nation and state".[19] The president seemed to have a similar view when he said "The whole nation cannot be sacrificed just for one or two persons".[20]

Could the military come back to power? Signs of military alienation from the new government appeared early. The military, which sees itself as the guardian of national unity, seemed unhappy with the tolerance shown by the government to separatists in Aceh and Irian Jaya and limitations imposed on military operations. In November, police and military leaders were pushing openly for the application of martial law in three *kabupaten* in Aceh but without success. It also appeared that the President may have been encouraging factionalism within the military at the expense of General Wiranto. The extraordinary leeway permitted to Major-General Agus Wirahadikusumah seemed to suggest some sort of presidential protection while the appointment in November of General Tyasno Sudarto, the former head of military intelligence, as army Chief of Staff was another indication of Wiranto's waning influence over the military. Agus Wirahadikusumah was presumably referring to Wiranto when he claimed at a public forum in the University of Indonesia that there were people who wanted to depose the president including "a person whose aspirations to become vice-president or to become president were not fulfilled".[21]

The possibility of a successful coup, however, still seemed remote at the end of 1999. The Defence Minister, Juwono Sudarsono, warned a parliamentary committee that "If civilian leaders aren't able to develop a healthy and independent political life then we will return to military rule sooner or later just like what we find in Pakistan and some African countries".[22] But the Pakistan coup took place after fourteen years of civilian rule. In Indonesia the legitimacy of the democratically elected government was, after only two months, still strong and expectations of civilian rule still high while memories of the military-backed Soeharto regime were still fresh. For the military in particular, the memory of the way in which a mix of student demonstrations and military factionalism had triggered the May 1998 rioting in Jakarta was still a potent warning. A military coup would almost certainly set off massive popular demonstrations that could easily trigger rioting. The result would be a further setback to the prospects of economic recovery and widespread international condemnation. The Defence Minister's warning was apt but it applied more to the distant than immediate future.

Conclusion

At the beginning of the year 2000, Indonesia faced four crucial challenges. First, the government needed to create a stable and effective political system based on democratic principles and capable of preventing a return of the military to political power. This required an effective party system that could produce both a stable coalition of support for the government and an effective means of making the government responsive to popular demands. Second, the government needed to find a formula for dealing with regions where public opinion is currently strongly in favour of separation from Indonesia as well as to satisfy the other regions of the country. Third, the government needed to deal with increasing signs of social disintegration, particularly ethnic and religious conflict. And fourth, the government needed to promote conditions conducive to economic recovery.

During 1999 significant progress towards the first goal had been made although Indonesia's new democracy was still far from entrenched. Some tentative steps had been taken towards the second goal. Despite the common foreign perception of Indonesian "Balkanization", Aceh and Papua were the only provinces with real potential for separatism. The third challenge in the form of conflict between ethnic and religious groups — what Indonesians often call "horizontal" as opposed to "vertical" conflict — continued at dangerous levels throughout the archipelago and were seemingly intractable in Maluku. And finally, although the economy had shown some signs of growth, it had yet to undergo the fundamental reforms needed to attract the investment that was necessary for long-term recovery. Unless economic recovery can get under way, the long-term prospects of democratization, national unity, and social peace will remain questionable.

NOTES

1. I wish to thank June Honna and Marcus Mietzner for helpful comments on an earlier draft of this chapter.
2. *Australian*, 26 May 1999.
3. *Carter Center Weekly Report on East Timor*, no. 18, September 1999.
4. *Kompas*, 2 September 1999.
5. *Kompas*, 9 September 1999.
6. *Kompas*, 2 September 1999.
7. *Republika*, 5 October 1999.
8. Agence France-Presse, *Australian Financial Review*, 13 September 1999.
9. *Kompas*, 24 December 1999.
10. *Kompas*, 13 December 1999.
11. Although East Timor left the republic, the number of provinces remained at twenty-seven when the new North Maluku province was formed in October.
12. Remarks in the author's presence at the Indonesia Next conference (Van Zorge, Heffernan & Associates) in Bali on 24 October 1999.
13. *Tempo*, 12 April 1999.
14. *Kompas*, 14 December 1999.
15. *Jakarta Post*, 23 December 1999.
16. *Jakarta Post, Kompas*, 23 November 1999.
17. *Kompas*, 26 December 1999.
18. <http://www.Detik.com>, 14 December 1999.
19. *Kompas*, 17 December 1999.
20. *Jakarta Post*, 23 December 1999.
21. <http://www.Detik.com>, 14 December 1999.
22. Associated Press, *Dow Jones Newslines*, 22 November 1999.

THE INDONESIAN ECONOMY
UNDER ABDURRAHMAN WAHID

Hadi Soesastro

The honeymoon period following the election of Abdurrahman Wahid as president under a more democratic system was only a brief one. It ended with the announcement of the National Unity cabinet. Wahid's cabinet was a great disappointment to many. Firstly, it did not reflect the spirit of *reformasi* because it was not free from individuals that have been associated with the *status quo* forces. Secondly, it was regarded as a "political" cabinet rather than a cabinet that can deliver the reforms because it incorporates all major political parties with diverse interests and agendas. Thirdly, the capability of the economic team is highly questionable as it consists of politicians from different parties (and some military officers) with no technocratic background.

Abdurrahman Wahid, also known as Gus Dur, is fully aware of these short-comings. He consciously made a political "trade-off" between effective govern-ment, on the one hand, and national unity and reconciliation, on the other hand. Gus Dur has been of the view, even before assuming the presidency, that national unity and reconciliation should be given highest priority. He has been deeply concerned with the political polarization in the country. This moti-vated him to run for the presidency himself in order to prevent a deepening rift within the nation between the nationalists, represented by Megawati, and the Muslims who are organized into different groups and factions that initially rallied behind Habibie. He has been worried about the weakening of the nation's social fabric. He is of the view, for example, that to punish former president Soeharto would tear apart this already fragile social fabric.

It is somewhat puzzling that the problems of Aceh, Irian Jaya, and Maluku did not initially figure prominently in Gus Dur's agenda although they pose a serious challenge to national unity. Gus Dur delegated the task of resolving the problems of Irian Jaya and Maluku to Vice-President Megawati and reserved Aceh for himself. They both moved only slowly and gave the impression that they did not know what to do. However, this could have been a calculated move. On Aceh, Gus Dur successfully kicked the ball back to the Acehnese court as the ball was too hot for him to handle. He would only burn his hands

Hadi Soesastro is Executive Director at the Centre for Strategic and International Studies (CSIS), Jakarta.

and there was not much that he could do unless the Acehnese themselves can come up with a credible representation to engage in serious negotiations with Jakarta. While the problem remains unresolved, Gus Dur has been able to defuse one of the many "time bombs" that were left by the previous governments. To further improve the situation in Aceh the military must restrain itself. Gus Dur appears to have taken over from Megawati the task of dealing with Irian Jaya and Maluku. He appears to have responded to the psychological demand of the Irianese by agreeing to adopt the name Papua. This could open the way for a peaceful resolution of the problem. The problems of Aceh and Irian have been (temporarily) defused by Gus Dur. More recently, the situation in Maluku also appears to be under control, especially following Gus Dur's successful move to change the leadership in the army. This suggests that there may be some truth in the allegations that elements in the army have been responsible for the outbreak of hostilities in Maluku.

The task for Jakarta now is to seriously tackle the problem of regional autonomy that involves a smooth devolution of power from the centre to the regions and a more fair sharing of resources between the centre and the regions. If these tasks are handled satisfactorily, there is a good chance that Aceh and Irian Jaya will not break away from the Republic. It remains to be seen how well Gus Dur can handle this difficult problem. His political skills are well recognized and people still have great confidence that he will be up to this task. Yet the issue is not merely one of political skill of the leader but one of effective government that is necessary to resolve the ongoing economic crisis and to rebuild the economy and the society. This article sets out the main challenges that the Abdurrahman administration faces in the economic area. This will be followed by an examination of the institutional setting and the policy agenda of the new government.

The Economic Setting

The deep economic and political crisis in Indonesia is clearly indicated by the dramatic deterioration in economic indicators. The value of the currency fell from about Rp 2,500 per U.S. dollar at the onset of the crisis to Rp 17,000 in January 1998 following a series of events of political significance, namely, Soeharto's illness and the nomination of Habibie as Soeharto's vice-president. The economy shrank by about 14 per cent in real terms in 1998, and inflation during that year reached almost 80 per cent. This was Indonesia's worst economic performance over the past thirty years. However, the most serious problem that emerged was the loss of confidence on the part of the populace and international investors in the economy and the government. This led to the huge outflow of capital and a series of bank runs. In an attempt to put an end to panic withdrawals of funds by depositors the government instituted a blanket guarantee. This has thus far cost the government about Rp 54 trillion or US$7.5 billion at the exchange rate in January 2000. However, a much larger amount of emergency liquidity assistance to banks was provided by Bank Indonesia as a lender of last resort. It remains a matter of dispute between Bank Indonesia and the Ministry of Finance as to how large that emergency liquidity was, but it is estimated to be in the order of US$25 billion to US$30 billion at the exchange rate in January 2000.

Banks have been the hardest hit by the crisis. On the one hand, depositors withdrew their money. On the other hand, their corporate borrowers ceased to pay interest or to repay their debt. Non-performing loans increased rapidly from around 14 per cent at the onset of the crisis to perhaps 50 per cent at the height of the crisis. In some state banks, the proportion of non-performing loans is estimated to have reached 70 per cent. A programme of bank and corporate restructuring was introduced as part of the agreement with the International Monetary Fund (IMF). A major component of this is bank recapitalization. The plan is to recapitalize all state banks, all regional development banks with a capital adequacy ratio (CAR) of less than 4 per cent, and so-called Category B private banks, namely, those with a CAR of between –25 and 4 per cent if they have a sound and realistic business plan and if the owners and management have passed a test for competence and propriety. The cost of bank recapitalization is huge. A major part of the cost is borne by the government and is financed by issuance of government bonds. This could amount to about US$45 billion to US$50 billion at the exchange rate in January 2000. Hence the total cost of bank restructuring would be about US$90 billion, which includes the cost of bank recapitalization, issuance of bonds to cover the emergency liquidity, and government blanket guarantee. This amount is about the same as the cost of bank restructuring in Mexico. In Mexico it accounted for about 25 per cent of gross domestic product (GDP), but in the case of Indonesia the cost of bank restructuring that is borne by the government accounts for about 85 per cent of GDP. This is a staggering amount. On top of this, the government has an external debt of about 60 per cent of GDP. The total public debt is about 145 per cent of GDP. The burden to the government is enormous. Total public debt service payments in fiscal year (FY) 1999/2000 (ending 31 March 2000) is about Rp 55 trillion, which amounts to 26 per cent of total expenditures or 4.5 per cent of GDP. In the year 2000 budget (1 April to 31 December 2000), total public debt service payments will increase to Rp 59 trillion, which amounts to 32 per cent of total expenditures or 6.5 per cent of GDP.

The restructuring and rehabilitation of the banking sector is entrusted to the Indonesian Banking Restructuring Agency (IBRA), an institution established under the Ministry of Finance with a lifetime of five years. IBRA has acquired assets from failed banks and banks that have been taken over, as well as non-performing loans of state banks and recapitalized banks. It has been estimated that over 50 per cent of corporate assets are now in the hands of the government. In a sense it is "nationalization by default". Since the government does not intend to control these assets it will have to dispose of them. In addition to restructuring banks, IBRA's task is to help recover government funds that have been used to restructure the banking sector. Maximizing asset recovery is thus a major objective of IBRA. The Asset Management Unit Credit (AMC) arm of IBRA manages about Rp 207 trillion of loan portfolio, which consists of approximately 170,000 debtors. Most of the value is concentrated in the large corporate loans. There are 1,339 corporate debtors (0.8 per cent of debtors) with loans above Rp 50 billion and with total loans of about Rp 172 trillion (82.8 per cent of loans). About 40 per cent of the loan portfolio is in manufacturing.

Disposing of the assets of these large corporations is not an easy task. Many of the large debtors are related to Soeharto. They have not been co-operative, and the Habibie government did little to help IBRA recover assets from Soeharto-related companies. IBRA also faces resistance from the original owners or the management as in the case of the sale of Bank Bali and Astra. IBRA has been estimated to achieve an asset recovery rate of about 32 per cent. Its plan is to dispose of the assets at a rate of about Rp 40 trillion per year from 2000 to 2004. Less than half of this amount will be contributed annually to the budget to help finance the cost of interest that accrue from issuance of government bonds to restructure the banks.

Restructuring of the banks is key to economic recovery, but its huge cost creates a major drag on the economy and raises the longer-term issue of fiscal sustainability.

The Institutional Setting

When installing the National Economic Council (Dewan Ekonomi Nasional) at the beginning of December 1999, President Abdurrahman stated that the Council's main task is to advise him on economic matters, specifically to provide him with a "second opinion". He further stated that this was deemed necessary because his cabinet was the result of "horse trading". He revealed that he wanted to have a smaller cabinet of eighteen ministers, doing away with the co-ordinating ministers that characterized Soeharto's cabinets, in order to be effective. Yet he ended up with a thirty-three-person cabinet and retained the structure of the three co-ordinating ministers, one for politics and security; one for the economy, finance, and industry; and another for social welfare. This large cabinet resulted from his own initiative to invite other political forces to have representatives in the cabinet. It is not a coalition government in the usual sense. Rather, Gus Dur tries to accommodate the different interests and to gather support from other political parties by having their representatives in the cabinet.

The problem with the cabinet is not so much its large size but that many of its members are in at the sponsorship of political parties (and the military). More precisely, they are being "guaranteed" by leaders of those political parties. Gus Dur did not personally know a number of the candidates but accepted them under that guarantee. It has become clear from the outset that these ministers have difficulties working together unless there is strong leadership from the President himself or from the co-ordinating ministers. In the first 100 days Gus Dur did not try to exert any leadership on economic matters, entrusting this to the co-ordinating minister, Kwik Kian Gie. This may be because Gus Dur's priority is in the area of politics, but it may also be because he feels less competent about economic affairs.

Minister Kwik was Gus Dur's own choice. He is in the cabinet not because of Megawati although he has been with the PDI-P (Partai Demokrasi Indonesia-Perjuangan) for many years and as one of the chairpersons of that party he has been in charge of research and planning. He has some experience in business but left it since joining politics. He has been one of the founders of one of the oldest graduate business schools in Indonesia and is still active in managing an undergraduate business school. With him in the economic team from the same party is Laksamana Sukardi, who is a state minister in charge of investment and state enterprises. Laksamana is Megawati's man in the cabinet. Another key person in the economic team, Minister of Finance Bambang Soedibyo is from Amien Rais' PAN (Partai Amanat Nasional) and is said to be the intellectual author of the Central Axis, the political alliance among a number of Muslim parties. Minister of Industry and Trade Jusuf Kalla is from Golkar, but he was suggested to Gus Dur as the person to represent South Sulawesi by the former Defence Minister M. Jusuf, who is also from that region. The background to the importance of having a representative from this region is to placate the people there who have been disappointed by the defeat of Habibie, who is also from the same region, in the presidential election in 1999. The minister of mines and energy as well as the minister of transportation, who traditionally are also under the co-ordinating minister of economic affairs, are both from the military. It is possible that their inclusion in the cabinet was to remove Wiranto's competitors from the armed forces as a price to get Wiranto in the cabinet or out of the cabinet.

The media has been full of reports about the lack of co-operation and co-ordination among members of the economic team. This is clearly demonstrated by two recent events. The first was the resignation of the President Director of the PLN (Perusahaan Listrik Negara), the state electricity company, because his policy of dealing with the foreign independent power producers (IPPs) was not supported by the new government, which prefers an out-of-court settlement. Had there been better communication and co-ordination in the government, the negotiations involving court procedures already set in motion by the PLN, which would have guaranteed a fairer outcome for Indonesia, need not have been terminated. The damage to the government is that it appears to be caving in to pressures by the U.S. government, which acted in the interest of the foreign power producers. Ironically, the U.S. government is seen to be backing those that allegedly were engaged in corrupt practices. The point here is that the government did not consult the PLN in resolving the problem. The second event was the issuance of a government regulation to amend another that was issued only five days before. At issue is who should be in control of state banks, the state minister for investment and state enterprises or the minister of finance. The media exposed this struggle between the two ministers as a struggle between the two political camps that each minister represents. Co-ordinating Minister Kwik admitted that there is a struggle for control, but he argued that it is based on technical rather than political grounds. Despite this statement, observers believe that the struggle for the control of resources by political parties for the next general elections (in 2004) has already begun. These developments have not helped to create confidence on the part of the public in the ability of the government, the economic team in particular, to resolve the country's grave economic problems.

Gus Dur was given 100 days by opinion-makers to prove that his "political" cabinet can deliver. This kind of pressure is without any constitutional basis. He has been legitimately elected by the People's Consultative Assembly (Majelis Permusyawaratan Rakyat, or MPR) and constitutionally only the MPR can unseat him. It is true that instead of meeting every five years the new MPR has decided to meet every year. A meeting is scheduled for August 2000. This means that the MPR need not call an extraordinary session to change the president. There is speculation that the chair of the MPR, Amien Rais, will make use of this opportunity if indeed the Gus Dur cabinet turns out to be totally incompetent. This "threat" of a constitutionally legitimate change of government before the term of the president is over may well provide an incentive for the Abdurrahman administration to shape up. On his part, Gus Dur had also given his ministers 100 days to get their act together, threatening to remove those that fail to do so. The Co-ordinating Minister for Social Welfare has already been replaced, perhaps largely for political reasons. Talks about an imminent cabinet reshuffle continue to feed the rumour mill, but any reshuffle is not likely before the end of the first six months, let alone the first 100 days. The end of the first 100 days was in fact overshadowed by tensions that developed between the President and General Wiranto whom the National Human Rights Committee report implicated in human rights abuses in East Timor. The President's subsequent suspension of Wiranto from his cabinet post as Co-ordinating Minister for Political and Security Affairs cleared the way for reforms in the armed forces in the direction of a more subdued role for the military in society, and in the short term it possibly will also put a stop to the sudden outbreaks of disturbances in the regions. The people and international markets have welcomed this development. However, investors' confidence will not be fully restored until Gus Dur shapes up his cabinet, his economic team in particular.

Seemingly, Gus Dur does not intend to do this yet. He has decided to take charge of the economy himself, acknowledging that economic leadership will not come from within his cabinet. In doing so he may want to rely more on the advice from the National Economic Council (Dewan Ekonomi Nasional, or DEN) and the National Council for Business Development (Dewan

Pengembangan Usaha Nasional, or DPUN). DEN is to advise the President on ways to recover the economy and to enhance Indonesia's economic position in international competition. The President has also asked DEN to formulate a new framework for the Indonesian economy. DPUN is to advise the President on how to revive the real sector. There are concerns that the existence of these different institutions could lead to conflicts that would further weaken the effectiveness of the government. DEN is conscious of this danger and has made it clear that while it is a body advising the President it will maintain open communication with members of the cabinet and other government institutions, such as the Central Bank (Bank Indonesia).

It is too early to assess whether DEN and DPUN can be effective. Even if they can become effective advisory bodies, they cannot and should not be involved in the execution of policies. Gus Dur has also strengthened his inner circle in the Palace. In addition to the Presidential Secretariat and the State Secretariat he has instituted a Secretariat for the Management of the Government and a cabinet Secretariat. It is likely that the governing of the state and policy-making, including economic policy-making, will be in the hands of this group rather than the cabinet.

In the final analysis, it is the executing agencies that are most important in the successful implementation of policies to revive the economy. To deal with the crisis the previous government had established new institutions. These include the Indonesian Banking Restructuring Agency (IBRA), the Indonesian Debt Restructuring Agency (INDRA), and the Jakarta Initiative Task Force (JITF). Together with Bank Indonesia, the Ministry of Finance, the State Minister for Investment and State Enterprises, all those "crisis" institutions are involved in the gigantic task of *credit restructuring*, which is key to the recovery of economic activities. Co-ordination amongst these institutions and agencies is at best very weak and of an *ad hoc* nature. This explains why banking and corporate restructuring has been very slow. During the Habibie administration there was a lot of political intervention in those "crisis" institutions, IBRA in particular, with the aim of mobilizing financial resources for political purposes. The Bank Bali scandal is a case in point. There was also intervention in the state banks to conceal huge non-performing loans of politically connected companies. The Texmaco scandal is believed to be just one of many similar cases that await to be exposed.

During the very first few days of the Abdurrahman administration there were attempts by certain political groups to gain control over IBRA, the institutions that is now in control of a lot of assets of banks that have been taken over and failed companies that owed to those banks. Gus Dur and the government initially gave conflicting signals as to what they want to do with IBRA. However, by late November it became clear that the government is serious in strengthening IBRA. The empowerment of IBRA is stipulated in the new three-year IMF-supported programme. There have been suggestions to further strengthen IBRA by making it a fully autonomous agency. Under an earlier

IMF-support programme, Bank Indonesia has become an independent institution since 17 May 1999.

It remains to be seen whether the independence of these institutions would help expedite the process towards banking and corporate restructuring by insulating them from political interests. The political environment under which these institutions have to operate has become more complex as the political system opens up. Insulating them from political influences has become a necessity but these institutions must also increase their transparency and accountability.

The Economic Agenda

The economic agenda of the Abdurrahman government is still being crafted. It will be guided by the Broad Outlines of State Policy (Garis-Garis Besar Haluan Negara, or GBHN) that were formulated by the MPR in October 1999. In essence they require the government to take steps to accelerate the recovery of the economy. Some critics have said that the government is too preoccupied with dealing with problems of KKN (Korupsi, Kolusi, Nepotesme, or corruption, collusion, and nepotism) and has not given sufficient attention to tackling the more urgent problem of reviving the economy. Others are of the view that the government has done nothing on the KKN problems. The government will have to find the right balance between tackling KKN and concrete efforts to revive the economy. KKN problems in the widest sense should include efforts to improve public and corporate governance.

In practice, the government already has an economic agenda for the next three years as formulated under the new three-year programme supported by the IMF. It incorporates a medium-term agenda that has four components, namely, a medium-term macroeconomic framework, restructuring policies, rebuilding economic institutions, and improvements in natural resource management. The medium-term macroeconomic framework aims at recovery while maintaining price stability. The targets are likely to be set for a 5 to 6 per cent growth over the medium term with inflation below 5 per cent. Other targets include gross international reserves at about six months of imports, and a gradual reduction of the ratio of public debt to GDP from the present high level to 65 per cent by the year 2004.

The financial system and corporate reforms remain at the core of the restructuring programme. In addition, new reform programmes have been introduced that are aimed at strengthening the agricultural sector, increasing opportunities to small and medium enterprises (SMEs), improving targeted spending programmes, upgrading human capital, and sustained poverty reduction. These new programmes have been accorded a high priority by Gus Dur. The third component of the medium-term agenda, namely, rebuilding of economic institutions, places the priority on the public sector (fiscal management, fiscal decentralization, and civil service reform), the financial sector (IBRA, state-owned banks, regulatory and supervisory institutions), the judiciary, and institutions responsible for corporate governance. The fourth component involves policy and institutional framework for natural resource management. This framework has three objectives, namely: (a) greater consultation and stakeholder participation in decisions affecting natural resources; (b) developing a pricing structure for natural resources that reflects true value; and, (c) improving forest management and ensuring a sustainable production of goods and services from forest resources.

The short-term economic agenda of the government has two main components, namely, macroeconomic policies and structural reform programmes for the year 2000. The macroeconomic targets for 2000 are as follows: a 3–4 per cent growth rate, single-digit inflation, and a fiscal deficit of up to 5 per cent of GDP, which will be financed about equally from domestic asset recovery and foreign sources.

The government appears to be reluctant to adopt even a slightly expansionary fiscal policy. The Finance Minister stated that the budget "will not be too contractive". The government has set a constraint to the budget by limiting foreign borrowing. Initially it started out with a policy to significantly reduce foreign borrowing, but later on decided to adopt this policy in a pragmatic manner. Minister Kwik has announced that the government will seek to maintain a level of foreign borrowing as deemed necessary.

A comparison of the budget for 2000 (for nine months) with estimated realization of the FY1999/2000 budget for nine months suggests that total expenditures would increase by about 30 per cent. However, about two-thirds of this increase will be accounted for by increased debt service payments on domestic debt. As discussed earlier, the huge jump in domestic debt resulted from the issuance of bonds to recapitalize banks. It is estimated that the cost of servicing these bonds would amount to about Rp 45 trillion a year. Every 1 per cent increase in interest adds about Rp 6 trillion to domestic debt service payments. This is the reason for the government targeting a low inflation rate.

There are three other issues that deserve mentioning. The first is the raise in civil service salaries. Official civil service salaries have always been low and they have been frozen since the crisis. However, the income of government officials is not necessarily low as there are many ways to earn additional income, such as through involvement (nominal or real) in the execution of development projects. A 20 per cent raise in salaries has been proposed by the government, but the increase will not be across the board. The government is of the view that in the first instance substantial increases should apply to the salary of the ministers and first echelon bureaucrats. The theory is that those at the top should be made clean before the system can be rid of the entrenched corruption. However, in addition to raising salaries there is need for civil service reforms and improving governance in general to fight corruption effectively. It remains to be seen whether the parliament (Dewan Perwakilan Rakyat, or DPR) subscribes to this theory and approves the huge increase in salaries at the top echelon or opts for an across-the-board increase.

The second is the problem of subsidies. Total subsidies in the current budget (FY1999/2000) are estimated to be about Rp 50 trillion, or about 25 per cent of total expenditures. Of this amount, more than 60 per cent is accounted for by fuel subsidies. Fuel prices in Indonesia have been highly distorted for many years for social and equity reasons. The price of kerosene has been kept low and is currently only about one-fifth of the cost of production. Automotive diesel oil (ADO) is also highly subsidized. Kerosene and ADO together account for about 75 per cent of total fuel subsidies. Various studies have shown that these subsidies are mostly received by those who do not need them. Yet the government continues to be cautious and will reduce these subsidies only gradually because of the political implications of higher prices. Student demonstrations in 1998 that led to the fall of Soeharto were triggered by the decision of the government to raise fuel prices. In the 2000 budget, fuel subsidies will be reduced by 15 per cent. Other subsidies (food and electricity) will also be reduced. However, there will be a significant increase in interest subsidies for small loans.

The third issue relates to fiscal decentralization. The two decentralization laws (No. 22/1999 and No. 25/1999) that were passed in parliament in May 1999 will not be in force until May 2001. However, demands for their earlier implementation have forced the government to begin with fiscal decentralization in the 2000 budget. About 60 per cent of development expenditures from domestic sources will now be managed by the regional governments directly.

The second component in the short-term agenda that deals with structural reforms is essentially a continuation of what had been stipulated in the earlier IMF-supported programmes but these programmes will be strengthened. A successful implementation of these programmes will require the strengthening of the institutions responsible for undertaking the programmes and better co-ordination among them.

Prospects for the Year 2000

Indonesia can expect a modest recovery in year 2000. Economic growth will be about 3 to 4 per cent. More optimistic projections suggest a growth rate of 4 per cent or more. It will be difficult for the government to maintain a low inflation rate of below 5 per cent. With increasing fuel and electricity prices and the raise in civil service salaries, inflation is likely to be higher but still below 10 per cent.

Institutional changes and the shaping up of the economic team will help accelerate banking and corporate restructuring, which is the key to recovery and sustained growth in the future.

The government is faced with an enormous task. It has to defuse a host of time bombs that have been left by the previous governments. There are demands on all fronts — economic, political, social, and even cultural. It has yet to develop an effective government machinery to deal with them. Fortunately, there is still a lot of goodwill on the part of the people to give the present government a chance to turn the country around. There is also much goodwill shown by the international community. But goodwill may run out if the government does not deliver.

The risk to this forecast, however, remains largely political: Will Gus Dur be able to maintain national unity and make progress on the democratization front? The chances are good. His political skills will help him manage the frail democratization process, but he must recognize as well that a significant improvement of the economy will make that task more manageable.

LAOS

LAOS
An Episode of Yo-Yo Economics

Yves Bourdet

The macroeconomic situation of Laos has become significantly worse over the past two years as a result of both external and internal factors. Of the external factors, the depressed international environment in the Southeast Asian region, in the wake of the Asian crisis, has played a critical role. The fact that Thailand, one of the countries most hit by the Asian crisis, is the main trading partner of Laos (and also its largest foreign investor) explains the high vulnerability of Laos. This is not the whole story, however.

Domestic factors in Laos have also contributed to fuelling macroeconomic fragility, as evidenced by the higher inflation and much larger exchange rate fluctuations than in neighbouring countries. Inflation reached 87 per cent in 1998 and was estimated to be more than 100 per cent in 1999. The Lao currency, the kip, depreciated by no less than 90 per cent in relation to the U.S. dollar between mid-1997 and mid-1999. Further, the kip fluctuated like a yo-yo during 1999: from some 5,000 kip per dollar in early January, it plunged to 10,000 kip per dollar in June, then appreciated to 5,800 kip in September and dropped again thereafter to 7,600 kip in December.[1] Political inertia contributed greatly to the rapid deterioration of the macroeconomic stance in 1998 and 1999 by slowing down, and in some cases even blocking, the introduction of a less accommodating macroeconomic policy and financial and banking reforms. On the other hand, economic growth has continued at a slower pace than before (4 per cent in 1998 compared with 6.6 per cent on average between 1991 and 1997) but better than in neighbouring countries, reflecting a kind of de-linkage of the real economy from the monetary economy.

The Legacy of the Sixth Party Congress
The current political situation in Laos and the balance of power between different groups and individuals go back to the changes that took place during the Sixth Congress of the Lao People's Revolutionary Party. This was held in Vientiane in 1996 and a major result of it was a change in the distribution of political power in favour of the military network and the faction of the party opposed to too rapid and comprehensive reforms. The military network is

YVES BOURDET is Associate Professor of Economics, University of Lund, Sweden.

made up of former and current members of the Lao People's Army. The fact that it is the only organized, well-structured, and officially accepted network outside the Lao People's Revolutionary Party explains its growing role in the political life of Laos. The change in the top leadership well illustrates this enhanced role. Of the nine members of the Politburo emanating from the Sixth Party Congress, no less than seven belong to the military forces (six generals and one colonel). The two most prominent political posts are occupied by the military. General Khamtay Siphandon, number one in the party hierarchy, is State President and General Sisavath Keobounphan, Prime Minister. The death of Vice-President Udom Khatthinha, one of the two non-military members of the Politburo and number four in the hierarchy on 9 December 1999 may further contribute to the political dominance of the military network in Laos.

In spite of the set-back for the most prominent advocates of comprehensive reforms, the 1996 congress reaffirmed its commitment to reform policy. (Reform policy in Laos was initiated in 1987 under the name of the New Economic Mechanism.) This seems at first sight paradoxical. But it is not that surprising if one considers the wide involvement of the military in business activities and the fact that the returns from these activities are highly dependent upon the development of market activities and the opening up of the Lao economy. It is worth noting that the attachment of the military to the liberalization process is limited to economic matters, strictly speaking, and does not concern politics.[2] No challenge to the monopoly power of the Lao People's Revolutionary Party over political life is tolerated in Laos.

The weakened position of the advocates of more rapid and comprehensive reforms at the Sixth Party Congress was illustrated by the eviction of their most active representative, Khamphoui Keoboualapha, from the Party's Politburo and the Central Committee. Nevertheless Khamphoui formally remained one of the two vice–prime ministers and was even appointed finance minister in 1998. But he retired in August 1999, at the age of sixty-eight officially for reasons of age. Bounyang Vorachith, who had already replaced him in 1996 as responsible for foreign investment management and economic co-operation with donors, replaced him as finance minister. Bounyang now combines the post of finance minister with that of president of the Foreign Investment Management and Co-operation Committee (FIMC), which was created in early 1999. Another political change included in the government reshuffle last summer concerns the post of governor of the Central Bank, with the former governor of Bokeo province, Soukanh Maharath, replacing Cheuang Sombounekhanh.

A main conclusion regarding the recent political changes in Laos is that they have contributed to manifesting (and cementing) the outcome of the Sixth Party Congress. The military network has consolidated its control over the government after reinforcing its position in both the Politburo and Central Committee of the Lao People's Revolutionary Party. That changes in the government reflect changes in the party hierarchy is natural in Laos because of the high dependency between the party and the government. The government is often described in official documents as the "administrative staff of the Party's Central Committee". If it takes some time for changes in the party hierarchy to be reflected in changes in the composition of the government, it is due to the time it takes for "newcomers" to work through the party bureaucracy, and the fact that human resources are scarce in Laos.

The consolidation of the outcome of the Sixth Party Congress has implications for the content of economic policy. A first implication concerns the primacy of political leadership over technocratic rule. The ideological vacuum that followed the collapse of communism in the East European countries and the Soviet Union was exploited by technocrats to increase their role in the design and implementation of reform policy. An ambition of the Sixth Party Congress is to better control technocratic rule and restore political leadership over development strategy. The "resignation" of Khamphoui in August 1999 is an illustrative episode of this development. In spite of his position as minister of finance, Khamphoui could not stop the introduction of a large-scale and under-financed irrigation project defended by Khamtay, with, as a result, a monetary financing of part of the project and an upsurge of inflation. A second illustration of the primacy of political leadership is the government effort to boost economic and commercial ties with Vietnam to put them in line with the close political ties. The opening up of a Vietnamese bank in Vientiane and the organization of trade fairs are the kind of measures introduced to achieve this goal.

The increased role of the armed forces in political life also affects the way political power is exercised in Laos. An illustration of this concerns the limited transparency commonly associated with increased participation of the army in political life. This has economic implications because limited transparency tends to encourage rent-seeking activities and the development of a form of bargaining economy. The structure of the Lao economy with a few actors in many sectors may also contribute to this development.

The Asian Crisis, Political Inertia, and Macroeconomic Instability

In the late 1980s, Laos embarked on the New Economic Mechanism, a main purpose of which was the development of an economy open to international trade and foreign investment.[3] The international environment is therefore critical for the outcome of reform policy. From the mid-1980s to the mid-1990s the economies of Southeast Asia experienced very high growth rates (between 7 and 10 per cent). In 1997–98, however, several countries of the region were hit by a severe financial and economic crisis, with dramatic consequences: significantly lower growth rates (even negative for some countries), declining real incomes, increased unemployment and poverty, massive capital flight, and large currency depreciation.

Thailand was one of the countries most hit by the 1997–98 turmoil. Growth rates in Thailand dropped from an average of 8.5 per cent between 1990 and

1996 to some –5 per cent on average in 1997–98 and the Thai currency, the baht, depreciated by some 38 per cent in relation to the U.S. dollar between the years 1996 and 1998.

The impact of the Asian crisis on Laos worked mostly through Thailand, Laos' main trading partner and principal source of foreign investments. The crisis affected principally the macroeconomic and financial situations. Macroeconomic instability in Thailand and the sharp depreciation of the Thai currency triggered a loss of confidence in the Lao currency, the kip, in 1997–98. The depreciation of the kip was, however, much larger than that of the baht. Between 1996 and 1998, the kip depreciated by some 75 per cent in relation to the U.S. dollar, compared with 38 per cent for the Thai currency. Further, the value of the baht stabilized (and even appreciated somewhat) in 1999 while the kip continued to depreciate considerably. In late 1999, one U.S. dollar was worth some 7,600 kip, compared with some 4,500 kip one year earlier (that is, a depreciation of some 40 per cent).

Domestic macroeconomic policy failures after 1997 explain the further erosion of confidence in the Lao currency, the large capital flight out of the kip and the divergent development of the Lao and Thai exchange rates. To some extent, the macroeconomic instability in Laos is the result of an expansive fiscal policy. Figure 1 illustrates the worsening of the fiscal situation in the late 1990s. The increase in the budget deficit is the result of two main factors: expanded capital expenditure and lower than expected tax revenue. The increase in capital expenditure in 1998 can, to a large extent, be ascribed to the large irrigation programme whose purpose was to achieve national rice self-sufficiency through a fourfold increase in the irrigated (lowland) rice-growing areas.

But lower than expected tax revenue also contributed to an increase of the budget deficit in the late 1990s (see Figure 1). The Lao tax system was profoundly reformed in the late 1980s to adapt it to the emerging market economy. It was again modified in 1995–96 with the objective of broadening the tax base so as to finance increased development expenditures. The most significant changes concerned: (a) the widening of the turnover tax, that now covers most domestically produced and imported goods, (b) the reduction and standardization of the profit tax, (c) the replacement of specific excise duties by *ad valorem* excise duties, and (d) the increase of income tax for the lowest bracket from 2 to 10 per cent. Figure 1 shows that the 1995 tax reform has failed to increase tax revenue in terms of gross domestic product (GDP), at least in the short term. Tax revenue, which increased steadily after the introduction of the first tax reform in the late 1980s, stopped increasing in 1996 and has even decreased thereafter. Two main reasons can be advanced to explain this relative failure. The new system is rather complicated, which, in view of the limited administrative capacity in Laos, makes its implementation difficult and limits the revenue potential of the tax system. Its complicated nature also favours the development of rent-seeking activities, which in this case take the form of tax

FIGURE 1
Government Budget, 1987–98
(As a percentage of GDP)

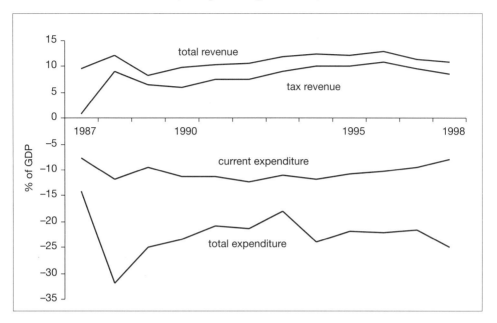

NOTE: Since 1992 the fiscal year has been from 1 October to 30 September.
SOURCE: Lao authorities.

exemptions. A second related reason is the inability of the Lao tax system to cope with high inflation situations, with nominal targets playing a central role.

The deterioration of the macroeconomic stance in Laos in the late 1990s also results from severe financial and monetary imbalances. Confidence in the Lao banking system is plummeting, mainly because of the huge volume of non-performing loans. An accommodating interest rate policy, with low (negative, that is, inferior to inflation) interest rates, and unwise loans explain the rapid increase in non-performing loans. According to a confidential audit, the ratio of non-performing loans ranges from 30 to 70 per cent in the state-owned commercial banks. A second reason behind the lack of confidence is the refusal by the Lao government to publish the findings of the audit and to implement rapidly a structural reform of the banking system. Instead, new loans were given by the central bank to enterprises and individuals that had difficulties in paying back their loans. The steep depreciation of the Lao currency was also the result of relatively low interest rates and monetary expansion. Part of the large irrigation programme was financed by the Lao Central Bank. This concerned the loans accorded to rice farmers to enable them to install the pumps purchased abroad with the help of the Central Bank's international reserves. Except for shorter periods, the interest rates administered by the Lao Central Bank have remained negative (inferior to inflation) since mid-1997, and strongly contributed to credit expansion.

The relationship between monetary expansion and the exchange rate is illustrated in Figure 2. The rapid increase in monetary liquidity, money (currency outside banks and deposits) and quasi-money (saving and foreign currency deposits) after 1996 is strongly correlated with the sharp depreciation of Lao currency. To a large extent, the increase in money supply is the automatic result of the increase in the value in kip of foreign deposits. But the increase in the domestic component of money supply since 1996 has contributed to the steep depreciation of the Lao currency. This was particularly true in 1998 when a marked increase in domestic liquidity led to a considerable depreciation of the exchange rate (Figure 2). This movement continued during 1999. A consequence of the rapid depreciation of the Lao currency is the enlarged

FIGURE 2
Money Supply and Nominal Exchange Rate, 1991–98

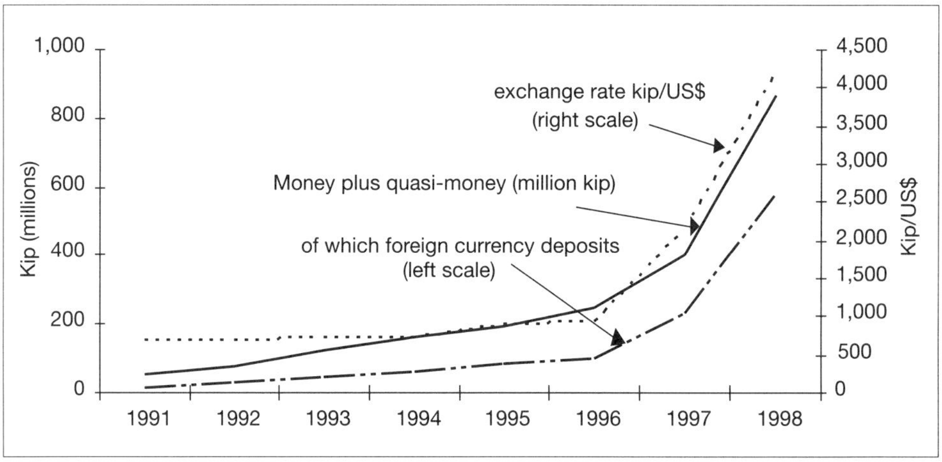

NOTE: The data pertain to the end of the year.
SOURCE: Bank of the Lao People's Democratic Republic.

role of foreign deposits in the money supply. Foreign currency deposits accounted for 67 per cent of the money supply in 1998 while they only accounted for 37 and 40 per cent in 1991 and 1996, respectively. Such a structural shift has far-reaching consequences for the conduct of monetary and economic policy in Laos. The steady depreciation of the kip was stopped in September 1999 when the Bank of the Lao People's Democratic Republic put restrictions on the credit policy of the commercial banks and introduced high-interest certificates (with an annual rate of 60 per cent) to absorb excess liquidity.[4]

Relatively Unaffected Economic Growth

The Asian crisis has affected the real sector in Laos through a decrease in the demand for its export products and a drop in direct foreign investments. The impact was limited, however, with economic growth averaging 5 per cent in 1997–98. The decrease in the demand for export products concerned mainly timber and wood products, which accounted for one-third of Laos' total exports during the second half of the 1990s. The decline in timber and wood exports, by some 30 per cent, was partly compensated for by an increase in garment exports following the reinstatement of Generalized System of Preferences status for the country by the European Union in 1997. Garment exports accounted for some 25 per cent of total exports in 1997–98 while it only accounted for 21 per cent in 1994–96.

A drastic fall in the volume of direct foreign investments also contributed to slowing down the rate of economic growth in Laos in the late 1990s, in particular in industry and manufacturing. But the impact was probably limited, since the impact on growth of the steep decrease in foreign investments will be felt mainly in the medium and long term. Figure 3 shows that the volume of approved foreign direct investment projects increased significantly in the mid-1990s. The volume of realized foreign investments was lower, however. Large-scale projects in the hydropower and mining sectors account for a large share of this increase. Foreign investments dropped markedly in the late 1990s and returned to their level of ten years earlier. Thai investors accounted for most of this decrease.

FIGURE 3
Approved Foreign Investment Flows in Laos, 1988–98
(Million US$)

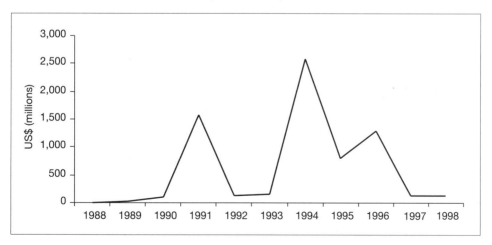

NOTE: The hydropower and Hongsa lignite projects are included in 1991, 1994, 1995, and 1996.
SOURCE: Foreign Investment Management Committee.

Weak linkages between the real economy and the monetary economy explain the limited impact of the Asian crisis on economic growth in Laos. This is illustrated in Figure 3, which compares the real GDP growth in Laos with that of Thailand, the main trading partner and foreign investor in Laos, and Vietnam, where a similar transition process is under way. Figure 4 shows that the Asian crisis had a considerable effect on growth in Thailand but only limited effect on growth in Laos (and Vietnam). However, Figure 4 shows that Laos and Vietnam have embarked on a lower growth path since 1997. The same factor explains the de-linkage of the Lao growth from the Thai growth after 1997, and the lower rate of economic growth in Laos relative to Vietnam. The existence of a large subsistence sector in Laos lies behind the limited correlation between the growth rates in Laos and Thailand. It also explains the lower rate of growth in Laos relative to Vietnam, where agriculture is more integrated in the economy and has exhibited significantly higher rates of growth during the 1990s.

The impact of the Asian crisis on the social sector and poverty is less severe due to the dominant position of the subsistence sector in the Lao economy. The crisis has mainly affected the urban population, which is more involved in the cash economy and more dependent on imported products. The civil servants have been hardest hit by the crisis, because their salaries have not increased in line with inflation. The impact of the crisis on rural areas has not been that dramatic and some rural areas may even have benefited from the huge depreciation of the Lao currency. The subsistence economy has worked as a buffer and it is mainly people without access to land or with insufficient land that have been adversely affected.[5] Further, there are indications that the depreciation of the kip has boosted exports of agricultural products to Thailand and improved living conditions in areas with road access to the Mekong and Thailand.

FIGURE 4
Real GDP Growth, 1993–99
(1993 = 100; estimates for 1999)

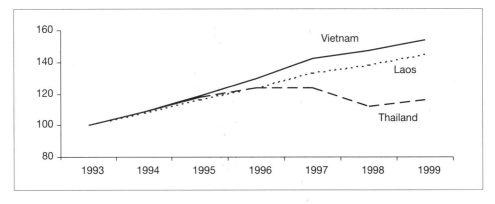

SOURCES: IMF and Lao authorities.

Table 1 shows that growth is unevenly distributed in Laos. It shows also that agriculture, which accounts for some 50 per cent of domestic production in Laos, tends to slow down the rate of GDP growth. Industry has exhibited the best performance, even if the growth rate has slowed down in the last two years. The growth of the service sector has been lower over the same period, although significantly higher than the growth rate observed in the agricultural sector. Table 1 confirms that the contraction of economic activity in the Southeast Asian region has had only limited effects in Laos. This applies in particular to the agricultural sector. The poor performance of the agricultural sector in 1998 was the result of adverse climatic conditions.

TABLE 1
Gross Domestic Product by Industrial Origin, 1991–98
(Percentage change)

	1991–93 Average	1994–96 Average	1997	1998
GDP	5.6	7.3	7.2	4.0
Industry	12.6	13.7	8.1	8.5
Services	6.0	8.1	7.5	4.8
Agriculture	3.1	4.7	7.0	3.7

SOURCE: Based on data provided by the Lao authorities.

ASEAN Integration and Beyond

Laos became a member of ASEAN in July 1997 together with Myanmar. A main objective of ASEAN is the development of a free trade area. In 1992 the member countries signed an agreement on the reduction of tariffs and non-tariff barriers and the creation of a free trade area, called AFTA (ASEAN Free Trade Area). The objective of AFTA is the establishment of intra-regional free trade (or rather preferential trade, since tariffs between members will only be reduced to 0–5 per cent), and the elaboration of a common legal framework that should facilitate the development of foreign direct investments in the region.

The integration of Laos into AFTA will stretch over a rather long period and vary by product group. Many import products already carry tariff rates of between 0 and 5 per cent and are thus not affected by the tariff cuts. Tariff reductions will only begin around 2003 and not be completed before 1 January 2015. On that date, tariff rates on intra-regional trade will be reduced to 0–5 per cent. For some products, however, tariff protection will remain higher. These products, included in an exception list, will be excluded from tariff reductions for reasons such as health, national security, and public morality.

Regional trade liberalization should be trade-creating and favour the export of products for which Laos has a comparative advantage.[6] These may be products that use natural resources intensively, because of Laos' rich endowment in natural resources and relative scarcity in physical and human (skilled labour) capital. But it may also be land-intensive agricultural products, such as livestock and certain export crops like coffee, because Laos has an abundance of land when compared with neighbouring countries. The cultivated area per capita in Laos is about twice that of other ASEAN countries like Vietnam or Indonesia. On the other hand, regional integration should facilitate the import of products that use skilled labour and capital intensively in their production. The positive impact of regional trade liberalization can, however, be expected to be rather limited, since the Lao economy is primarily complementary to the economies of the other ASEAN countries, and integration between complementary economies usually has small trade-creating effects. Another factor that may limit the volume of future trade creation is the tariff cuts, which have been undertaken by Laos since the start of the reform process and resulted in relatively low tariff rates in the late 1990s.

The positive trade effects of regional integration will not materialize before the period 2003–15 because of the extended time-frame for Laos. But there may be earlier positive export effects for Laos since the more developed ASEAN countries decided in late 1999 to accelerate the process of tariff liberalization on intra-regional trade. The negative trade-diverting effects, that is, the replacement of imports from non-ASEAN countries by more expensive imports from ASEAN countries, should be more limited than the trade-creating effects. Lao foreign trade is already concentrated on neighbouring ASEAN countries, and thus the risk of trade diversion can be considered minimal.

In addition to its impact on trade and specialization patterns, ASEAN integration will affect fiscal policy. Import duties account for some 20–25 per cent of budgetary revenue in Laos. The removal or large reduction in tariffs on intra-regional trade will tend to reduce this source of revenue and might result in fiscal instability and inflationary pressures. It can also jeopardize capital expenditures that are necessary for long-term growth. It is therefore important for Laos to use the next few years to find alternative sources of revenue and improve the efficiency of the public sector. A broadening of the tax base could be a solution, but this is a rather difficult task in Laos. (Laos has replaced tariffs with excise duties on imports of motor vehicles. This permits the country to keep an important source of revenue, but the positive effects of ASEAN integration on trade creation are thereby limited.) Another solution could be a rapid increase in hydropower and timber exports, which would generate new royalties. A third solution could be a contraction of budgetary expenditures that are not so important for long-term growth. Laos seems to have chosen a combination of the first two sets of solutions. It is also worth adding that the membership in ASEAN has resulted in not negligible administrative costs that have affected the expenditure side of the budget (training of Lao officials, ASEAN meetings, language courses, and so forth).

In summary, the integration of Laos into ASEAN will result in some costs for the country in the short and medium term. These costs are more of fiscal and macroeconomic nature and are to some extent anticipated by the market, as illustrated by the current macroeconomic instability in Laos. The difficulties met by the government in reforming the fiscal system and increasing tax revenue, and hence in finding alternative sources of revenue, contribute to fuelling inflationary anticipations. In the longer term, specialization gains should outweigh these costs. The gains should be concentrated in the private sector and certain provinces (or districts) close to growth regions in other member countries.

The Regional Dimension

Laos is a big country with a relatively small population that is scattered unevenly. This dispersion over large areas is accompanied by wide disparities between the provinces (and within them) in terms of well-being and economic development. Figure 5 illustrates the large differences in income per capita in 1997–98. Income per capita in the wealthiest province of Vientiane Municipality is more than four times larger than that of the poorest northern provinces of Oudomxay and Phongsaly. The two wealthiest provinces after Vientiane Municipality are Xayabury and Champasack, both bordering (and relatively well integrated economically with) Thailand. In 1997–98 the income per capita in Vientiane Municipality was around 780,000 kip, that is, about US$460 (US$1 = 1,680 kip on average between March 1997 and February 1998). In the poorest northern province of Oudomxay, it amounted to a little more than US$100. Other northern provinces also show significantly lower per capita incomes than the average for Laos.

Figure 5 also shows that the differences between the provinces have increased significantly since 1992. It is the rapid increase in income per capita in the provinces of Vientiane Municipality, Xayaboury, and, to a lesser extent, Champasack that lies behind this result. Income per capita in Vientiane Municipality was on average twice that of Laos in 1997–98, while it only was 1.5 times higher in 1992–93. The increase is still more pronounced in Xayaboury. It is noteworthy that these three provinces are along the border with Thailand and economically partly integrated with that country.

To a large extent, the inter-provincial differences in income per capita reflect differences in human capital endowment and infrastructure.[7] The impact of these two factors works through labour productivity. Poor human capital endowment and poor infrastructure result in low labour productivity and low levels of per capita production and income. The process is cumulative in the sense that low levels of income in turn limit the capacity to save and to invest, and hence the potential for improved productivity. In addition, low income limits purchasing power, which means that inducements to expand non-rural activities and develop rural-urban linkages are small.

Human capital endowment varies considerably between provinces in Laos. Literacy, one of its main components, varies from 32–35 per cent of the population aged fifteen and above in the northern provinces of Phongsaly and

FIGURE 5
Income Per Capita by Province, 1992–93 and 1997–98
(Laos average = 100)

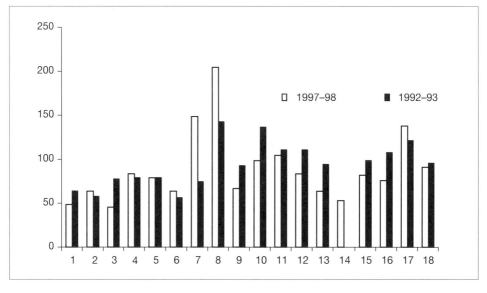

NOTE: The provinces in the figure are (1) Phongsaly, (2) Luangnamtha, (3) Oudomxay, (4) Bokeo, (5) Luangprabang, (6) Huaphanh, (7) Xayaboury, (8) Vientiane Municipality, (9) Xiengkhuang, (10) Vientiane, (11) Borikhamsay, (12) Khammuane, (13) Savannakhet, (14) Xayasomboon SR (Xaysomboon SR is a new province formed using parts of Vientiane province and Xiengkhuang), (15) Saravane, (16) Sekong, (17) Champasack, and (18) Attapeu.
SOURCE: Lao Expenditure and Consumption Survey, 1993 and 1998.

Luangnamtha, to 71–72 per cent in the provinces of Vientiane and Champasack, and 85.5 per cent in Vientiane Municipality. The figures pertain to the year 1995 but have only changed marginally since then. Illiteracy in Laos is particularly extensive and thus probably hinders the development effort most of all in the northern provinces along the Chinese and Myanmar frontiers and in the southern province of Sekong. As in other low-income countries, literacy rates for women are significantly lower than for men in Laos. The northern, remote provinces exhibit the lowest literacy rates for women, often two to three times lower than those in the provinces of Vientiane Municipality, Vientiane and Champasack. The gender gap is also very large in the southern region, except for the province of Champasack. Literacy rates are the result of past investments in education, and thus the supply of schools, quality of education and duration of schooling are decisive for literacy. It takes between five and eight years of schooling to acquire the basic skills, literacy and numeracy. The variation in literacy rates across the provinces reflects to a large extent the existence of large (past and current) differences in access to education.

Another factor that has a strong impact on labour productivity is infrastructure. Infrastructure should be understood in the broad sense of the term to include roads, irrigation, access to safe water and sanitation, electricity, telecommunications, and so forth. It is more easily supplied in urban than in rural areas because of higher population density and because the unit cost declines with production. The provision of infrastructure has a clear, positive effect on economic performance, reducing production costs and raising productivity. It encourages the growth and diversification of production, and hence has a positive effect on incomes. In rural regions, the improvement of infrastructure, in particular irrigation, is necessary for the growth of farm productivity and expansion of non-farm rural employment. In general, the state of infrastructure in Laos is rudimentary and there is considerable variation both between and within provinces in the provision (and probably the efficiency) of infrastructure. One example concerns access to safe water. In 1995, for example, only 15 per cent of Lao households had access to safe water, but the percentage varied from 0.4 per cent in the northern Phongsaly province to some 48 per cent in Vientiane Municipality. Large differences exist between the three main regions, with the central region benefiting from the best access to safe water, followed by the southern and the northern regions. In five of the eight northern provinces, less than 2.5 per cent of all households had access to safe water in 1995. Similar wide disparities across regions and provinces can be observed for other infrastructures.

The AFTA integration process is likely to affect the distribution of economic activities across the provinces and hence the distribution of income and well-being. AFTA integration should favour economic development in those regions (and provinces) that are close to growth regions abroad and benefit from comparative advantages. The regions bordering Thailand will probably be the first to benefit from the dynamics of international integration. The ongoing improvement of the road infrastructure in the southern region will also provide development opportunities for this region. On the other hand, the remote provinces (and districts), which are isolated by high transport costs and disadvantaged by the small size of the provincial markets, will only be slightly affected by the integration process. Household incomes in these provinces will tend to stagnate, and income disparities between the provinces that benefit from localization advantages and the others will tend to increase in Laos.

An Isolated Episode of Yo-Yo Economics?

Our analysis above has shown that during the past two years Laos had been through severe macroeconomic imbalances but has maintained relatively good growth performance. This raises the question of the nature of the Lao economic (and political) system and its interaction with economic policy. At first sight the recent macroeconomic turmoil might be regarded as resulting from the Asian crisis. However, it could be argued that several, more structural features of economic, institutional, and political character lie behind not only this episode but the large macroeconomic fluctuations in Laos, which we some-what provocatively have named yo-yo economics.

A feature of yo-yo economics is the small size of the domestic currency economy and the large size of the subsistence sector. The former is illustrated by the small role of the kip in the Lao economy: the kip broad money stock corresponds to less than 10 per cent of GDP. And the latter is due to the predominantly subsistence character of the agricultural sector that still ac-counts for more than 50 per cent of GDP.

A second feature is the existence of several currencies in circulation, with the implication that the monetized economy is larger than the kip-based economy. The other currencies in circulation are the Thai baht and the U.S. dollar. The government at times tried to limit the use of foreign currencies within the country but gave up some years ago. The existence of several cur-rencies implies that loss of (or improved) confidence in the domestic currency results in rapid and large movements out of (or into) the kip. Because of the relatively small size of the kip exchange market, such large supply and demand movements have sizeable upward and downward effects on the exchange rate. Laos formally adopted a managed floating exchange rate system in September 1995. However, from time to time the government has introduced restrictions in order to limit exchange rate fluctuations with, as a main consequence, an increase in the gap between the official and parallel market rates.

A third feature is the accommodating monetary policy. This consists in the monetary financing of part of the public deficit, as illustrated by the financing of the large-scale irrigation schemes in the late 1990s. But it consists also in unwise loans and in low (often negative) interest rates that encourage credit expansion. An important aspect of interest rate policy in Laos is the interest rate differential between domestic and foreign currency deposits, since this differential affects movements in or out of the domestic currency.

A fourth feature is the financial fragility of the banking system and the large role played by state-owned commercial banks. Financial fragility results from the existence and persistence of soft constraints in the banking system and takes the form of a large volume of non-performing loans on the balance sheets of the banks. There is a strong relationship between financial fragility and low interest rate policy. Low interest rates contribute to credit expansion. Eventually an increase in interest rates becomes inevitable, which leads to an augmentation in the volume of non-performing loans, further worsening the fragility of the banking system.

A fifth central feature is the pervasive role of political constraints in the conduct of economic policy. There are two main channels through which political influence operates. The first one works through the Central Bank and concerns the primacy of political decisions over consideration of monetary stability. Some autonomy was granted to the Central Bank during the first half of the 1990s, but the role of the Ministry of Finance in the conduct of mon-etary policy has increased since the mid-1990s. Note that this change is not formally reflected in the Bank's organizational structure, which has remained the same over the whole period, with the Minister of Finance as Chairman of the Board of Governors. The second channel works through public decisions. The lack of transparency in government-business relations, the one-party state, the absence of political competition and a weak civil society have resulted in a form of bargaining economy, slow and poor public decision-making and a multiplication of rent-seeking activities. This means that public decision-making is rather stochastic, which affects both the revenue and expenditure sides of the budget and eventually monetary stability.

A sixth feature is the multinational donors (and some bilateral donors) that demand fiscal and monetary discipline before resuming (or increasing) their financial aid. Their intervention usually puts an end to an expansive period and launches a restrictive period. A recent illustration of this is the joint intervention of the International Monetary Fund, the World Bank, and the Asian Development Bank in March 1999 to "encourage" the Lao government to conduct a more restrictive budgetary and monetary policy.

It is the interaction between these features that explains the emergence and resurgence of yo-yo economics in Laos. ASEAN integration is likely to put a straitjacket on Lao trade policy and limit the extent of rent-seeking activities. But nothing in ASEAN integration will secure the macroeconomic and financial discipline that is necessary to dampen macroeconomic fluctuations. Yo-yo economics is, therefore, likely to resurface from time to time unless structural reforms, which address its structural and institutional foundations, are introduced.

NOTES

1. These huge exchange rate fluctuations occasioned a funny article in the *Bangkok Post* (10 September 1999): "The US dollar is also under heavy attack by the gnomes in Vientiane. Early last week it was trading on the free market at about 9,400 kip. Today it is well under 6,000 and plunging toward 4,000, a figure rumour says is the target."
2. The interest of the army in economic matters is not new. The army actually played a decisive role when reform policy was initiated in the mid-1980s. In the struggle between the traditionalists, like former State President Nouhak Phoumsavan, and those who wanted economic reforms, like the Party General Secretary, Kaysone Phomvihan, the army supported the latter. Economic privileges, like timber contracts and trading rights, were the price paid for this support. The best-known representatives of the army in this horse-trading were Generals Khamtay Siphandon and Sisavath Keobounphan. On this episode, see Martin Stuart-Fox, *A History of Laos* (Cambridge: Cambridge University Press, 1997), p. 195.
3. For an evaluation of reform policy, see Yves Bourdet, *The Economics of Transition in Laos — From Socialism to ASEAN Integration* (Cheltenham and Northampton: Edward Elgar, 2000).
4. The Minister of Finance, Khamphoui, introduced a similar measure in April 1999. The measure was heavily criticized by the members of the Central Committee and the sale of certificates ended rapidly. This policy failure resulted in an upsurge of inflation and a further, steep depreciation of the kip.

5. World Bank, *Effects of the Asian Crisis on Lao PDR — A Preliminary Assessment* (1999), pp. 38–39.
6. For a more exhaustive analysis of the impact of ASEAN on Laos, see Jayant Menon, *Lao PDR: ASEAN Membership and Macroeconomic Policy Issues*, ADB T.A. No. 5713 (Asian Development Bank, 1998).
7. For a more complete analysis, see Yves Bourdet, "The Dynamics of Regional Disparities in Laos", *Asian Survey* 38, no. 7 (1998): 629–52.

MALAYSIA

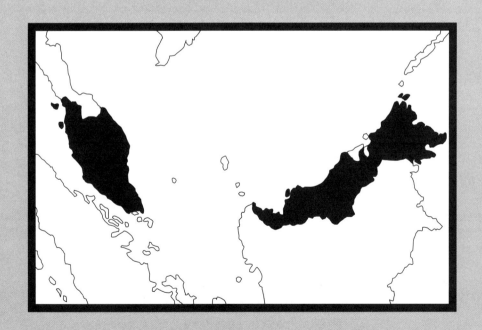

UNFINISHED CRISES
Malaysian Politics in 1999

Khoo Boo Teik

A biological disease appeared in peninsular Malaysia in 1998 and spread surreptitiously until September when medical authorities recognized that they faced an epidemic of viral encephalitis. In early 1999 the disease spread terrifyingly. Only in the latter half of 1999 did it abate. By then it had killed 104 people, forced the destruction of hundreds of thousands of pigs and devastated a multi-billion ringgit pig-farming industry.

Coincidentally, the body politic was gripped by a metaphorical disease on 2 September 1998 when Prime Minister Dr Mahathir Mohamad sacked his deputy, Anwar Ibrahim. Two days later, Anwar, who was also deputy president of the United Malays National Organization (UMNO), was expelled by the party's Supreme Council. From then on, the affliction invaded Malaysia's institutional organs, convulsed its political system, and damaged the underpinnings of the Malaysian polity. By year's end any faith that Dr Mahathir placed in the healing powers of Malaysia's tenth general election was seriously shaken, although the incumbent Barisan Nasional (BN) triumphed.

The Scourge of the Nipah Virus
During the third quarter of 1998, large numbers of pigs were reported to be sick and dying in major pig-rearing localities in Perak, around the Ipoh area and the Tambun district. Between December 1998 and January 1999, the disease spread to other states as infected livestock were transferred out of Perak. By March 1999, Bukit Pelandok, Negeri Sembilan, the location of Southeast Asia's biggest pig farm, was in the clutch of the lethal epidemic.[1]

When the administrators, and medical, veterinary, and public health officers of the Ministry of Health first sought to control the epidemic, they thought the pigs were suffering from an outbreak of Japanese encephalitis (JE). A mass inoculation of pigs against JE was conducted in suspect localities. (There was also a voluntary inoculation of people.) The inter-farm and inter-state movement of pigs was progressively banned. Eventually, the government opted to cull the pig population and evacuate the human population in the worst af-

KHOO BOO TEIK is Associate Professor in the School of Social Sciences, Universiti Sains Malaysia.

fected areas. By March almost half of some two million pigs in peninsular Malaysia had been targeted for destruction.

As the epidemic persisted, experienced pig breeders and some medical experts expressed reservations about JE being the probable cause.[2] They noted that JE occurred commonly enough, even seasonally, but rarely killed adult pigs, and definitely not on the prevailing scale. The scale of human illness and fatalities was also perplexing. Typical JE outbreaks showed a very low baseline of deaths, usually confined to children and the elderly. But serious illnesses and fatalities were rising at an alarming rate among cohorts of people not normally regarded as at high risk, notably pig farmers, their family members and workers, as well as other handlers of live pigs.

The epidemic exacted an appalling economic and social toll. The human deaths, the culling of so many pigs, and the evacuation of stricken localities threatened the collapse of this multi-billion ringgit branch of domestic animal husbandry. For pig farmers the loss of a business often backed by loans and credit was disastrous, as was immediate unemployment for thousands of households involved in related businesses. For an economy still reeling from the East Asian crisis of July 1997, the loss of pig export earnings, the replacement of domestic pork with imported meat, and the costs of culling and epidemic control (not to mention the likely loss of revenues from tourism) were a substantial burden.

Moreover there were potentially serious political ramifications arising from contrasting ethnic and religious sensitivities towards pigs and pork. In Malaysia, pig-rearing is an exclusively Chinese activity, and pork an important part of the Chinese diet. But pigs are anathema to the majority Malay-Muslim community because the consumption of pork is forbidden by Islam.

Hence, the Barisan Nasional (BN) government could find itself damned if it did (or did too much) and damned if it did not (or did not do enough). If this were indeed the government's dilemma, it was not publicly mentioned or debated. At most some BN politicians insinuated that the government could not do more to help the pig farmers for fear of losing its Malay-Muslim support to Parti Islam SeMalaysia (PAS, or Islamic Party). To the credit of Malaysian society, the opposition parties, including PAS, refrained from politicizing the pig farmers' tragedy along communal or religious lines. The government did not take advantage of that restraint to promote a freer flow of information, professional exchanges of opinion and public education on the epidemic.

On 19 March, the Director-General of the Ministry of Health announced that local researchers and their foreign counterparts (notably from the Centers for Disease Control [CDC], United States, but also from Japan and Australia) had isolated a "Hendra-like" virus, or paramyxovirus and identified it — not the JE virus — as the most likely pathogen. Continuing CDC-based research established in April that the epidemic was caused by a new virus, given the name of the Nipah virus after Sungai Nipah, in Negri Sembilan, the village residence of the patient from whom the first virus isolate was cultured.

Yet the Ministry of Health, the cabinet task force headed by Health Minister Chua Jui Meng, the Malaysian Chinese Association (MCA), and the mass media persisted in claiming that the country faced a "JE" epidemic, or even a "dual JE/Nipah epidemic", which some local experts and international medical opinion considered to be a sign of an official "denial syndrome".[3] But the thrust of the government's "public education" campaign, conducted via a tightly controlled mass media and unquestioned by the domestic medical and scientific establishment, was to pre-empt criticism of the government's wrong diagnosis of the epidemic and irrelevant if not counterproductive "anti-JE" measures.[4]

Likewise, the government barely acknowledged that a national crisis had struck. In the wake of the "speculator's disease" of July 1997, the government had instituted massive rescue plans for selected sectors and corporations, bought over corporate non-performing loans, recapitalized the banking sector, and repeatedly reduced interest rates to reflate the economy. Confronted with the Nipah virus, the government would only bear the cost of culling the pigs but would not compensate the pig farmers for their destroyed livestock. Compensation of RM50 per pig was finally offered in late March, but the pig farmers regarded the amount to be inadequate. Even this compensation would not be paid out of government funds but provided from public donations being solicited by an MCA-sponsored "JE Humanitarian Fund". Nor were provisions made for other forms of assistance, such as credit relief for pig farmers facing imminent bankruptcy, financial backing for a post-epidemic revitalization of the pig-rearing sector, or workmen's compensation for infected or dead farm workers.

At the height of its mobilization of charity for the epidemic victims, the MCA organized a lottery. Perhaps the lottery was a politically expedient throwback to the MCA's origin as a pre-independence organizer of lotteries for "Chinese welfare". But even a lottery run on good intention would preclude Malay-Muslim contributions since Islam prohibited gaming and gambling. In effect, the government and the MCA stayed true to their ethnic fixation by posing the worst epidemic in the living memory of most Malaysians not as a *national* emergency requiring a *comprehensive* solution but as a *Chinese* problem requiring a *communal* remedy.

In response, the Federation of Livestock Farmers' Associations of Malaysia, Chinese guilds and associations, opposition parties and non-governmental organizations (NGOs), the Citizens' Health Initiative, and concerned experts and individuals collectively demanded greater transparency in epidemic control, a national approach to the crisis, greater responsiveness to local and foreign expert opinion, more effective public education, and increased assistance to the victims of the epidemic. Joint memoranda were issued, protests made, and appeals launched. The government made a tacit concession to popular discontent over its crisis management by appointing Deputy Prime Minister Abdullah Ahmad Badawi to replace Chua Jui Meng as the head of the cabinet's "JE" committee. However, the government would not bow to popular pressure.

Only an expert epidemiological assessment can conclusively establish how far official intervention, and not fortuitous circumstances, arrested the spread of the epidemic. But the government's management of the epidemic will long be remembered for the "denial syndrome" shown by the official attachment to "JE", lack of transparency, reluctance to bail out a commercially important but politically weak sector, ethnicization of a national crisis, and resistance to popular pressure.

Anwar Ibrahim's Trials and Tribulations

After his arrest, Anwar was arraigned on ten separate charges, five relating to corruption (abuse of power) and five sodomy.[5] He was presented in two separate trials during 1999. The first, which had opened on 2 November 1998, was for four counts of corruption, involving the misuse of police to prevent prosecution for sexual misconduct and sodomy — under legislation repealed by the House of Representatives in October 1998 but still before the Senate.

The trial was highly politicized, given the manner of Anwar's sacking, sensational accusations laid against him, growing public opposition to Dr Mahathir, arrests of several Anwar associates, and domestic and international protests against an assault on Anwar while in custody — the infamous black eye. Several circumstances surrounding the trial were bizarre, such as the arrests in early September of Sukma Dermawan (Anwar's adopted brother) and Munawar Anees (Anwar's former speech writer) and their summary trial, conviction, and sentencing (six months' imprisonment) — just a few days later — after they had pleaded guilty to sodomy, allegedly perpetrated on them by Anwar. Shortly after, both recanted their guilty pleas and said their confessions had been extracted under duress while in police detention. There was a parallel trial of Datuk S. Nallakaruppan, described as Anwar's "tennis partner". Nallakaruppan, who was charged with illegal possession of firearms under the Internal Security Act — for failing to return 125 bullets when a gun permit had expired some years earlier — faced a mandatory death sentence if convicted. During Nallakaruppan's trial, his lawyer gave evidence the prosecution had wanted Nallakaruppan to incriminate Anwar.

Anwar's case provoked strong public emotions, with many moved to demonstrate against the regime, or keep a supporting vigil outside the Kuala Lumpur High Court. Even before his trial began, Anwar, it was felt, had been ignominiously convicted by Mahathir, UMNO, and the mass media they controlled. In January the Attorney-General blamed the police for Anwar's assault and the Inspector-General of Police had resigned, but no one was charged with beating Anwar. Many sections of the public were also incensed over certain kinds of evidence — such as a mattress said to be stained with Anwar's semen — and repulsed by media presentation of lurid details of sexual acts allegedly committed by Anwar.

To many observers — including Malaysia's Bar Council, international law-yers, Amnesty International, and the U.S. State Department — the conduct of the trial was unfair.[6] The judge's strictures to the defence to answer only to the charges laid against Anwar and to leave out the defence's counter-charges of a high-level conspiracy against Anwar belied the political character of the trial. The judge, Augustine Paul, frequently ruled as "irrelevant" the testimony of defence witnesses. At one point, one of Anwar's lawyers, Zainur Zakaria, was handed a three-month jail sentence for contempt of court. In the public view, nothing was so prejudicial to Anwar's defence as the prosecution's sudden move, at the conclusion of its case, to amend the corruption charges against Anwar so that the prosecution need not prove his sexual misconduct. If this was not controversial enough, the judge followed up by "expunging" all evi-dence given in relation to those dropped charges. The defence protested in vain that all the doubt the defence had cast upon the testimony of key pros-ecution witnesses had come to nothing.

The trial was dogged by other developments. In February Anwar gave evidence before a royal commission of inquiry investigating the assault he had suffered in police custody the previous September. Then the former inspector-general of police, Rahim Noor, through his lawyer, confessed before the com-mission to the assault on Anwar. In March, the trial was almost halted as Anwar's lawyers were threatened with arrest when they refused to make their closing arguments in protest against the conduct of the trial thus far. The defence team applied to have Paul discharge himself on grounds of bias; the judge rejected the application.

Anwar's first trial ended in April 1999. Paul found Anwar guilty of all four charges of corruption and sentenced him to six years' imprisonment. In a courtroom statement, Anwar maintained his innocence, praised his lawyers, thanked his supporters, and urged *Reformasi*.

April 1999 brought the legal verdict that the prosecution had wanted. Barring a successful appeal, Anwar was thereby disqualified as a member of parliament and could not stand for election for five years after his sentence was served. The verdict was also a political triumph for Mahathir. But the mass demonstrations in Kuala Lumpur and nation-wide protests against the verdict showed that Paul's judgement had not secured the moral victory that "justice" — "done and seen to be done" — alone could confer.[7]

Perhaps it was some such realization that led to the second trial of Anwar in June, this time for alleged sodomy. At the time of writing, the case is in progress. But the progress of the second trial, like the first, has been equally troubled. The prosecution has twice amended the dates of the alleged of-fences. The trial was adjourned in September when the defence produced international expert certification that Anwar showed symptoms consistent with arsenic poisoning. Anwar's family and supporters claimed that Anwar may have been poisoned in jail by his enemies. Once again mass demonstrations broke out even as the judge, Ariffin Jaka, ordered Anwar to be delivered into the care of Universiti Kebangsaan Malaysia's hospital for medical tests and check-ups. Eventually the tests pronounced Anwar free of arsenic poisoning but did not account for the symptoms Anwar exhibited which the original diagnosis associated with high arsenic levels.

While the trial was on, Anwar lodged several police reports, accompanied by copies of official documents, alleging corruption on the part of several of Mahathir's closest political associates, including Daim Zainuddin, Rafidah Aziz, and Rahim Thamby Chik. These police reports, ignored by the mainstream media, found their way into the Internet. On the other hand, Murad Khalid, a former assistant governor of Bank Negara — someone once regarded as "close to Anwar" and under investigation for alleged corruption — made a statutory declaration containing accusations of corruption against Anwar and many individuals and organizations (all opposition supporters). As Murad then took off to an undeclared destination, his statutory declaration was greatly publicized by the mainstream media, and the director of the Anti-Corruption Agency declared his agency ready to investigate all portions of the statutory declaration.

Around that time, Anwar's trial was again adjourned, because the judge had a bad back. The adjournment began on the day Dr Mahathir announced a general election. From then on, Anwar was held in seclusion. His communications from prison, police reports, courtroom remarks, and off-the-cuff statements came to an end for 1999.

The Meanings of *Reformasi*
At a rally held in his home town of Cherok To'kun, Penang, in mid-September 1998, before his arrest, Anwar issued a call for *Reformasi* which resonated beyond expectations: *Reformasi* blossomed into a social movement.

At one level, *Reformasi* was an inchoate movement of cultural opposition born of mostly Malay revulsion at Anwar's maltreatment. Perhaps Dr Mahathir and the UMNO élite had expected that allegations of sodomy made against Anwar would stun the Malay-Muslim community into acceptance of Anwar's guilt. If so, an intensifying defiance of the regime showed how far the politicians had miscalculated. They had transgressed, in fact, an ancient but deeply held cultural code that forbade a ruler from shaming the ruled. Malay popular opinion found in towns and villages, within the civil service, on university campuses, among students studying overseas, and even at UMNO's lower levels equated the shaming of Anwar and the humiliation of his family with the disgrace of an entire community and nation.[8] Non-Malay opinion sympathetic towards Anwar was not anchored to a comparable cultural code, but took the Anwar affair to symbolize all that was morally and politically wrong in Malaysian public life.

At another level, *Reformasi* became the site of an alternative media of expression, communication, and public debate which were free of state censorship, if not quite liberated from fear of state retribution. New and sophisticated forms of social criticism came from a young satirist, Amir Muhammad (who mixed political irreverence with literary criticism in his "Perforated Sheets" column in the *New Straits Times*), a middle-aged diarist, Sabri Zain (whose internet *Reformasi Diary* provided an evocative record of the 1998–99 street demonstrations), and an elderly allegorist, Shahnon Ahmad (whose best-selling novel *SHIT!* transformed vernacular profanity into an anti-regime code). Defying legal restrictions on the sale of party newspapers to non-party members, PAS's twice-weekly, and bilingual, *Harakah*, rose in circulation to 300,000 copies from 70,000 before *Reformasi*. The paper was available on the Internet, too. Malay-language magazines such as *Tamadun, Detik, Wasilah,* and *Eksklusif* and the online bilingual *Saksi*, brought together writers, analysts, and artists, and maintained a steady stream of commentary and criticism.

Internet *Reformasi* websites mushroomed. Some were the websites of established organizations, particularly the opposition parties and non-NGOs. Some sites were anonymously maintained but their designations made clear the principal concerns and objectives of those who maintained, supported, and visited them: *Laman Reformasi* (Reformasi Website), *Jiwa Merdeka* (Soul of Independence), *Anwar Online,* and *freeMalaysia.* Other sites, like Sabri Zain's *Reformasi Diary* and Raja Petra Kamaruddin's *The Malaysian* and *Kini* were maintained by individuals who disdained to conceal their names or goals. Yet others flaunted names like *Mahafiraun* (Great Pharoah) or *Mahazalim* (Great Tyrant), which were sneeringly open about the target of their derision.

The *Reformasi* websites carried countless postings in Malay and English, and, frequently, translations from one language to the other. The postings were breathtaking in their diversity: announcements of *Reformasi* events, reproductions and translations of news reports, unofficial transcripts of trial proceedings, transcripts of interviews, press releases, eyewitness accounts of protests and public events, economic and political analyses, summaries of public talks, letters, appeals for support, petitions, reminders on voter registration, rebuttals of official statements, diatribes against leading politicians, denunciations of senior public officials, accusations against corporate figures, police reports, copies of official and purportedly official documents, poems, modern fables, photographs, cartoons, recordings of speeches, and video clips. Not all the postings were thoughtful; some were scarcely readable. But the Internet "voices of *Reformasi*" defied the regime's monopoly of mainstream media. The Internet *Reformasi* output was ultimately purposeful: demand justice, democracy, and reform.

In that sense *Reformasi*, at a third level, meant the erosion of the regime's ideological hegemony over Malaysian civil society.[9] Mahathirist politics was premised on rapid growth and continued prosperity, nationalist vision and popular support, and strong leadership and managed succession. The July 1997 economic crisis had shaken the regime's claim to being able to ensure rapid growth and continued prosperity. The events of September 1998 undermined its insistence on strong leadership and managed succession. It fell to

Reformasi supporters to mock at all three of the regime's premises. They characterized post–July 1997 economic management as being captive to "corruption, cronyism, and nepotism". They wanted an end to Dr Mahathir's leadership, and rejected the succession implied by Abdullah Ahmad Badawi's appointment as deputy prime minister. And they refused to go along with Mahathir's anti-Westernism.

Such positions were bound by a loose ideological unity. In economic matters, for instance, *Reformasi* counted among its adherents free marketeers, supporters of the New Economic Policy, Keynesians, populists, socialists, and Islamicists — but all wanted an end to "corruption, cronyism, and nepotism".

Reformasi supporters were united in deploring the state or conduct of key public institutions. They disbelieved the judiciary's impartiality, attacked the police force for suppressing peaceful demonstrations and dismissed the media for subservience and untruth. They criticized university administrators for "disciplining" arrested student protestors, and economic or financial regulatory agencies for lacking in professionalism or independence. Muslim supporters of *Reformasi* spurned state-appointed religious officers for collaborating with the regime. And since Dr Mahathir personified to them the emasculation or degradation of key institutions, *Reformasi* supporters were agreed on a fundamental point: *Undur Mahathir!* (Resign, Mahathir!).

Had Mahathir decided to retire in 1999, or been persuaded to do so by UMNO, *Reformasi* might have come to an early end. However, the UMNO general assembly's support for Mahathir in late June — after Anwar's conviction and the commencement of his second trial — precluded an early, politically acceptable, conclusion to the Anwar affair. By then, the Mahathir regime was preparing for a general election, in which it hoped to gain from management of the July 1997 crisis, and its focus on alleged external threats, in order to quieten the September 1998 crisis. Thus, the crucial question for the regime's opponents was not whether, but how, to transform *Reformasi*'s moral revolt into an organized opposition.

The Emergence of Barisan Alternatif

Reformasi had achieved a critical cross-cultural breakthrough which created novel possibilities of multiethnic alliances.[10] The Anwar affair had eroded Malay support for UMNO. Malay attitudes towards the Democratic Action Party (DAP) had changed, too. Weeks before Anwar's sacking, DAP's Lim Guan Eng had been jailed for sedition arising out of an UMNO leader's alleged statutory rape of an underaged Malay girl. Many Malays reviewed their former antagonism towards the "Chinese chauvinist", the DAP, because they held that Lim Guan Eng had sacrificed his career and liberty for the sake of a girl "who was not of his race or religion". Many NGOs, whose membership was largely non-Malay, had joined *Reformasi* to support Anwar but also to continue the 1980s struggles against the Mahathir government over several scandals and crises. With the opposition parties — PAS, DAP, and Parti Rakyat

Malaysia (PRM) — making common cause, *Reformasi* drew into its fold "Anwaristas", Islamicists, "Malaysianists", social democrats, NGO activists, women, concerned Christians, and students. Within *Reformasi*, the ethnic divide blurred. Malaysia's new or reinvented leaders of dissent became figures identified with a political standpoint, not the colour of their skin. They included Dr Wan Azizah Wan Ismail (Anwar's wife), the leaders of the opposition parties, Anwar's team of lawyers, the lawyers voluntarily helping arrested demonstrators, and prominent NGO activists.

If *Reformasi* had an institutional expression, that would be Gerak (Majlis Gerakan Keadilan Nasional, or Council of the National Justice Movement), an *ad hoc* coalition of PAS, DAP, PRM, and many NGOs, including ADIL (the precursor of Parti keADILan Nasional [keADILan, or National Justice Party, which was established in April, one week before Anwar's conviction]). Established in September 1998, Gerak operated on the basis of regular consultation among its members. For some time, Gerak seemed experimental and reflective of the fluidity of *Reformasi* which, like social movements elsewhere, blended bits of the future with bites of the past. Gerak's own dialogues were often disagreements among its partners. Its fresh vision of broad-based multiethnic co-operation had to contend with the old suspicions of formerly opposed parties as well as NGOs having their own programmes and objectives. Its alliances were untested in an election but already it faced several sets of difficulties.

Some of Gerak's greatest difficulties were ideological. Gerak's parties typically appealed to specific constituencies. PAS's support came almost entirely from Malay voters. But non-Muslims and "liberal-minded" Muslims were often hostile to its Islamic programme and its "ultimate goal" of an Islamic state. The DAP's "Malaysian Malaysia" programme had always depended on non-Malay support but it was regarded by most Malays as an ill-disguised Chinese opposition to affirmation action under the New Economic Policy (NEP). The PRM had variations of a radical Malay nationalist and socialist platform. KeADILan was most closely associated with Anwar but there were doubts whether its untried multiethnic politics of "national justice" and "reform" could draw many Anwar supporters or much Malay support away from UMNO. Hence, many questioned whether Gerak's combination of PAS's Islam, the DAP's multiculturalism, the PRM's social democracy, and keADILan's "national justice" was ideologically sustainable.

The two major parties in Gerak also seemed to diverge in electoral goals. PAS wanted a maximalist goal of replacing the BN government while the DAP argued more modestly for denying the BN a two-thirds majority in parliament. PAS's confidence was influenced by three factors: its 1990 and 1995 electoral successes, deepening Malay disaffection, and the logical argument that Gerak could not pose as an alternative to the BN without being prepared to take power. The DAP's caution stemmed from the rout it suffered when it tried to capture the Penang state government in 1995, and non-Malay unease over the consequences of a BN defeat and of having PAS in power.

Gerak had to forge a power-sharing framework if it were to present a unified opposition to the BN. The ethnic limitations of Malaysian politics gave PAS and the DAP natural targets: the pronounced Malay-majority constituencies for PAS, and obvious non-Malay (essentially Chinese)-majority ones for the DAP. The smallest party, the PRM, was not expected to contest many seats. Still, the PRM had (never successfully) contested urban middle-class constituencies with small non-Malay majorities which could equally be DAP targets. KeADILan's situation was more complex. It was new and undeveloped, but, having a predominantly Malay membership and a multiethnic "*Reformasi* leadership", it might contest a mix of Malay-majority and non-Malay majority constituencies. That could lead to conflicts with PAS and the DAP over seat allocation. Finally, some NGOs in Gerak were either interested in fielding candidates, or could provide candidates for one or another party, for the election.

Against many kinds of domestic and foreign criticisms, Gerak overcame its internal difficulties in quite original ways. By August, Gerak had reached an agreement on three critical matters: a common election manifesto, a "one-on-one" strategy that would field only one opposition candidate in any contested constituency, and an undertaking to resolve issues of potential divisiveness by institutional procedures. This unprecedented level of co-operation and collective leadership among the Malaysian opposition led to Gerak's being called "Barisan Alternatif" (BA, or Alternative Front). The road from *Reformasi* to Gerak and to the BA was paved with more internal problems than a summary account can capture. And yet, by November, the BA had become sufficiently unified and it was prepared to offer itself as the alternative to the BN, if not in 1999 then in a future election.

On 24 October, the BA released its common manifesto, *Towards a Just Malaysia*.[11] In its political analysis, the manifesto linked the Anwar affair to the government's post–July 1997 and particularly post–September 1998 economic policies. It questioned the entire system of administration of justice over Anwar's prosecution and conviction, the imprisonment of Lim Guan Eng, and other controversial court cases, all of which, the manifesto argued, had turned the judiciary into an instrument of the executive. It attacked the government's intolerance of dissent and its use of police force against peaceful demonstrations. And it offered a wide-ranging programme of political, economic, and social reform that would investigate allegations of high-level corruption, reassess prevailing practices of privatization, and restore civil rights and liberties. While Gerak had not definitively addressed the differences between PAS's Islam and the DAP's "Malaysian Malaysia", the BA's manifesto affirmed the importance of a constitutional framework for dialogues between Muslims and non-Muslims. Set against the "Malay dominance" parameters of BN politics, *Towards a Just Malaysia* shows how far the BA had succeeded in building a "rainbow coalition".

The BA went further. In November, just prior to the tabling of the 2000 budget, the BA presented its "people's budget". This outlined a "vision" of what an alternative plan of economic development might be should the BA come to power.[12] The "people's budget", clarified the BA's positions on several economic and financial matters, including capital controls, taxation, investment policies, and development priorities. Its cornerstone was a populist commitment to dismantling "corruption, cronyism, and nepotism", providing a safety net for neglected social groups, reversing the privatization of core social services, restoring professional integrity to planning and regulatory agencies, and terminating the regime's predilection for "mega projects". To that extent, the budget strategy indicated the social base to which the BA appealed: the rural populace, urban poor, middle classes, professionals, small and medium-sized businesses, and the civil service. That was a broad social base that could non-antagonistically respond to the various platforms of the BA's partners.

Internal Resources and External Threats?

All through 1999, the government pinned its hopes for political support on a strategy of economic recovery that had evidently been devised before Anwar's dismissal. The key to Mahathir and Daim Zainuddin's management of recession was a set of capital controls and currency peg. The capital controls of 1 September 1998 halted the post–July 1997 trend of capital flight — if only by trapping remaining foreign funds for at least a year — and reversed it somewhat — if only by forcing the return of some offshore funds after 31 October 1998 when the ringgit could no longer be traded outside Malaysia. An accompanying currency peg of RM3.80 to US$1 gave domestic businesses and foreign direct investment a measure of stability to plan, contract, and manage. Behind this "shield" (as public officials described the capital controls and currency peg) the government implemented its strategy of crisis management and economic reflation.[13]

The government used Danaharta, an "asset management company" established as part of the National Economic Recovery Plan, to acquire about RM23 billion in non-performing loans (by mid-1999) from banks heavily saddled with corporate debt. Another "special-purpose vehicle", Danamodal, helped to recapitalize the financial sector by giving "credit injections" (totalling RM6.4 billion) to leading banks. Bank Negara, the central bank, moved to increase liquidity, ease corporate debt burdens, and facilitate loans to the corporate sector — by lowering banks' statutory reserve requirements, reducing interest rates, reclassifying non-performing loans, and directing higher levels of bank lending. A third body, the Corporate Debt Restructuring Committee, managed applications for debt restructuring, the best known and most controversial of which involved conglomerates such as the UMNO-owned Renong, the state-owned Bank Bumiputra, and Sime Bank.

While trade surpluses and the country's reserves began to build up in 1999, because of increasing exports and declining imports, most of the funds used in recapitalization and reflation were drawn from three sources: public funds (notably the Employees Provident Fund and the reserves of the national oil company, Petronas), external loans (extended by Japan and the World Bank), and bonds (raised in the money market by the government and Petronas). Credit was also made more easily available for private consumption as credit card regulations were relaxed, and loans were extended to consumers and purchasers at more favourable terms (than pre–July 1997 ones) to stimulate or support key economic sectors, such as the automobile industry and the property market. In the latter sector, for example, the government mobilized property developers via "roadshows" to mass market their unsold residential premises and commercial space at reduced prices.

There was intense controversy over the government's recovery plan. Government spokespeople defended the measures as a strategy

> to restructure and consolidate the financial sector, with the aim of relieving the banks of their non-performing assets, strengthening and recapitalizing banking institutions, improving the efficiency of the intermediation process and facilitating corporate debt restructuring.[14]

The government's opponents saw them in a very different light. The opposition leader, Lim Kit Siang, for instance, charged that the policies had

> three thrusts — to pump liquidity into the system to prime the pump, to isolate the economy from the discipline of markets, and behind the curtain to hand out public resources to the chosen few.[15]

Even as the economy began emerging from recession by mid-1999, controversy continued. The government claimed to have successfully managed recovery based on internal resources and the reversal of "the wrong turns taken during the initial stage of the crisis"[16] (that is, during Anwar's last year as minister of finance). Critics, however, attributed the end of recession to a regional recovery, and a fortuitous growth in (mostly electronic) exports, and warned of the long-term costs of capital controls and the absence of far-reaching reforms within the banking and corporate sectors:

> Those who pat Mr Mahathir on the back now are misframing the argument. There was never any doubt that preventing money from fleeing Malaysia could provide short-lived relief to the beleaguered economy. By bringing an abrupt end to capital flight, capital controls allowed Kuala Lumpur to lower interest rates and pump cash into the economy to the pressure of overleveraged companies without fear of further devaluation. The cash spigot is still on, so today it should surprise no one that the stocks of companies that might otherwise have been forced to the brink are rallying.
>
> The real question is whether the short-term gain was worth the cost, and what Malaysia's long-term prospects are. Here the picture is more gloomy.[17]

Many economic and financial matters remained points of contention between

Mahathir's government and other domestic and foreign parties. A Bank Negara plan to merge Malaysia's fifty-eight banks and finance companies into six large banking groups — rationalized as an attempt to make domestic banking more competitive — was opposed by many critics as a move to centralize the control of the banking sector in the hands of politically favoured groups. The proposed bank merger was also opposed by many banks, in particular those "controlled by Chinese interests", and was still unimplemented by year's end.[18] Diplomatic relations between Singapore and Malaysia failed to improve, not least because of the continued suspension of over RM10 billion in Malaysian shares formerly traded under the (Singapore-based) Central Limit Order Book (CLOB) International. The issue of capital controls, arguably the most intractable one to pit the regime against the international money market, was partially resolved as capital controls were relaxed, beginning in February, to permit the repatriation of foreign funds subject to a graduated exit tax. What the government offered as a pragmatic compromise, others regarded as a retreat from politically motivated controls that could not work in the long run but had already harmed Malaysia's position as a destination of foreign investment.[19]

Some investment funds (notably Templeton) were adamant about staying away from Malaysia under Dr Mahathir. By mid-year onwards, however, influential money market "voices" had toned down the hostility they had shown towards Mahathir's government in the aftermath of July 1997.[20] The government and Petronas were able to raise bonds of US$1 billion and US$500 million, respectively, from the international money market, albeit at "punitive" premiums. Subsequently, Morgan Stanley Capital International announced its plan to reincorporate Malaysia into its index by early 2000. This *rapprochement* between Mahathir's government and the money market was perhaps best signalled by the *Asian Wall Street Journal* editorial of 23 June 1999, which concluded:

> The longer it hides behind capital controls, the wider the gap between Malaysia and the other Tigers grows. Now that the pressure of the Asian crisis has abated, it's time to declare victory and rejoin the global economy.

It was in any case an ambivalent *rapprochement*. To be sure, hard-nosed considerations of financial matters toned down the hostility between Mahathir's government and the money market. But while the latter, in tandem with Western states, was unremitting in its promotion of "globalizing forces", the former was obdurate in its "nationalism". This nationalism had economic expressions — in the semi-autarkic character of the capital controls, the claim that "internal resources" had effected economic recovery, the MCA-led "Buy Malaysia" campaigns, and the insinuations that Anwar was pro–International Monetary Fund.

But the nationalism found targets elsewhere. The Anwar trials, verdict, and sentence occasioned criticism of the Mahathir government by some ASEAN and Western states to which Mahathir and his supporters responded with scorn.

The unresolved conflicts between Malaysia and Singapore were often subsumed under allegations that CLOB had been manipulated to damage Malaysian companies listed under the Kuala Lumpur Stock Exchange.[21] When post-referendum East Timor was engulfed in violence, Malaysia sided with Indonesia, and became entangled in altercations with Australia over the latter's role and command in the dispatch of the United Nations' INTERFET troops to East Timor.

There were exceptions to this theme of cantankerous diplomacy. Malaysia's relations with China were probably never better, as seen in the very cordial visits by Mahathir to China and by Zhu Rongji to Malaysia. Malaysia-China relations were promoted out of mutual opposition to Western domination and business interests, but also by the BN's need to preserve the support of Chinese Malaysians to offset the loss of Malay backing. UMNO's loss of credibility among the Malay-Muslim community was scarcely improved by revelations of secretive diplomatic communications and contacts between the Malaysian Minister of Foreign Affairs, Syed Hamid Albar, and his Israeli counterpart.

Over the years, Mahathir has frequently made calls for "national unity" against external threats and foreign forces. In 1999, with the fall-out from the economic crisis of July 1997 — for which the Mahathir government admitted no responsibility — and the political crisis of Anwar's sacking — in which it admitted no wrong — such calls were woven into a persistent theme that only wholesale support for the BN could thwart the recolonization of Malaysia.

The "Minus 681,000" Election

Malaysia's tenth general election was held on 29 November 1999, about eight months ahead of its constitutional deadline. One hundred and ninety-three parliamentary seats were contested. Elections were concurrently held for all state legislative assemblies in peninsular Malaysia but not in Sarawak, which had held its last state election in 1996, or Sabah, where the BN had won the state election of 12–13 March 1999. In the previous general election of 1995, the BN won 162 out of 192 parliamentary seats and all but one state government. (A coalition of PAS and UMNO-breakaway Parti Semangat 46 ruled Kelantan from 1990 to 1996, before the latter dissolved itself and its members rejoined UMNO, leaving PAS to rule alone.)

After fourteen months of post-Anwar turmoil, the BN's electoral objectives were straightforward: preserve its customary two-thirds majority in parliament, win all state assemblies, and thereby abort the BA's emergence as a credible "alternative coalition". The BA aimed to win at least one-third of the parliamentary seats, retain control of Kelantan, defeat the BN in other states, and introduce a vibrant opposition into Malaysian politics. The basic tenor of the electioneering reflected the objectives of the principal antagonists. The BN argued that only its coalition could guarantee continued economic development, political stability, and, above all, untroubled interethnic relations. In a shrill campaign that made the most of ethnic fears, the BN told Malay voters that only UMNO could preserve "Malay dominance" even as it warned non-Malay voters that only an UMNO-led coalition could be their safeguard against ethnic violence and (PAS's) "Islamic state". On the other hand, the BA appealed for an end to the BN's monopoly of state power, and the institution of a process of political and social reform as a constitutional bulwark against the BN's increasing authoritarianism and corruption.

As in previous elections, the electoral contest took place on a "non-level playing field". The BN wielded an unchallenged control over the electoral process, state machinery, public resources, and the mass media. The mainstream press conducted its habitual publicity blitz for the BN, and either ran down or blacked out the opposition's campaign. The radio and television stations, all owned by the state or companies close to UMNO, became part of the BN's electoral machinery while they refused the opposition any meaningful access to their election coverage or air time. The opposition's media handicap was accentuated by the brevity of the campaign period: in eight days, its candidates had to contend with police restrictions on public rallies and the "caretaker" government's refusal to allow the opposition to use public meeting places. The use of postal ballots (essentially the votes of uniformed personnel) remained non-transparent since the opposition was not permitted to scrutinize the casting or the deployment of such ballots.

However, the BA suffered its most crippling disadvantage when the Election Commission decided, against objections from all quarters except the BN, to use electoral rolls certified in January 1999. Between April and May 1999, the Election Commission had conducted a voter registration exercise. This exercise drew in 681,120 eligible citizens, or almost half a million more than the average 200,000 people who participated in a typical voter registration exercise. It was widely conceded that the additional half million were overwhelmingly young and/or opposition-minded people who had registered as "first-time voters" precisely to "teach the BN a lesson". On grounds that it could not prepare new electoral rolls before February 2000, the Election Commission disenfranchised these newly registered voters.

Despite all this, had the election been conducted on the basis of proportional representation, *Reformasi*'s impact and the BA's unified opposition would have transformed Malaysian politics into a meaningful "two-coalition system". The BA secured 40.3 per cent of the popular vote (out of a combined opposition share of 43.5 per cent) against the BN's 56.5 per cent, the latter being close to a 9 per cent decline in popular support compared with the BN's share of the popular vote in 1995. But Malaysia's "first past the post system", distorted by electoral gerrymandering, heavily favoured the BN in power terms: the BN took 148 parliamentary seats (almost 77 per cent of the total) while the BA obtained only forty-two seats (and Parti Bersatu Sabah, three).

Hence, the BN was returned to power. But that fact alone would obscure UMNO's severe losses. The BN lost more than half of the parliamentary seats (eight out of fifteen) in Mahathir's home state of Kedah, where UMNO won only five out of the thirteen seats it contested. In Kelantan the BN was again routed (this time by PAS and keADILan): former S46 leader, Tengku Razaleigh Hamzah, scored the BN's sole victory amidst its thirteen defeats. The BN also suffered a historic defeat in Terengganu where it lost all eight parliamentary contests. In total, UMNO's parliamentary representation fell to 72 from 94, a 22-seat (or 23.4 per cent) decline. The scale of UMNO's set-back was dramatized by the defeat of four UMNO cabinet ministers and five deputy ministers, the highest number ever.

At the state level, the BN won 281 out of a peninsular Malaysian total of 394 seats, a 17 per cent decline from its command of 339 seats in 1995. Of this 58-seat loss, UMNO alone accounted for 55 (which coincidentally was the total number of opposition seats in 1995). Once again, UMNO was virtually shut out in Kelantan, winning two out of 43 seats. And, forty years after winning the Terengganu state election in 1959, PAS regained control of the state government by winning 28 out of 32 seats.

Still, the BA had failed to deny the BN its two-thirds majority. The extent of the BA's failure could be gauged by comparing its component parties' individual performances with those of the opposition in recent elections. KeADILan won five seats, which was not a bad showing for a party that was only a few months old. Yet the number was less than the eight seats that the UMNO dissidents in S46 obtained in the 1990s. And while Wan Azizah won Anwar's constituency of Permatang Pauh, keADILan's most prominent *Reformasi* leaders — Chandra Muzaffar, Tian Chua, and Zainur Zakaria — lost, albeit by slim margins. Again, the PRM did not win any seat. The DAP won an extra seat over 1995, but its ten seats were half what it won in 1990, and its secretary-general, the long-serving opposition leader, Lim Kit Siang, as well as other veteran parliamentarians, were defeated. Only PAS truly advanced by winning 27 seats where it had only seven in 1990 and eight in 1995, and taking over the leadership of the opposition from the DAP.

For many observers, the most important factor in the BA's failure was a non-Malay reluctance to vote against the BN for fear of jeopardizing an economic recovery that had begun in the months preceding the election, or to vote for the BA out of apprehension that a "PAS-dominated" BA would adversely affect non-Muslim interests. Consequently, strong non-Malay support for the BN offset the Malay voters' swing against UMNO and its partners. Such reasoning must be taken seriously to the extent that ethnic sentiments, especially when heightened or alarmed, critically influence Malaysian electoral behaviour at any one point. After all variants of this reasoning had simultaneously supplied the emotive edge of the BN campaign, and worried DAP that its coalition with PAS would lose the DAP enormous non-Malay support.

Yet the 1999 election, seen within a longer view of Malaysian politics, raises far more complex issues related to social change than can be addressed by habitual ethnic explanations of Malaysian politics. First, UMNO's dominance in the so-called "Malay heartland" of Kelantan, Terengganu, and Kedah had been regularly challenged since the mid-1980s, always by PAS, but also by different sets of UMNO dissidents. What explanation can adequately clarify why UMNO was finally battered by PAS (in more places than Kelantan) in November 1999? Second, the definitive shift of non-Malay support from the DAP to the MCA and Gerakan Rakyat Malaysia in the large and traditionally oppositionist urban constituencies took place in 1995, at the height of non-Malay adulation for Dr Mahathir, and not in 1999 under the shadow of a resurgent PAS. What crucial or subtle changes in Malaysian political economy and social attitudes account for the occurrence and the persistence of that shift? And third, what local and regional factors have enabled UMNO and the BN's "local partners" to entrench themselves in Sabah and Sarawak, respectively, and hence create a major underpinning of the BN's national power? And, fourth, if the BA consolidates as a stable coalition, how will the parameters and assumptions of Malaysian politics be affected?

An Unfinished Business

The year 1999 came to an end in Malaysia with the month of Ramadan bringing a lull onto the political terrain. As year 2000 approached, however, this much was clear: beneath the calm lay unresolved the tensions and contradictions of Malaysian society which were exposed by Anwar's fall, reflected in *Reformasi*, partially mediated through the BA, and temporarily checked by the November election.

Mahathir had led the BN to an electoral victory for the fifth time, only victory in this "dirtiest election" (as he himself had warned before it was held, although he meant to accuse the opposition) was not cheaply purchased. The swing against the government was large, and considering that 6,659,000 valid votes were cast, would have been more pronounced had the Election Commission not disenfranchized the 681,000 voters. Malay disaffection with UMNO has changed qualitatively, too. There is now Malay sentiment, unthinkable before, that UMNO has become "irrelevant". No one can predict whether this sentiment will subside before the next election, or gather sufficient momentum to threaten UMNO's ability to remain in power.

One critical factor will be how UMNO deals with intra-party disaffection. In 1999 Mahathir had pre-empted open expression of dissent linked to Anwar's expulsion and Abdullah Badawi's promotion to deputy premiership by postponing the party election, originally scheduled for June 1999, to the year 2000. To that dissent must now be added a brooding unhappiness over the loss of 22 parliamentary and 55 state assembly seats and the state government of Terengganu, as well as a niggling unease that UMNO could truly become irrelevant to the Malay masses.

No one can be happy in prison. But one can imagine Anwar confident that Mahathir's "Anwar affair" is far from finished. Its incidence and impact testify to a festering crisis within UMNO which makes the party's chronic factionalism — rather than the DAP's once alleged and now irrelevant "Chinese chauvinism", or PAS's once contained but presently dreaded "Islamic state" — the real source of political instability within Malaysia.

NOTES

The research and most of the writing of this article were conducted when the author was Visiting Fellow at the Asia Research Centre, Murdoch University, Western Australia. He gratefully acknowledges the support of the Asia Research Centre, and thanks Richard Robison, Kanishka Jayasuriya, and Garry Rodan for many engaging discussions of a critical period of Malaysian politics.

   1. M.N. Mohd. Nor, C.H. Gan, and B.L. Ong, "Nipah Virus Infection of Pigs in Peninsular Malaysia", Report submitted to the Office International des Epizooties (OIE) Chapter of *Scientific and Technical Review*, 8 August 1999.
   2. D.K.L. Quek, "Viral Encephalitis Outbreak: More Questions Than Answers", *Berita MMA* 29, no. 3 (1999): 1, 5; Chan Chee Khoon, "'Japanese' Encephalitis: A Re-Emergent Nightmare?", *Aliran Monthly* 19, no. 3 (April 1999): 7–8.
   3. Martin Enserink, "New Virus Fingered in Malaysian Epidemic", *Science* 284 (16 April 1999): 407–9.
   4. See <http://dph.gov.my/special/outbreak/je/press%20release/awsj.html> for an exchange between the *Asian Wall Street Journal* and the Malaysian Ministry of Health between April and July 1999, on these and related issues of the management of the epidemic.
   5. It is not feasible here to provide an adequate citation of the extensive coverage of Anwar Ibrahim's trials. The British Broadcasting Corporation has a series of useful reports on the trials, "arsenic poisoning" episode, and popular protests at various points between September 1998 and November 1999; see "A Crisis Unfolds: Timeline" <http://news.bbc.co.uk/hi/english/special_report/1998/10/98/malaysia_crisis/newsid_204000/204632.stm>.
   6. See, for instance, Bar Council Statement, 16 April 1999 available on <http://www.jaring.my/bar-mal/fr_mess.htm>; Amnesty International, News Release, ASA 28/02/99, 14 April 1999, "Malaysia. Anwar Verdict — A Door Has Opened That Cannot Be Closed"; Frances Webber and Geoffrey Bindman, "Anatomy of Corruption", *New Law Journal*, 4 June 1999; and "Malaysia: 1999 Country Reports on Human Rights Practices" (Bureau of Democracy, Human Rights, and Labor, U.S. Department of State, 25 February 2000).
   7. Philip Khoo, "Thinking the Unthinkable", *Aliran Monthly*, June 1999, provides a thoughtful commentary on the political ramifications of the "Anwar Affair", verdict of the first trial, sentence on Anwar, and the growing dissent, particularly among Malays.
   8. See the preceding reference for this important insight. A scholarly discussion of this cultural code as a "social contract" is available in Cheah Boon Kheng, "The Rise and Fall of the Great Melakan Empire: Moral Judgement in Tun Bambang's *Sejarah Melayu*", *Journal of the Malaysian Branch of the Royal Asiatic Society* 71, part 2, no. 275 (December 1998): 103–21.
   9. An interesting, post-modernist reading of *Reformasi* is offered by Farish A. Noor, "Looking for Reformasi: The Discursive Dynamics of the Reformasi Movement and Its Prospects as a Political Project", *Indonesia and the Malay World* 27, no. 77 (March 1999): 5–18.
  10. Khoo Boo Teik, "Malaysia's 'Reformasi' Breaks Cultural Lines", *Nation* (Bangkok), 9 August 1999.
  11. *Towards a Just Malaysia* is available at <http://www.malaysia.net/dap/ba-ind.htm>.
  12. There is no official English translation of the BA's budget strategy, *Belanjawan*

Rakyat 2000: Demi pemulihan, pembangunan dan keadilan [The people's budget 2000: Towards recovery, development and justice]. The original document is available at <http://www.malaysia.net/dapmnet/bljw.html>.

13. The fullest official version of the government's policies is set out in the April 1999 White Paper, *Status of the Malaysian Economy* <http://www.topspot.com/NEAC>.

14. Ibid.

15. Lim Kit Siang, Speech on the White Paper (*Status of the Malaysian Economy*), *Dewan Rakyat*, 6 April 1999 <http://www.freemalaysia.com/archive/kitsiang-whitepaper.htm>.

16. *Status of the Malaysian Economy*, Box 1.

17. "Malaysia Needs to End Isolation", *Asian Wall Street Journal*, 23 June 1999. On the point of reforms, Jorgen Borhnoft, the outgoing president of the Malaysian International Chamber of Commerce and Industry expressed MICCI's "concern that there does not seem to be enough strong action against those people who were responsible for that massive spate of irresponsible borrowing, and just as irresponsible lending", "hoped that the improvements which are being afforded to the troubled corporates [*sic*] are not just financial", mentioned that MICCI supported the capital controls of September 1999 "on the basis that they are clearly seen to be short-term measures", and urged "serious structural adjustments" to some troubled companies. (Dow Jones, "Foreign Investors Want More Reform: MICCI", 15 June 1999 <http://freemalaysia.com/reformasi_investors.htm>.

18. S. Jayasankaran, "Merger by Decree", *Far Eastern Economic Review*, 9 September 1999, pp. 10–14.

19. For a neo-liberal criticism of the capital controls and other recovery measures, see "Capital Controls Erode" <http://www.freemalaysia.com/economic/loss_of_control.htm>, 21 February 1999.

20. Despite appearances, foreign media attitudes became more favourable towards the Mahathir regime in 1999. See Khoo Boo Teik, "Mahathir, Foreign Media No Bitter Foes", *Nation* (Bangkok), 5 August 1999; and John Funston, "Malaysia/Thailand, A Mid-Year Review: Contrasting Political Trajectories", *Trends in Southeast Asia* (Singapore: Institute of Southeast Asian Studies), 4 September 1999.

21. For a discussion of the Malaysia-Singapore conflicts, probably the most serious in this respect, see John Funston, "Malaysia: A Fateful September", in *Southeast Asian Affairs 1999*, edited by Daljit Singh and John Funston (Singapore: Institute of Southeast Asian Studies, 1999), pp. 165–84.

MALAYSIA'S ALTERNATIVE APPROACH
TO CRISIS MANAGEMENT

Mahani Zainal Abidin

The severity of the crisis and the speed of its recovery surprised not only the affected countries but the market as well.[1] After a decade of high economic growth supported by an outward-looking strategy, active participation by foreign investors and prudent fiscal policy, the East Asian economies had been touted as the global growth centre for the next century. Within six months of the onset of the crisis in July 1997, the affected East Asian economies were threatened with economic implosion and hardship. Their economic contraction in 1998 was the worst ever experienced. Similarly, the recovery also came swiftly, if only to some. In 1999, most of the crisis-hit countries grew between 4 and 10 per cent. Short-term capital, which had drained from the region, flooded back, thus pushing the stock markets past their pre-crisis levels.

The Malaysian experience of fall and recovery generally follows that of other affected countries. The initial impact of the crisis was delayed and Malaysia managed to register a reasonably strong growth rate of 7.7 per cent in 1997. The severity of the crisis was really felt in the first quarter of 1998 when the gross domestic product (GDP) declined by 3.1 per cent, but by the third quarter the GDP fell by 10.9 per cent, its largest contraction. This sharp contraction was caused by the collapse of aggregate demand by 20.3 per cent, which primarily came from a decline of private sector investment of 50.5 per cent. Higher cost of funds and shortage of credit, excess capacity, and the expectation of decreasing consumption triggered cut-backs in private investment. Although there was a reduction in public consumption (–7.2 per cent), public investment (0.4 per cent), and private consumption (–7.5 per cent), these were relatively small compared with the drop in private investment. But unlike some other crisis-hit economies, the severe economic contraction in Malaysia did not translate into hyperinflation and widespread unemployment. In 1998, inflation rose to 5.3 per cent, double that of 1997, and unemployment climbed to 3.2 per cent from 2.5 per cent.

Apart from the GDP contraction, the most striking effects of the crisis were the steep depreciation of the ringgit and the massive short-term capital out-

Mahani Zainal Abidin is Professor at the Faculty of Economics and Administration, University of Malaya.

flow. On 14 July 1997, the Malaysian government floated the ringgit after finding the existing *de facto* exchange regime to be unsustainable. With the flotation, the ringgit slipped from RM2.50 to the U.S. dollar prior to the crisis to its lowest level of RM4.88 on 7 January 1998. In 1998, RM21.7 billion of short-term capital left Malaysia. One effect of the massive outflow of short-term capital was the collapse of the equity market. The Kuala Lumpur Stock Market (KLSE) lost 80 per cent of its market valuation: from a high of RM917 billion in February 1997, the KLSE market valuation sank to RM182 billion in September 1998 when the selective capital controls were imposed. In index terms, the KLSE composite index fell from 1271 points to 262 points during the same period.

The deflationary effect of the regional contagion had weakened the demand for Malaysian exports. But the sharply devalued ringgit increased export revenue even though in terms of volume, exports had decreased. This is shown when a comparison is made between export growth measured in ringgit and in U.S. dollar. In ringgit terms, exports increased by 29.8 per cent in 1998, but in U.S. dollars they declined by 2 per cent. In contrast, imports only grew by 3 per cent due to dampened consumer demand and low investment. As a result of high export revenue and a slowdown in imports, Malaysia recorded a large trade surplus of RM69 billion, or 24 per cent of the GDP.

The crisis started as an exchange rate depreciation, but had soon pushed the economy into recession and finally threatened the stability of the financial system. The collapse of the stock market, reduced economic activities, high interest rates, a credit crunch, and credit restriction increased the level of non-performing loans (NPLs) in the banking sector and eroded the banks' capital base. The banking sector's NPLs jumped from 4 per cent in 1997 to a high of 15.8 per cent in August 1998.

Measures to Overcome the Crisis
As an initial response to the crisis, Malaysia had embraced a tight fiscal and monetary policy in the second half of 1997. But these measures did not produce the expected results and the economy continued to deteriorate by the end of 1997 and in early 1998. Domestic conditions (such as a high domestic debt of about 160 per cent of GDP) and the low level of short-term external debt (15 per cent of GDP) enabled Malaysia to seek a different set of policies to revive the economy. Malaysia adopted six key strategies:

- relaxation of the tight fiscal policy to boost the domestic economy
- easing the monetary stance
- reform and restructuring of the financial and corporate sectors
- selective capital controls
- liberalization
- corporate governance

Fiscal Policy

Since the private sector was unable to spur growth during the crisis period, the public sector had to take the initiative to generate economic activities by increasing its consumption and investment. For this purpose, the budget stance was reversed from a surplus of 3.2 per cent of GDP in 1998 to a deficit of 6 per cent in 1999. Fiscal stimulus programmes were undertaken in agriculture, low- and medium-cost housing, education, healthcare, infrastructure, rural development, and technology upgrading.

Monetary Policy

For the economy to stabilize and grow, there must be sufficient liquidity and a reasonable level of interest rates which will allow companies to borrow again and resume their activities. Relaxation of the monetary policy included:

- Reduction of the statutory reserves requirement from 13.5 per cent in February 1998 to 4 per cent in 16 September 1998. This injected RM38 billion into the banking system.
- The lowering of interest rates: the base lending rate was reduced from the peak of 12.27 per cent in June 1998 to 6.79 per cent by October 1999, while average lending rates were consequently decreased from a high of 24 per cent in February 1998 to 7.91 per cent in October 1999.
- The period for classification of loans as NPLs was changed back to six months in September 1998 from three months in March 1998.

Reform and Restructuring of the Financial and Corporate Sectors

An asset management company (Danaharta) was established in June 1998 to manage the NPLs of financial institutions. Its main objectives were to remove NPLs from the balance sheets of financial institutions at fair market value and to maximize their recovery value. This would free the banks from the burden of debts that had prevented them from providing loans to their customers. As the capital base of banks had been affected by the decline in share prices and by the NPLs, these banks needed to be recapitalized. For this purpose the Special-Purpose Vehicle (Danamodal) was set up to recapitalize and consolidate the banking sector, that is, to inject capital into banks facing difficulties. This would restore the resilience of banks, increase their capacity to grant new loans, and consequently speed up the economic recovery. To complement the restructuring of the financial system by Danaharta and Danamodal, the Corporate Debt Restructuring Committee (CDRC) was set up in August 1998 to facilitate debt restructuring of viable companies. The aim was to minimize losses to creditors, shareholders, and other stockholders and avoid placing viable companies into liquidation or receivership and to enable banking institutions to play a greater role in the rehabilitation of the corporate sector.

Stabilization of the Ringgit

The Malaysian response to the East Asian crisis created some controversy when it implemented selective capital control measures on 1 September 1998. The selective capital controls have two inter-related parts: the stabilization of the ringgit and the restriction of the outflow of short-term capital. Stability of the currency is guaranteed by pegging the ringgit to the U.S. dollar at a rate of RM3.80:US$1.00. For the fixed exchange rate system to work, the outflow of short-term capital had to be controlled. Specifically, the measures are:

- All settlement of exports and imports must be made in foreign currency.
- Travellers are allowed to import and export ringgit not exceeding RM1,000 per person.
- Export of foreign currency by resident travellers is limited to a maximum of RM10,000.
- Residents are required to seek prior approval for remitting funds in excess of RM10,000 for overseas investment purposes.
- Residents are permitted to obtain credit facilities in foreign currency up to the equivalent of RM5 million. Any amount exceeding the permitted limit would require prior approval.
- Residents are not allowed to obtain credit facilities in ringgit from non-residents except with prior approval.
- Proceeds in ringgit received by non-residents from the sale of any security must be retained in the external account and be converted into foreign currency after one year.
- The ringgit is not a legal tender outside Malaysia.

Thus, the capital control measures affect the transfer of funds among non-residents, import and export of ringgit by travellers (both residents and non-residents), and investment abroad by Malaysian residents. Similarly, non-residents are restricted from raising credit domestically for the purchase of shares. Non-resident portfolio investors are required to hold their investment for at least twelve months in Malaysia. The outflow of short-term capital was also restricted with the banning of Central Limit Order Book (CLOB) International.[2]

The selective capital controls were modified effective 15 February 1999 when the quantitative control (the requirement that proceeds from the sale of ringgit assets be kept in the country for one year) was replaced by a price-based regulation. The new control on capital flows is governed by a graduated exit levy system based on the length of time that the funds are kept in Malaysia.[3] Further relaxation was introduced on 21 September 1999 on the exit levy where the two-tier system was reduced to a flat rate of 10 per cent on profits repatriated.

Liberalization

Although the focus of the recovery measures has been on the expansion of the domestic economy through fiscal stimulus and easing of the monetary policy, Malaysia also realizes the importance of long-term foreign capital inflow. Malaysia liberalized selected sectors where it is comfortable with foreign presence and it can maximize the gains from foreign capital injection:

- In the manufacturing sector, the Malaysian government relaxed the rule on equity ownership by allowing 100 per cent foreign ownership for investments made before 31 December 2000.[4]
- It allowed 61 per cent of foreign ownership in the telecommunication sector but this will have to be reduced to 49 per cent after five years. Prior to the crisis, there was a 30 per cent limit on foreign ownership in telecommunications, stockbroking, and insurance industries.
- It allowed foreign ownership in stockbroking companies to be increased to 49 per cent while for the insurance sector the limit was raised to 51 per cent;
- Foreigners were permitted to purchase all types of properties above RM250,000 in new projects or when the projects are less than 50 per cent completed. Previously, there were restrictions on foreigners buying landed properties.

Corporate Governance

The crisis highlighted the need to strengthen corporate governance, which is a much more difficult and lengthy process than the other measures introduced. More importantly, it requires the political will and commitment to guarantee that corporate governance framework is fully and effectively implemented. Malaysia has adequate laws and regulations to govern its public and private sectors. However, additional measures were introduced to further strengthen governance and there were calls for more effective execution. The additional measures are:

- improve transparency and disclosure standards
- enhance monitoring and surveillance
- enhance accountability of directors of companies
- protect the rights of minority shareholders
- review codes and acts such as the Securities Industry Act to eliminate any weaknesses that can lead to breaches of the Act
- make changes in the rules of the KLSE and its clearing and depository system to ensure orderly and transparent trading of securities.

The government also established a committee on corporate governance and this committee has produced a comprehensive report on measures to enhance governance.

Sustainability of the Recovery

When Malaysia experienced a quick and sharp recovery in 1999, many analysts questioned its sustainability. The Malaysian recovery process, which began in the second quarter of 1999, initially looked weak. The 1999 GDP was initially estimated to grow only by 1 per cent but as recovery indicators firmed up, this forecast was revised upwards to 4.3 per cent in October 1999. The real 1999 GDP growth rate announced in early 2000 was 5.4 per cent and the estimated growth for 2000 was increased from 5 per cent to 5.8 per cent.[5] Market forecasts of the Malaysian economic recovery were more bullish than the early estimates made by the Malaysian government — for example, the Malaysian Institute of Economic Research forecast 1999 GDP growth at 4.8 per cent while Goldman Sachs forecast it at 5.2 per cent. The International Monetary Fund also expected a strong growth of 6 per cent for Malaysia in 1999.[6] Nevertheless, it is useful to analyse the sources of the recovery and its possible downside risks.

The external sector was the engine of recovery with its strong performance reviving domestic production. In addition, the large trade surplus provided the liquidity needed to boost domestic consumption and strengthened international reserves. Revival of domestic demand also helped the recovery, although domestic private investment was still weak. The selective capital controls deterred short-term capital inflow but foreign direct investment (FDI) continued to come in. An essential element of the recovery was the management of the non-performing loans (NPLs) and the recapitalization of financial institutions. In short, a strong recovery was made possible and sustainable by both external and internal factors, as indicated below:

- External sector: In 1999, Malaysian exports increased by 12 per cent in U.S. dollar terms, one of the strongest among crisis-hit economies. On the other hand, imports growth was still slower, at 9 per cent. Consequently, Malaysia registered its largest trade surplus of RM72 billion in 1999, or 27 per cent of the gross national product (GNP). The strong trade balance has bolstered significantly the current account position, so that in 1999 the current account surplus was RM47 billion, or 17 per cent of the GNP. The large export proceeds that are locked in by the selective capital controls provide the liquidity to revive domestic demand and strengthen the international reserves position. The country's international reserves increased from US$20.2 billion in August 1998 to US$33 billion in January 2000.

  Export growth has been driven by a boom in the global electronic industry and strong imports by a vibrant U.S. economy. Any downturn in the electronic cycle and a slowdown of the U.S. economy, which may dampen the demand for Malaysian exports, can weaken the recovery. However, this risk is minimized by the continuing expansion in the global electronic industry, which is fuelled by the exploding demand for information technology products and activities. Furthermore, the U.S. economy has proven to be very resilient as its ongoing growth is predicated on productivity gains and price stability.

- Industrial production: After a twelve-month decline, industrial production expanded by 3.8 per cent in February 1999. By June 1999, the industrial production index had increased by 8.3 per cent and reached a peak of 23 per cent in November 1999. Within the industrial sector, manufacturing was the fastest-growing sector, with growth of 19.5 per cent in the third quarter of 1999. The construction sector has yet to enter a period of expansion, but its fall has been arrested as it recorded a small growth rate of 0.9 per cent in the third quarter of 1999. The expansion of industrial activities has helped Malaysia to contain the level of unemployment to 3 per cent during the crisis period.

- Loan growth: Interest rates have also decreased significantly: for example, the base lending rate was reduced to 6.79 per cent in October 1999 from a high of 12.27 per cent in June 1998. The lower cost of borrowings has saved many businesses from bankruptcies, and put a lid on the level of NPLs.[7] The low level of interest rate, however, did not spur loan growth and the government set a target of 8 per cent loan growth for 1998 and 1999 to encourage financial institutions to resume their intermediation role. For 1998, the banking sector did not meet the loan growth target and this raised doubts about the sustainability of the recovery process. But low loan growth is not uncommon during the early stage of recovery because of the excess capacity that emerged as a consequence of high investment during the pre-crisis period and the collapse in production during the crisis. The revival of industrial production has raised the average rate of capacity utilization to 80 per cent and loan disbursement will only increase when excess capacity has been exhausted.

- Aggregate consumer demand: Among the economic components, consumer demand was the slowest to recover. Although the demand for some consumer durables such as vehicles recovered quickly, others such as commercial property remained sluggish. However, following the increase in liquidity and the return of market confidence, consumer demand recovery became stronger in the second half of 1999 and this is shown by a higher rate of increase in imports and house purchases and a larger collection of sales tax.

- Inflationary pressure: Malaysia was successful in containing the upward price pressures during the crisis. The consumer price index rose from 2.7 per cent in 1997 to 5.3 per cent in 1998 but had declined to 2.8 per cent in October 1999. There were concerns that liquidity from fiscal stimulus and trade surpluses, which is confined in the domestic economy by the selective capital controls, would quickly push up inflation. The existence of excess capacity, particularly in the property sector, will absorb much of the liquidity; and the capacity to expand output by increasing foreign labour will also reduce the inflationary pressure.

- Short-term capital flows: One of the dire predictions concerning the selective capital controls was that there would be a massive foreign capital outflow at the end of the twelve-month locking-in period, on 1 September 1999. However, this deadline was a non-event, with only an outflow of US$800 million, which was well below the projected outflow of between US$5 billion and US$7 billion. Nevertheless, the stock market performance was lacklustre until December 1999. The KLSE rebounded strongly from the first week of the year 2000 because foreign institutional funds came in to take a position before the reinstatement of Malaysia in the Morgan Stanley Capital International (MSCI) index in May 2000. The Kuala Lumpur Composite Index rose from its low of 262 points on 2 September 1998 to 1009 points on 24 February 2000. In terms of market capitalization, it has increased by 304 per cent from RM181 billion to RM732 billion during the same period.

- Long-term capital flows: FDI continued to flow in after the introduction of the selective capital controls: approved FDI investment in the first half of 1999 was RM7 billion as compared with RM6.8 billion during the same period in 1998. Unlike other crisis-hit economies, the long-term foreign investment into Malaysia is encouraged mainly for the manufacturing sector while liberalization in non-manufacturing areas is still limited.

- Financial and Corporate Sector Restructuring: Malaysia's effort in financial sector restructuring, particularly the work done by Danaharta and Danamodal, is considered as one of the key factors in overcoming the crisis. On the other hand, although there are some successes, corporate debt-restructuring is slow due to the nature and complexity of the process.

(a) Danaharta

Danaharta has successfully completed the first phase of its mandate — to carve out the NPLs. As at 31 December 1999, it had acquired a total of RM45.5 billion NPLs, reducing the level of NPLs in the banking sector to 12.4 per cent. The purchase of the NPLs was completed in six months, much faster than the original time target of one year. Financial institutions have had to take losses from the sales. The average discount rate for NPLs was 57 per cent. The second stage of Danaharta operation is asset management. Thus far, Danaharta is in the final stages of resolving NPLs worth about RM17.6 billion. Danaharta's role of taking over the NPLs is critical in removing the stress from the banking system while at the same time avoiding depressing the market prices of the assets used as collateral for the bad loans. In carrying out its tasks, Danaharta has to balance a number of objectives — not to warehouse the NPLs, maximize recovery value, not to depress market prices when it sells the assets, and provide a return to Danaharta's capital.

(b) Danamodal

Danamodal has injected RM7.59 billion into ten financial institutions, pre-empting any potential systemic risk to the financial sector. As a result, the capital adequacy ratio of the banking system was increased to 12.7 per cent. The capital injection was accompanied by absorption of losses by shareholders through reduced shareholding in troubled institutions, change in the composition of boards of directors and/or change in management. Danamodal has also appointed its representatives in the recapitalized institutions to ensure that these institutions are managed prudently and efficiently as well as to institute changes that will strengthen these institutions.

(c) Corporate Debt Restructuring Committee (CDRC)

The CDRC has received sixty-seven applications with debts totalling RM36.3 billion. Of these, nineteen debt restructuring schemes involving RM14.1 billion have been resolved. The slow progress of the work of the CDRC can be attributed to two factors. First, unlike Danaharta, which has extensive powers because it was established by an act of parliament, and Danamodal, which has the full backing of the central bank, the CDRC is only a voluntary unit that mediates between borrowers and lenders. It has no legal power to enforce any debt-restructuring solutions. Second, solutions to debt restructuring are difficult to obtain because all creditors must agree to the restructuring proposal. Banks, in particular, are reluctant to settle the debt without full repayment. Negotiations have therefore been long because even disagreement from one creditor will jeopardize the whole restructuring process.

(d) Bank Restructuring

Malaysia has moved to another stage of the restructuring process with the introduction of a merger exercise of financial institutions. As a preparation to meet the challenges of a liberalized and global financial system, Malaysia has decided that financial institutions should be merged into bigger entities to allow them to have stronger capital and a larger capacity to invest in information technology and to increase productivity. In early February 2000, Bank Negara Malaysia (the central bank) announced the consolidation of fifty-eight financial institutions into ten banking groups. Each of the banking groups may offer a complete range of financial services such as merchant banking, fund management, and stockbroking services. Plans are also under way to consolidate the stockbroking industry to create strong, efficient, and competitive stockbroking companies. These initiatives are consistent with the earlier plan of financial sector restructuring, which was announced at the beginning of the crisis, and a Financial Sector Master Plan is being formulated for this purpose.

Was the Malaysian Response to the Crisis Different from Those Taken by the Other Affected Countries and Does It Work?

Many regard the measures taken by Malaysia to respond to the crisis as different from those taken by other affected countries. Malaysia did not follow the International Monetary Fund (IMF) assistance programme and instead it advocated a reversal of the tight fiscal and monetary policies set by the IMF for South Korea, Thailand, and Indonesia.[8] Malaysia also singled out currency speculators as the primary cause of the crisis and believed that its economy was fundamentally strong. More controversially, Malaysia imposed selective capital controls that fixed the ringgit exchange rate against the U.S. dollar and restricted short-term capital outflows.

As other crisis-hit economies have also recovered, some very dramatically such as South Korea, it is important to evaluate why the Malaysian measures differ from those taken by the other countries and whether they have worked. In particular, many doubted the effectiveness of the selective capital controls, with some critics declaring that these measures were introduced to postpone the much needed economic reform and restructuring. Even views from the multilateral agencies are mixed: the IMF, for example, concludes that it is unclear whether the selective capital controls did make a significant contribution to the Malaysian recovery process while the World Bank views the controls as giving Malaysia an opportunity to deal with the crisis. There are also concerns about the long-term effects of the controls, namely, the distortion that could be created by a prolonged pegging of the ringgit.

Malaysia initially implemented the IMF-type measures because they were supposed to restore market confidence and stabilize the economy and the exchange rate. When these measures failed to produce the expected result, Malaysia began to examine other options. Since Malaysia had relatively low short-term external debt and had adequate reserves to meet its short-term obligations, it did not have to seek IMF assistance and therefore had greater freedom to choose a set of recovery measures that could halt the economic meltdown and minimize social costs. The search for new measures started with an examination of the underlying conditions of the Malaysian economy. After the economic recession in the middle of the 1980s, the Malaysian government had decided to reduce its role in leading the nation's economic activities and made the private sector as the engine of growth. Public sector investment decreased and development expenditure was taken over by the private sector via privatization projects. The subsequent high economic growth, driven largely by the private sector, had been funded by a high level of private sector domestic debt because of restrictions on raising foreign loans.[9] Under such circumstances, a high interest rate policy and tightening of credit, which created a liquidity crunch, would choke businesses. For businesses to continue their activities and for the domestic economy to expand, it was necessary to restore liquidity and to lower the cost of funding. Furthermore, as the private sector was in trouble and could not continue to function as the generator of economic activities, it fell to the public sector to re-assume the role of the engine of growth, by increasing its consumption and investment to expand the domestic economy.

Malaysia had the internal resources to finance expansionary fiscal and monetary policies. Following years of fiscal surpluses from higher revenue and smaller investment, the government could finance fiscal stimulus such as rural infrastructure projects. There was also adequate domestic private saving through a compulsory savings scheme (the Employees Provident Fund) as well as voluntary ones (such as insurance). In addition, there were also savings by the banking sector in the form of a requirement for statutory reserves, which were placed with the central bank and which could be used to increase liquidity in the financial system. Malaysia could also seek external financial assistance. With a high sovereign rating and a low level of official borrowings, Malaysia could seek international official financial assistance from multilateral or bilateral sources.

The socio-economic and political dimensions provided another important reason why Malaysia could not implement the measures suggested by the IMF. Malaysia is an ethnically diverse country, with a delicate social and political balance.[10] The stability of the country is very much dependent on its ability to expand the economy to meet its restructuring and distribution objectives as set out in the New Economic Policy (NEP). The economic restructuring and redistribution process gives preferential treatment to *bumiputera* (sons of the soil), who lagged in economic areas and this process is based on the assumption that the economy would continue to grow. Any attempt to remove the *bumiputera*'s special status in the name of reform and restructuring would have serious implications on national political and social stability. Moreover, a deep economic contraction would negate any achievements made to improve the economic position of the *bumiputera*. For example, the reduction of *bumiputera*'s corporate equity through the sales of troubled companies to non-*bumiputera* or foreign investors would be unacceptable. It was, therefore, imperative that the economic contraction caused by the crisis be reversed with a policy to expand the domestic economy.

Two key instruments to boost the domestic economy were the implementation of fiscal stimulus programmes and the lowering of interest rates. For these to work, it was imperative that Malaysia regained its monetary policy independence. The existence of active securities and ringgit offshore markets could erode the effectiveness of Malaysia's efforts to ease its fiscal and monetary policies.[11] Without restrictions on the repatriation of short-term capital and the ban on securities trading outside the KLSE, some of the liquidity injected in the domestic economy by fiscal stimulus programmes and the lowering of the statutory reserves requirement would have left the country and made the recovery measures ineffective. Thus, the selective capital controls, which restrict the outflow of short-term capital, were an important part of the recovery. In addition, the selective capital controls, which also fixed the ringgit exchange rate against the U.S. dollar, were necessary to de-link the interest rate from the exchange rate: under a floating exchange rate regime, a lowering of the interest rate would depreciate the ringgit.

Did the Measures Work?

A cursory look at the economic figures shows that the recovery measures have worked. But such an analysis is incomplete because the impact the crisis may have had on society is not included. The Malaysian recovery can be considered a success because it maintained Malaysia's social cohesion. Compared with some other affected countries, Malaysia was able to minimize the social impact of the crisis. The unemployment level was kept at a manageable level (3.2 per cent in 1998) and there was no massive retrenchment. Creative schemes such as flexible work arrangements allowed workers to seek part-time jobs while maintaining their existing jobs, thus allowing troubled companies to reduce their payroll cost without retrenching workers. Similarly, Malaysia also avoided high inflation: the highest price increases were for food items and the government introduced price controls and food subsidies to mitigate the problem. Another indicator of the social impact of the crisis is the poverty level. There was no serious increase in the poverty level in Malaysia.

As an ethnically diverse society, the success of Malaysia's recovery can also be measured by its ability to maintain social stability during the crisis. A sharp erosion of economic welfare can create tension among the various races and fuel social instability. In the Malaysian case, the situation was even more challenging because there was political instability during the crisis. However, the economic hardship was not too severe and the gains that had been made in narrowing the interethnic economic disparity and the existence of a significant middle class have averted social and ethnic tension.

In its recovery process, Malaysia has resisted the pressure to sell its assets to foreign buyers at "fire sale" prices. The crisis put tremendous stress on Malaysian corporations, many of which have high debts. As a result, many corporations, some in strategic industries, were financially troubled and needed fresh equity injection or debt rescheduling. Malaysia was reluctant to allow foreign participation in the resolution of the problems faced by its corporate sectors and only permitted foreign purchase in selected areas.[12] The preferred solution to this corporate stress is through domestic mechanisms such as the purchases of NPLs by Danaharta and debt restructuring by the CDRC. The issue of foreign purchase of Malaysian assets is particularly important for two reasons. First, if these assets were sold under stress to foreign buyers, Malaysia may not get the best value from the sales and when the economy recovers they will cost much more if Malaysia were to want to re-purchase these assets. Second, any sales that reduce the *bumiputera* corporate equity holding would be very sensitive and have wide ramifications. In some cases, corporate holdings represent the *bumiputera* institutional interest. Sales of these assets will negate the gains that have been made to increase *bumiputera* participation in the corporate sector.

Contrary to dire predictions, the selective capital controls have achieved their objectives. The "undervalued" ringgit gives Malaysian exports a price edge, resulting in double-digit export growth in 1999, a large trade surplus, and the strengthening of the current account and international reserves position. As the capital control measures only restrict the movement of short-term capital, which is normally invested in the equity market, FDI has continued to flow in. The selective capital controls were designed not to impede the current account transactions (trade transactions for goods and services), repatriation of interest, dividends, fees, commissions, and income from portfolio investments, and other forms of ringgit assets and FDI inflows and outflows (including income and capital gains). But the selective capital controls also had an important implicit objective, namely, to renew domestic confidence that had been battered by the crisis. Revival of domestic confidence was vital for the resumption of domestic economic and business activities and for social stability. With the pegging of the ringgit, domestic producers were able to restart production because exchange rate uncertainties had been removed. After making the necessary adjustments, most businesses could operate at any exchange rate level so long as there was some degree of stability. Multinational companies, which import most of their inputs and export all their products, face no foreign exchange risks when the ringgit exchange rate is fixed. As a result, the business community welcomed the fixing of the ringgit exchange rate. In an ethnically diverse society such as Malaysia, social and economic stability is critical to growth and development and thus any threat of conflict among the various ethnic groups arising from an economic slowdown must be avoided. By insulating the economy from further deterioration and stabilizing the ringgit, the government managed to revive domestic confidence, thus averting any serious social dislocation.

Malaysia has made serious efforts and registered good progress in restructuring its financial and corporate sectors. NPLs were taken out from the banking system and troubled financial institutions were recapitalized. In fact, Malaysia's efforts in these two areas have been regarded as a critical part of the recovery because they were executed efficiently, in a transparent manner and at a cost much lower than that incurred by the other crisis-hit countries. Moreover, the banking sector consolidation exercise shows Malaysia's commitment to further strengthen its financial sector and to increase efficiency. Rules governing the equity market have also been tightened to ensure a more orderly market.

Challenges

Although Malaysia has made a good recovery, it still faces the challenges of creating a competitive economy that can produce sustained long-term high growth. The recovery measures must be monitored and changed, if necessary, so that they do not jeopardize the long-term goals of Malaysia's economic development. The development experience of the 1990s has shown that a high-growth policy can place serious stress on the economy, causing both shortages of resources and a lower quality of life. The estimated potential growth rate for Malaysia is 6.7 per cent per annum and therefore future economic growth targets should recognize this limit. Malaysia should aim for a growth rate that is compatible with its available resources.

The fixed exchange rate regime has contributed to Malaysia's economic recovery by ensuring the efficacy of the recovery measures, providing exchange rate stability, ensuring export competitiveness, and restoring domestic confidence. Nevertheless, if the ringgit were to become overvalued as a result of a substantial depreciation of other regional currencies, the present strong export performance may cease. Conversely, foreign investors and analysts may consider the ringgit undervalued relative to other regional currencies and eventually this may lead to re-pegging at a higher level (appreciation) to reflect the strong recovery. This possibility may attract short-term capital inflows, which, together with the existing excess liquidity coming from the trade surplus, will create inflationary pressure, and ultimately result in pressures for further appreciation of the ringgit. In such a situation, the adjustment cost to the economy can be significant. Hence, Malaysia has to find an exchange rate regime that can balance two goals, namely, exchange rate stability and the need to smooth and include price and market signals in the determination of the exchange rate.

The crisis has shown that short-term capital flows, which are expected to increase, can determine a country's economic performance. Short-term capital flows are determined both by a county's economic fundamentals as well as market confidence. In a situation of uncertainties, market perception overrides economic fundamentals and as a result, even a country with strong fundamentals can suffer from capital flight. In such a situation, it is perhaps imperative to minimize the exit of capital until market confidence has returned. Thus, selective capital controls should be viewed as measures to calm the market and allow the country to put a brake on economic deterioration. However, countries must strengthen their fundamentals because capital controls can only give a temporary relief and the medium- and long-term growth prospects will only be determined by fundamentals.

In conclusion, the Malaysian recovery measures were formulated after evaluating the domestic circumstances, with the aim of reviving the economy without weakening its fundamentals. These measures were designed to respond to extreme situations and some have labelled them as market-unfriendly. The question is whether these measures have cast doubts over Malaysia's pro-business approach and created fear of policy inconsistency. Malaysia's recovery approach shows there is an alternative way to deal with an economic and financial crisis but it does not run contrary to the overall pragmatism of the Malaysian economic development strategy.

NOTES

1. The South Korean economy was expected to grow by 8 per cent in 1999 while Taiwan, Singapore, and Thailand's growth rate was expected to range between 4 and 5 per cent. Indonesia, which experienced the worst economic recession, is estimated to grow by 1 per cent in 1999.

2. The measure that significantly affects portfolio investors requires all dealings in securities listed on the KLSE to be effected only through the KLSE or through a stock exchange recognized by the Malaysian authority. Consequently, trading of the 112 Malaysian companies on the Central Limit Order Book (CLOB) International, an over-the-counter market in Singapore, was discontinued by the Singapore Stock Exchange.

3. The aim of relaxing the twelve-month holding period is to enable foreign short-term investors to estimate the cost of investing in Malaysia. This easing of capital controls contains two parts:

    (a) For capital that was brought in before 15 February 1999, a levy was imposed on the principal at the following rates:
       • 30 per cent for a maturity period of seven months
       • 20 per cent for a maturity period of nine months
       • 10 per cent for a maturity period of twelve months
       • capital with maturity period of more than twelve months will not have to pay any levy.

    (b) For capital that was brought in after 15 February 1999, a levy was imposed on the profits made at the following rates:
       • 30 per cent for a maturity period of less than twelve months
       • 10 per cent for a maturity period of more than twelve months

4. Previously, only companies that exported all of their output were allowed full foreign ownership but with this relaxation, companies can have 100 per cent foreign equity regardless of the level of products exported.

5. The new revised figures were announced during the retabling of the 2000 Budget on 25 February 2000; see *New Straits Times*, 26 February 2000.

6. Malaysian Institute of Economic Research, "Malaysian Economic Outlook" (2000); Meesook, K.M., "The World Economic Outlook and Implications for Malaysia" (Papers presented at the National Economic Outlook 2000 Conference, the Malaysian Institute of Economic Research, 18–19 January 2000, Kuala Lumpur); and Goldman Sachs, *Asian Economic Quarterly* (Hong Kong), 1999.

7. Market analysts had predicted that NPLs in the Malaysian banking sector could reach 30 per cent because the high level of domestic debt was very sensitive to any interest rate hike. Prior to the crisis, the NPLs of the financial institutions were only 4.9 per cent but they rose to a high of 15 per cent at the height of the crisis. The reduction of interest rates and the formation of Danaharta have reduced the level of NPLs substantially.

8. These three countries had eased their tight fiscal and monetary policies in the second half of 1998 to help their economies recover from the crisis. Due to this policy shift, some analysts considered the recovery measures of these countries as not too different from those of Malaysia's, with the exception of the selective capital controls. However, there were also arguments that the IMF prescription brought along social upheaval, which inflicted substantial pain on the population in the affected countries.

9. The Bank Negara Malaysia only permits Malaysian companies to raise foreign loans if they have a natural foreign exchange hedge, such as foreign income. Consequently, companies have to raise financing in the local market, which resulted in domestic debt of about 160 per cent of the GDP.

10. Malaysia comprises 50 per cent *bumiputera*, 30 per cent Chinese, 10 per cent Indians, and 10 per cent other races. The ruling coalition, which has ruled Ma-

laysia since Independence in 1957, consists of parties representing the major races of the country, with the *bumiputera* party, UMNO, dominating the coalition. As a result of the racial riots in 1969, a New Economic Policy (NEP) was introduced to eradicate poverty and restructure society. The key measure in the NEP was the affirmative action for the *bumiputera*, which targeted a 30 per cent equity owner-ship and employment by the 1990.

11. For a discussion on Malaysian securities and currency offshore markets and their influence on Malaysian monetary policy, see Mahani Z.A., "Implications of the Malaysian Experience on the Future International Financial Arrangement", *ASEAN Economic Bulletin* (Institute of Southeast Asian Studies, Singapore), forthcoming.

12. For example, Blue Circle (a British company) was allowed to purchase a cement company and British Telecom became a strategic partner of a telecommunications company.

MYANMAR

MYANMAR
Political Stasis and a Precarious Economy

Tom Wingfield

By most accounts, 1999 had not been a good year for Myanmar. Politically, the country remained in stasis. The ruling military junta, the State Peace and Development Council (SPDC), had yet to finish drafting a new constitution and continued to rule by decree. Meanwhile, repression of the opposition National League for Democracy (NLD) intensified and there were no indications that the two sides were closer to dialogue. Several international initiatives that aimed to end the stalemate also failed to bear fruit. While the country's politics remained in limbo, the economy deteriorated. The boom of the mid-1990s turned to bust and there were few signs of an imminent upturn. The day-to-day life of the majority of the country's population continued to decline, with the World Bank warning of a "silent emergency" in child malnutrition. The crisis in education and health services continued. Internationally, Myanmar remained isolated and sanctions were renewed by the United States and the European Union (EU). Myanmar's relations with its immediate neighbour, Thailand, also deteriorated.

Political Limbo and the Marginalization of the NLD
It has now been more than a decade since the military took power in a *sui* coup in 1988 following widespread public demonstrations against military rule. Despite the oft-repeated pledge that the junta would transfer power to an elected government once the new constitution is completed, this appears no closer to reality. The body tasked with drafting the new constitution, the National Convention, has not met since it went into recess in 1996. While a timetable for the completion of the new constitution is still unknown, it is clear that the pace of Myanmar's political transition will be dictated by the military. In all likelihood, the constitution will only be completed if, and when, the military is confident that it will win the test of an election. Despite consolidating its power over the past decade, the junta appears to remain deeply uncertain about such a prospect. In an interview with *Asiaweek* in December, the SPDC's intelligence chief, Lieutenant-General Khin Nyunt, warned that

Tom Wingfield is Lecturer in the Department of East Asian Studies, University of Leeds, United Kingdom.

the junta was "still in the process of building democracy" and that it was "better to be safe and sound rather than to be precipitous".

One precondition before elections are held appears to be the elimination of any potential opposition from the NLD led by Nobel laureate Daw Aung San Suu Kyi. In a clear reference to the party, Khin Nyunt commented that the transition to "democracy" would happen "a lot faster if the negative elements inside the country would stop hindering the process by trying to create unrest and by fomenting other conditions that threaten the present stability and sound economic foundation of Myanmar". These allegations, however, illustrate the junta's strategy to pillory the country's civilian opposition. Meanwhile, perhaps in preparation for a future election, the junta has continued building a mass-based political organization, known as the United Solidarity Development Association (USDA). Membership of the USDA had risen to eleven million by early 1999, representing around 40 per cent of the adult population.

The Military: Unity Maintained

Despite anecdotal evidence of a power struggle between the army chief General Maung Aye and Lieutenant-General Khin Nyunt, there were no signs that this led to open conflict in 1999. After the infusion of new blood into the ruling junta in 1997, there were only minor changes in the executive during the year indicating relative stability and unity within the ruling group. In November, Brigadier-General Pyi Sone replaced Major-General Kyaw Than in the key commerce and trade portfolio. He is said to be a member of Khin Nyunt's clique. The sports minister, Major-General Kyaw Than, also retired in October.

The decisive question in the post–Ne Win period (the former leader turned ninety in June 1999) is whether the military can maintain unity within its ranks. Khin Nyunt, a Ne Win protégé, is seen as representing a more pragmatic and less xenophobic face of the military, but may be resented by other more "professional soldiers" who have combat experience. He is also understood to have backed a relatively restrained approach to dealing with the NLD and pushed for the country's membership in the Association of Southeast Asian Nations (ASEAN). The NLD's continued defiance and the growing criticism within ASEAN against Myanmar could compromise his position (see below).

The military's monopoly on power and its assumption of permanency in office may lead to the same complacency that has dogged previous regimes. The junta regularly warns members of the armed forces to "represent the entire mass of the people" and has publicly recognized rising corruption among the rank and file of the army. Such exhortations to virtue rarely work and there is little prospect of the SPDC developing any degree of genuine legitimacy in the eyes of the population following its brutal crushing of the pro-democracy movement in 1988 and the poor state of the economy. Several senior generals were relieved of their posts in 1997 and were widely believed to be guilty of blatant corruption, resulting particularly from opportunities provided by the opening up of the economy.

Containing Dissent

The junta's success in stifling dissent was aptly illustrated in September, when calls for nation-wide demonstrations against military rule were effectively quashed. In August, the All Burma Students' Democratic Front (ABSDF), an exiled opposition group active on the Thai-Myanmar border, called for a general strike on 9 September. The date, referred to as the "four nines" (9/9/99), was chosen because it is numerically auspicious and parallels 8 August 1988 (8/8/88), when demonstrations against military rule were crushed, with the loss of an estimated 3,000 lives. Although the ABSDF predicted that the "four nines movement" would mark "the beginning of a wave of force that would topple the regime", there were few signs that the military's position was under threat.[1] In a pre-emptive strike, the junta vowed to "annihilate" any agitator, and in mid-August it announced that thirty-six people had been arrested in connection with the planned protests. Another twenty were held in the first week of September, according to the NLD, while the U.N. special rapporteur reported that more than one hundred people had been arrested in the three months leading up to September.

Despite these measures, a small protest by around twenty students took place near the Shwedagon Pagoda in Yangon and sporadic hit-and-run protests took place outside the capital. Between thirty and forty people were reported to have taken part in protests at Dagon, Okkalapa, and Pazundung townships. The largest protest was in the city of Meiktila in central Mandalay division, where about 1,000 people reportedly took part in a demonstration.

Bizarrely, two British activists were also arrested in September. James Mawdsley, aged twenty-six, was jailed after illegally entering Myanmar to distribute pro-democracy leaflets. Although he remains in prison, another Briton, Rachel Goldwyn, was released in November after serving less than two months of a seven-year jail term for singing pro-democracy songs in Yangon on 7 September.

Education: The Lost Generation

As a sign of the junta's growing confidence in its ability to stifle opposition, it announced in December that some universities would be reopened. Few details of the decision have emerged, but it was reported that some third and fourth year students at the Yangon Institute of Technology had been told to contact the institute to re-enrol in classes. It appears that the Yangon campus will remain closed and students will attend classes in three satellite towns on Yangon's outskirts where campuses have been relocated. In January, four medical institutes were reopened. The country's thirty-odd universities have remained closed since December 1996 following a series of student protests.

Earlier in the year, 270 Yangon University students were sentenced to fourteen years in prison for staging demonstrations in 1998 in favour of the Committee Representing the People's Parliament (CRPP). One, a student leader, Thet Win Aung, was imprisoned for fifty-three years.

Since universities were closed, about 100,000 students, who were due to take their final exams, were reported to be affected. A further 300,000 to 400,000 students who passed entrance exams in 1996, 1997, 1998, and 1999 have been waiting to enter universities.[2] Once one of Asia's most literate countries, Myanmar also faces a crisis in primary education. According to the United Nations International Children's Fund (UNICEF), it now has one of the lowest levels of primary school attendance in the world, with less than 30 per cent of children completing primary school, compared with around 80 per cent in Vietnam. Government spending on education as a share of national income is also among the world's lowest, with official data showing that real public spending per child has fallen from about 1,200 kyat in 1990/91 to a dismal 100 kyat in 1999/2000.

The Military and the NLD: The Impasse Continues

There was no progress on the issue of initiation of talks between the army leadership and the NLD in 1999. During the year, however, the NLD offered a number of concessions which the junta studiously ignored. In April the party announced that it would be willing to offer a blanket amnesty to army officers involved in the killing of pro-democracy demonstrators in 1988. Two months later it offered to hold low-level talks with the military without the presence of Daw Aung San Suu Kyi as a first step to resolving the political deadlock. In the past the junta had claimed that the question of the Aung San Suu Kyi's participation was blocking negotiations.

Despite these gestures, the junta has reiterated that the NLD must rescind the Committee Representing the People's Parliament (CRPP) — a panel set up to represent a parliament of members elected in 1990 — before any talks could begin. In July, for example, it issued a statement saying it viewed the CRPP with "great concern" and called on the NLD to be "more pragmatic and sensible so that a positive and meaningful interaction can be resumed without interruption again".[3] It has also accused Daw Aung San Suu Kyi of being more intransigent than ever.

The NLD is unlikely to disband the CRPP. Since it was established in September last year, it has been the focal point of its activities. Given the military's monopoly on power and the NLD's inherently weak bargaining position, the party has little room to manoeuvre. With a compliant judiciary, the NLD has little recourse to legal means to prevent the arbitrary detention of its members or to convene parliament. For example, in December the Supreme Court dismissed a complaint by the NLD that the military government was harassing its supporters. In this context, abolishing the CRPP would risk the NLD being forgotten as a political irrelevance and be tantamount to

giving up the 1990 election results. In September, during a meeting to celebrate the committee's anniversary, the party stated that it "would never re-
tract our call to convene a parliament and ... will never dissolve the committee
representing parliament".[4]

Some within the party and outside have been critical of the NLD's stand
on the CRPP, arguing it has widened the gulf between the opposition and
military, thereby lessening the chances of dialogue taking place. In May, a
letter signed by twenty-five NLD deputies was sent to the party leadership,
criticizing the tactic and arguing that the party's confrontational stance had
backfired by encouraging further military repression. In response, the NLD
issued a statement accusing the three main authors of the letter of collusion
with the junta, labelling them "lackeys", and of attempting to sow disunity
within the party. Indeed, all three had earlier been arrested by the junta,
suggesting they may have agreed to write the letter in return for being released.

Since the NLD floated the People's Parliament proposal, the regime has
stepped up its pressure on the party, forcing members to resign and disbanding the party's local offices. This has been effective and it has made it increasingly difficult for the NLD to operate as a political party. According to a
statement made by the U.N. special rapporteur on 4 November to the General
Assembly, "all means appear to be exerted to compel members of the NLD, in
particular to abandon their party or, at least, to abandon political activities".
Daw Aung San Suu Kyi stated in September that the party had "suffered far
more over the last year than over the last seven years".[5] Repression of the party
has included the arrest or resignation of the 392 members of parliament
elected in 1990. Many of the 200 members-elect of parliament detained when
the CRPP was announced last year have been released, but only after agreeing
to resign from the party. Throughout the year, a number of constituency
members gathered to denounce their elected NLD candidates using the formation of the CRPP as the pretext for their change of heart. According to the
state press, some meetings were attended by more than 50,000 people and it
is more than likely that these were organized by the military. In March, Daw
Aung San Suu Kyi conceded that 145 members of her party have been detained by the government and persuaded to resign from the party. She declared the resignations invalid, however, because there is no parliament to
which they can submit their resignation. By mid-November more than forty
elected parliamentarians were still being held, including the Speaker-Designate
Dr Saw Mra Aung. According to a report by the Election Commission in late
May cited by *Xinhua*, a total of 263 NLD deputies have been struck off: ninety-
one had resigned, thirty-one had died, seventy-two had been disqualified, and
108 had been removed due to a "breach of law", a government euphemism for
imprisonment or detention.

The NLD is also being gradually worn down at the local level. In September 1999, the SPDC announced the closure of over fifty NLD party offices and

the resignation of more than 34,000 NLD members. According to the U.N. special rapporteur, in Kachin state alone, NLD membership had fallen from over 4,000 to just about thirty, while a number of NLD working committees throughout the country were "dismantled by the authorities and their offices forcibly shut down".

These actions, combined with the detentions described above, have crippled the NLD's nation-wide organizational capacity. Meanwhile, the junta has continued its campaign to discredit the party's leader. Throughout late 1998 and early 1999, the SPDC organized mass rallies denouncing Daw Aung San Suu Kyi. The state-controlled media accompanied these rallies with virulent personal attacks on Daw Aung San Suu Kyi, which continued unabated throughout the year. In a move condemned by the international community, the junta refused the party leader's husband — British academic, Michael Aris — a visa to enter Myanmar during the last stages of his terminal illness. Daw Aung San Suu Kyi chose not to attend his funeral in England since the military refused to guarantee that she would be allowed back into the country. The junta's behaviour during Dr Aris' illness has evoked international rebuke, including an expression of "dismay" by U.N. Secretary-General Kofi Annan. The opposition leader has remained stoic to the end, saying many people in Myanmar face similarly cruel situations imposed by the military.

Poverty, Malnutrition, and Myanmar's "Silent Emergency"
Despite the junta's aim to create a "modern developed nation", a World Bank draft report leaked to the press concludes that poverty and human development indicators in Myanmar have fallen behind most developing countries.[6] Life expectancy at birth is sixty years compared with an average in East Asia of sixty-eight; infant mortality is seventy-nine per thousand births, compared with the East Asian average of thirty-four; child malnutrition rates are very high and represent a "silent emergency". Data collected by both the Ministry of Health and UNICEF show high levels of moderate and severe malnutrition among preschool-age children. According to a government-determined poverty line, about one-quarter of the population lives below minimal subsistence levels. The highest rates of poverty are in the Chin state, Magway division, and Kayah state. At the same time, the quality of healthcare has deteriorated: public use of hospitals and dispensaries had fallen by 80 per cent over the last ten years, while the junta allocates only 0.2 per cent of its budget to healthcare, far below regional and developing country averages. For example, Cambodia, which has a smaller income per capita than Myanmar, spends three times more on public health as a share of gross domestic product (GDP). The United Nations AIDS (acquired immune deficiency syndrome) programme accused the junta of ignoring a mounting AIDS epidemic in the country, estimating that there are 440,000 human immunodeficiency virus (HIV) positive cases.

The World Bank puts the blame for Myanmar's "silent emergency" squarely on the shoulders of the military junta, arguing its policies have disproportionately hurt the poor and ethnic groups. According to the U.N. special rapporteur, it attributes the problem to

> flawed policies that afflict a twin blow: policy distortions retard the ability of farms and firms to create income-earning opportunities, and poor public finances prevent adequate response to the needs of the diverse population.

Military spending also continues to drain the government budget: defence spending in the 1998/99 budget accounted for 32 per cent of expenditure. On a per capita basis, this is nine times that spent on health and two times that spent on education. The report warns that failure to improve living standards "could have devastating consequences for poverty, human development, and social cohesion in Myanmar".

Prison Visits Lauded, but Forced Labour Condemned

The regime surprised its critics by granting permission to the International Committee of the Red Cross (ICRC) to inspect the country's prisons. In September, the organization stated that it had been granted access to 19,000 inmates and registered over 700 security detainees. It also stated that the junta had agreed to allow ICRC delegates to revisit the prisons on a regular basis. Daw Aung San Suu Kyi criticized the ICRC for not consulting the NLD beforehand and claimed that hundreds of prisoners had been transferred ahead of the inspection.

In a separate development, the International Labour Organization (ILO) ejected Myanmar in June, accusing it of the widespread use of forced labour. It has prohibited any further participation by Myanmar in its activities and banned ILO technical assistance. A report issued by the French parliament in October also concluded that forced labour was used during the construction of a pipeline for the Yadana gas project, led by France's Totalfina (see below). It concluded that Totalfina's continued involvement in Myanmar was damaging to France and hampered progress towards democracy in the country. This raises the possibility that France may, like the United States, call for a freeze on future investment.

Drug Production, Drought, and Border Tension

Myanmar is the world's largest producer of opium, accounting for about 90 per cent of Southeast Asian production and about half of the world's supply. In the wake of widespread international condemnation, the junta has stepped up its counter-narcotics efforts in recent years. Poppy cultivation and opium production fell by 31 per cent and 38 per cent, respectively, in 1999. The U.N. Drug Control Programme (UNDCP) said it believed drought rather than government-led eradication efforts was the main reason for the decline. The junta has pledged to eradicate opium production by the year 2014, but according to a U.S. State Department report issued on 3 November, the government "implicitly tolerates continued involvement in drug trafficking by ethnic insurgents who have signed cease-fire agreements".

Amphetamine production in Myanmar has also strained relations with neighbouring Thailand. According to the U.S. State Department, amphetamine seizures tripled between 1997 and 1998 and also increased in 1999. Nevertheless, in August Thailand closed the border crossing at San Ton Du, which has traditionally been used to ship amphetamines across the border. Earlier, Myanmar had turned down a Thai suggestion that the two countries' anti-drug forces undergo joint training exercises with the U.S. Drug Enforcement Agency and insisted that amphetamines did not come from Myanmar.

External Relations: The Failure of International Mediation
There were several international attempts during the year to end the deadlock between the junta and the NLD. In an unusual break from the past, the EU sent a delegation to Yangon in July to discuss the country's humanitarian needs and examine the political stalemate. There were no breakthroughs, however. Reflecting on the visit, the NLD vice-chairman stated that the delegation "didn't offer anything or come back with new initiatives".[7] Foreign Minister Win Aung also poured cold water over the idea of foreign mediation when he told the international press that Myanmar could solve its own problems. The EU's lack of progress was reflected in its decision to extend sanctions against Myanmar for another six months in October. The Myanmar issue has dogged EU relations with ASEAN since Myanmar joined the regional grouping in 1997. Since 1996 the EU has banned visas for Myanmar officials, effectively preventing ASEAN-EU talks from being held in Europe.

The failed EU initiative was followed in October by the visit of the U.N. special envoy, Alvaro de Soto. Representatives from the World Bank and International Monetary Fund were also included in the delegation. The visit, which had been postponed by the junta twice during the year, involved separate meetings with Khin Nyunt and Daw Aung San Suu Kyi. There were few signs of progress. Shortly after his visit, de Soto was named U.N. Special Representative to Cyprus, suggesting his continued lack of progress and frustration with the political stalemate. A measure of the failure of de Soto's mission came with the announcement that the authorities had arrested the leaders of two ethnic minority parties who took part in talks with him during his October visit. No announcements have been made about de Soto's successor or the future of the Myanmar mission.

The most interesting international initiative came earlier in 1999 from Australia. In June, it proposed setting up an independent human rights institution in Myanmar, similar to a body set up in Indonesia during the Soeharto regime. The proposal was discussed further during the visit to Yangon of Australia's Commissioner for Human Rights, Chris Sidoti, in August. While the junta's initial response to the proposal has been positive, it was resolutely criticized by the NLD. Daw Aung San Suu Kyi was quoted as saying that it was "ironic that anybody imagines that they will be able to cooperate with the junta to improve the human rights situation in Burma", stating that it was "a bit like asking the fox to look after the chickens".[8] Later, in a video message delivered to the Australian parliament, she stepped up her criticism, describing the proposal as "ill-advised". She told the parliament that at a time when the military authorities "are at their most oppressive", the proposal could be mis-construed "as an endorsement of their policies" and "tacit approval of what they are doing to the democratic forces of Burma", which could hurt the opposition "very badly".

Australia has remained steadfast in its defence of the plan, however. In a letter published in the *International Herald Tribune* on 23 August, Australia's Foreign Minister, Alexander Downer, said the time was ripe to "engage the regime in a serious dialogue on the protection and promotion of human rights". Alluding to the sanctions imposed by the United States and the EU, he commented that "simply shouting from the sidelines has apparently achieved nothing". Instead, Australia foresees an "incremental process" with the first objective being to engage the military leadership "in a process of dialogue to better promote and protect human rights". Despite the initial approval from the junta, Downer admitted that it "has yet to make up its mind about how it would work" but he took solace from the fact that the junta "can see the point of such a body".

Towards the end of the year, there were also signs that Japan is seeking a more proactive role in Myanmar. Japanese foreign policy in Myanmar has been low-key since it played a crucial role in negotiating the release of Aung San Suu Kyi from house arrest in 1995. Following Suu Kyi's release, Japan agreed to lift the freeze on humanitarian assistance imposed since the crack-down in 1988.

In November, Keizo Obuchi became the first Japanese premier in fifteen years to meet his Myanmar counterpart when talks were held with General Than Shwe during the ASEAN summit in Manila. Mr Obuchi reportedly told the Myanmar leader that Japan was ready to support the regime if it reformed the economy and undertook dialogue with the opposition. His senior foreign policy adviser and former premier, Ryutaro Hashimoto, followed this up with a four-day unofficial visit to Myanmar. During the visit, Hashimoto reportedly criticized the stance of the United States and Europe. Sanctions, he argued, only served to "drive the Burmese leadership into a corner and make it more and more obstinate".[9] The former premier expressed hope that continued bilateral talks with the country's leaders would eventually lead to changes in the military government.

At about the same time as Mr Hashimoto's visit, a forty-eight-member delegation from the Keidanren business organization was also in Myanmar. This is a further indication that the Japanese government may be considering a plan to release Overseas Development Assistance in exchange for political concessions. The Keidanren is strongly backed by the pro-business ruling Liberal Democratic Party. By the end of the year there were no concrete signs that Japan was considering stepping up aid to Myanmar. As with the resumption of humanitarian aid, it is unlikely it will do so without concrete concessions from the military.

Myanmar and Thailand: Turbulent Relations
The year proved to be a tumultuous one for Thai-Myanmar relations. Bilateral ties, which showed signs of improving earlier in the year with the visit of the Thai Foreign Minister to Yangon in March quickly deteriorated after the Myanmar embassy in Bangkok was stormed by five exiled Myanmar students on 1 October. They demanded the release of all political prisoners, the convening of parliament, and the start of dialogue between the NLD and the military. Diplomats and foreign hostages were held in the embassy at gunpoint for twenty-six hours until Thai officials defused the crisis by trading the eighty-nine hostages for Thailand's Deputy Foreign Minister, Sukhumbhand Paribatra. They were then given safe passage to the Thai-Myanmar border and released, much to the displeasure of Yangon, which openly criticized Thailand's handling of the siege and its failure to arrest the offenders.

Bilateral tension escalated following remarks by the Thai Interior Minister that he did not consider those who seized the embassy to be terrorists, but rather regarded them as "student activists fighting for democracy". The junta responded by closing down the 2,100-kilometre border with Thailand and ordering Thai fishing vessels out of Myanmar waters, stating they would not be reopened until the student exiles were arrested and handed over. In a tit-for-tat gesture, Thailand announced that all illegal Myanmar workers — numbering about 600,000 — would be deported. When the Thai authorities attempted to begin the first deportations, many were reportedly forced back at gunpoint by Myanmar troops stationed on the border. Bangkok also stepped up its efforts to repatriate the more than three thousand exiled student dissidents based in Thailand to third countries.

The crisis in relations was only defused following the visit of the Thai Foreign Minister to Yangon in November. The restoration of cordial relations and reopening of the border may have been dictated more by the economic interests of the two countries than any genuine *rapprochement* and relations remain volatile.

Myanmar and ASEAN: The Loss of an Indonesian Role Model?
Throughout the dispute with Thailand, the ASEAN member countries remained conspicuously silent. The actions of fellow member Indonesia brought little comfort to the Myanmar regime, however. Prior to a visit to Myanmar in November, Indonesia's new president, Abdurrahman Wahid, stated that he sympathized with Daw Aung San Suu Kyi and hoped to meet her during his visit to Yangon. Although, on the advice of the authorities, Abdurrahman did

not in the end meet with the opposition leader, his comments went some way in breaking the ASEAN tradition of non-interference in the politics of member countries. Suggestions from Thailand and the Philippines that the policy of "constructive engagement" be abandoned in favour of "constructive intervention" may be a source of further concern for the junta. In the past, former president Soeharto's military-backed rule of Indonesia had been in some ways an example and a source of comfort for the Myanmar military.

The Economy: Declining Growth, Budget Cuts, and the Foreign Exchange Drought

The economic malaise in the late 1980s was a catalyst to civilian unrest in 1988. Although the economic anomie which helped ignite the protests in 1988 is now absent, Myanmar's economy remains in a perilous state and has clearly been on the decline since the mini-boom of the mid-1990s. The pace of GDP growth has steadily slowed since fiscal year 1994/95, falling to 6.4 per cent in 1996/97 and 5.7 per cent in 1997/98. Perhaps as an indication of the worsening state of the economy, the junta failed to publish economic data for the fiscal year ending 31 March 1999. However, according to statements in the state-controlled press, the rate of GDP growth again declined in 1998/99, falling to a rate of 5.6 per cent — well below the official target of 6.2 per cent. This figure has been greeted with scepticism by many analysts. The Asian Development Bank, for example, estimates growth of only 3 to 4 per cent, while the Economist Intelligence Unit puts the figure slightly higher, at 4.4 per cent. The International Monetary Fund, which estimates the rate at 4 per cent, expects growth to slow to a "grim" 2.5 per cent in the medium term unless there is a "significant policy overhaul".[10] A number of reasons have been attributed for the poor performance of the economy: weak demand; power shortages — due to a cut in hydroelectricity output caused by dry weather — which stymied industrial production; and the combination of adverse weather and shortages of key inputs (such as fertilizer and diesel fuel), which have constrained agricultural output.[11] The construction sector has also suffered in the wake of the collapsing real estate market.

The economic slowdown is clearly having an impact on government spending targets. The 1999/2000 budget announced in March 1999 proposed cutting the deficit by almost two-thirds. Revenue is forecast to rise by 3.1 per cent, helped by the introduction of an 8 per cent levy in March on exchange earnings from most exports. Expenditure, on the other hand, is to be cut by 13.2 per cent. The planned reduction in the deficit may be unrealistic, given that Myanmar has one of the world's worst tax collection rates: the ratio of taxes to GDP, at 3.5 per cent, is very low by international standards. The high defence expenditure is expected to continue.

One piece of good news for junta was that inflation slowed to 20.1 per cent year-on-year in the second quarter of 1999 compared with a year-on-year average of 30.5 per cent in the first quarter. These figures represent a considerable drop on 1998's annual average rate of 51.5 per cent. Nevertheless, the official data is merely indicative: it only covers prices of select goods in Yangon and does not take into account parallel market prices. Fuel prices, for example, were estimated to be 50 per cent higher than the official price in the middle of 1999.

The World Bank's Critical Assessment

A draft World Bank report on Myanmar's economy, excerpts of which were leaked to the *International Herald Tribune* in November, argues that recent economic growth has been accompanied by dangerous macroeconomic imbalances which "do not bode well for Myanmar's economic future". The report warns that a dangerous buildup of debt due to agricultural subsidies could erupt into a systemic banking crisis. In addition, the kyat "faces irresistible downward pressure" and the economy is rapidly becoming "dollarized": more than 20 per cent of bank deposits are now denominated in foreign currency, twice that two years ago. The rationing of foreign exchange, which began during the economic slowdown in 1997, has also created a large degree of protection for state-owned enterprises in their imports and encouraged rent-seeking. Another effect has been to distort relative prices, which has hindered development in the private sector. It also notes that bad economic policies have led to the doubling of deforestation rates since the late 1980s. The report concludes that there is little commitment to economic reform within the junta's high command and that "the capacity to undertake reform does not currently exist".[12] The report, which was prepared with the co-operation of the junta, was immediately dismissed by government officials as "over-exaggerated".

Foreign Investment: The Well Runs Dry

In the last two years, Myanmar has rapidly shifted from an "emerging" to a "submerging" market in the eyes of foreign investors. From a peak of US$2.8 billion in 1996/97, approved foreign investment has dramatically collapsed, falling from US$777.4 million in 1997/98 to only US$29.5 million in 1998/99. This trend continued into the first six months of 1999 with investment contracting by 95 per cent to US$11.8 million compared with the same period in 1998, which was already a bad year. This is despite a series of measures introduced by the junta to encourage investment, including tax breaks for those with projects in the country as well as extending grace periods for delayed projects. Approvals have been hit by the regional financial crisis and sanctions imposed by United States on new investments in April 1997. In April it was announced that twenty-six companies from Southeast Asia had pulled out of Myanmar. Many Thai investors have either left or are putting projects in Myanmar on hold. On a recent trip to Yangon by Singapore's Deputy Prime Minister, Lee Hsien Loong, Singaporean investors complained that foreign exchange restrictions imposed by the junta have penalized foreign investors. In particular, hoteliers have been affected by the ban on "luxury" imports. The ban on the export of rice, groundnut, oil, sesame, and sesame oil has also hit foreign companies, who are required to export Myanmar products before they can import goods. The new tax on private traders' foreign currency receipts introduced in March to retroactive to the 1 January, cut into exporter's margins. The World Bank estimates that only half of approved investments generally come to fruition in Myanmar.

In December the junta overhauled the Myanmar Investment Commission (MIC), which is responsible for encouraging foreign investment. The influential MIC secretary Brigadier-General Maung Maung was replaced by the deputy minister of electric power, another brigadier-general of the same name. Rear Admiral Maung Maung Khin was appointed MIC chairman, while the Minister for Electric Power, Major-General Tin Tut, became vice-chair.

The junta hopes to make up for the shortfall by boosting domestic investment. Tax breaks as well as other benefits granted foreign investors have been extended to local companies. Despite high inflation, which had kept interest rates steeply negative in real terms for the last two years, interest rates were cut in the second quarter of 1999. No explanation was given for the move, but some analysts speculate that it may be due to the government's own need for cheap credit or an attempt to stimulate private investment due to the economic slowdown. Domestic savings in Myanmar are traditionally very low, remaining at only 9.9 per cent of GDP in 1997/98, which has limited the sources of capital for domestic investment. According to the head of the Directorate of Investment and Company Administration, Thin Maung, 22.6 billion kyat (US$3.6 billion at the official exchange rate) in domestic investment was approved in the first ten months of 1998/99. This represents a sharp increase of 53.8 per cent on the 13.8 billion kyat (US$2.3 billion) approved for the whole of 1997/98. However, the rise is minimal if one takes into account inflation, which averaged over 50 per cent in 1998.

Agriculture: Saviour of the Economy?
With the collapse of foreign investment, economic policy has shifted towards self-reliance and boosting agricultural production. In late 1998, the junta announced a new policy to increase output in the rural sector involving a combined strategy of bringing unused land into production and private sector investment to encourage larger, more capital-intensive farming. According to the state-owned press, some 467,370 hectares were reclaimed under the scheme in 1999, compared with an estimated eight million hectares which lie fallow. Priority has been placed on rice production and under the scheme, private-sector companies are permitted to export half of their output after selling the other half to the state at fixed prices. According to the Agriculture Ministry, some seventy-six companies have reclaimed 1.2 million hectares for rice production since December 1998. This may go some way in explaining the sharp rise in rice exports in 1998/99, despite a reported low harvest. Nevertheless, the land reclamation scheme has been sharply criticized by the World Bank.

According to one official, the Bank has "serious questions about the environmental and economic cost of the scheme" and has "suggested that there be a halt until further study and debate can take place".[13]

The Kyat: Hints of a Realignment
In early October, Brigadier-General David Abel suggested to foreign journalists that the official and free-market exchange rates for the kyat might be realigned. He refrained from indicating when the junta might make the adjustment and there have been no further reports on the subject. The announcement came after sharp downwards pressure on the free-market exchange rate in September when the rate fell to 364 kyat : US$1, a depreciation of just over 9 per cent since the start of August, in response to the call for public demonstrations on 9 September. Later in the month, the junta detained black-market currency traders in the capital in an effort to halt the slide in value. The currency strengthened to 356 kyat : US$1 in the first week of October and to 340 kyat : US$1 in the first week of November. The official rate for the kyat remained stable throughout the year at around 6 kyat : US$1.

Balance of Payments: Dwindling Foreign Exchange and Shrinking Reserves
Myanmar's worrying trade statistics continued in fiscal year 1998/99. The trade deficit widened to 9.8 billion kyat in 1998/99 — up nearly 2 billion kyat on the previous year — as import growth outpaced exports. Imports increased by 18.5 per cent in 1998/99 to 16.9 billion kyat, while exports expanded by only 12.6 per cent to 7.1 billion kyat.

Exports of pulses — one of Myanmar's leading sources of foreign exchange — declined in both volume and value terms in 1998/99, and rubber exports also fell sharply. However, rice exports appear to have recovered from their slump of the past two years, rising in value terms by over 500 per cent. Exports of teak also remained buoyant. Import growth was driven by capital goods, rising by 40.6 per cent in 1998/98 over the previous year. Despite restrictions on the import of "luxury" goods, consumer goods imports remained high, expanding by over 30 per cent in the same period.

The widening trade deficit has continued to put pressure on the current account and reserves. By the end of May 1999, total international reserves were US$350.5 million, which the central bank governor admitted was only enough to finance two months' of imports. Myanmar has little access to external capital, major donors having cut off aid after 1988. This together with the collapse in foreign investment has created a balance of payments crisis.

Tourist arrivals also declined, by 14.7 per cent in the first quarter of 1999/ 2000 to 56,772. Although the numbers were up slightly in 1998/99 — 286,882 visitors, representing a rise of 8.2 per cent over the previous year — these were far below official expectations. There is a glut of luxury hotels in Yangon in the wake of the mid-1990s property boom. During the low season, hotel occupancy rates are said to be as low as 15 per cent. The NLD's efforts to discourage tourists to visit the country could have also contributed to the low numbers.

Plans to generate foreign exchange by exporting more gas from the Yadana and Yetagun gas fields are behind schedule. In mid-1999 the Petroleum Authority of Thailand (PTT) renegotiated its contract to buy gas from the Yadana consortium. The consortium comprises Totalfina of France (31.2 per cent), U.S.-based Unocal (28.3 per cent), the PTT (25.5 per cent), and the state-owned Myanmar Oil and Gas Enterprise (15 per cent). The PTT had been originally contracted to buy 65 million cubic feet/day starting in July 1998, rising to over 500 million cubic feet/day by October 1999. However, because of delays in completing a power plant at Ratchaburi on the Thai side of the border, the PTT had been taking only 5 million cubic feet/day and had not paid the first US$62 million tranche owed under the take-or-pay deal. Under the terms of the new agreement, the PTT will pay the Yadana consortium $50.5 million by the end of August. The sum was reduced when the PTT complained about the quality of gas. This may cause some problems for the junta as anecdotal evidence suggests it may have already mortgaged loans based on future oil and gas earnings. Meanwhile, onshore oil production has fallen steadily. According to official figures, output of crude oil by Myanmar Oil and Gas Enterprise fell by 7 per cent to 3.4 million barrels in 1998/99. Myanmar imports about 300,000 tons of crude oil a year as well as around 100,000 to 150,000 tons of diesel.

Conclusion: Power Without Legitimacy

Despite its monopoly on power and complete control over the political transition process, Myanmar's ruling military junta failed to address a number of outstanding political and economic issues in 1999. It continues to rule the country without a constitution, it has stepped up its repression of the opposition, and its policies have exacerbated the country's economic woes. Although none of these directly threaten the SPDC's control over state power, they do undercut its undisputed authority and threaten its credibility. Moreover, key questions surrounding the country's political future remain unresolved.

If, and when, the National Convention finalizes the constitution, it will have little legitimacy in the eyes of the opposition and important sections of the international community. The NLD walked out of the convention in 1995 when it became clear that its proceedings were undemocratic. Genuine political legitimacy — and the resumption of much needed international aid — is unlikely to be forthcoming until dialogue with the opposition takes place. This begs the wider question of what that dialogue would be about. Under another scenario, reconciliation with the opposition may not be required if, as recent developments suggest, the USDA is developed into a mass-based party capable of endorsing a new constitution or backing the SPDC if elections are held. This strategy is unlikely to be successful if the economy remains in its current perilous state, however.

Notes

1. Reuters, 9 September 1999.
2. The figure of 400,000 is given in "Burma Students Gear Up for Campus Reopening", Reuters, 8 December 1999. The U.S. State Department report *Conditions in Burma and US Policy to Burma* (3 November 1999) gives the figure as "more than 300,000".
3. Reuters, 14 July 1999.
4. Associated Press, 16 September 1999.
5. *Asian Age*, 9 September 1999.
6. See *International Herald Tribune*, 15 November 1999; Bradley Babson, senior adviser, World Bank, "Talking Points for Burma Roundtable at Human Rights Watch", 16 December 1999, cited in *Burma Net News*, 21 December 1999, issue 1417; and "Statement by Rajsmoor Lallah, Special Rapporteur on the Situation of Human Rights in Myanmar, 4 November 1999".
7. Reuters, 10 July 1999.
8. Agence France-Presse, 2 September 1999.
9. *Nation*, 5 December 1999.
10. *Wall Street Journal*, 28 December 1999.
11. *EIU Country Reports* (1999).
12. *Time*, 15 November 1999.
13. Bradley Babson, senior adviser, World Bank, "Talking Points for Burma Roundtable at Human Rights Watch", 16 December 1999.

THE FAILURE OF MYANMAR'S AGRICULTURAL POLICIES

Peter G. Warr

Significant economic reform was reportedly a condition for the resumption of international assistance to Myanmar, suspended for several years, but the required reforms have not been forthcoming.[1] Agriculture is central to Myanmar's poor economic performance and to the lack of reform. It represents 43 per cent of gross domestic product (GDP) (Table 1), employs 70 per cent of the population, and accounts for at least that proportion of Myanmar's poor people. But the performance of the agricultural sector has been deteriorating and current policy directions seem unlikely to improve it. This article focuses on the problems of agriculture within the Myanmar economy and the reforms that are required for improved agricultural performance.

Agricultural growth has been declining since 1995 and yields have been static. There are two ways yields could be improved: by cultivating existing farming lands more intensively, or by opening new lands to cultivation. Elsewhere in Asia, the "green revolution" made the first of these approaches possible. It required that new agricultural technologies were available and that farmers had the economic incentives to apply them. In Myanmar, neither condition applies. New technologies have not been adapted to local conditions because domestic agricultural research and extension capabilities are almost non-existent. More important, the prices of agricultural commodities and the markets for the inputs required for agricultural expansion are suppressed to such an extent that farmers lack incentives to expand production.

The government's response to static yields in agriculture has been surprising. Rather than encouraging the more intensive cultivation of existing cropped areas, by addressing the causes of poor performance, the government has instead given high weight to expanding the areas under cultivation by granting large tracts of uncultivated land to "local entrepreneurs" and offering preferential conditions for production on these large farms. It is argued in this article that this approach is economically wasteful and environmentally dangerous and that it threatens to exacerbate the already serious problem of rural poverty. We discuss first the disappointing performance of agriculture in Myanmar, then the policy environment that has brought this about, and finally the reforms that seem most urgently required.

PETER G. WARR is the John Crawford Professor of Agricultural Economics at the Australian National University, Canberra.

TABLE 1

Myanmar: Gross Domestic Product by Ownership
and Sectoral Contribution, 1998/99

Sector	Distribution of GDP by Ownership			Real GDP 1998/99 (million kyat)	Share of GDP (%)	Growth in 1998/99 (%)
	State	Co-operative	Private			
Crops	0.2	1.9	97.9	27,154	34.5	2.5
Livestock and fishery	0.3	1.1	98.6	5,709	7.2	4.3
Forestry	46.2	0.6	53.2	765	1.0	−0.9
Energy	99.9	0.1	—	148	0.2	−3.8
Mining	10.8	1.0	88.2	1,245	1.6	16.8
Manufacturing	28.2	0.9	70.9	7,259	9.2	6.7
Power	99.9	0.1	—	819	1.0	−4.4
Construction	45.8	0.2	54.0	3,868	4.9	6.5
Transportation	29.8	1.0	69.2	3,383	4.3	6.3
Communications	100.0	—	—	1,510	1.9	14.6
Financial institutions	54.8	14.4	30.8	1,614	2.0	16.0
Administrative services	88.8	0.5	10.7	5,362	6.8	6.8
Rental services	3.9	2.9	93.2	3,356	4.3	6.5
Trade	21.3	2.4	76.3	16,583	21.1	5.2
GDP	21.8	1.9	76.3	78,775	100.0	5.0

SOURCE: Planning Department, Ministry of National Planning and Economic Development, Yangon.

PERFORMANCE

Over the decade since the disastrous year of 1988/89, during which real GDP declined by 11 per cent, Myanmar's overall real growth rate recovered briefly in fiscal year 1989/90, declined to 1991/92, recovered again in 1992/93, and has declined since (Figure 1). Agricultural output has mirrored the overall performance of the economy, but its worsening performance since the early 1990s has been the most dramatic (Figure 2). The deteriorating performance of agriculture in recent years is indicated by the growth of real agricultural output per head of the total population. It grew at 4.8 per cent in 1994/95, 3.6 per cent in 1995/96, 1.7 per cent in 1996/97, 1.3 per cent in 1997/98, and 0.6 per cent in 1998/99. At the end of the century, real agricultural output per head of population remains below its level in 1985.

About 25 per cent of Myanmar's total land mass is arable. Roughly half of the arable land, 23 million acres, is cultivated, mostly by farm families holding small plots of land. The average size of a farm holding is around 5.6 acres. About 86 per cent of Myanmar's farms are less than 10 acres in size and they

FIGURE 1
Myanmar: Growth of Real GDP, 1989/90–1998/99

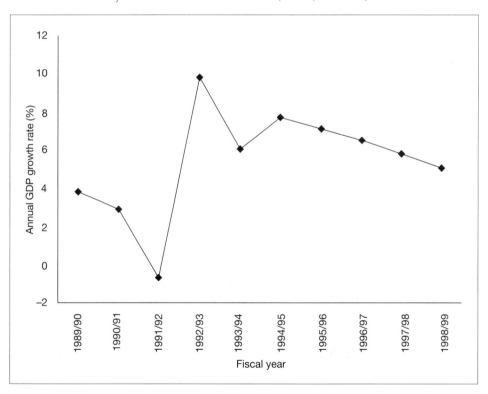

SOURCE: Ministry of Agriculture and Irrigation, Yangon.

FIGURE 2
Myanmar: Sectoral Components of Real GDP Growth, 1989/90 to 1998/99

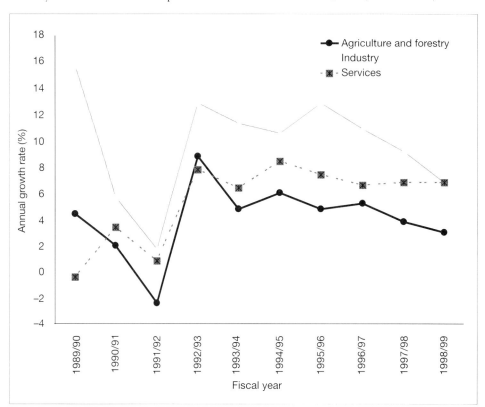

SOURCE: Ministry of Agriculture and Irrigation, Yangon.

account for 58 per cent of the total cultivated area.[2] Farms over 50 acres comprise less than 1 per cent of the total number and they account for only about 3 per cent of total cultivated land (Table 2). Beyond these cultivated lands, a further 20 million arable acres are classified as "cultivable waste land". The government views this land as an abundant resource, available for agricultural exploitation. Much of this land is already under environmental pressure related to population growth, increased fuelwood cutting, land clearing for cultivation, and unofficial logging. As of June 1999, 1.1 million acres had been granted to the private sector for the establishment of large-scale farming and much more is planned. This policy is discussed further below.

Cultivation
Paddy remains the dominant crop, with 14.5 million acres sown in 1998/99, accounting for just under half of total net sown acreage (Table 3). Whereas paddy acreage increased by over a quarter from 1990 to 1995, over the following five-year period the area sown remained static. Pulses have become the

TABLE 2
Myanmar: Distribution of Cultivated Land Holding Sizes, 1997/98

Size of Holding (acres)	Holdings		Area	
	No.	%	Acres	%
<5	2,804,000	62	6,719,400	27
5 and <10	1,139,400	25	8,133,500	32
10 and <20	493,400	11	6,852,200	27
20 and <50	101,000	2	2,783,800	11
50 and <100	1,900	0	121,500	0
≥100	1,100	0	599,200	2
Total	4,540,800	100	25,209,600	100

SOURCE: Ministry of Agriculture and Irrigation, Land Records and Settlement Department, Yangon.

TABLE 3
Myanmar: Sown Area for Major Crops
(Thousands of acres)

	1994/95	1995/96	1996/97	1997/98	1998/99
Paddy	14,637	15,161	14,514	14,289	14,452
Wheat	269	230	225	217	252
Maize	615	412	412	400	457
Pulses	4,313	5,054	4,849	5,167	6,069
Groundnut	1,252	1,302	1,183	1,112	1,168
Sesame	3,285	3,176	2,828	2,556	2,875
Sunflower	492	546	309	296	743
Cotton	504	936	823	659	808
Jute	96	124	116	94	99
Sugarcane	264	331	412	499	583
Myanmar tobacco	69	62	72	84	69
Virginia tobacco	7	10	10	10	12
Rubber	220	259	294	333	368
Others	3,969	4,221	4,364	4,607	4,636
Total	29,993	31,823	30,411	30,324	32,592

SOURCE: Ministry of Agriculture and Irrigation, Yangon.

next most important crop, with 6 million acres under cultivation in 1998/99, representing 22 per cent of total sown area. Similarly, sunflower and cotton acreages increased by 50 to 60 per cent during the period 1990–95. Sesame is the third largest crop in terms of acreage, but an export ban on sesame has severely affected its cultivation. Acreage cultivated declined 13 per cent between 1994/95 and 1998/99. Sugarcane cultivation has more than doubled in acreage since 1994/95 as eight new state-owned sugar mills are being built.

TABLE 4
Myanmar: Output of Major Crops
(Thousands of metric tons)

	1994/95	1995/96	1996/97	1997/98	1998/99
Paddy	18,195	17,953	17,673	16,651	17,848
Wheat	89	78	87	92	92
Maize	284	275	286	308	303
Pulses	1,109	1,337	1,370	1,597	1,678
Groundnut	500	593	559	540	502
Sesame	304	304	344	296	186
Sunflower	117	164	92	90	184
Cotton	86	165	168	164	189
Jute	35	43	39	33	33
Sugarcane	2,375	3,342	4,042	5,136	5,927
Myanmar tobacco	35	41	47	57	46
Virginia tobacco	18	22	23	25	29
Rubber	27	26	26	27	26

SOURCE: Ministry of Agriculture and Irrigation, Yangon.

Output

Rice production achieved its largest gains (22 per cent increase in output) between 1992 and 1994 (Table 4), mostly due to the introduction of summer paddy cropping. Since then, rice output has fallen about 4 per cent from a maximum of 18.2 million metric tons in 1994/95, and later stabilizing at an average annual output of 17.5 million tons. The output of pulses has risen by 50 per cent, from 1.1 million tons in 1994/95 to 1.7 million tons in 1998/99. Sugarcane and cotton output have more than doubled since 1994/95, reflecting the government's new encouragement of these "pillar crops". Sesame production declined, under the ongoing export ban referred to above, to a level 40 per cent below the 1994/95 level.

Yields

Between 1994 and 1999, yields for paddy declined and they continue to stagnate (Table 5). Yields of wheat, pulses, and groundnut showed very slight increases of around 7 per cent. Sesame and sunflower yields showed strong increases of 42 per cent and 20 per cent, respectively, over the period to 1997/98, but a severe drought in 1998/99 caused yields to drop sharply back to their 1994/95 levels. Cotton was the only exception, showing consistent yield increases, adding to over 25 per cent during this five-year period.

Exports

Pulses and beans have become a leading export product, surpassing teak and rice in value of exports. In 1998/99, pulses and beans contributed 18 per cent of total export earnings, followed by teak logs (11 per cent), and rubber and

TABLE 5
Myanmar: Yields of Major Crops
(Kilograms per acre of harvested area)

	1994/95	1995/96	1996/97	1997/98	1998/99
Paddy	1,283	1,205	1,240	1,247	1,251
Wheat	337	347	389	424	367
Maize	689	691	701	249	214
Pulses	265	270	287	316	284
Groundnut	407	466	473	486	438
Sesame	109	136	137	155	112
Sunflower	265	307	307	318	259
Cotton	196	206	228	269	245
Jute	383	370	370	394	363
Sugarcane	18	21	20	20	19
Myanmar tobacco	506	664	658	685	668
Virginia tobacco	2,429	2,227	2,137	2,380	2,350
Rubber	210	215	229	229	214

SOURCE: Ministry of Agriculture and Irrigation, Yangon.

other agricultural products (7.3 per cent). Rice exports have fluctuated widely, from a high of over 1 million tons in 1994/95, contributing 22 per cent of the total value of exports, to a low of 28,000 tons in 1997/98 as a result of crop loss from flooding. In 1998/99, 250,000 tons of rice were exported, which was worth a mere 5 per cent of total exports and 2 per cent of total production.

Poverty
Between April 1996 and January 1997 the United Nations Development Program (UNDP) financed a representative survey of 20,000 households in twenty-three townships across Myanmar.[3] The results of this survey, known as the Human Development Baseline Survey (HDBS), included an estimate that 77 per cent of rural households are directly engaged in agricultural production as their main source of income. Although 70 per cent of Myanmar's poor households are located in rural areas, only 56 per cent of poor rural households are directly engaged in agricultural production. Clearly, rural poverty and farming are not synonymous. The HDBS estimated that 35 per cent of rural households were landless, 40 per cent owned no livestock, and 24 per cent owned neither land nor livestock. Moreover, many households who do own land are poor. Although the minimum size of plot required for reasonable subsistence varies across agro-climatic zones, 5 acres is considered a good guide, given current levels of productivity. The HDBS found that of the 4.7 million households who owned land, over 60 per cent owned less than 5 acres. The 1993 Agricultural Census estimated that 45 per cent of all land-owning households employed workers, and had an average farm size of 8 acres. The 55 per cent of farms which did not employ workers averaged 3.7 acres in size.

For the landless rural poor, off-farm employment and petty trading supplement the seasonal availability of agricultural employment, the latter accounting for just over 60 per cent of their total incomes.

Environment

Myanmar's forests cover around half of the total land area and represent more than half of all closed forest areas in Southeast Asia. Nevertheless, agricultural encroachment, commercial logging and cutting for fuelwood increasingly threaten these forests. According to the World Resources Institute, from 1980 to 1990, East Asia experienced the highest rate of deforestation in the world, at 1.4 per cent per year. Recent data from the Food and Agricultural Organization (FAO) suggest that Myanmar's annual rate of deforestation was exactly the same, at 1.4 per cent, over the period 1990 to 1995, double the rate of 1973–85 estimated in an earlier study.

Wood is the principal fuel source for rural people and cutting for fuelwood is a major source of deforestation. In the Dry Zone especially, supplies of fuelwood are increasingly insufficient to meet demand. UNDP estimates of fuelwood supplies in the Dry Zone for 1995 suggested that the sustainable yield of fuelwood was 4.14 million metric tons per year, with crop residues contributing another 1.48 million tons. These supplies add to just half the annual rate of Dry Zone consumption. The study projected the deficit to increase over time, implying above sustainable pressure on Dry Zone forest resources.[4]

Deforestation has led to soil erosion and subsequent siltation problems in several waterways. For example, deforestation of the catchment areas of Inle Lake has led to siltation of the lake causing the lake bed to rise by between six and eight feet in the last decade. Depletion of mangrove forests in the delta zone is especially problematic. The Forestry Department has estimated that in the three coastal townships of Bogalay, Laputta, and Mawlamyaing, over the period 1985–95, 320,000 acres of mangroves, representing 82 per cent of the total mangrove area, have been destroyed.

In summary, during the second half of the 1990s, Myanmar's agricultural sector has stagnated. By Southeast Asian standards, Myanmar's growth in total agricultural output per head of population has been low since the mid-1980s (Table 6). Paddy yields are also low, especially considering Myanmar's natural advantages as a rice producer. Once the largest exporter of rice in Southeast Asia, Myanmar is no longer a significant participant in the international rice market. With some exceptions, such as pulse and bean production for export, the gains in agricultural performance achieved during the first half of the 1990s have not been sustained. In the case of rice, these earlier gains derived primarily from expansion of the effective area planted through double cropping rather than from increased yields per crop planted. We now turn to the policy environment that has produced these outcomes.

TABLE 6
Average Annual Growth of Agricultural Output
and Paddy Yields, 1974–84 and 1985–96

| | Average Annual Growth Rate of Agricultural Output per Capita | | Paddy Yields (tons/acre) 1994–96 |
	1974–84	1985–96	
Indonesia	2.2	1.6	1.78
Malaysia	1.0	1.3	1.25
Philippines	0.7	0.6	1.00
Thailand	1.8	0.7	0.86
Vietnam	2.8	2.4	1.28
Myanmar	2.8	0.7	1.07

SOURCE: Calculated from the Food and Agricultural Organization, *Production Yearbook* (1985, 1996).

POLICY

Myanmar's socialist agricultural programme operated from 1962 until its demise in 1988. It consisted of taxation and suppression of the agricultural sector by means of compulsory government procurement of agricultural products at a fraction of market prices, severe restrictions on domestic trade, and restrictions on farmers' choice of crops. Government agencies monopolized processing, domestic marketing, and international trade in agricultural products. Private export of agricultural commodities was prohibited. By the early 1980s the official price of paddy, which farmers were paid for rice procured by the government, was less than one-quarter of the unofficial market price. Agricultural output collapsed after 1986, falling by 6 per cent in 1987/88 and by 13 per cent in 1988/89.

In the late 1980s important market reforms were introduced. Controls over domestic trade in rice and other key commodities were abolished and private trading was permitted. Private exports of some commodities, not including rice, was permitted. Production and export of beans and pulses was privatized, resulting in the export boom described above. Farmers were able to make cropping choices relatively freely, except that the government continued to encourage production of the "four pillar crops", rice, beans and pulses, sugar, and cotton. Fertilizer importation was decontrolled and the government ceased to monopolize its distribution. Domestic production of fertilizer remains a public sector monopoly, however, with large, antiquated plants delivering poor-quality supplies at high cost. Fertilizer subsidies have been abolished. These subsidies were intended to encourage fertilizer use by reducing its price to the farmer in an environment where the farm gate prices of rice and other commodities were suppressed. The fertilizer subsidies were thus intended as a form of price compensation.[5] But although the fertilizer subsidies have now been abandoned, the suppression of commodity prices continues. Fertilizer use remains low, not because of unavailability of supplies but because of lack of demand, reflecting output prices.

Agriculture's problems have not been caused by neglect. Official statements continue to emphasize the urgency of raising agricultural output and in the allocation of public capital expenditures, agriculture and agriculture-related expenditures have received high priority. Public capital expenditures in agriculture increased from 0.6 per cent of GDP in 1994/95 to 0.9 per cent by 1998/99. By the latter year agriculture was receiving 13 per cent of total public sector capital spending (not including defence). Large, capital-intensive public works, such as irrigation facilities and rural roads and bridges have been relatively well funded, especially in the rice-growing areas.

The reforms of the late 1980s and early 1990s produced a short-term supply response, with output increasing at an average of 7 per cent per year over the first half of the 1990s. As shown above, these gains were not sustained in the second half of the decade. Government sources emphasize climatic problems as the causes of these outcomes, but the decline in fertilizer use, lack of access to credit, and inflation combined with continued suppression of farm-gate prices of key commodities are more significant factors.

The theme of this discussion is that poor performance of agriculture derives from the inadequate incentive structure facing the farmer. There are two types of taxes implicitly levelled on rice production, both of which reduce incentives for farmers to produce rice. The first is an implicit rice export tax, which arises from the difference between domestic rice prices and f.o.b. export prices. The second is an implicit tax on land used for rice cultivation, which arises from the difference between market prices and the procurement price at which the government's rice trading company compulsorily acquires rice from farmers. These policies are remnants of the earlier socialist programme. Both have the effect of suppressing agricultural output prices, thereby taxing agricultural producers for the benefit of urban consumers and the government itself.

Export Restrictions

Rice

Rice exports are a legal monopoly of Myanmar Agricultural Produce Trading (MAPT), a government-owned enterprise under the control of the Ministry of Commerce. In 1999, Myanmar's rice exports received f.o.b. prices of between US$200 and US$220 per metric ton. These were relatively low average prices, compared with exports from neighbouring countries, such as Thailand, reflecting the generally low quality of rice available for export from Myanmar. To see the degree of taxation of rice exports implicit in the rice export monopoly, it is necessary to compare the above f.o.b. prices with domestic prices of rice of similar quality.

Domestic farm gate prices of export-quality rice currently average around 500 kyat per basket of paddy. Around eighty baskets of paddy produce 1 metric ton of milled rice, so this farm gate price is equivalent to 40,000 kyat per metric ton. The MAPT reports that transport, milling, and handling costs for delivery to the port are equivalent to 4,400 kyat per metric ton, bringing the domestic price, landed at the port and comparable to the f.o.b. prices cited above, of 44,400 kyat per metric ton. At the 1999 market exchange rate of 340 kyat to US$1, this converts to f.o.b. prices of US$130.60 per metric ton. The implicit rate of export tax, using the export price as the base, is thus 35 per cent. At US$210, a farm gate price of 500 kyat implies a rate of export tax of 38 per cent; and at US$220, the implicit tax is 41 per cent.[6]

Other Crops

Government agencies also exert monopoly control over exports of cotton, rubber, jute, and sugar. The individual agencies controlling these exports are each under the auspices of the Ministry of Agriculture. The effect is to depress domestic prices relative to export prices. In several other commodities control over domestic prices is exerted on an intermittent basis by banning exports temporarily. Exports of *gram dal* have been banned for the past four years and oil seed exports, including sesame, groundnuts, and Niger beans are frequently banned without prior notice, sometimes even after shipments have already been loaded.

Government Procurement

The MAPT procures paddy from farmers in quantities that are compulsory for the farmers concerned. The procurement quotas are fixed per acre and reflect land quality. This procurement system is made administratively feasible by the detailed land records maintained by the Land Records and Settlement Department of the Ministry of Agriculture. The rice obtained in this manner is used as the supply delivered to civil servants and other fixed income groups at subsidized prices and is also the stock used for export.[7] In crop year 1998/99, the price at which the procurement took place averaged 320 kyat per basket of paddy. This was the same procurement price used in the previous crop year and will be retained for the following crop year.[8] With inflation at 30 per cent, it is obvious that the real value of the procurement price is declining rapidly and the gap between this price and the market price is widening.

At farm gate prices of 500 kyat per basket, the procurement price is equivalent to a tax of 36 per cent of the market farm gate price.[9] However, since the quantity of rice required to be delivered at these (below market) prices is fixed per unit of paddy land, the system is equivalent to a land tax.[10] Overall, the quantity of paddy procured in this manner (2 million metric tons) is around 10 per cent of the total crop. As a proportion of total production, procurement quotas are close to 20 per cent of output in highly fertile areas and much lower in upland areas.

The effect of this procurement system is to tax land used for rice production relative to land used for other purposes. The system has a perverse effect on the quality of rice available for export and for distribution to civil servants. Because the procurement price is so low, farmers have an obvious incentive to supply their worst rice to the procurement agency, subject to meeting the minimum requirements as to the quantity and quality demanded of them. But because the MAPT is the sole exporter, this rice becomes the stock available for export, with obvious consequences for the prices subsequently received from foreign purchasers.

Credit

Credit is supplied to farmers through the government-owned Myanmar Agricultural Development Bank (MADB), which lends at 17 per cent interest. Since this is well below the 30 per cent current rate of inflation, real interest rates charged to farmers are significantly negative. However, the amounts lent are small. Table 7 summarizes seasonal crop loans for the year 1998. Paddy receives by far the largest share of total loans, but the average loan per acre of 1,235 kyat may be compared with the price of fertilizer of 4,000 to 5,000 kyat per bag (50 kilograms). Recommended fertilizer use is two bags per acre in paddy production and average use is around one bag. But the average loan from the MADB would finance the purchase of around one-fourth to one-third of a bag.

Since loans from the MADB are at substantially negative real interest rates, they must be rationed. The total coverage by the MADB of 5.9 million acres accounts for 40 per cent of all paddy land and the 6.7 million acres of total crop land covered accounts for 24 per cent of total cultivated crop land. Deposits must be held by farmers wishing to receive loans and because negative real interest rates are paid on these deposits, the only reason for holding such deposits is to retain the right to borrow. Capacity to repay loans is taken into account by the MADB in allocating its loans and the effect is that small land holders receive a disproportionately small proportion of total loans.

The problem of credit provision is closely linked to the legal status of agricultural land usage in Myanmar. Legally, the state owns all land and private agents may possess use rights, subject to not leaving the land idle for more than three years, in which case use rights lapse. Land taxes are levied, but these tax rates per acre have been held fixed in nominal terms for several decades and the amounts are now trivial. The problem with these arrangements from the point of view of agricultural performance is the legal status of the land use rights. Legally, land cannot be freely sold, but active markets in land do exist. Use rights for land cannot be used as legal collateral for loans from formal banks. Since land is the major non-human asset of most poor rural households, the inability to mortgage land presents a major problem for financing agricultural production activities.

Because the amounts lent by the MADB are so small, even farmers receiv-

TABLE 7
Myanmar: Seasonal Loans, Myanmar Agricultural Development Bank, 1998

| Crop | Maximum Loan (kyat/acre) | Loan Disbursement | | Average Loan (kyat/acre) | % of Total Disbursement |
		Thousand Acres	Million Kyat		
Paddy	4,000 to 5,000	5,883	7,202.4	1,235	84.4
Groundnut	2,000	135	250.3	1,854	2.7
Sesame	1,500	265	371.9	1,019	4.5
Beans	3,000	322	286.4	889	3.4
Soybeans	1,000	2.9	2.9	1,000	0.1
Cotton	2,500	175	418.2	2,389	4.9
Total		6,734	8,532.2		100

SOURCE: Myanmar Agricultural Development Bank, Yangon.

ing MADB loans are normally compelled to borrow from informal money lenders. There interest rates are 10 to 15 per cent per month for farmers without legal collateral and 5 to 8 per cent with collateral. Lacking legal collateral, poorer farmers tend to be, on the one hand, ineligible for even the small amounts of formal (MADB) credit that are available and, on the other, are required to pay a heavy risk premium to informal money lenders as well. Over a six-month crop season, the informal interest rate without collateral means that the cost of inputs which must be financed by loans, such as fertilizer and seeds, is roughly doubled. A single year of crop failure or family illness is therefore frequently sufficient to generate such problems of indebtedness as to compel small farmers to abandon their land. Paradoxically, the inability of small farmers to mortgage land legally is a significant cause of rural landlessness.

Land Reclamation Schemes
The government has decided to develop large tracts of land, to be farmed by private, national entrepreneurs. Of the land area of Myanmar, a total of 45 million acres are considered potentially cultivable. Of these, 23 million acres are presently cultivated, leaving a further 22 million acres of currently "vacant" land. A high proportion of this land is considered potentially eligible for the reclamation programme, which began in late 1998. The land concerned includes wetlands, coastal land, and dry zone land not presently under cultivation. To date, around 1.1 million acres have been allocated to around eighty-two business groups. Its distribution is summarized in Table 8. The average size of these holdings is thus 13,400 acres, but aside from a few very large holdings, the largest of which is 72,000 acres, most are around 3,000 to 5,000 acres. The objective of the project is to expand agricultural production, both for domestic consumption and for export.

The government of Myanmar provides assistance for these projects in the following ways.

- The land itself is made available in a thirty-year lease, provided free of charge, under the condition that the land be developed for agricultural production within three years.
- The public works required for flood control, drainage, and irrigation are provided to the project area free of charge.
- Government agencies assist in supplying the heavy earth moving machinery used to create the level fields to be used for paddy production. They do this under contract with the developer, but at subsidized rates.
- The government assists in providing technical assistance in developing the project, free of charge.
- Local private banks are encouraged to provide loans to the projects on a preferential basis.
- Fuel required for project construction and land preparation is provided

TABLE 8
Myanmar: Land Reclamation Scheme, June 1999
(acres)

State/Division	Total Area Leased	Total Area Developed
Ayeyarwaddy division	246,366	65,456
Yangon division	58,368	22,134
Bago division	101,890	6,835
Total of delta region	*406,624*	*94,425*
Magwe division	233,037	3,625
Total of dry region	*233,037*	*3,625*
Tanintharyi division	464,744	415
Total of coastal region	*464,744*	*415*
Shan state	21,675	15,017
Kachin state	33,036	1,409
Kayin state	1,000	400
Total of upland region	*55,711*	*16,826*
Union total	*1,160,116*	*115,291*

SOURCE: Ministry of Agriculture and Irrigation, Yangon.

at the government price of 160 kyat per gallon, compared with the current market rate of 320 kyat per gallon.

- Project investors may export 50 per cent of the rice they produce and are exempted from the rice procurement system operated by the government agency, the Myanmar Agricultural Produce Trading (MAPT).
- Preferential provision of telephone services, including cellular phones and land-based phone lines.
- Provision of security services to protect project staff and equipment, free of charge.
- Permission to import equipment, including water pumps, tractors, bulldozers, excavators, duty-free and without limit, and without the need to demonstrate foreign exchange earnings through approved channels, which applies to other importers.

An Appendix to this article describes one such large reclamation scheme, which involves draining a wetlands area for intensive irrigated production. Large-scale capital works are required for drainage, flood control, and irrigation for the project. It is argued in the Appendix that in purely economic terms the social costs of the project exceed its social value in that the combined social opportunity cost of the publicly supplied or subsidized inputs used by the project exceeds the value of the reclaimed land "produced", even if it is assumed that the land would have had zero social value in the absence of the project. In addition, the social implications of the project are potentially significant. Local communities lose access to the wetlands being drained. In place of these wetlands, very large, capital-intensive agricultural enterprises are created which are more typical of Latin America than Asia. The long-term social and environmental consequences of these developments could be even more costly than the purely economic considerations summarized above.

Land reclamation schemes are also under way in upland and coastal areas. The business groups given access to the land are required to "develop" the sites within three years as a condition for the grant of the land. In the case of upland areas this means clearing the entire area and establishing crop culti-vation on at least part of it within this period. The potential for avoidable but permanent ecological damage caused by this haste is obvious, not least the danger of land degradation in fragile upland areas. There is also the potential for enduring social conflict between the local groups now denied access to these lands and the business groups being established on large agricultural estates.

REFORM

It is one thing to criticize policy, another to suggest workable reforms. Drawing upon the above discussion and lessons from elsewhere in Southeast Asia, this section summarizes policy suggestions that, in the author's judgement, could contribute to more rapid and equitable growth in Myanmar. The details are intended to be indicative only. Liberalization of rice exports is central, but to have its most beneficial effect this liberalization needs to be accompanied by protection of vulnerable consumer groups on the demand side, and comple-mentary measures on the supply side which will enhance the production re-sponse resulting from the improvement of farmer incentives.[11]

Rice Export Liberalization

If the prohibition on private sector exports of rice were removed, the domestic price of export quality grades of rice would increase by around 35 per cent and the prices of non-export grades of rice would increase also, but by a smaller proportion, and with a delay. Export earnings would increase, along with farm incomes. Farmers could be expected to respond to the increased prices by increasing their production through greater use of fertilizer and more intensive cultivation. In addition to the overall increase in rice supply, there would also be a quality shift. High-quality grades of rice receive substan-tially higher export prices and under a competitive market environment these price differentials would be transmitted to the farm gate level. The increased price differential between different grades of rice thus give farmers a price incentive to shift production towards higher-value grades of rice, compared with the present situation.

The prohibition of private sector rice exports should be eliminated, but phased over, say, five years. Private sector exports should start with only the highest-quality grades of rice and be extended gradually, and on a pre-announced schedule, to lower-quality grades of rice because of the social necessity of protecting vulnerable low-income groups. Since poorer groups consume lower-quality grades of rice, the phased liberalization provides time for the administrative machinery of the government to prepare the mitigating mechanisms which will shield these groups from the price increases which will reach them.

Similar effects to the above would also be experienced for non-rice exports such as jute, cotton, and sugar. The liberalization of exports of these commodities is also appropriate and should be conducted in a pre-announced phased manner, beginning with the highest export quality grades. For agricultural exports not presently controlled by the government, the problem is that prohibitions on exports are common and unpredictable. Costs of doing business would be reduced if exporting firms operated under a more predicable policy environment and this would mean higher farm gate prices and thus higher incomes for rural people.

A Rice Consumption Subsidy for Low-Quality Grades of Rice

Liberalization of rice exports would mean increased prices for consumers. Particularly for low-income groups other that rice producers, this would present a significant problem. The price of the lower-quality grades of rice consumed by these groups could increase by as much as 25 per cent. In the absence of corrective measures, rates of poverty incidence could rise. To alleviate these effects, it is recommended that consumption of lower-quality grades of rice be subsidized. These subsidies should apply only to the lowest-quality grades of rice, which are consumed only by low-income groups, to ensure that the effect of the subsidy is automatically targeted to these groups. The grades of rice which would qualify for this subsidy might be the lowest-quality 20 per cent of rice consumed. The rate of subsidy required would be around 25 per cent. Introduction of the subsidy would need to occur within a year of the export liberalization.

Abolition of Compulsory Rice Procurement, Introduction of Land Tax

The present rice procurement system provides the rice used for export and for civil service distribution, but since it is acquired compulsorily at substantially less than market prices, it gives farmers an incentive to supply their lowest-quality rice. This rice then becomes the stock available for export. This system could be replaced with direct purchase of rice by the MAPT at market prices at the wholesale level, combined with an explicit land tax system levied in cash, rather than kind, as at present. The rate of tax per acre would depend on the quality of land (as is the case with the present procurement quotas) and could be progressive with respect to farm size. That is, the rate of tax per acre could be lower for small-sized farms than for larger farms.

The advantage of this proposed system is that by market-based purchasing of the rice it wishes to deliver to civil servants and others, the MAPT would be able to control the quality of rice it receives. Procurement would be substantially more efficient because the MAPT would not be required to procure small quantities of rice from large numbers of farmers, the latter understandably reluctant to deliver. The collection of the land tax would similarly be more efficient if conducted in cash than in kind and would not need to be confined to rice land. Finally, the perverse effect on the quality of rice available for export which arises under the present compulsory procurement system would be eliminated.

Legal Mechanism for Mortgage, Sale, and Transfer of Land-Use Rights

If farmers could use their land-use rights as loan collateral, the provision of credit could be greatly enhanced and credit costs to farmers could be significantly reduced, thereby improving the profitability (and incomes) of many small farms. The current, informal land rights market could be made more transparent and secure, by establishing a legal mechanism for private mortgage, sale, and transfer of land-use rights. It should be noted that most countries which pursue land reforms must first establish land registration and titling. Myanmar has an advantage in that much of this necessary work is already in place, through the work of the Land Records and Settlement Department.

Suspension of Land Reclamation Scheme

The present land reclamation scheme is unnecessarily costly. It is financially attractive to the business groups participating in it because of provision by the public sector of inputs priced below their social opportunity costs, including the land itself. Moreover, the scheme is likely to have unfavourable and significant social and environmental effects. The additional food supplies this scheme may deliver would be more efficiently obtained by improving productivity on land already in intensive cultivation. As described above, this requires improving the price incentives facing farmers and improving the supply of crucial inputs.

APPENDIX
Myanmar Billion Group (MBG)

This project, being developed by a group of local Myanmar entrepreneurs, covers a total of 72,000 acres, divided into two parts, one of 40,000 and the other 32,000 acres. The MBG believes it can develop the entire 72,000 acres within three years. The area is low-lying wetlands and during the monsoon season the land is submerged under more than 10 feet of water. The project involves draining the wetlands, building bunds and dikes to prevent inflow of water during the monsoon, levelling the fields for paddy production and installing irrigation facilities for dry season production.

One paddy crop of 1,729 acres was harvested in early 1999 and a similar-sized crop is planned for the current year. Highly mechanized methods of cultivation are in use, including large, heavy-duty tractors for cultivation, mechanical rice planters and weeders, and mechanical rice harvesters. Because the drained soil is highly fertile, with high organic matter content, low levels of fertilizer input are sufficient to obtain high yields.

The private costs of the development, incurred by the MBG, included:

- Cleaning and establishing bunds, 10,000 kyat per acre, paid to Agricultural Mechanization Department of the Ministry of Agriculture and Irrigation, which arranged the work.
- Further earth-moving work conducted by the MBG itself, including land levelling, consolidation, and establishment of irrigation system, 70,000 kyat per acre.

The social costs of this work, evaluated at market prices, exceed these costs because the inputs used in the construction work were priced below market prices. For example, the earth moving work uses large quantities of diesel fuel, which is provided to the Agricultural Mechanization Department and the MBG project itself at prices below the market value of the diesel. The bund establishment above used 80,000 gallons of diesel for a 6,000 acre site, which implies that the social cost of the diesel fuel alone exceeded the private cost by 2,133 kyat per acre. Applying a similar calculation to the second item of cost above (incurred directly by the MBG) suggests an additional divergence between social and private costs of around 15,000 kyat per acre, a total of 17,200 kyat per acre, raising the social cost of the land development at the site itself to no less than 97,200 kyat per acre. It should be emphasized that these calculations make no allowance for divergence between the accounting cost of machinery supplied to the government and its social opportunity cost, allowance for which would raise further the divergence between social and private costs.

In addition to these costs incurred at the site itself, the government, through the Ministry of Construction, provides irrigation and drainage facilities to the project through the development of the Nyaundone Island area. The public investment in this development has to date been 645 million kyat, with an output of 90,000 acres of cultivable land, including the MBG site described above. The cost per acre is thus 7,200 kyat, of which 30 per cent are again fuel costs, implying a market equivalent social cost of not less than 9,300 kyat, again making no allowance for divergence between the accounting cost of machinery supplied to the government and its social opportunity cost, allowance for which would raise further the divergence between social and private costs.

The above calculations imply that the aggregate social cost of developing the land for agricultural use is not less than 106,400 kyat per acre, considering only the sources of social cost mentioned above and disregarding public provision of technical support, security, improved roads, and so forth. We now turn to the value of the project.

Suppose, initially, that in the absence of the project the social value of the land under development would have been zero. Under this assumption, the project creates usable agricultural land from an area which would have otherwise have been wasteland. Land of a quality similar to that developed by the project has a market value of 100,000 kyat if directly adjacent to the sealed road. Land further distant from the road has a market value of 50,000 to 70,000 kyat per acre depending on the distance. The agricultural land established by the MBG project includes areas close to and distant from the sealed road. The mean market value of this land would be thus no more than 85,000 kyat per acre.

That is, the project "creates" agricultural land worth, say, 85,000 kyat per acre at a social cost of at least 106,400 kyat per acre. The project is privately profitable because of the special privileges extended to the project, but without these privileges the project could not be viable. It should be recalled that the above calculations assume that in the absence of the project the land would have no value. This is clearly not the case. Allowance for the social value of the wetlands drained by the project, and therefore lost to Myanmar because of it, in terms of fishing amenities to the local population, wildlife habitat, hydrological value in terms of water course movement and other ecological values, will increase the social cost of the project further, reinforcing the above conclusions.

NOTES

1. *The Economist*, 12 February 2000, p. 14.
2. Government of Myanmar, *1993 Myanmar Census of Agriculture* (Yangon: Ministry of Agriculture and Irrigation, 1994).
3. P. Shaffer, "Studies in Social Deprivation in Myanmar" (Report prepared for the United Nations Development Program [UNDP] and the United Nations Department for Economic and Social Affairs [UNDESA]), MYA/98/004, April 1999.
4. C.J. Johnson, "Planting, Conservation and Conversion: Multiple Strategies to Sustain Myanmar's Environment" (Report prepared for the UNDP), February 1995.
5. S. Larkin, and U San Thein, "Myanmar Research: Agriculture Sector" (Paper prepared for Irrawaddy Advisors Ltd.), February 1999.
6. Farm gate prices as high as 600 kyat per basket have been reported in some areas. When the above calculations are repeated, the equivalent price at the port is US$154. Prices at the f.o.b. level of US$200, US$210, and US$220 imply rates of export tax equivalent of 24, 27, and 30 per cent, respectively.
7. Approximate disbursement of the 1.2 million metric tons of milled rice equivalent (2 million tons of paddy) procured in 1998/99 was: subsidized distribution, 0.7 million tons; export, 0.1 million tons; addition to stocks, 0.2 million tons; and commercial domestic sales, 0.2 million tons.
8. Performing the above calculation for delivery to the port, this rice costs the MAPT around US$88 delivered at the port. At f.o.b. US$200, the implicit rate of export tax on this rice is 56 per cent.
9. At a farm gate price of 600 kyat, the implicit tax is 47 per cent.
10. For example, for farmers required to deliver twelve baskets per acre, the equivalent tax is 2,160 kyat per acre, assuming a market price of 500 kyat and at a market price of 600 kyat the equivalent tax is 3,360 kyat per acre.
11. See also D. Taylor, "Investing for Growth and Equity: Evaluation and Selection of Rural Projects" (Report prepared for the UNDP), September 1995; and "Agricultural Mechanization in Myanmar: Policy Choices Affecting Poverty Alleviation and Rural Growth" (Report prepared for the UNDP), May 1996.

THE PHILIPPINES

THE PHILIPPINES
Governance Issues Come to the Fore

Miriam Coronel Ferrer

All three Philippine presidents following Ferdinand Marcos have their respective claims to fame. Corazon Aquino is credited for the restoration of formal democratic institutions and rights. Fidel Ramos's term from 1992 to 1998 saw the real economic growth rate reaching to its highest levels in over fifteen years at 6 per cent and market reforms put on track. Joseph "Erap" Ejercito Estrada, on the other hand, vowed to help the poor ride the wave of economic development through what has been described as an ambitious synthesis of pro-poor and pro-market polices. This promise of social and economic reforms and individual charisma catapulted him to an overwhelming electoral victory in May 1998 and gave him tremendous confidence in his stature as head of state.

As year 1999 drew to a close, however, national newspapers feasted on the reported dip in the Philippine President's popularity. The growing disaffection stemmed from the spate of corruption and cronyism scandals that struck the administration, and from President Estrada's drive to initiate a constitutional change amid other pressing concerns. Multiple hikes in oil prices and the slow delivery of pro-poor programmes further dampened enthusiasm for the populist president. Two big rallies in Metro Manila and other cities in August and September 1999, attended by former President Corazon Aquino and Manila Archbishop Cardinal Jaime Sin, signalled the downslide. The year also saw an upsurge in rebel activity in the country.

Disappointment over the poor national leadership overshadowed the relative success in stabilizing the economy, the judicial reforms that have been introduced by Hilarion Davide, the new chief justice of the Supreme Court, and the decline in cases of kidnapping of rich ethnic Chinese as a result of the tough anti-crime policy of Estrada's controversial Philippine National Police chief Panfilo "Ping" Lacson.

The Philippine economy inched slowly towards some measure of recovery from the 1997 financial crisis. Inflation fell from 10 per cent in January to 3.9 per cent by November 1999, and the peso/dollar exchange rate was stable at

Miriam Coronel Ferrer teaches at the Department of Political Science and is Director of the Third World Studies Center, University of the Philippines.

roughly 40 pesos (P) to 1 U.S. dollar. Gross national product (GNP) grew from
0.1 per cent in July 1998 to 3.8 per cent in July 1999, while the gross domestic
product (GDP) rose from 0.5 per cent to around 3 per cent by the end of
1999. Agriculture contributed the bulk of GDP growth from a previous low
share because of the prolonged drought in 1998.

The Ramos administration's economic liberalization thrust was continued
and foreign relations were primarily geared towards attracting investments. In
September, President Estrada travelled to New Zealand for the Asia-Pacific
Economic Co-operation (APEC) Summit and proceeded to Latin America for
a series of state visits dubbed as an "economic diplomacy mission".

The bruised relationship with the United States since the non-renewal of
the U.S. lease on Philippine military bases in 1991 was salved in May when
Estrada signed the Visiting Forces Agreement (VFA) with the concurrence of
the Senate. The VFA provides the legal framework for the conduct of joint
U.S.-Philippine military training exercises in the Philippines.

Disputes with China over the Spratly Islands claimed by the Philippines
posed the toughest diplomatic challenge to the foreign affairs and defence
departments in 1999, following several alleged provocations on both sides. By
and large, the Philippines has not played any significant role in directing
regional affairs apart from hosting the ASEAN informal summit in November
and deploying a significant number of troops and medical workers to the
International Force in East Timor (INTERFET). A Filipino general was subsequently appointed to head the peacekeeping forces of the United Nations
Transitional Authority in East Timor (UNTAET).

In all, the year saw governance issues emerging as the paramount concern
of the populace. To a growing number, the government had not met the three
fundamentals of good governance — accountability, transparency, and efficiency. What they saw was a government in disarray and unable to deliver the
goods.

Poor Governance

One-third of the way through the six-year presidential term, the cabinet remained fractious and burdened by overlapping appointments and the absence
of a coherent programme. Failure to uphold a high standard of integrity
among members of the administration had also contributed to its poor rating
in popularity. The Social Weather Station series of surveys revealed an abrupt
downward slide in Estrada's approval rating: from a high 65 per cent in June
to 28 per cent in October 1999 and, finally to a low positive 5 per cent in
December.

Estrada's management style is a poor contrast to his predecessor's rigour
in mobilizing government instrumentalities and monitoring the progress in
the programmes of his cabinet. It is generally believed that Estrada meets
more often with his friends whom he has appointed to various advisory posts
than with his professional managers. A list made by the *Philippine Daily Inquirer*

identified twenty presidential consultants, twenty-two presidential advisers, and twenty-eight presidential assistants, or a total of seventy, in November 1999.[1] Their individual assignments may be as specific as computer education, overseas Chinese investors, and the disadvantaged, or as broad as "Foreign Affairs and Poverty Alleviation" and "Special Concerns". The presidential spokesperson admitted that this coterie of advisers and consultants dish out advice but are not accountable for the consequences.

The overlap in missions among the advisers and with the various government agencies has inevitably led to squabbles over turf, prerogatives, and policies. Stabilizing the economy did not come without the conflicts in perspectives among the economic managers. The finance secretary and the Central Bank governor clashed publicly over interest rates, with the former (supported by the National Treasurer) preferring low rates. Estrada himself has not interfered much in managing the economy, much less provided a coherent framework. With nobody really in charge, his budget, finance, economic development, and treasury lieutenants negotiated policy matters among themselves. But such a diffused centre has not been able to hold nor move things fast enough for the long haul.

The President has on several occasions changed his position on policy issues. In November he announced a cabinet revamp, denied it, then affirmed it again. New Year's eve passed with the revamp still to take place. Overlapping appointments and Executive Orders have been issued on several occasions. For example, the Northern Luzon Growth Commission was created in June and the Central East Asia Growth Circle programme in September. Both Acts put three regions in Northern Luzon under two different bodies with almost similar functions. To address Muslim Filipinos' concerns, an administrative order[2] created a development council covering three Mindanao provinces, areas already covered under the Southern Philippines Council for Peace and Development and falling under the mandate of other existing bodies and processes. The creation of the Presidential Commission on Mass Housing in October also duplicates the functions already given to the Housing and Urban Development Coordinating Council under the Philippine Medium Term Development Plan for Shelter approved by Estrada in June. These developments have raised questions about the President's leadership and suspicion over the personal agenda of the various people surrounding him.

Scandals involving cabinet secretaries have further distracted from the main function of governance. Local government chief Ricardo Puno is facing charges of corruption for the supply of radio parts by a firm owned by his brother to a government agency. Environment and Natural Resources Secretary Antonio Cerilles, who was a key Estrada campaigner in Mindanao, has been criticized for his numerous appointments of hometown friends and relatives whose qualifications are far from suitable for the job.

The President has not been spared embarrassment. With his blessing, fifty-two luxury cars impounded by the Bureau of Customs were given out to favoured government officials and legislators. Rather than being auctioned off, smuggled boxes of used clothing and canned sardines seized by the Bureau were diverted to the Palace for distribution in one of its civic action programmes. Following public uproar, the "hot cars" were eventually returned and scheduled for auction as required by the Tariff and Customs Code.

The President's choice of Philippine National Police chief was contentious. The police chief is known for his liberal use of heavy-handed methods, including wire-tapping and summary executions in past cases. Estrada's presidential adviser on Latin American affairs until his dismissal in July 1999, Mark Jimenez, is facing extradition charges from the United States for alleged crimes such as tax evasion and illegal campaign donations. These shadowy men constitute one flank of the Estrada administration, which includes former Marcos cronies, former high-school classmates, his election campaigners, and on a smaller scale, university economics and public administration professors, and a segment of the non-governmental organization (NGO) community who believed that the president's populism could be a takeoff point for social change.

Weak Executive-Legislative Team Up

Even though the ruling party was able to gain a majority in the House of Representatives, largely through post-election defections, and hold the post of Speaker, the Executive has not been very successful in pushing for legislative reforms needed for economic restructuring. This has been blamed on an apparent lack of appreciation on the part of the President of the role of the legislature in the reform process.[3] The weak leadership in the House of Representatives under House Speaker Manuel Villar, a defector to Estrada's Laban ng Masang Pilipino (LAMP) party, compounded the problem for the Executive. In contrast, the Ramos administration had forged a tight relationship with Congress through his LAKAS-NUCD partymates led by former House Speaker and unsuccessful presidential candidate Jose de Venecia.

Only nine laws of significance had been enacted as of November 1999, and one on economic reform was passed in December amid opposition from nationalist sectors. This is the retail trade liberalization law which allows foreigners to own and operate retail stores in the country with a capitalization of at least P100 million. Bills on the overhaul of the tax system, strengthening the supervision of the stock market and banks, and the controversial privatization of the power sector remain pending. Even the Bill for the year 2000 national budget failed to pass through the Senate in time for the new fiscal year.

Moreover, the Executive had not effectively lobbied budget appropriations for its pro-poor programmes. In the House-approved budget for 2000, no funds were allocated for its centrepiece anti-poverty programme and the budget of the National Anti-Poverty Commission itself was slashed by 50 per cent. Earlier, the 1999 funds of the Department of Agrarian Reform (DAR) for land acquisition were cut. Indications are the year 2000 budget will give less than half of its proposed P1.2 billion to the agrarian reform fund. The Comprehensive Agrarian Reform Program (CARP) is now in its last budgeted phase of distributing big private landholdings where stiff resistance has been put up by landowners. Lack of funds will further curtail the administration's ability to acquire large landholdings for distribution.

Cronyism Resurrected

The word "cronyism", popularized by critics of the Marcos regime, has witnessed a revival under the new administration. A survey of top executives of Makati Business Club in July 1999 showed their growing worries about this type of influence peddling. Other foreign and local business groups have subsequently expressed the same concern.

Several prominent presidential friends, a good number of them the so-called taipans or very rich ethnic Chinese businessmen, have been using their close ties with the presidency for access to business ventures. They include plastics tycoon and Presidential Adviser for the Welfare of Overseas Filipino Workers William Gatchalian, who is owner of Wellex Industries and Waterfront Philippines.[4] Gatchalian is reportedly interested in procuring some of the assets of the soon-to-be privatized National Power Corporation. Another presidential friend, Eusebio Tanco, was reportedly interested in buying the Tiwi Mak-Ban geothermal plant for a bargain price of US$201 million. The National Power Corporation has placed the plant's book value at US$600 million.

Businessman-friend Dante Tan got the exclusive government franchise to run an online bingo business in the country. Estrada defended the support given to the online bingo franchise, saying that earnings from this gambling activity will go to his anti-poverty programme. In November the Philippine Stock Exchange began a short-lived investigation of Dante Tan and certain stockbrokers for the alleged rigging of trading transactions of Tan's BW Resources. Also an investor in BW Resources is Stanley Ho, a gambling magnate from Macau whom Estrada feted during his visit to the country. Ho was enticed to transfer his gambling business in Macau to the Philippines after the former Portuguese colony reverted to China in December.

With government assistance, tobacco and airline magnate Lucio Tan succeeded in suspending for ten years the collective bargaining agreement with the trade union of Philippine Airlines (PAL). To help PAL further, the government cancelled or limited the landing rights of some Asian airlines plying lucrative routes such as Taiwan and Hong Kong, effectively compromising the former administration's "open skies policy". Despite his financial woes, Tan has been buying government shares in the Philippine National Bank through his commercial bank, the Allied Banking Corporation. He was also reported to have taken over Air Philippines, a competitor domestic airline, and by June 1999 was able to raise the US$200 million fresh capital to rehabilitate the PAL.

Some of Estrada's appointments have also raised eyebrows because of apparent conflict of interests. For example, Presidential Adviser for Iron and Steel Johnny Ng is part-owner of Cathay Pacific Steel. Ng, along with Lucio

Tan who is his relative, was reported to be interested in the purchase of the bankrupt National Steel Corporation. The family of Estrada's adviser on computer education and the chair of the Presidential Commission on Y2K Compliance, businessman Amable R. Aguiluz V, is owner of a computer college. The Aguiluz family reportedly set up a subsidiary outfit in their group of companies which sold to private and public agencies computer cards designed to deal with the Y2K problem. Estrada's ex-adviser on mass housing, Jose Luis Yulo, is in the real estate business. Both Aguiluz and Yulo were eventually forced to resign.

The President, for his part, accused the media of negative reporting on his administration. Estrada filed a P100 million libel suit against *Manila Times* for a photo caption stating that he was an "unwitting godfather" to a rigged contract awarded to an Argentinian firm. He withdrew the charges in May, after *Manila Times* publisher Robina Gokongwei issued an apology. The Gokongwei family makes up one of the country's fifty largest commercial groups. To avoid further problems, they sold the paper to a party known to have close ties with the President.

The *Philippine Daily Inquirer* also suffered income losses after movie producers, who were friends of Estrada, and government corporations pulled out their advertisements from the top-selling newspaper. Estrada was angry at the newspaper for its scathing reviews on the presidency. The shake-up affecting the two newspapers was graphically dubbed by the press as "death by corporate strangulation" and revived press freedom issues reminiscent of martial law days.

In response to accusations of cronyism, Estrada denied he had cronies. He narrowly defined cronies as presidential friends who received favourable access to loans and programmes of government financial institutions.[5] Other observers have also argued that the present administration's corruption is no different from past administrations' rent-seeking activities. The Philippines ranked no. 54 in Transparency International's 1999 corruption rating of ninety-nine countries surveyed, more or less the same spot it held over the years. But as one University of the Philippines economist pointed out, "The remarkable fact is that all these have occurred in just one year".[6]

Continuing Economic Difficulties
Oil prices rose seven times from April to October 1999, pushing workers to demand wage increases. The administration, however, could only offer a P25.50 compromise adjustment, pegging the minimum daily wage to P223.50 in Metro Manila effective 30 October 1999. The adjustment satisfied neither the trade unions nor the employers' federations. (A family of six in Metro Manila needs at least P441 daily to live decently; and in agricultural and non-agricultural areas in other regions, a family needs P335 and P355, respectively, to rise above the poverty threshold.)

While aimed at opening the field to new competitors, the Oil Deregulation

Law allowed the three big oil companies (Shell, Caltex, and Petron) to jack up prices. In December the Supreme Court dismissed a petition by a legislator to declare unconstitutional the lifting of price controls on oil products on the grounds that it was contrary to public interest and that the deregulation had not broken the monopoly of these oil companies.

Alarm bells also rang on the impending privatization of the National Power Corporation (NAPOCOR) and the water supply in outlying provinces which would inevitably lead to lifting of subsidies and higher power and water rates. In 1999 NAPOCOR secured a 3 per cent increase in its basic tariff so that it could reduce its net loss from P3.6 billion in 1998 to P2.1 billion in 1999. NAPOCOR also needs to raise its return-of-rate to qualify for funds from the World Bank and the Asian Development Bank.[7] Electricity rates are already the highest in the region.

Other developments indicate continuing obstacles to full economic recovery. According to the Board of Investments (BOI), investments declined by 37 per cent in the first three quarters of 1999 compared with the same period in 1998. This has forced the BOI to lower its investment targets for 1999 from P300 billion to P200 billion. With only P40 billion in new investments by May, even this adjusted target may be difficult to realize. The biggest individual projects approved by the BOI are in the power industry but more than half of the approved investments are in the manufacturing sector.

While rice and corn production recovered from the 1998 El Nino–related drought, sugar and coconut production levels remain below the previous year's, necessitating increased imports of sugar and coconut oil substitutes. Rice imports are projected to remain slightly above the historical average, at 1.1 million tons.

The 1999 budget deficit is estimated at slightly over P100 billion, exceeding the P85.319 billion ceiling promised by the administration to the International Monetary Fund (IMF) in exchange for a US$1.4 billion support programme. The sale of government equity in the country's copper smelter corporation, the Philippine Associated Smelting and Refining Corporation, and in the Manila Electric Company has made only a relatively modest contribution to the budget income.[8]

Both the Bureaus of Customs and Revenues failed to meet their revenue targets. Poor collection was compensated only by enforced cuts in government expenditures. For instance, the government refused to give an amelioration pay to government employees, resulting in protest rallies of public school teachers and other government personnel. The government hopes to raise revenues from new tax proposals but these have not yet been enacted.

There were thirty-six pending tax evasion cases amounting to P70.7 billion, excluding the P26.5 billion tax case against Lucio Tan, at the Bureau of Internal Revenue (BIR). Tax credit scams have also deprived the government of sources of funds. Sixteen finance officials were being investigated for alleged fraudulent issuance of tax credit certificates to big companies totalling P245 million. In 1999 the BIR projected to collect only P413 billion, a mere 7 per cent increase from 1998.

The Philippines ranks among the lowest in Southeast Asia in tax collection effectiveness. BIR statistics show that only 35 per cent of 35 million taxable Filipinos pay their taxes. If the House-approved budget of P651 billion for year 2000 is passed, and without any improvement in tax collection, the deficit could double next year to P153 billion and the government may have to rely on more loans.

Charter Change

To boost economic recovery, Estrada sought constitutional changes that would allow foreigners to own land and more than 40 per cent of stakes in utility, media and advertising, education, and mining and exploration companies, claiming that the constitutional prohibition on ownership has discouraged foreign investment. The 1987 Constitution, as in past Philippine constitutions since 1935, protects the national patrimony from foreign incursion by requiring at least 60 per cent Filipino ownership in sensitive industries.

A twenty-three-member constitutional reform preparatory committee led by retired Supreme Court Chief Justice Andres Narvasa was formed but the charter changes initiative did not seem to come from this committee but from a smaller circle around the President. The Committee submitted a report on 20 December echoing the need for the amendments.

In a speech before the Manila Overseas Press Club in August 1999, Estrada had proposed that the Congress be constituted as a constituent assembly to introduce the economic reforms. At the same time, he suggested convening a Constitutional Convention that would deliberate on the political reforms. More recently, he announced that instead of synchronizing the vote for the constitutional amendment with the scheduled elections in 2001, a plebiscite may be held as early as October 2000.

The churches, NGOs, and several legislators fear that the proposed charter changes called the Constitutional Correction and Development (CONCORD) programme will open the constitution not only to the economic but also to other unwanted changes, notably extension of terms and lifting of term limits on government officials, including the president. The present constitution, drafted in the immediate post-Marcos period, sought to prevent monopolization of power by imposing a single-term limit on the presidency and three consecutive three-year term limits on local government officials and House legislators, and by introducing a party-list system to enhance representation of different sectors in Congress.

Pro-charter change House representatives have already publicly stated that they want the following amendments: an extension of the term of office of local government officials and House representatives from a maximum of three three-year terms to a maximum of four three-year terms, the restoration of the two-party system and removal of the party-list system, among others. In

1997, President Ramos also pushed for charter change (Chacha) but stiff opposition from the public forced him to retreat from his plans.

Poverty Eradication: A Letdown

Key pro-poor programmes have been stymied by flawed approaches and politicization of the function of governance. Not that the need for comprehensive solutions is not appreciated. The Convergence Strategy of the Office of the President, for one, called on the agrarian reform, agriculture, and environment departments to co-ordinate their efforts. As noted by a social scientist,

> The government is already aware that the causes of poverty are interlinked and must be tackled in a coordinated way. However, it could not move beyond conventional and sectoral approaches because of poor bureaucratic coordination, heavy politicization of government service delivery, and poor support for micro-level participatory development initiatives.[9]

The plight of two basic pro-poor programmes — housing and poverty alleviation — manifests these dismal dynamics.

Anti-Poverty Programme

Despite poverty alleviation being the touted as the linchpin of this presidency, its anti-poverty programme took time to take off. The original head of the National Anti-Poverty Commission (NAPC) Orlando Sacay was replaced after six months for slow action. The Commission itself was convened only in late April 1999. As a result, some of its 1998 unused funds were allocated to other departments. By September 1999, only 30 per cent of its funds for the year had been released.

Based on the Social Reform and Poverty Alleviation Act (Republic Act 8425) passed in December 1997, the NAPC will serve as the lead agency, acting as a co-ordinating and advisory body of the President's poverty eradication programme. The Commission is chaired by the President, and members include the heads of ten departments, three agencies, the leagues of government units (provinces, cities, municipalities, and *barangays*), and representatives of fourteen basic sectors, including the urban poor, children, victims of disasters and calamities, and indigenous peoples.

The Lingap para sa Mahirap (Care for the Poor) programme serves as the centrepiece of NAPC's intervention. Lingap will target the poorest 100 families at the village level in each province and city. These families will cluster themselves into cooperative-like enterprises bound by mutual guarantees for the loans they take out. As for medical assistance to the poor, under the "Food, Nutrition and Medical Assistance Component" of Lingap, a certain amount will be allotted to all legislators for release to their identified government hospital beneficiary. The Department of Health (DOH) will also issue a "Health Passport" to Lingap beneficiaries, which they will use to avail themselves of services and assistance in government hospitals.

Through the P2.5 billion Lingap programme, the government hopes to meet its target of poverty reduction of 2 per cent per year. But as an economist pointed out, the 100 selected families in the seventy-eight provinces and eighty-four cities of the country (for a total of 16,200 families) have to achieve a multiplier effect of 1:2,000 to reach this poverty reduction goal. Considering the smallness of the scale of the activities that will be introduced and the fact that the very poor are lacking in human and social capital needed in entrepreneurial activity, such a high multiplier rate is unlikely to be reached.[10]

The programme's approach has also been criticized as welfarist. The idea of delivering government services to a select segment is only an extension on a larger scale of the Presidential Action Center, which made promises of employment, money, and goods to the poor who lined up in front of Malacanang Palace. This earlier programme was stopped after two people died in a stampede. Critics have also pointed out that the programme will only reinforce patronage since the key role of identifying beneficiaries is given to government officials and legislators, building up their role as benefactors. The NAPC itself only plays a co-ordinative role whose power over the line agencies is only as good as the President's backing.

Finally, the Erap para sa Mahirap Program with its five components (food security, modernization of agriculture and fisheries within the context of sustainable development, low-cost mass housing, protection of the poor against crime and violence, and active participation of the Local Government Units [LGUs] in implementation) has also been criticized for not placing enough stress on structural reform. In contrast, land reform and recognition of ancestral domains were integral to the anti-poverty framework of the Social Reform Agenda drafted by multi-sectoral groups during the previous administration's term.

Housing Programme
Mass housing is supposedly another centrepiece of Estrada's pro-poor programme. In 1998, 100,000 mass housing units were constructed, already one-half of the 200,000 built during the six-year term of the Ramos administration. In October, Estrada pledged to build 350,000 houses for the poor every year of his term. Of this number, roughly 70 per cent will be socialized housing costing a maximum of P180,000 per unit while approximately 30 per cent will be low-cost mass housing units costing a maximum of P500,000 per unit. He also appointed himself as chair of the Presidential Commission on Mass Housing.

This effort to address the basic needs of the burgeoning urban poor population was, however, marred by several housing controversies. In October, Housing and Urban Development Coordinating Council (HUDCC) chair Karina David, an NGO leader with a track record in working for urban poor and women's rights, resigned from her post. The resignation of David was interpreted by many sectors as a further weakening of Erap's pro-poor commitment and a victory of the real estate developers' lobby. David was one of the few cabinet-ranking members recruited from the NGO sector.

The HUDCC co-ordinates and supervises all shelter agencies of the government. David quit after Estrada created the Presidential Commission on Mass Housing, which *de facto* subordinated David's agency to the new commission and appointed a businessman-friend engaged in the real estate business, Jose Luis Yulo (who was a council member of the HUDCC under David's chair), as co-chair of the new Presidential Commission. A few weeks before, David had told a Senate committee that the government had squandered P42 billion allotted for socialized housing. The amount was borrowed by private developers with only about 50 per cent returned and only 19 per cent going to socialized housing.

The new appointee was not able to stay in the post long, however. After twenty-eight days, Yulo was forced to resign amid reports of numerous court cases lodged against him. Embarrassed by the expose, Estrada replaced Yulo with Home Insurance Guaranty Corporation (HIGC) chair Wilfredo Hernandez and the Presidential Management Staff Executive Director Lenny de Jesus as presidential adviser on socialized housing and HUDCC chair, respectively. Hernandez is, however, facing congressional investigation for HIGC's anomalous guarantees made on flagship construction projects during the Ramos administration. For one such project, the HIGC had paid P488 million to cover up the defaulted loans of the private contractor who built the luxury villas in Subic for the 1996 APEC Summit. Not surprisingly, the HIGC's pending congressional request for P50 billion recapitalization to realize the present administration's centrepiece shelter programme of creating several so-called Erap Cities in key metropolitan areas is being opposed.

Upsurge in Armed Conflict and Rebel Activity

The new administration inherited the 1996 Peace Agreement with the Moro National Liberation Front (MNLF), and the negotiations with the Communist Party of the Philippines–National Democratic Front (CPP-NDF) and with the Moro Islamic Liberation Front (MILF). But negotiations with rebels was not a key plank in the administration's own programme. Consequently, it did not provide a serious and co-ordinated support to its peace negotiators.

But the rebel groups share blame for the failure to negotiate a political settlement. The communists are ideologically opposed to the constitutional framework as a starting point for the talks and are largely using negotiations for tactical purposes. The goal of seizing the state through armed struggle remains the strategic frame of the party guided by its founder-in-exile, Jose M. Sison, and its armed wing, the New People's Army (NPA). The MILF has no clear strategy for negotiations and shifts from calling for autonomy to full independence. It is also adopting a wait-and-see stance to assess progress in the implementation of the agreement with the MNLF. The MNLF was the leading Moro rebel group fighting the war with the government in the 1970s. The MILF broke away from the MNLF in 1984.

The peace and order situation relating to the insurgency has consequently taken a turn for the worse. By the end of 1999, negotiations with the CPP-NDF were called off. Fighting had resumed between government and communist and MILF forces while the MNLF was becoming restless over what it perceived as a lack of government support in implementing the 1996 Peace Agreement.

The first part of the 1996 Peace Agreement with the MNLF called for the setting up of a Southern Philippines Council for Peace and Development (SPCPD) that would co-ordinate development initiatives in the region as a preliminary step to the creation of a new autonomous region that would re-place the existing Autonomous Region for Muslim Mindanao (ARMM). The MNLF, whose Chair Nur Misuari is also the SPCPD chair and ARMM governor, has complained that the government has not extended enough development assistance outside the funding given through the regular line agencies. Most development initiatives were funded by U.N. agencies and a set of donor countries which responded to the call for assistance. Assistance was channelled through the MNLF State Revolutionary Committees or co-operatives that were put up for capability building and livelihood enterprises. By and large, the SPCPD itself did not exercise the initiative over development, dependent as it was on such external and governmental funding and existing line agencies.

Implementation of the terms of the agreement was also set back by delay in the drafting of a new Organic Act for the Southern Philippines. As a result, the referendum that would have defined the new terms and the geographical extent of the autonomy for the region had not taken place and the current transition phase had to be extended for at least another year. In July 1999, the House of Representatives held special sessions that enabled the passage of the pertinent Bill. At the end of 1999 the Bill was with the Senate for amendment or adoption. It hopes to finalize the Act and hold the referendum by Septem-ber 2000.

The MNLF remains unhappy over certain provisions determining the area of coverage of autonomy, allocation of government properties, and power and control over key economic activities such as mineral extraction. Because no real demobilization nor disarmament has taken place as a result of the agree-ment, the MNLF can easily revert to a war strategy if it is not satisfied with the outcome of the transition phase.

On other fronts, fighting has resumed intermittently. The government went ahead with the opening of formal talks with the MILF on 25 October 1999. It agreed to continue with the process of acknowledging MILF camps in parts of Maguindanao and Cotabato in Mindanao. However, it remained un-clear how negotiations would proceed and how a political settlement with the MILF would interface with the agreement already in place with the MNLF.

Fighting broke out between the government and the MILF again in North Cotabato, Lanao, and Sultan Kudarat provinces shortly after the opening of the talks. By December the fighting had resulted in more than 40,000 evacuees who took refuge in safer areas in Bukidnon and North Cotabato.

The MILF alternates between asking for full independence and peace within the Philippine state. In October, inspired by developments in East Timor, massive rallies by the Muslims in the provinces of Cotabato, Maguindanao, and Lanao were staged calling for independence. When new Indonesian President Abdurrahman Wahid came to Manila for the ASEAN Informal Summit in November, he indicated his interest in meeting with MILF Chair Hashim Salamat. The government, however, discouraged such a meeting. President Abdurrahman invited Salamat to meet with him in Indonesia instead.

In June, talks with the CPP-NDF ended, resulting in the disbanding of the government's Negotiating Panel for the NDF and the invalidation of the immunity from arrest of NDF negotiators and consultants. Estrada replaced the negotiating panel with the National Peace Forum that will co-ordinate the holding of dialogues at the local levels. Talks with a breakaway faction of the CPP, the Rebolusyonaryong Partido ng Manggagawa sa Pilipinas, and the armed urban-based Alex Boncayao Brigade were also held in December.

CPP-NPA founding Chair Jose Ma. Sison and the NDF have refused to co-operate with this new tack. By the second half of the year, rebel activity intensified in remote areas of Southern Luzon, the Visayas, and Mindanao as reflected in increased incidence of reports of ambushes, raids, and arrests.

The Commission on Human Rights (CHR) in Southern Mindanao reported an increase in abuses committed against civilians by the Army. According to the CHR, from January to August 1999 twenty-three cases were filed against the army compared with only three cases over the same period in 1998. The CHR attributes the increase in complaints to renewed military offensive against the NPA. Elements of the Philippine National Police, however, continue to be the subject of most complaints in the last two years, followed by civilian complaints against other civilians.[11] The army, on the other hand, capitalized on the arrest of wounded guerrillas of minor age, claiming NPA violation of the International Humanitarian Law against recruitment of minors.

High Stakes Bargaining
Like all past Philippine presidents, Estrada is the chief mediator in the bargaining table called the Philippine state where various socio-political actors haggle. However, bargaining today has become more complicated and multi-sided. The liberalization of the economy has allowed for the entry of more varied enterprises, each wanting to enter the open, supposedly level, fields. The old and new entrants have ensured what Hutchcroft has noted a certain social mobility, a "steady creation of *nouveaux riches*" whose "anarchy of particularistic demands" continuously choke the state apparatus.[12]

Bargaining has also been set within the parameters of law and a constitutional set-up that allows the legislative, judicial, and executive branches to check on each other. The Senate, for instance, has been undertaking several investigations on reported anomalies, though the presidency does remain the most powerful political institution in the country; and Congress itself suffers from low popularity.[13] It is also argued that private enterprises can be both rent-seekers and entrepreneurs at the same time[14] and that rent-seeking may also register significant production growth.[15] The increasing demands of an economy dependent on international aid and foreign investments could thus force a modicum of economic rationality.

Another contention is that incoherence in the bureaucracy allows for "islands of flexibility and relative autonomy within the state". For example, while the Department of Finance's neo-liberal prescriptions may clash with the Departments of Agriculture and Agrarian Reform's credit programmes for small-holder farms, the different lines of march enable these more reform-oriented agencies to undertake their programmes.[16]

Moreover, because government is constantly under the scrutiny of various reform-minded sectors in society, including a very intrusive and opinionated mass media and ubiquitous NGOs, each bargain has to be explained and justified. In several instances, bargains have been rescinded due to public outcry, and some backward flips had to be made to save the face of government. These manifest that in key moments, political imperatives can prevail over crony satisfaction.

For the most part, however, certain groups and certain policies whose agenda go against a developmental state's reform agenda have prevailed. This shows that the Philippine state remains weak and unable to assert autonomy from various societal groups. One can thus see it stagnating into a pseudo-industrializing pseudo-democracy, with variations from one administration to another only in leadership personality and style, extent of profligacy and rent-seeking, and corresponding degree of effectiveness.

NOTES

1. *Philippine Daily Inquirer*, 13 November 1999.
2. This is Administrative Order No. 48 creating the Maglanco (Maguindanao-Lanao del Sur-Cotabato City) Development Council.
3. Rigoberto Tiglao, "Timid Speaker", *Far Eastern Economic Review*, 4 November 1999.
4. Sheila S. Coronel, "The Pare Principle", *i Investigative Reporting Magazine*, no. 4 (October–December 1998).
5. *Philippine Daily Inquirer*, 23 October 1993, p. 1.
6. Emmanuel De Dios, "A Crisis Without Consequence, Recovery Without Reform" (Revised paper delivered before Kilosbayan, 9 July 1999).
7. Economist Intelligence Unit, *Country Report on the Philippines, 3rd Quarter 1999.*
8. Ibid.
9. Leonora Angeles, "Women, Bureaucracy and the Governance of Poverty: Integrating Gender and Good Governance in Poverty Alleviation Plans and Programs in the Philippines" (Paper presented at the annual Philippine Political Science Association conference, 23 July 1999, Balay Kalinaw, University of the Philippines).
10. Emmanuel De Dios, "Can He Do It? Assessing the Estrada Administration's Anti-

Poverty Program" (Paper presented at the annual Philippine Political Science Association conference, 23 July 1999, Balay Kalinaw, University of the Philippines).

11. "Army Rights Abuses Rising", *Today*, 21 October 1999.

12. Paul Hutchcroft, "Booty Capitalism: Business-Government Relations in the Philippines", in *Business and Government in Industrialising Asia*, edited by Andrew MacIntyre (Sydney: Allen & Unwin, 1994).

13. The Social Weather Station surveys show a dismal performance rating for both Houses: from 31 per cent in March to negative 2 per cent in December for the Lower House, and from 35 per cent to 1 per cent for the Senate. Legislators are criticized largely for their interest in securing "pork-barrel" funds for themselves which they use for supporting projects in their respective constituencies in order to secure votes.

14. Shinggo Mikama, "Economic Policy-Making in the Philippines", *UP-CIDS Chronicle* (University of Philippines), July–December 1997, p. 69.

15. Hutchcroft, "Booty Capitalism".

16. Pancho Lara, "Agrarian Reform: *Pasado rin ba tayo* [Do we make it to the passing mark]?" *Conjuncture*, August 1999.

SINGAPORE

SINGAPORE
A Vision for the New Millennium

Jasmine S. Chan

For Singapore the year 1999 was marked with trepidation about the uncertainties of the new millenium and with anticipation for a new beginning. Even as some argued that the last year of the old millennium was really the year 2000, and not 1999, it hardly mattered. Departmental stores touted the last sale of the century to would-be shoppers. Travel agencies advertised tours to view the first sunrise of the new century. Singaporeans looked forward to several big parties to be held on the eve of the new millennium. A vision for the Singapore nation of the twenty-first century (the Singapore 21 vision) was unveiled, a vision derived from a major project of consultation in which Singaporeans were asked to frame their ideas for the future. This led to the catch-phrase "every Singaporean matters". Lending action to talk, the Prime Minister led with a proposal to study the possibility of introducing compulsory education for every child to help each reach his or her potential. Terms like "civil society", "active citizenship", "heartlanders", and "cosmopolitans" abounded in discussions in parliament and on the streets. This led to a sense of optimism and anticipation that the nation would continue to evolve to become a "world-class home".

At the same time there were worries that ranged from the technological to the political. Institutions and organizations raced against time to protect themselves against the potentially destructive powers of the Y2K bug which, it was feared, could bring the world to a standstill, with Singapore Airlines announcing that flights on some routes would either be cancelled or re-timed from 30 December to 1 January 2000.[1] Economists pessimistically forecast that the impact of the regional economic crisis would still be felt, and politicians cautioned that the road to economic recovery would be a long hard one. Uncertainties about relations with neighbouring countries that were undergoing changes or challenges to their leadership were also being closely watched not only by the Singaporean leaders but also by the common citizen for their possible effects on the nation.

Jasmine S. Chan is Assistant Professor at the Department of Sociology, National University of Singapore.

"Singapore 21: Make It Our Best Home"
The Singapore 21 Report was launched in April 1999. It has been hailed as a blueprint for the future, a plan to guide Singapore and Singaporeans through difficulties and challenges that the coming millennium may bring.

Singapore 21 came out of the People's Action Party (PAP) manifesto for the 1997 General Elections that outlined the PAP's vision to make Singapore the "best home". At the PAP's twenty-fourth ordinary party conference in 1996, Prime Minister (PM) Goh Chok Tong highlighted five key goals: to "create wealth for the country, share its success among Singaporeans, invest in the young, look after the old and build ties among the people".[2]

In his speech launching the Report, PM Goh referred to the "21" as a metaphor to signify Singapore's adulthood. The major emphasis was on social aspects and on the need to go beyond material concerns and economic survivalism. PM Goh highlighted the need to create emotional ties among Singaporeans to the Singapore nation.

A Singapore 21 committee, headed by Education Minister Teo Chee Hean, was set up in 1997 to garner feedback on the non-material needs of Singaporeans. The committee's main task was to suggest new ideas to reinforce the notion of Singapore as a home in an age of globalization. A total of sixty-six Singaporeans were appointed to assist the five Singapore 21 subject committees in gathering Singaporeans' views through a variety of methods from focus group discussions to seminars and forums. In all, feedback was obtained from about 6,000 Singaporeans over a period of more than a year. Each subject committee was given the task of looking into one of five dilemmas: (a) the drive towards internationalization/regionalization versus the need to make Singapore a home, (b) a less stressful life versus retaining the drive to achieve, (c) attracting foreign talent versus looking after Singaporeans, (d) the needs of senior citizens versus the aspirations of the younger generation, and (e) consultation and consensus versus decisiveness and quick action.

The large-scale feedback sessions eventually led to the Singapore 21 Report. With the launch of the Report, a new committee comprising twenty-one members, headed by Minister of State (Defence and Information and the Arts) David Lim, was asked to turn the Singapore 21 vision into reality. The Report was distilled into the following five rallying calls:

- All Singaporeans matter.
- Strong families are our foundation.
- Opportunities for all.
- The Singapore heartbeat.
- Active citizens: making a difference.

Some of these catch-phrases are familiar such as the call to build a strong family as the foundation of society, a view reminiscent of the *White Paper on Shared Values*.[3] One cannot help but read some of these slogans as having a strong pragmatic streak to them. The call for a strong family was expected in the light of the greying population and declining fertility rate, which raised concerns about the country's ability to support an ageing population. In the past, legislation such as the Family Maintenance Bill[4] was passed in view of this anticipated problem. In fact, President S.R. Nathan himself expressed this view in his maiden speech to parliament when he described the family as the "first line of care for its older members".

The other calls may be located in worries about the consequences of globalization. Given that the principles of economic pragmatism and survivalism guide both economic policies and social life in so far as material incentives and disincentives are used to regulate facets of life from road usage to family size, the very success of the system has inevitably reinforced a mindset that gives precedence to economic considerations.

> If Singaporeans are just economic animals, materialistic with no sense of belonging, they will be like migratory birds, seeking their fortunes in other lands when the season changes. If it ever comes to this, Singapore will not survive as a sovereign nation.[5]

Moreover, globalization means that Singaporeans who wish to leave have more opportunities to do so. Economic considerations play a role in these decisions as well, albeit in opposing ways. There are those who leave Singapore in pursuit of financial success — to be global players in a world economy — and there are those who desire to leave behind a culture that emphasizes the material. Paradoxically, those who are able to leave and make homes abroad are precisely those who have the means and qualifications that are desired by other countries, leading to fears about the consequences that such a "brain drain" may have on the nation. It is in part this concern that, during a year of financial hardship, led to focus on the contentious issue of "foreign talent". It is the successful inculcation of values that have economics as a fundamental principle which pushes the government to constantly reiterate its commitment to the principles outlined in Singapore 21. This is seen in President Nathan's maiden speech to parliament, which veered away from the economic to focus on people.

However, even though PM Goh said, as early as in 1997, that "we need to move beyond material progress, to a society which places people at its very centre",[6] in a more recent interview, Brigadier-General (NS) Lee Hsien Loong emphasized that while priorities will be given to education and to making Singapore 21 a reality, the overarching objectives for Singapore in the millenium are still economic.[7] In view of this, it will be interesting to see how these "people-centred" ideals get translated into concrete policies.

All Singaporeans Matter
The idea that all Singaporeans matter seems rather self-evident, given that the government has a moral obligation to improve the lives of all citizens. Yet this particular phrasing of a Singapore 21 objective is timely, in view of the percep-

tion that the PAP government is an élitist one, whose policies tend to disproportionately benefit those with resources and especially those with high educational qualifications. Past policies such as the graduate mother scheme bear
evidence of this élitist stance.

Part of this perception was reinforced when the Prime Minister in his
National Day Rally speech used two terms "cosmopolitans" and "heartlanders"
to refer to two broad categories of Singaporeans with different marketable
skills and opportunities in the global economy. The cosmopolitan is highly
educated, with skills that are marketable globally. He or she is at ease in the
world and is mobile. The heartlander, on the other hand, forms the core of
Singaporean society. He or she has made his or her home in Singapore, and
is less mobile.[8] However, feedback from Singaporeans indicates that they feel
the terms are divisive, which may pose another problem in relation to creating
a single Singapore heartbeat.

Singaporeans are told that they will be given the chance to fulfil their
potential wherever that may lie, including Singaporeans who face special hard-
ships in their everyday lives. One concrete step in this direction was the pledge
to make education compulsory, which means that all children, including those
with special needs, will be given opportunities to attend school. This pledge
has been hailed by many, especially those in the social service sector, as timely.

However, stating that all *Singaporeans* matter also goes to the heart of
another issue. The Singapore 21 Report called for the creation of a cosmopolitan city where opportunities and wealth are created by encouraging people to
come to Singapore, bringing with them ideas, resources, and expertise. It was
this reference to foreign talent that stirred the most emotions, given the difficulties that many Singaporeans faced in 1999, a year when they were seeking
reassurance that their interests and needs are first protected. There also exists
a perception that the PAP government holds a favoured stance towards foreign
talent. The term foreign *talent* is telling, since this favoured stance does not
necessarily include the many unskilled foreigners who come here to work in
the service sector as cleaners and maids or in the construction business.

The subject sparked a discussion in which members of parliament (MPs)
like Dr Tan Cheng Bok asked for restraint in the call for foreign talent during
a time of rising unemployment. The issue became a politically sensitive one
when the media ran reports about Singaporeans being retrenched from their
jobs while at the same time carrying announcements about major local companies employing top foreign talent. Despite the government's assurances that
the foreign talent policy would help to create more jobs and better opportunities for Singapore, the fear that the policy might be at the expense of local
talent remained, especially in a country where the private sector is accustomed
to following the government lead. Hence, stating that "All Singaporeans matter" is necessary to assure Singaporeans that their needs will not be forgotten
in the rush towards a knowledge-based economy, which involves a drive to
recruit foreign (albeit talented) labour.

The situation was exacerbated by the fact that this recession, unlike the 1985 recession, had hit hard at the middle-management level, the level at which "foreign talent" is being recruited to fill positions. While it is expected and understandable that foreign companies may recruit from their homeland, the fear that Singaporean companies may look elsewhere first to fill these positions created a sense of insecurity, which prompted a call for Singaporeans to be considered first by the government. The emergence of the debate is also an indication that this recession had hit the higher-educated, the more vocal group of people who are able to make their dissatisfaction known through their MPs and through letters to the press.[9]

However, foreign talent is recruited not merely for their expertise, but also to replace those who leave Singapore every year. This is evident in the call to integrate foreigners into Singapore society,[10] and in some cases, to encourage them to become Singaporean citizens, as approximately 2,000 Singaporeans emigrate every year. Out of these, more than 50 per cent are women married to foreign men.[11] The Prime Minister brought up this statistic to show why Singapore must encourage foreigners to make Singapore their home.

This author argues that one reason why the Singapore woman follows her husband is the patriarchal system, which the Singapore government proudly claims for its own. Under an overtly patriarchal system, benefits to the woman are made through the husband, who is set up as the head of household. This in turn has both material and psychological consequences for women. On the material level a patriarchal system rewards men more readily than women for similar jobs performed. This is evident by the different job benefits given to men and women and by the salary differences between the two sexes for similar job experiences and educational qualifications. Hence, materially it makes logical sense to develop the husband's career rather than the wife's when choices have to be made. Another consequence is that a country that constantly harps on being patriarchal sends the message to women that they are second-class citizens, whose positions and benefits are tied to their men. Thus, a mindset is encouraged that to place women's needs and interests first is unthinkable, a mindset that then encourages Singaporean women to leave with their foreign husbands.

The Other Half: A Vision for Women?
Dr Aline Wong, Senior Minister of State for Education, gave an unprecedented speech at the tenth anniversary of the PAP Women's Wing concerning the party's attitude towards women. She stated that some women party members are "impatient at the slow progress women have been making both inside and outside the party". She called upon the PAP to apply the same critieria in encouraging men to stand for elections as are applied to women. "To qualify, women not only have to be good as wives, mothers and in their chosen careers, they have to be exemplary".[12] The Singapore parliament has only six women; and at 6 per cent, this is one of the lowest proportion in the world. As such,

Dr Wong called upon the party to include single women and married non-working women in their search for candidates to stand for elections. In particular, she pointed to the lack of women in top positions in the civil service, statutory boards, and government-linked companies. She focused on the double burden that women face at the home and at work, and suggested that resources like flexi-time, no-pay leave, and childcare leave should be shared by the family. Allocating such resources to women and only women reinforced stereotypical notions that their role is located in the home, as mothers and wives. Hence, sick leave for a child should be shared between spouses rather than being allocated only to the mother. Various women's organizations such as the Association of Women for Action and Research (AWARE) and the Singapore Council of Women's Organizations (SCWO), as well as individual women voiced their support for her observations and her call for more progress in getting women into top positions.

It was soon after this speech that the first woman permanent secretary Madam Lim Soo Hoon was appointed on 1 October this year. However, in contrast to Dr Wong's observations, Madam Lim claimed that the civil service is gender-blind, that there is no glass ceiling, and that she had never felt any sexual discrimination. Madam Lim focused on her work, without reference to any contradictory demands placed upon her as mother, wife, or worker. The claim that there is no sexual discrimination is based on the fact that she works like men do and as such "whoever meets the grade will be given the opportunity". The implication here is that women who give priority to other aspects of their lives cannot or choose not to put in the requisite hours and energies into work, and as such do not make the grade. They are then deserving of the positions that they occupy within the organizations.

There is thus a lack of recognition of the different roles that women play and the different resources available to some women and not to others. At one level, women are judged by different criteria — as mothers and wives in addition to their role as workers. For example, family policies are mainly geared towards women as mothers. However, in assessing women's capabilities at work, only one standard criterion is applied — the male criterion — in judging women's dedication. It is this mis-recognition of the male criteria as an objective standard that places women at a disadvantage, both at work and in politics.

Given the push towards a knowledge-based economy, the tight labour market, the need for skilled workers, and falling birthrates, Singapore can no longer afford to take a position that the problems of family life are purely private ones. One of the more innovative ways in which Singapore can become a first-class home and a global economy is to rethink and experiment with schemes that can help integrate family and work rather than expect individuals, mainly women, to continually seek *ad hoc* solutions to a balancing act that inevitably fails.

However, it was not only gender issues that came to the forefront in 1999. The issue of race, especially with regard to the creation of a Singapore heartbeat, also touched off some discussion about the emotional rootedness of individuals and of the different races to the nation.

Multiracialism and the Singapore Heartbeat

> What makes you and I Singaporean is our shared sense of belonging, a collective memory of our shared past, and total commitment to our shared future. This emotional rootedness is The Singapore Heartbeat.[13]

Creating a Singapore heartbeat means strengthening emotional ties to Singapore, focusing on the need to create a Singapore nation, a Singapore tribe. The government has long realized that the basic need for survival of the country having been assured, Singaporeans are seeking to have their other needs fulfilled. A 1997 survey which showed that 20 per cent of Singaporeans wish to emigrate merely confirmed this observation. Despite economic success and fulfilment, some Singaporeans have chosen to opt out of the economic rat race, and to seek a different life-style elsewhere. While material welfare is necessary, it is not sufficient in defining a meaningful life.

The issue of race came to the forefront in the debate about what makes Singapore a city state but not yet a nation. How race could affect the creation of a Singapore nation was highlighted at a Singapore 21 forum at Tanjong Pagar on 18 September, when in response to a question from the audience, Senior Minister Lee Kuan Yew stated:

> If, for instance, you put in a Malay officer who's very religious and who has family ties in Malaysia in charge of a machine gun unit, that's a very tricky business. We've got to know his background. I'm saying these things because they are real, and if I don't think that, and I think even if today the Prime Minister doesn't think carefully about this, we could have a tragedy.[14]

This raised a *furor* among some in the Malay-Muslim community, with two groups — Taman Bacaan, a grassroots group and Majlis Pusat, the central organizing body for thirty-eight Malay-Muslim cultural bodies — asking for a dialogue with the Senior Minister. However, Minister-in-Charge of Muslim Affairs Abdullah Tarmugi rejected the calls for such a dialogue, asking instead that such energies be put into preparing the community for a knowledge-based economy. Once again, economic priorities outweigh the ideological.

In line with his known thinking, Senior Minister Lee Kuan Yew also said that the community self-help group approach works best for Singapore, given the realities today. The reality he referred to is that while Singapore has made progress in integrating the different races, certain emotional bonds are instinctive and cannot be removed overnight. However, these sentiments may at the same time reify differences between the races through a pragmatic attitude that people would rather help their "own kind" or are best suited to do so, for example, through racially based welfare organizations like Mendaki for the Malays, the Chinese Development Assistance Council (CDAC) for the Chinese, and the Singapore Indian Development Assistance (SINDA) for the Indians.

It is believed that some of these potentially divisive identities can be overcome only through the creation of a Singapore tribe. PM Goh Chok Tong referred to this Singapore tribe in his speech to parliament in May 1999, as the "common Singapore family, with its distinct core values and social traits and sharing a common destiny".[15] In elaborating, he reiterated those values embodied in the *White Paper on Shared Values* such as the family as the basic social unit, society before self, and consensus rather than conflict. At the same time he emphasized that this is to be created within a multiracial context, that ethnic and racial identities and sentiments are part of the foundations of what makes Singapore "one family, one people and one nation".

Building a common identity upon differences is not necessarily impossible. Indeed the ideal, as PM Goh described it, would be one where Singapore society is a mosaic, with different groups retaining their different identities, yet having an overarching Singaporean identity pulling groups together.[16] However, one should beware of any tendency to emphasize differences and to translate them into practices that exaggerate these differences, making it seem as if distinct racial groups have the appropriate characteristics. For this may breed stereotypes and some may use such stereotypes in their interactions with other groups.

Civil Society

Part of the push for a Singapore heartbeat is to initiate a people sector, as part of a new three-way relationship with the private and public sectors. The people sector was to provide feedback on policies, even creating a process of "constructive disagreement". Citizens are encouraged to "participate in the nation's affairs"[17] in the hope that they will have a stronger stake in the nation's success.

The Singapore 21 vision of active citizenship, which goes beyond governmental consultation of prominent individuals in society as well as selected ordinary individuals, calls for the involvement of every citizen in some aspect of the Singapore community. Singaporeans are now asked to develop a mindset that does not necessarily depend on the government to initiate change. Instead, should something need to be done, citizens can start to organize and participate in effecting change within Singapore. Active citizens are deemed to have "an obligation to the society and country that nurtures" them, and through participation they are both giving back to the country and at the same time making a difference to the lives of others. However, the definition of what active citizenship means is still being hotly debated, particularly within the framework of civil society.

Indeed, the definition of "civil society" came to the forefront, with PAP leaders in the past intending it to mean active citizenship in a limited welfarist fashion which included the people's initiative to help others in need. This does not necessarily mean an invitation to political commentary. This distinction between civil and civic society has in the past opened up a discussion on out-of-bound (OB) markers, as exemplified by the case of Catherine Lim, whose commentary on political styles received a hard-hitting response from the government. The government took the stand that any citizen who wants to make political comment should join a political party. This in turn evoked responses that citizens have a right to political comment as much as politicians. Such hard responses had not helped to encourage active citizenship in the past.

In a response to a query, it was clarified that active citizenship means that the people have to take the initiative to create space for civil society rather than wait for the government to do so. However, in order to encourage people to do so, the government could help by dismantling some structural impediments to a flourishing civil society, such as the Societies Act and the Internal Security Act (ISA). The people must have confidence that the actions that they may take as conscientious citizens will not result in a heavy-handed response that the PAP government is well known for. OB markers that define the political from the non-political to demarcate the boundaries of civil society will simply continue to inhibit Singaporeans from taking action.

On critical political comment, it was said that "the government will defend its policies, principles and programmes openly and robustly",[18] and that those "without mischievious intention or a hidden agenda need not fear rebuttal". However, it is the statement that "those out to undermine the government or wrest political power must expect a political response" which sends one wondering again about OB markers. A political response could include the might of governmental machinery that may deter some from fully participating in the process of active citizenship. Does challenging government policies constitute undermining the government? Would a political response include the ISA? The call for active citizenship is still very much dependent upon the government's definition of what "constructive debate" is.

It is then little wonder that the first response to the government's call upon Singaporeans to initiate change was to ask the government what it is doing on its part to encourage active citizenship and participation and to open up civil society. Indeed, PAP members themselves such as MP Davinder Singh called for a clearer statement on the rights, responsibilities, and expectations of those who choose to become active citizens. While this, as the government claims, would be contrary to its wanting Singaporeans to take the initiative, it is but an expected response in the light of the ambiguous statements suggesting dire consequences for overstepping the boundaries of the permissible.

That the meaning of active citizenship remains ambiguous is true for now. However, it is recognized that, as the education system is changed to develop creative and critical thinking minds, as the economy demands a highly educated people, Singaporeans' relationship to and expectations of the government will necessarily change. As more of us become linked globally through the Internet and have greater access to information and more exposure to alternative ideas, the demand for change in governance style cannot be ignored. It is this that the government itself is trying to foster, yet at the same time, it itself does not have a consensus on how much change to encourage.

Having seen the costs of overstepping the boundaries, most Singaporeans would rather take a wait-and-see attitude. It is not merely the "embarrassment of having our arguments torn apart", as MP Davinder Singh put it,[20] but the knowledge that the power of various state apparatus may follow that silences.

Elected President

One of the more significant political events of 1999 had to do with the presidential election. Mr Ong Teng Cheong, who became Singapore's first elected president in 1993, announced on 17 July 1999 that he was not standing for re-election. In 1990 the Elected Presidency Bill was passed which conferred some executive powers to the head of state; also, instead of being appointed, the president would in the future be directly elected by the people. The elected president's executive powers include veto power over the national reserves and over key public appointments. However, his ability to utilize his powers may be limited by the Council of Presidential Advisers (CPA), which consists of six appointed members.[21] Before the president is able to exercise his veto power, the majority of the CPA must agree with his decision, otherwise the veto may be overturned by a two-thirds majority in parliament — which is not difficult to do in Singapore, where the PAP has virtually monopolized parliament since independence.

The media ran articles speculating on potential and possible candidates for the post, many of whom when interviewed replied that they had not been "asked" to stand for election. Considering that the stated objective of having an elected president was to provide a check on possible governmental abuses with regard to the national reserves, it is significant that eligible individuals who had indicated that they were interested in standing for election would not consider doing so without the cabinet's support.

Shortly after Mr Ong made known his decision not to run for re-election, it was announced that the cabinet had asked Mr S.R. Nathan to consider standing for election. Despite speculation relating to some other eligible candidates, none of them stepped forth to challenge Mr Nathan, and on nomination day he was the only candidate to qualify. Two other candidates who had submitted nomination forms were not given certificates of suitability; that is, they failed to fulfil the criterion that required experience in a top government position or in running a company with a paid-up capital of at least S\$100 million for a minimum of three years. Mr Nathan then became president without an election.

The *Straits Times* conducted two surveys, which indicated that approximately 80 per cent surveyed wanted an election.[22] Many felt that it was a chance to have a voice in choosing the president. Indeed, at the previous election the government had to persuade Mr Chua Kim Yeow, former

Accountant-General, to run against Mr Ong. Without a campaign, Mr Chua garnered 41.3 per cent of the votes. This is in part because Singaporeans wanted the president to be a true check on the government, and the perception of Mr Ong as a PAP man did not, at that time, bode well for the independent powers of the president.

The walkover also led to a discussion on the mandate of Mr Nathan to assume the role of president. Overall, the change of president might have been a non-event, were it not for Mr Ong Teng Cheong's unprecedented public airing of the difficulties he, as an elected president, encountered with the government,[23] bearing in mind the fact that Mr Ong was at one time a leading member of the PAP and a former deputy prime minister. This happened during his end-of-term press conference on 16 July and opened up an intense debate on the role of the elected president, compelling the Prime Minister and other cabinet members to respond during parliament on 17 August. Their response included not only rebuttals to substantive points raised by the President, but also criticism of his decision to go public with his disagreements with the government.

> I did not expect him to cast doubts on the Government, that it was unwilling or reluctant to give him full access to all information and documents for him to discharge his constitutional duties.[24]

This public airing of the conflict between the President and the government could be interpreted in two ways. One interpretation accepted PM Goh's statement that Mr Ong had asked to run for a second term and that the cabinet had decided against supporting Mr Ong because of concern over his health, in view of medical reports that Mr Ong's low-grade lymphoma had developed into high-grade lymphoma. So, according to this interpretation, Mr Ong's public disagreement with the government indicated his disgruntled feelings towards the government's decision not to support him. The second interpretation was that the cabinet did not support a second term for the president because he had taken his role as a check on the government's powers seriously, which resulted in conflict with the government. This latter interpretation was found to have cast the "most serious doubt which the Government must clear up".[25] While PM Goh, among others, gave details to dispel these doubts, the fact that the cabinet had chosen to support the nomination of a 75-year-old who had undergone a coronory artery bypass operation, did not quite put the doubts to rest. However, President Nathan voluntarily submitted his medical report to the cabinet, a report which stated that while he was still on medication for hypertension, diabetes, benign prostate enlargement, and coronary artery disease, all these were under control.[26]

The whole episode reinforced the preception among many Singaporeans of the powerful role that the government continues to play in respect of the office of a directly elected president. Another significant consequence of the debate was the change within the political discourse of the description of the president's powers. The president was now described as not having *executive* powers, but only *custodial* ones, terms which, as nominated member of parliament (NMP) Simon Tay pointed out, were not found in the Constitution. Indeed, PM Goh's speech constantly and consistently referred to the presidency as a custodial position, which protects and guards over specific areas of the nation's welfare, rather than having powers to initiate changes. Hence, this custodial president is not an alternative centre of power. The president's custodial powers are only "reactive or blocking powers",[27] and the exercise of even these was dependent upon the consent of the CPA. Yet the elected president does have the power to override the cabinet's decisions, albeit in a limited fashion, in areas which come under his custodial oversight. It is this — that the president is a check on the government — which led to the desire of citizens to choose their president through an election.

The Economy: Recovery and Challenges
The 1999 economic performance proved to be better than expected. While growth in the first quarter was 0.6 per cent, it shot up to 6.7 per cent in the second quarter of the year. The growth was in part helped by the recovery of the electronics industry, the recovering regional economies of Thailand, South Korea, and Malaysia, and by a strong U.S. economy.[28] Growth of 6.7 per cent was maintained in the third quarter of the year. With recovery firmly in sight, the Ministry of Trade and Industry revised its forecast for the year to around 5 per cent for 1999 compared with an earlier projection of 0 to 2 per cent.

A sustained recovery was evident in all sectors except construction, which contracted by 15.6 per cent. Manufacturing led the growth at 16.7 per cent, followed by the wholesale and retail sector at 9.3 per cent, transport and communications at 7.6 per cent, and financial services at 4.3 per cent. Inflation also increased, rising continuously from 0.1 per cent in May to 0.6 per cent in July, and to 1.2 per cent in September. This rise in the consumer price index may suggest a recovering economy, a suggestion that bore out when the third quarter figures were announced.

The third quarter held the best news for the economy with several negative trends reversing themselves. Private consumption rose by 9.1 per cent, domestic demand by 13 per cent, and capital spending by only 1.7 per cent. However, the unemployment rate increased to 4 per cent, up from 3.3 per cent in the second quarter. Approximately 3,200 persons lost their jobs, making it a total of about 10,000 jobs lost by the end of September.[29] The economic outlook for the rest of the year remained bullish, with only two external risks, namely, an excessive appreciation of the Japanese yen and the possibility of a stock market crash in the United States, both of which did not occur by the end of 1999.

The importance of the push towards a knowledge-based economy was highlighted by announcements made by various companies such as Western Digital Corp and Seagate Technology to transfer parts of their production process to Malaysia, given the lower costs there. Singapore seemed poised to face new competitive challenges from other recovering economies in the region, which can provide infrastructural support and lower costs to businesses. A knowledge-based economy requires the preparation of the population for more skilled work, and increasing the educational qualifications of workers. The government announced in September that it would invest S$200 million into continuing education and training programmes.

Human capital was the buzzword of the year, with emphasis on tapping that capital to the fullest through retraining programmes, upgrading skills, and formulating plans to revamp the education system to encourage creative thinking.[30] Nevertheless, manufacturing will remain the "key pillar of the Singapore economy", PM Goh announced. Indeed, manufacturing is seen as essential to ensure the continued growth of the services sector, given its ties to the global market.[31] The goal is then to move into high-technology manufacturing, research and development, and product design, and to encourage companies that require skilled and knowledgeable, rather than low-cost, labour to set up bases in Singapore.

The year also saw various attempts by the Ministry of Trade and Industry to promote the new economic plan. Singaporeans were encouraged to be techno-entrepreneurs, or technopreneurs. Various funds such as the Local Enterprise Technical Assistance Scheme provided grants to help aspiring entrepreneurs or local companies to go global and use new technology. Reforms have been taking place, mainly in the financial and banking sector, with wide-ranging incentives given to organizations providing fund management services, the development of a bond market, and loosening up regulations that allow foreign banks to compete with local ones in retail banking.

On 23 November 1999, it was announced that employers' contribution to workers' Central Provident Fund (CPF), which was cut from 20 per cent to 10 per cent in January 1999, will be increased by 2 per cent in April 2000 due to good economic growth in 1999. This 2 per cent will go into workers' CPF Special Account. The goal is to fully restore employers' contribution of 20 per cent by the end of five years, depending upon the economy's performance.[32]

Overall, there was an upbeat mood at the end of the year, which hailed the end of the economic crisis, placing Singapore firmly on the road to a sustainable recovery.

Regional Affairs

Indonesia

The election of Abdurrahman Wahid as President of Indonesia and his decision to make Singapore his first stop during a nine-country tour in Southeast Asia signalled to both the Singaporean leaders and its people that relations between the two countries were warming up. Relations with Indonesia had deteriorated soon after President Habibie came into power in July 1998 when he accused Singapore of not being "a friend in need", describing it derisively as a little red dot in a sea of green that is Indonesia.

Relations did not improve when, in February 1999, asked by Taiwanese reporters regarding discrimination against the Chinese in Indonesia, President Habibie declared that there was no discrimination against the Chinese as Indonesia had "abolished all racist policies and signed the United Nations human rights declaration",[33] and that reports on the rapes of ethnic Chinese women were greatly exaggerated. Instead, he made a comparison of the two countries: "The situation in Singapore is worse. In Singapore, if you are a Malay, you can never become a military officer. They are the real racists, not here. You can go and check it out."

Apart from being erroneous in factual terms, since Singapore has Malay military officers, his perception of Singapore as being racially discriminatory was not unexpected. When statements concerning the conflicting loyalties of Malay officers, like the one SM Lee made in September, are made openly at public forums, such statements become public fodder for the consumption of readers abroad. Political leaders, Malay MPs, and various Malay organizations such as Taman Bacaan and the Association of Muslim Professionals protested against the inaccuracy of President Habibie's statement. This statement came amidst other dissatisfaction he had with Singapore such as Singapore's requirement that sons of Indonesian permanent residents serve national service in the Singapore military. President Habibie had declared that Indonesians undergoing national service in Singapore would have their citizenship revoked.[34]

On the other hand, President Abdurrahman deliberately took steps to improve relations with Singapore in a variety of ways. His decision to visit Singapore first was a signal not missed by both Singaporeans and Chinese Indonesians. During his visit, the President reassured both the Singapore government and the business community that his government was intent on weeding out corruption, and that it would practise the separation of religion from the state. He announced his plan to invite Senior Minister Lee Kuan Yew as an international adviser to his government. He assured the business community that market forces and profit margins would rule the economy, and tried to dispel racial unease by claiming some Chinese ancestry. The outcome of the visit was positive, with PM Goh announcing that he would personally lead a business delegation to Jakarta to show Singapore's sincerity in wanting to play a role in helping the Indonesian economy.[35]

Malaysia

Ties with Malaysia continued their roller-coaster ride, with contentious issues as yet unresolved by year-end 1999. In January, the new Malaysian Foreign Minister, Datuk Syed Hamid Albar, said that his top priority was to ease tension in Singapore-Malaysia relations. It was after this that meetings were set up to discuss a range of issues left over from 1998 which had aroused acrimony on both sides of the causeway.[36] These included Customs, Immigration and Quarantine (CIQ) facilities for Malaysia in Singapore, Malaysia's continued water supply to Singapore, the withdrawal of CPF savings for West Malaysians who worked in Singapore, and the Singapore Air Force's alleged intrusions into Malaysian air space.

However, Professor S. Jayakumar, Singapore's Foreign Minister, announced that as long as Malaysia claimed a legal right to retain its CIQ facilities at Tanjong Pagar, the other bilateral issues could not proceed since the CIQ issue involved Singapore's sovereignty.[37] On 10 February, the Singapore government received a paper from Malaysia stating that Malaysia did not claim a legal right to operate CIQ facilities at Tanjong Pagar, and it was then announced that Singapore was ready to proceed with a bilateral discussion on all issues.[38] However, by July 1999 it was announced that no settlement on the various issues was in sight,[39] although both Singapore and Malaysia would continue to work on them.

Another issue unrelated to the above drew political ire as well. The Malaysian media took up a report in Singapore which stated that Istana Kampung Glam which housed the descendents of Sultan Hussain Shah would be turned into the Malay Heritage Centre. The Malaysian media described the process as a sudden seizing of the property from its rightful owners, portraying this as the erasing of a part of Malay history in Singapore. This compelled cabinet minister Jayakumar to lead other MPs in chiding the Malaysian media for distorted reporting on Istana Kampong Glam, describing such reports as "irresponsible and mischievous" which had "deliberately distorted and played up the facts of a sensitive racial and internal issue, without regard to the possible damage to the racial harmony and social stability in Singapore".[40] Others including *Berita Harian*, Singapore's Malay newspaper, too joined in the fray, condemning the Malaysian media for interfering in the internal affairs of another country. There was some speculation that these unfavourable Malaysian media reports were retribution for an 18 June 1999 *Business Times* report on the upcoming Malaysian elections suggesting that a new team could better lead Malaysia into the millennium. Both Prime Minister Mahathir and the Malaysian media criticized *Business Times* for interference with domestic Malaysian politics.[41] Prime Minister Goh Chok Tong through his press secretary wrote a letter to *Business Times* as well, rebuking the newspaper for its commentary, describing it as "rash, unwise and inappropriate".[42] Referring to this, Professor Jayakumar stated in parliament: "Non-interference cannot be a one-sided matter. The Malaysian media should not practise double standards. They should heed their own advice and refrain from interfering in Singapore's internal affairs."[43]

Another continuing contentious issue was the freezing of Central Limit Order Book (CLOB) shares worth RM$12 billion when Malaysia imposed capital controls in September 1998. Although it was initially announced that CLOB might be discussed along with other bilateral issues, the Malaysian government later decided to let the Singapore and Malaysia stock exchanges handle the issue.[44] In January it was announced that the status of Singapore's Central

Depository Pte. Ltd. (CDP) as the authorized nominee for CLOB shares would be extended until 31 December 1999 to give it more time to resolve the matter. By year end, the CLOB issue was as still unresolved, and the possibility of another extension was mooted by Prime Minister Mahathir in an interview. He also gave reassurance to investors that Malaysia cannot seize these shares.[45] Prime Minister Mahathir also referred to CLOB as an illegal stock exchange. The Singapore government has always denied this, claiming instead that CLOB was a legal offshore over-the-counter market. Indeed, the Singapore government has said it might refer the matter to the World Trade Organization if it was not satisfactorily resolved by Malaysia. By 31 December 1999, there were five private sector proposals offered to CLOB investors to unfreeze their shares.

Conclusion

On the whole, 1999 was an eventful year on all fronts — political, social, and economic. On the political scene, Singapore had a new president, and there was a flourishing debate on civil society. On the social front, a new vision for the millennium was unfolded, plans were made for a greying population, and women raised their voices about their position in Singapore. Economically, the news was mainly good, although the unemployment rate remained relatively high, which probably added to the resentment towards the "foreign talent" policy. Plans were made to hasten the transition towards a knowledge-based economy. With newly elected Indonesian President Abdurrahman making Singapore his first stop overseas, relations with Indonesia improved materially, while those with Malaysia remained problematic.

Notes

1. *Straits Times*, 22 September 1999.
2. *Straits Times*, 19 November 1996.
3. The *White Paper on Shared Values* was presented to the Singapore parliament by the President on 2 January 1991. It contains a description of values which Singaporeans of all races and faiths can subscribe to and live by, and which would form a national ideology. These five values are (a) nation before community and society above self, b) family as a basic unit of society, (c) regard and community support for the individual, (d) consensus instead of contention, and (e) racial and religious harmony.
4. The Maintenance of Parents Bill was first mooted by NMP Walter Woon, and was passed in parliament on 2 November 1995. It allows the setting up of a tribunal to help listen and settle claims of maintenance by parents of their children. Only those parents who do not have any means of supporting themselves will be able to claim such maintenance (*Straits Times*, 3 November 1995).
5. PM Goh Chok Tong, *Business Times*, 7 July 1997.
6. *Straits Times*, 5 October 1999.
7. *Straits Times*, 13 June 1999.
8. *Straits Times*, 8 and 13 September 1999.
9. *Straits Times*, 28 March 1999.
10. *Straits Times*, 5 October 1999.

11. *Straits Times*, 15 October 1999.
12. *Straits Times*, 30 July 1999.
13. PM Goh Chok Tong, *Business Times*, 26 April 1999.
14. *Straits Times*, 30 September 1999.
15. *Straits Times*, 12 May 1999.
16. *Straits Times*, 8 May 1999.
17. *Straits Times*, 5 October 1999.
18. PM Goh Chok Tong, *Straits Times*, 14 October 1999.
19. *Straits Times*, 26 May 1999.
20. *Straits Times*, 12 October 1999.
21. *Straits Times*, 22 September 1999.
22. *Straits Times*, 12 August 1999.
23. *Asiaweek*, 30 July 1999.
24. PM Goh Chok Tong, *Straits Times*, 18 August 1999.
25. PM Goh Chok Tong, *Straits Times*, 18 August 1999.
26. *Straits Times*, 29 August 1999.
27. PM Goh Chok Tong, *Straits Times*, 18 August 1999.
28. *Straits Times*, 9 August 1999.
29. *Straits Times*, 19 November 1999.
30. *Straits Times*, 24 August 1999.
31. *Straits Times*, 15 October 1999.
32. *Straits Times*, 24 November 1999.
33. *Straits Times*, 10 February 1999.
34. *Business Times*, 29 January 1999.
35. *Straits Times*, 7 November 1999.
36. *Straits Times*, 27 January 1999.
37. *Straits Times*, 21 January 1999.
38. *Straits Times*, 16 March 1999.
39. *Straits Times*, 22 July 1999.
40. *Straits Times*, 7 July 1999.
41. *Asiaweek*, 2 July 1999.
42. *Straits Times*, 21 June 1999.
43. *Straits Times*, 8 July 1999.
44. *Straits Times*, 26 May 1999.
45. *Straits Times*, 31 December 1999.

SINGAPORE
Information Technology for an Intelligent Island

Arun Mahizhnan

Singapore's Senior Minister Lee Kuan Yew presided over a midnight launch party in April 2000 for a new telephone company in Singapore and it was front page news in local newspapers.[1] This was not just news about a new telephone company. It is a sign of the times — only a few years ago, it would have been almost inconceivable that the most venerable political leader of Singapore, especially someone of Lee's stature and inclinations, would be part of a midnight bash for the launch of a commercial operation. Lee is now presumably game for this sort of ceremonies because the big game has changed. The big game in Singapore is information and communication technology (ICT). It is not just the technology sector that is changing but indeed the entire economy is going through significant shifts. These changes are reflected in terms like Knowledge-Based Economy (KBE) or, even more briefly, the New Economy, which punctuate public discourse these days. This article traces the development of Singapore's ICT strategies and policies — especially in the areas of infrastructure, commerce, and education — to meet the challenges of the KBE.

Genesis of an Intelligent Island
Though technology has always been part of Singapore's economic growth from the time it embarked on its major industrialization programme in the 1960s, the role of technology as a primary and central source of national development and economic growth is a relatively recent phenomenon. Singapore had been referred to as the "Emporium of the East" and "New York of the East" and by other such monikers in the past, by many writers outside Singapore. But there is one name that the government has given itself: "Intelligent Island". In 1992, the then National Computer Board released a document entitled "A Vision of an Intelligent Island: IT 2000 Report", outlining the government's strategic vision of Singapore in the information age. In painting a futuristic picture of the Intelligent Island, the report said:

ARUN MAHIZHNAN is Deputy Director of the Institute of Policy Studies, Singapore.

> In our vision, some 15 years from now, Singapore, the Intelligent Island, will be among the first countries in the world with an advanced nation-wide information infrastructure. It will interconnect computers in virtually every home, office, school, and factory.[2]

At the beginning of 2000, the target year, Singapore is almost the Intelligent Island that was imagined just eight years ago — at least in some key aspects. For example, by June 1999, 98 per cent of all homes in Singapore could be connected to the broadband network called Singapore ONE.[3] ONE stands for One Network for Everyone and it is a nation-wide multimedia network capable of delivering high-speed, high-capacity information services to almost "everyone, everywhere".[4] These services include a wide range of information and transactional facilities. Government information and services, public databases, directories, educational materials, travel information, music, movies, games, access to cybermarts, e-commerce malls, banking and trading facilities, and business-to-business applications are some examples of what are available through Singapore ONE.

ICT 21

Even before the dust settled on the IT 2000 Masterplan, the government has come up with yet another called the Information and Communication Technology 21 (ICT 21). Realizing the tremendous speed and complexity with which the ICT industries have been growing around the world in the past decade, the government revamped some of its own ministries and created a new one — Ministry of Communications and Information Technology (MCIT) — to cope with ICT developments. In addition, it merged two existing statutory boards, the National Computer Board (NCB) and the Telecommunication Authority of Singapore (TAS), into a new one: Infocomm Development Authority (IDA).

IDA's primary role is to develop, promote, as well as regulate ICT developments in an integrated manner so as to position Singapore as a leading ICT centre in the world.[5] This would appear to be a tall order. It is rather difficult for a regulatory authority to be, simultaneously, a developer and promoter. These roles, especially the first and the next two are somewhat mutually exclusive. The ethos of the regulator would be an ill-fitting cloak for the promoter to wear and vice versa. But this is not the first time such arrangements have been made in Singapore. Only a few years ago, the Singapore Broadcasting Authority (SBA) was set up with a similar mission with regard to the broadcasting industries. As there is no research available on the conduct of the SBA, it is difficult to judge its performance. However, if one were to go by the general performance of the Singapore government in its market intervention policies over the past decades, the success of the Singapore economy would clearly suggest that Singapore regulators could be market-enabling and not just market-distorting, as is generally assumed. In any case, as the IDA was established only in December 1999, it is far too early to make even cursory observations on its efficacy.

IDA's new masterplan has three strategic thrusts: (a) to develop the ICT sector as a major sector of growth, (b) to leverage on ICT as an enabler to boost the competitiveness of key economic sectors, and (c) to prepare Singapore for the information society of the future.[6]

E-Infrastructure

One of the key foundation stones of the above-mentioned vision is the electronic infrastructure for information and communication technologies. This e-infrastructure is not just confined to the national boundaries but need to be interconnected to the major ICT centres of the globe. Though the national electronic superhighway such as Singapore ONE has already been built, it is hardly enough for the complex needs of an ICT node. There are numerous other electronic services that should be in place to make Singapore a competitive, innovative, and leading player.

The ICT world is undergoing such rapid changes that even a fleet-footed government like Singapore's finds itself caught off-guard sometimes. One illustration of this situation is the sudden and, to some, shocking reversal of its earlier policy on the liberalization of the telecommunications industry in Singapore. In 1997, when it opened up the basic telecommunications services market, the government had committed itself to only partial liberalization up to March 2002. This obviously attracted certain kinds of companies to test the market, whose calculus of profit and loss was based on a restricted market. StarHub succeeded in getting the only other licence to compete with incumbent monopoly SingTel, effective April 2000. But in January 2000, the government announced that it was bringing forward the full liberalization plan by two years, to be effective April 2000, the very date StarHub was to begin operations.

In explaining the government's surprising reversal of policy, the Minister for Communications and Information Technology said:

> ... info-communications industry is changing so dramatically, and industry players and other countries are moving so quickly, that Singapore would be left totally out of the game if we waited two years till 2002. In the national interest, we therefore have to move now.[7]

The Minister also conceded that both SingTel and StarHub would need to be compensated for certain potential losses.

This episode is reflective of the changing administrative culture of Singapore as it is of the technology field. Policy reversals are rare in Singapore, certainly those that are publicly admitted. But lately the government has not flinched from doing just that and also taken a far more entrepreneurial approach to public administration. "Swift response" and "Light touch" have become common refrains among government regulatory authorities these days.

Another key focus of the ICT 21 is what the MCIT has called "dot-coming the people sector".[8] Fearing the potential risks of a digital divide between those who become net-savvy and those who do not, the MCIT and IDA are focusing on the ubiquitous adoption of computer and Internet usage. All Singaporeans, regardless of socio-economic or demographic differences, are expected to have easy and ready access to electronic information. In fact, with the advent of hand-held and wrist-worn devices, even personal computers (PCs) may no longer be the primary instrument for e-communication. With every Singapore resident plugged into some form of electronic device, there would, in effect, be an e-infrastructure in human form. What is missing so far is a government masterplan to do just that.

E-Commerce

Singapore's economic success over a thirty-year period had earned the epithet "an economic miracle". But for this miracle to be sustained, the very fundamentals of economic planning and implementation have had to be reviewed in recent times. It was increasingly becoming apparent that Singapore could not remain a leading production centre for multinational corporations (MNCs) as it had been for decades because of mounting competition from other countries. Singapore needed a very different business platform to maintain its leadership position and two intersecting phenomena provided that platform: the spread of IT and globalization. Though some forms of information technologies such as telephone, facsimile, and television have been in use for many decades, a revolutionary breakthrough occurred with the invention of the computer and even more significantly with the introduction of the Internet in the 1990s. Few countries caught on to these new technologies as Singapore did. Also in the 1990s, globalization of trade and investment took off at a feverish pitch. While the economic crisis of the late 1990s in Asia is partly a result of that phenomenon, there is little doubt about the opportunities it provides — especially for countries like Singapore. In addition to the obvious advantages of a clean and efficient government and a talented work-force, reliable high-speed, high-capacity communication channels are a vital requirement for globalizing companies. These channels form the lifelines of transaction and management for the MNCs. But in a surprising manner, these same channels also provide unprecedented opportunities for very small enterprises to conduct their business locally or globally at very little incremental cost, once the basic infrastructure is in place. Which is why there are now so many start-up companies that have grown into multi-billion dollar businesses in such a short time, as Amazon.com and Ebay.com have demonstrated. In contrast to the few thousand large corporations, Singapore now has more than 100,000 small and medium enterprises and many of them have the potential to grow to unprecedented levels through e-commerce.

In characteristic fashion, the government once again drew up another masterplan — the Electronic Commerce Masterplan — in 1998. It was designed as a comprehensive national initiative to bring e-commerce to mainstream businesses and the average citizen.[9] The plan has five main thrusts:

Develop an internationally linked e-commerce infrastructure; jump-start Singapore as an e-commerce hub; encourage businesses to use e-commerce strategically; promote usage of e-commerce by the public and businesses; and harmonize cross-border e-commerce laws and policies.

The second-mentioned initiative requires not only local efforts but also foreign support and involvement. It requires major international companies which are digital infrastructure providers, online service developers, trading and distribution companies, and retailers and wholesalers to use Singapore as their e-commerce hub. To attract them, incentive schemes and other support programmes are being put in place. The Approved Cyber Trader (ACT) is an example of such programmes. The ACT offers a 10 per cent tax concession on offshore income derived through e-commerce. Other schemes include the Development Expansion Incentive, Innovation Development Scheme, and Cluster Development Fund. In response, several companies, including Citibank, Sterling Commerce, and Hewlett Packard (HP), are reported to have committed to anchor substantial e-commerce activities here.[10]

E-Education

However, it is not just in laying the electronic infrastructure or building electronic commerce that some of the greatest challenges of incorporating ICT into the Intelligent Island lie. Like many fundamental social and economic changes, the shift towards a KBE, which will provide the sustenance for the Intelligent Island, requires the transformation of the mindset of the people. One of the best ways of achieving that is to catch them young — before the mind becomes too set. While many adult education programmes are going on around the country to induct the older generation into the world of computers and the Internet, the biggest and most productive effort is being channelled into the education system. In fact, a slogan has been coined by the government to reflect this focus: Thinking Schools, Learning Nation. Though some might wonder if it should not be the other way round, the government is keen to make "learning schools" — which is perhaps a traditional way of thinking of schools — into "thinking schools" — which is perhaps what many have criticized Singapore schools of not being! Singapore has taken specific and sustainable steps to align the education system to meet the challenges of the new century. The masterplan for IT in Education, drawn up in 1997 by the Ministry of Education (MOE), set out clear goals and specific milestones for the schools. The goals include enhancing creative thinking, lifelong learning, and social responsibility. The milestones include completing core computer training for teachers in every school by the year 2000, and achieving a 2:1 ratio between pupils and computers in schools, with 30 per cent of curriculum time devoted to IT-based learning by 2002.[11]

In addition to providing hardware and software infrastructure to transform the education system, the MOE is also focusing on the more important aspect of curriculum development and teaching. Information technology is seen as a means to expand and enrich the learning process itself. School children are now routinely doing project work that necessitates surfing the net and looking for materials that are normally not available within Singapore itself. They are also exposed to different technological possibilities in assembling and presenting these materials in ways never before done. In the process, they are not only learning different things but also learning things differently. There are also virtual classrooms now whereby pupils may remain in their respective homes but join their classmates in cyberspace with the teacher conducting lessons through the computer or a nifty hand-held device called Edupad. Several libraries are digitizing their collections to create virtual books that could be accessed anywhere, anytime. All these seem to add to the children's ability to learn independently, to think innovatively, and even to co-operate constructively. These are attributes that any Intelligent Island would consider prerequisites.

Conclusion

Though every one understands Rome was not built in a day, increasingly the challenge for the modern metropolis is one of coping with the task of never-ending building. As Singapore has learnt, there is no completion date for building the Intelligent Island. Even as one part is being built, another part becomes obsolete, or worse still, what one is building becomes obsolete even before completion. This is the nature of information and communication technologies. The most famous of the computer-related laws, Moore's law, which stated that computing power doubles every eighteen months, is itself becoming outdated. Thus, the Intelligent Island may never be completed but it seems likely to flourish even in an unfinished state.

Notes

The author would like to acknowledge the considerable research assistance of Mr Obood Talib, Research Assistant, Institute of Policy Studies.

1. *Straits Times*, 1 April 2000, p. 1.
2. National Computer Board, *A Vision of an Intelligent Island: IT 200 Report* (Singapore, 1992), p. 10.
3. National Computer Board, Press Release on 22 June 1999 <www.ncb.gov.sg/ncb/press/220699.asp>.
4. <http://www.s-one.gov.sg/overview>, p. 1.
5. <www.ncb.gov.sg/ncb/press/301199.asp>.
6. Ibid.
7. <www.ida.gov.sg/website/IDAContent.nsf/>.
8. Ibid.
9. <regent.ncb.gov.sg/ncb/press/1998/230998.asp>.
10. <www.ida.gov.sg/website/idac>.
11. <www.ida.gov.sg/website/IDAContent.nsf/>.

THAILAND

THAILAND
Farewell to Old-Style Politics?

Suchit Bunbongkarn

When Chuan Leekpai became Prime Minister again in November 1997, there was high hope that not only would the economic crisis be resolved, but the fragility of democracy and the corrupt practices among politicians would also be reduced. It was his impressive record of integrity and his economic dream team led by respected and competent former financial managers that stimulated this optimism among the Thai public. However, after two years in power, Chuan was unable to impress the Thai with his economic and political performance. In 1999, although the economy showed signs of recovery, the Thai, especially the urban middle class were still unhappy with its slow pace. In the political sphere, the democratic weakness and political corruption continued despite the new constitution aimed at reforming the political system. Chuan's government continued to face conflict and bickering among the coalition partners. The Prime Minister had to reshuffle the cabinet again in July to ensure support in the House of Representatives. He survived two no-confidence votes but his government had been discredited considerably. On the eve of the new millennium, Chuan had to rely on his personal strengths like integrity and honesty to maintain public support. The old-style politics showed no sign of withering away. However, some are optimistic that when the new constitution is fully in effect and the new election system and the new parliament start to function in the year 2000, Thai democracy will move gradually towards a more stable, accountable, and transparent system.

Politics of Economic Reform

How to resolve the economic crisis continued to be one of the main issues debated throughout 1999. The government introduced a number of bills to reform the financial sector and state enterprises and to enforce debt restructuring in the private sector. The bills, especially the Bankruptcy Amendment Bill, and the State Enterprise Capital Bill, intensified debates in the National

---

SUCHIT BUNBONGKARN is Judge of the Constitutional Court of Thailand. He previously served as Dean of the Faculty of Political Science, Chulalongkorn University, Bangkok, and Director of the Institute of Security and International Studies at the same university.

Assembly over the government's economic policy. A number of senators and business leaders were unhappy with the reform measures, which followed the IMF (International Monetary Fund) conditionality. Some sincerely believed that they were not the best prescription for economic recovery. There were also politicians and businessmen who were adversely affected by the measures and who tried to rally nationalist sentiments against the government's pro-IMF policy. In January when the Senate began to deliberate the Bankruptcy Amendment Bill, a group of senators came out against it, arguing that the bill would help foreign creditors to take over local enterprises cheaply. They questioned the timing of the passing of the bills when the IMF-prescribed economic reforms had not yet led the country out of the recession. One senator was quoted as saying that if the bills became laws, 90 per cent of the Thai people would become bankrupt. Another blasted the government for surrendering to the IMF and accused the international financial institutions of fooling the government to help foreigners collect their debts.[1]

Those who came out against the government economic bills were industrialists whose companies were outstanding debtors and would be affected once the bills became laws. The passing of the bankruptcy and foreclosure bills would deny corporate owners any opportunity to delay paying their debts. The opposition of such businessmen, however, did not produce broader public opposition against the government as the public was aware that those who opposed the bills were doing so for their private business interests. After some compromises had been made with the Senate to ensure a smooth and quick passage, the bankruptcy and foreclosure bills were passed to become laws.

Another controversial bill was the state enterprise capital bill, which was designed to facilitate privatization of state enterprises. The Chuan government had adopted the privatization policy as one of the measures to deal with the economic crisis but it was opposed by state enterprise employees organizations, of which the most vocal was the Electricity Generating Authority of Thailand (EGAT). One of EGAT's power plants was in the government plans for privatization. Those against the bill were concerned that it might be against the public interest as regulatory mechanisms governing the would-be privatized businesses were not yet in place. Another concern was the job security of the state enterprises' employees. However, the government stood firm on the bill and despite some delay, protests, and criticisms, it was finally passed by the parliament in November 1999.

The nexus between economics and politics was also reflected in the public's reaction to the government's economic stimulus package announced on 30 March 1999. This was a package of measures to induce people to invest and spend more. Earlier, the government was criticized for paying too much attention to financial institutions and overlooking the real sector. The 14 August 1998 measures were intended to reform the financial sector and there had been no other measures to stimulate the real sector until the stimulus package of 30 March 1999. The public response to it was not enthusiastic. The government had hoped that the package would also raise its credibility and popularity even though the measures were intended for long-term effects. One of the dilemmas the government faced was that if it wanted to gain popular support, especially among the urban middle class, it needed to put emphasis on short-term policies to please those who wanted a quick relief from the crisis and did not care much about a longer-term solution. But since the government decided to concentrate on a long-term policy and on fundamental change in the private sector, it was not easy to win the confidence of the middle class because the impact of the measures was not immediate. The Thai would not spend more unless they had confidence in the economy, while an economic turnaround was difficult to achieve if the people did not spend. As one commentator said, the stimulus package took into account the economic reality, but seemed to ignore the importance of the psychological factor.[2] More importantly, the government was unable to resolve the banking problems, especially those connected with non-performing loans (NPLs). As the rate of NPLs was still very high in most of the banks, they were not willing to give out loans. Thus, despite the stimulus package, it was anticipated that the economic recovery would continue to be slow.

Finance Minister Tarrin Nimmanahaeminda was a major target of criticism as he was responsible for financial reforms and was the Prime Minister's most trusted man. He was accused of mishandling the economy and of protecting his brother, the former chief executive officer of Krung Thai Bank, the largest state-owned bank. Those who wanted to see more drastic reform criticized him for not being tough enough in cleaning up this bank. The opposition accused him of trying to cover up the mismanagement of the bank, especially in the areas of lending practices, in order to protect Sirin Nimmanahaeminda, his brother. The high level of NPLs at the bank led people to think that there might be some wrong-doings on the part of the management. In October the Minister set up a committee made up of respectable figures in the financial sector to investigate these accusations. Although the committee found no credible evidence to file a complaint against the management, the public still believed that some dubious lending practices might exist. As pressure built up on him, the Minister asked the Bank of Thailand, which supervised commercial banks, to look into the matter while he continued to stand firm that he had done nothing to protect his brother or Krung Thai Bank.[3]

At the beginning of 1999, Tarrin was one of three ministers who were grilled by the opposition during the no-confidence debate. A promising young politician of the New Aspiration Party, Chaturon Chaisang, led the attacks. The Minister was accused of adopting wrong economic policies and lacking transparency. The opposition was trying to convince the people during the debate that the government, in particular the Finance Minister, had failed to reform the financial sector and bring about economic recovery. Never before had economic issues been politicized to this extent to discredit the prime minister and his finance minister.

The Economic Crisis, Political Corruption, and the No-Confidence Debate

The Chuan government entered the year 1999 with a no-confidence motion by the opposition parties. The debate took place on 28 to 30 January 1999. Instead of targeting the whole cabinet, the opposition adopted a new strategy of attacking only three key ministers who were close to Prime Minister Chuan and who were key figures in the Democrat Party. Apart from Minister of Finance Tarrin Nimmanahaeminda, the other two were Sanan Kachornprasat, the Interior Minister, and Suthep Tueksuban, the Communications Minister. Sanan served as the party's secretary-general and was known to be one of the most powerful figures in the party. There had been speculation that Suthep would succeed Sanan as the secretary-general. The opposition hoped to damage the three in order to destabilize the coalition.

As mentioned above, economic issues were some of the debate topics. But corruption, malpractices, and mismanagement in various government agencies were also featured. Chuan was known for his integrity, and he had emphasized time and again that honesty and transparent management were his top priorities. Thus, if the opposition could prove that his ministers had been guilty of corruption, the Prime Minister could be in trouble.

During the three-day debate, Interior Minister Sanan was assailed on a number of issues, ranging from the Kanchanaburi land scandal and the controversial expressway toll hike, to the mishandling of legal aspects of the upgrading of the Police Department into the National Police Bureau. The opposition, led by the New Aspiration Party, claimed that they had enough evidence to prove Sanan's abuse of power and corruption and believed that after the debate the Democrat secretary-general and the Interior Minister would be isolated from the rest of the party. The Communications Minister was attacked on a number of issues, including the synchronous digital hierarchy (SDH) telephone scandal. In 1998, Suthep had been accused by Thawee Kraikupt, a Democrat member of parliament (MP) from Ratchburi, of endorsing the results of the bidding for the SDH telephone project despite some dubious practices that allowed the project to be divided into smaller sub-projects so that each of the bidders could win a Suthep project.

All three ministers survived the three days of heavy assault. The coalition partners continued to stick together. The opposition was unable to isolate the Democrat Party from the others. They failed to mobilize public pressure to force the resignation of the three ministers or the Prime Minister though the debate had damaged them. Perhaps the Thai electorate continued to trust the Prime Minister. Another explanation for the government's survival was that, from the point of view of the public, the opposition was not a better alternative. The people still remembered their experiences with Chavalit Yongchaiyuth and the opposition when they were in power.

Nevertheless, the New Aspiration Party did not give up easily. Having failed in the censure vote, the party wanted to try the impeachment channel provided in the new constitution to remove the Prime Minister and the Interior Minister. Its members of parliament filed a complaint against the two for corruption and abuse of power in relation to the election of provincial assemblies, the expressway toll hike, and the move of the National Police Bureau from the control of the Interior Ministry to the Prime Minister's Office. The National Counter Corruption Commission (NCCC) were asked to investigate into these matters. If the NCCC found them guilty, the case would be submitted to parliament to have them removed from office. After some months of investigation, however, the NCCC found no evidence to impeach them and decided to drop the case.

The Increasing Strength of Civil Society

Despite the economic crisis, the year 1999 saw the growing strength of civil society or the people's sector. Several non-governmental organizations (NGOs), social groups, and rural farmers were more assertive, demanding justice, participation in the decision-making process to protect the environment and natural resources, and more government attention to the problems of the rural poor. One of the cases worth mentioning was the protest of local residents against the construction of two power plants in Prachuab province. The demonstration in December 1998 ended after a few days with violent clashes between the protesters and the police. The opponents of the power plants continued to campaign against their construction, claiming that the coal-fired plants would pollute the environment. Some believed that the pollution would affect the seashore, killing baby fish, plankton, and other small creatures as well as damaging coral reefs. They were not convinced that the use of low-sulphur coal would not produce air pollution and acid rain. Some even went further to argue that they were against the intrusion of industry into their communities, as represented by the two power plants and preferred a simple way of life. The protesters were backed by environmental groups and the local government administration.

The two companies' management and other proponents of the projects argued that the plants would have high standards of environmental protection. They also pointed out that the coal to be used would be low-sulphur, which would produce no air pollution. The Union Power Development Company, one of the two campanies, explained that the project would benefit the community and promised to continue to contribute to a better living environment in the area. Nonetheless, a large number of local residents still rejected the projects.

With no solution in sight, the government decided to resort to a public hearing. But those who were against the project rejected the hearing on the grounds that it came too late, arguing that it should have been held before the project was launched. Nevertheless, it was decided to move ahead with the hearing, which was organized at Bor Nok sub-district, one of the construction sites, in September 1999. Despite the boycott by most of the opponents, the hearing went off smoothly. However, the report submitted to the government did not suggest whether they should proceed with the project. By the end of the year the government had yet to decide what to do with the project.

The above case suggests that the voice of the people was becoming more powerful. This, coupled with the fact that the new constitution guarantees the right of the people to participate in the decision-making process of a project that would affect their community's environment, would have a more significant impact on the government's development projects. Protests by poor farmers occurred throughout the year. In January and February, more than 600 families from a village in Khon Kaen province in the northeast, led by the Assembly of Northeastern Small-Scale Farmers, illegally entered Dong Larn's forest plantation and began cutting down trees. These people had been affected by government projects to develop the Dong Larn area. Five projects were launched between 1979 and 1990 and a large number of villagers were removed. The idea was to move villagers out of the forest and provide them with resettlement in a deteriorated forest. The villagers claimed that they were promised a plot of land but many had not yet received it. Some claimed that the land they obtained could not be used for farming. After a series of negotiations, the government agreed to allow the villagers to stay in Dong Larn temporarily while the authorities concerned looked for alternative land for them.

Another interesting protest was the one organized by tapioca farmers in the northeast region in November. Because of falling prices in the world markets, the farmers wanted the government to guarantee the tapioca price. The government agreed but the protesters claimed that the price guaranteed was too low. The rally by the farmers to pressurize the government to guarantee higher prices took place in front of Government House but it could not force the government to change its stand. The issue became politicized when Interior Minister Sanan claimed that Chat Pattana Party, one of the coalition partners, was behind the rally, as canvassers of Korn Taparangsri, the Chat Pattana's leader and an MP from Korat, where the protesters came from, were found to be organizing it. After a series of negotiations, the farmers decided to return home without obtaining any commitment from the government.

The strength of civil society could be seen not only in its fight for the rural poor but also in its campaigning against corruption. One of the outstanding examples of the latter related to the alleged corruption of politicians and public health officers in purchasing medicine and medical equipment for public hospitals nation-wide. This scandal occurred in 1998 and a group of NGOs had then pressed the government to investigate the matter. A preliminary investigation by the Counter Corruption Committee (CCC)[4] came to the conclusion that there was enough evidence for further investigations into corruption against one political appointee and some officers at the Public Health Ministry. The case was sent to the police for criminal investigation and to the Ministry for disciplinary action. However, the NGOs were not pleased with the result and in 1999 they continued to put pressure on the CCC for further investigation. The CCC again found enough evidence for disciplinary action against some more public health officers but none for any criminal charges. The NGOs were still unhappy with the results as they were unable to obtain the prosecution of people at the ministerial level. What they had done, nonetheless, raised the public's awareness on corruption issues, and pushed the government agencies, especially the CCC and their officers, towards transparency, including, in this instance, the release of the full investigation report to the public.[5]

Another case that reflected the increasing influence of civil society was that of Dhammachayo, the former abbot of Dhammakaya Temple. The press had been attacking the abbot for several months on a number of issues, including embezzlement of the temple's funds. Prominent and respectable monks also accused one of his clerical assistants of distorting the Buddha's teachings. A Buddhist association and a group of respectable figures in society also filed a complaint with Mahatherasamakhom, or the Supreme Sangha Council, and the Department of Religious Affairs for investigation. In fact, the Dhammakaya Temple had developed its influence and wealth for more than two decades to represent a new image of the Sangha. The temple was very popular among intellectuals, university students, and the younger generation for its strict discipline. It is believed that the temple had more than a hundred thousand followers, a number of whom came from wealthy families. It has focused on university students and only those who have attained a satisfactory level of success in the Dhammakaya meditation system are accepted for ordination. As Peter Jackson puts it: "The selection process appears to be oriented towards ensuring that the students who complete Dhammadayada training are those who are most likely to succeed in future careers in business and government".[6] The major concern of the Sangha was the wealth of the temple, and the commercial-like manner in which it ran its property. Eventually, the police issued a warrant to arrest Dhammachayo in August 1999 for the abuse of temple funds. The abbot agreed to surrender himself to the police and after several hours of interrogation, the police released him on a bail of 2 million baht. Dhammachayo insisted that he was innocent. The police had no intention of detaining or defrocking him — they wanted to avoid possible unrest by the temple's followers.

The trial will be a long one and no one is sure how it will end. The Dhammakaya's followers are known to be in all the professions and at every level of society. The case reflects the inadequacies of monastic disciplinary procedures. The government was under criticism for being unable to resolve this complex problem and to come up with a long-term solution.

The Year-End No-Confidence Debate
The year 1999 ended with a no-confidence debate, just as it had begun with one. No-confidence debates are a common feature of Thai democracy and the hidden agenda is to discredit the government or to split the coalition. The no-

confidence debate that took place on 15–18 December was different from the one in January in that it was against the government as a whole.

The motion, submitted by the opposition to the House Speaker on 24 November, accused the Chuan government of corruption and supporting irregularities in government agencies. It alleged that the Prime Minister lacked vision and was unable to run the country, allowing foreign interests to exploit national resources, treating protesters cruelly, and infringing on the people's right to information and on the freedom of the press. It was anticipated that in addition to the Prime Minister, the key Democrat ministers including Finance Minister Tarrin, Interior Minister Sanan, and Communications Minister Suthep would be the major targets. Issues to be raised were expected to include the Krung Thai Bank's dubious lending practices, the conflict between the Forestry Department and the National Police Bureau over the legality of the issuance of a land title deed in Kanchanaburi and the financial and economic reform policy.

Without waiting for the start of the debate, Prime Minister Chuan launched an offensive against the opposition. A day before the submission of the debate motion, the Prime Minister, Finance Minister Tarrin, and Minister Abhisit of the Prime Minister's Office went on television to explain the government's achievements and to thank the people for helping the government to put Thailand's economy on the road of recovery. Chuan assured the people that the economic measures carried out by the government were on the right track and that they could expect more good news in the future. His humble style and his avoidance of attacks against the opposition swayed the mood of the people as indicated by the results of the Dusit poll that showed that most respondents surveyed were satisfied with the Prime Minister's performance.[7] However, some were dissatisfied with his answers relating to allegations of corruption on the part of his ministers. On the Krung Thai Bank issue, Finance Minister Tarrin remained steadfast to his position that there was no favouritism or nepotism in his dealing with the problem.

The debate went on for five days and the attacks were centred on the Prime Minister, Interior Minister Sanan, and Finance Minister Tarrin on issues such as economic performance, corruption, and lack of vision. The government eventually won the vote, which to some extent reflected coalition solidarity. The public continued to support the Prime Minister although the responses of some ministers, especially the Interior Minister, to the opposition's accusations were not convincing. The opposition was able to discredit the Interior Minister and the Finance Minister but not the Prime Minister and was still unable to convince the public that they were the better alternative.

Foreign Relations

Thailand's relationship with Myanmar continued to be problematic. Since the two countries share 2,000 kilometres of a common border, perhaps it is not surprising that there are problems such as disputed boundaries, smuggling, illegal migration and drug trafficking. The most serious related to Myanmar refugees — mostly students — in Thailand and the alleged violations of Myanmar territorial waters and economic zone by Thai fishing vessels.

In December 1998, an armed fishing trawler carrying no national identification attacked a Thai naval vessel in the Andaman Sea, killing two Thai naval officers. An armed clash between a Thai naval vessel and an unidentified fishing boat while the Thai ship was patrolling off the Ranong coast in the Andaman Sea occurred again on 12 January 1999. Each side accused the other of intrusion into territorial waters. Fortunately, the clashes did not escalate into a more violent and larger-scale conflict. In their meeting in March in a Thai northern city, Thai Prime Minister Chuan and Myanmar Prime Minister Than Shwe agreed to explore measures to reduce tensions on the border.

The worst incident between the two countries was the seizure of the Myanmar embassy in Bangkok by a group of Myanmar students on 1 October 1999. Armed with assault rifles, and hand grenades, five Myanmar dissident students stormed the embassy and held Myanmar diplomats, foreigners, and Thai as hostages. They demanded that Yangon release all political prisoners, open a dialogue with pro-democracy politicians, and convene the parliament that was elected in Myanmar in May 1990. The embassy seizure caught everyone by surprise. Nonetheless, the government wanted to end the occupation as quickly as possible, and without bloodshed. Luckily, the hostage takers were not professional terrorists, and so were not too difficult to deal with. After two days of intense negotiations, the students decided to release the hostages when the government agreed to provide them with a helicopter to fly them to the border with Deputy Foreign Minister M.R. Sukhumbhand Paribatra who offered himself as a hostage. Everyone was relieved when the Minister came back safely from the border after letting the dissidents disappear into the border area.

The government was praised at home and abroad for a quick and peaceful end to the occupation. But the Myanmar military junta, although expressing gratitude for this, decided to close the border and withdraw a fishery concession for Thai fishermen. There was no official explanation for the border closure, but it is believed that Yangon was unhappy because the Thai government did not make any serious effort to apprehend and punish the students involved. The Myanmar junta was also displeased with the leniency the Thai authorities showed to the Myanmar refugees at Maneeloy Camp in Ratchburi. As for the withdrawal of the fishery concession, the Myanmar authorities said that they wanted to review the fees. The Thai government stood its ground on what it had done to end the seizure of the embassy and made it known that everything must be done in accordance with Thai law and that it could not be forced to act otherwise. In fact, the Thai police issued arrest warrants for the five students and insisted that they would be arrested if found in Thai territory.

The political gap between Thailand and Myanmar was a major obstacle in the way of fostering bilateral ties and settling disputes. As a democratic country, Thailand could not afford to use harsh measures against the refugees and leniency was applied to them as long as they did not create trouble. However, the Thai authorities have tightened control at Maneeloy Camp and started looking for the possibility of moving the refugees to a third country to avoid future trouble that may affect the relationship with Myanmar.

Myanmar re-opened the border several weeks later after Thai Foreign Minister Surin returned from talks with the Myanmar leaders in Yangon. It was believed that Myanmar could not afford to close the border for long since some of its border towns such as Tachelek had to rely on the Thai side for food and fuel supplies. The Myanmar junta agreed that it would comply with international law in closing the border in future. Nonetheless, several border problems remained unresolved and Thai-Myanmar relations continued to be far from cordial.

One of new developments in Thai foreign relations was the decision to join the International Force for East Timor (INTERFET) to restore peace in East Timor. Thailand went along with the position of the Association of South-east Asian Nations (ASEAN) on the East Timor issue. As the principle of non-intervention in each other's internal affairs was still upheld, the ASEAN members did not make any move to deal with the conflict, an inaction that surely made the regional grouping less relevant. ASEAN agreed to leave the matter to the United Nations, which allowed non-ASEAN countries especially Australia, the United States, and the European Union to take initiatives. When the U.N. Security Council adopted a resolution to send an international force to East Timor, Australia was named to lead it. Thailand agreed to an Australian request to join the force after the discussion between Prime Minister Chuan and his Australian counterpart John Howard while they were attending the Asia-Pacific Economic Co-operation (APEC) meeting in New Zealand. To avoid any misunderstanding by Indonesia, the Thai Foreign Ministry spokesman reiterated that Thailand was willing to help Indonesia, which was a friend in ASEAN. Thai Foreign Minister Surin rushed to meet with President Habibie to discuss the sending of Thai troops to ensure his endorsement.

There were no significant negative reactions at home regarding Thailand's participation in the INTERFET. The army chief, General Surayud Chulanond, fully co-operated with the government and agreed to send an infantry battalion, while the navy would send a supply ship. Criticisms were focused on the funding, however. The United Nations did not provide funds for the INTERFET and it had to depend on the contributions of some members such as Japan. As Thailand was in the midst of the economic crisis, the question of where the money to pay for the troops would come from was a legitimate though sensitive one despite the promise of the U.N. secretary-general that there would be funding for the INTERFET.

The case of East Timor demonstrated that ASEAN is now at the crossroads. With its enlargement to cover all ten Southeast Asian countries, it is interesting to see how ASEAN can make itself more relevant to the changing political, security, and economic environment in the region. ASEAN is becoming more diversified economically, socially, and politically. This has made it more diffi-cult for ASEAN to reach consensus on sensitive issues. It is true that the political gap within ASEAN between different political systems and regimes is not easy to bridge, but the gap between the rich ASEAN and poor ASEAN can and should be reduced. In this context Foreign Minister Surin has proposed that ASEAN should give priority to the development of the Greater Mekong basin. However, if violence erupts again in some parts of Indonesia such as Aceh and the situation requires international intervention, Thailand will find itself in a dilemma as the chair of ASEAN Standing Committee on how to react and make ASEAN more relevant to the regional peace and security without revoking the principle of non-intervention.

Conclusion

Despite the frailty of its financial institutions in 1999 and its fragile democracy plagued by scandals and corruption, one institution that has united the na-tion, and of which the Thai are very proud, is the monarchy. 1999 was an exceptional year as Thai celebrated King Bhumipol's seventy-second birthday, an event of special significance to them. The public sector, the business com-munity, and the people at large expressed their gratitude and appreciation to their beloved King for his dedication and contribution to the development of the country and the well-being of the people.

The new millennium would bring a number of challenges for the Thai. They will, for the first time, vote in the Senate election in March 2000 and, very likely, in the lower House election a few months later. These elections will be conducted under a new electoral system stipulated in the new constitution. The Thai people were not sure that the new system would produce a capable and honest political leadership as well as good governance. However, there was at least hope that with the full implementation of the new constitution and the convening of a new parliament, new-style politics will come with the new millennium.

NOTES

1. "Contrasting Claims over Guarantors' Clause in Key Legislation", *Nation*, 18 Janu-ary 1999, p. A2.
2. "News Analysis", *Nation*, 31 March 1999, p. A1.
3. For a well-balanced account on the role of Finance Minister Tarrin in his dealing with the financial crisis, see *Far Eastern Economic Review*, 4 November 1999, p. 11.
4. The CCC preceded the NCCC. The NCCC was appointed in April 1999 and took over the functions of the CCC when it was dissolved in November 1999.
5. For the full text of the CCC's investigation report, see *Matichon*, 8 July 1999, pp. 1–19.
6. Peter Jackson, *Buddhism, Legitimation and Conflict: The Political Functions of Urban Thai Buddhism in the 19th and 20th Centuries* (Singapore: Institute of Southeast Asian Studies, 1989), p. 212.
7. *Nation*, 25 November 1999, p. A3.

THE THAI ECONOMY
Stabilization and Reforms

Pichit Likitkijsomboon

The economic crisis that erupted in 1997 was the most severe in Thailand's modern history. Its impact was not confined to the low and lower-middle income classes in urban centres alone; a wide range of socio-economic groups were adversely affected, from high-level industrialists, bankers, financiers, and white-collar employees to factory workers, farmers, petty traders, and street vendors. The hardest hit initially were those in the urban centres, particularly company employees and factory workers who had been laid off. New hiring was slowed down and even halted, causing new entrants to the labour market to have few employment prospects, while those who managed to keep their jobs were under constant threat of falling income and unemployment. The crisis thus resulted in large-scale unemployment in urban centres, a phenomenon previously unseen in Thailand. The number of those laid off during the second half of 1997, as estimated by the National Economic and Social Development Board (NESDB), was 42,200, with unemployment reaching 1.15 million, or 3.5 per cent of the labour force, at the end of 1997. By the end of 1998, unemployment as a result of the crisis was believed to exceed 2 million.

The Economy in 1999
In contrast, 1999 was the year of stabilization and creeping recovery. Various economic indicators show that the economy started recovering very slowly in the second quarter of 1999.

Different investment spending indicators do not show a consistent pattern of recovery. The private investment index, as calculated by the Bank of Thailand (BOT), improved by falling at a slower rate in the first nine months of 1999. The manufacturing output index growth rose from 0.4 per cent in January 1999 to 12 per cent in June and to 15.4 per cent in September 1999. Capital goods imports were unstable, with 2 per cent growth in April 1999, a contraction of 6.3 per cent in May and then a surge of 28.9 per cent in June 1999. Cement consumption followed a similar pattern. Steel bar and galvanized iron sheet sales managed to retain positive growth. Capacity utilization, which had been falling since early 1997, bottomed at 50 per cent in January

PICHIT LIKITKIJSOMBOON is Assistant Professor at the Faculty of Economics, Thammasat University, Bangkok.

1998 and fluctuated around 50 to 55 per cent for the rest of 1998 before improving gradually in 1999, from 52.6 per cent in January to 59.9 per cent in June 1999. It lingered between 58.6 and 60.8 per cent during the third quarter of 1999.

Most consumption spending indicators have recovered slowly since the beginning of 1999, although the trend remains fragile. Consumer goods imports and automobile and tyre sales recovered strongly, while department store sales remained depressed. Beer sales registered strong growth but soft drink sales showed a decline.

After 0.8 per cent growth in the first half of 1999, exports registered 10.2 per cent growth in third quarter of 1999, resulting in 3.9 per cent growth for the first nine months of 1999. However, imports registered higher growth rates of 5.9 per cent in the first six months of 1999 and 20.9 per cent in the third quarter of 1999. Thus, the merchandise trade surplus for the first six months of 1999 was 16.4 per cent lower than for the same period of the previous year, and 22 per cent lower in the third quarter of 1999. The service balance also deteriorated. Consequently, the current account surplus in the first nine months of 1999 fell by 13.4 per cent as against the same period in 1998.

The capital account recorded a deficit of US$2,872 million for the first half of 1999, a significant improvement of 50.2 per cent from a deficit of US$5,772 million for the same period the previous year. During July–August 1999, the capital account deficit was 18.0 per cent lower than for the same period in 1998. The long-term net private capital outflow since early 1997 was the result of foreign debt repayments by Thai corporations. Due to a continual budget deficit, the public debt at end June 1999 was 41.1 per cent higher than the amount outstanding at end September 1998. The government responded by issuing a series of debt instruments to finance its budget deficit.

A decline in prices or negative inflation has persisted since May 1999. The impact of rising oil prices in September 1999 was moderated by weak domestic spending and excess capacity. Real interest rates (nominal interest rates net of inflation) gradually increased and became higher than their pre-crisis levels. This could potentially slow down the recovery process. Bank lending was still declining, due to large non-performing loans (NPLs), high risk, and the slow recovery of the economy.

Asset Sales of Fifty-Six Defunct Finance Companies

The Financial Sector Restructuring Authority (FRA) was established by the government on 24 October 1997 in accordance with the Emergency Decree on Financial Sector Restructuring BE 2540 (1997). The FRA was created to oversee the rehabilitation of fifty-eight finance companies whose operations had been suspended by the order of the Finance Minister. Only two of the fifty-eight finance companies were allowed to resume operations in December 1997, while the remaining fifty-six companies were closed down permanently and their assets taken over by the FRA.

The assets were divided into core assets (consisting of hire purchase loans, residential mortgages, and commercial loans) and non-core assets (comprising office vehicles, capital investment, and other assets such as office equipment). The total asset sales for 1998 amounted to 105.3 billion baht, consisting of 75.4 billion baht core assets, or 71.6 per cent of the total, and 29.9 billion baht non-core assets, or 28.4 per cent of the total. The first asset auction for 1999 was held on 19 March 1999, consisting of commercial loans worth 221.5 billion baht. This round managed to realize only 40.3 billion baht, or 18.2 per cent of the outstanding balance.

The second asset auction, held on 6 July 1999, consisted of construction loans worth 1.3 billion baht. The auction garnered only 157.3 million baht, or 12.1 per cent of the outstanding balance. The third round of asset sales, held on 11 August 1999, comprised commercial and other loans worth 129 billion baht. This auction fetched 31 billion baht, or 24 per cent of the outstanding balance. The final round of core asset sales, for commercial and other loans worth 17.8 billion baht, was held on 10 November 1999. This round fetched 5.4 billion baht, or 30.1 per cent of the outstanding value. The remaining core assets of 86 billion baht will have to undergo a bankruptcy procedure, as they are too low in quality for auction. Some non-core assets consisting mainly of capital (securities) investments were auctioned in December 1999 and early 2000.

Corporate Debt Restructuring

The most serious obstacle preventing commercial banks from expanding lending, and hence injecting liquidity into businesses — necessary precursers for an economic recovery — is their huge NPLs, namely, loans with unpaid interest of more than three months. The authorities tackled the NPL problem with a two-pronged strategy: debt restructuring to reduce the size of NPLs and recapitalization to strengthen bank capital bases.

The Corporate Debt Restructuring Advisory Committee (CDRAC), headed by the Central Bank governor, was established by the Ministry of Finance (MOF) on 25 June 1998 with the assistance of the Federation of Thai Industries, the Board of Trade, and the Thai Bankers Association to co-ordinate debt restructuring between debtors and creditors. To facilitate such restructuring, incentives were granted that allowed financial institutions to upgrade a doubtful or loss loan to a substandard loan under certain conditions;[1] a new loan to be extended even if a client's previous loan was classified as non-performing;[2] a waiver of various taxes[3] in transferring assets, revising debt repayment conditions, and converting debt into equity for companies undergoing debt restructuring.

Debts in the restructuring process amounted to 271.1 billion baht in July 1998 (of which debts of only 9.3 billion baht, or 3.4 per cent, were restructured successfully), 378.3 billion in August 1998, 437.7 billion in September 1998, and 569.5 billion in October 1998, while restructured debts increased to

11.8 billion baht, 16.7 billion baht, and 36.6 billion baht, respectively. Thus the success rate gradually improved, from 3.1 per cent in August to 3.8 per cent in September and to 6.4 per cent in October 1998.

The slow pace of debt restructuring was in large part due to the commercial banks' reluctance to incur large realized losses from restructuring their NPLs. To accelerate the process, the BOT issued more incentives during the last quarter of 1998.[4] Following this, debt restructuring gathered pace. In January 1999 alone, Thai companies completed debt restructuring worth 31.8 billion baht, or 20 per cent higher than the 26.5 billion baht completed in December 1998. By end August 1999, Thai companies had completed debt restructuring worth 680.2 billion baht, while 1,204.6 billion baht of loans were still in the restructuring process. These figures were 142.1 per cent and 52.4 per cent higher than the completed 280.9 billion baht and 790.4 billion baht in process at end March 1999, respectively.

Non-performing loans as a percentage of total loans, which were as high as 45 per cent at end 1998, peaked at 47.7 per cent in May 1999. Despite the rapid progress in debt restructuring, the figure was slow to come down. On 18 August 1999, the BOT modified the definition of NPLs to facilitate the lowering of NPL figures. From the financial period ending 30 September 1999, NPLs must be defined as non-performing loans outstanding per account instead of per individual borrower, since the same individual borrower may have several loan accounts, some of which may still be performing financially. Moreover, those NPLs that have passed through a successful debt restructuring process can now be taken off the NPL list from the day of contract conclusion, without needing to fulfil the three-month consecutive payment requirement.

Restructured loans totalled 762.7 trillion baht as of 30 September 1999.[5] The debt restructuring process will increasingly separate viable firms adversely affected by short-term interest rates, exchange rates, and domestic demand volatility from those firms suffering from structural overcapacity and inefficiency. Restructuring rates varied significantly across sectors. The telecommunications, services, and wholesale trade sectors showed high rates of successful restructuring, while the construction materials, steel, and real estate sectors lagged behind.

The slow decline of NPLs signifies problems in the debt restructuring process, such as unclear measures and guidelines for operational restructuring and a lack of co-operation among creditors. Moreover, there were a number of cases in which certain restructured debts became NPLs again and had to re-enter a new round of debt restructuring as a result of poor general economic conditions and the debtors' attempts to renegotiate better deals as interest rates fell. It is estimated that around 15 per cent of restructured debt would return for a second round of restructuring in the third quarter of 1999. The successful restructuring outcomes seem to focus on small debtors, single lenders, and syndicate lenders with a lead creditor, resulting in an average case size of 7.5 million baht.

In contrast to the improvement of the NPL problem in commercial banks, NPLs in the state-owned banks worsened, rising from 989 billion baht in January 1999 to 1.18 trillion baht in June 1999. This reflected poor NPL management and slow debt restructuring in that sector. As the authorities took over ailing financial institutions without well-prepared measures, such action simply amassed substantial bad assets in state-owned banks and led to soaring NPL figures in that sector. By end September 1999, state-owned banks showed the worst NPL problems, with 65.6 per cent of total loans, while private banks provided better results, with 39.8 per cent.

Non-performing loans at end September 1999 amounted to 2.57 trillion baht, the fourth month in a row where outstanding NPLs had declined. However, NPLs for the whole financial system were still as high as 45.3 per cent of total loan portfolios. It is expected that the figure will come down more rapidly during the first half of 2000, as the rapid progress in debt restructuring starts to have a significant effect on the size of NPLs.

Financial Sector Restructuring Plan

On 14 August 1998, the MOF and BOT jointly announced the Financial Sector Restructuring Plan, under which twelve finance companies and six commercial banks previously taken over by the authorities would be consolidated and restructured. The heart of the plan is the capital support facilities for bank recapitalization. These capital support facilities consist of those for Tier-1 capital — mainly common and preferred shares and retained earnings — and Tier-2 capital — largely warrants and subordinated debt. Tier-1 and 2 capital would be made available to participating financial institutions that fulfil certain conditions.[6]

The authorities are also encouraging institutions to set up, capitalize, and fund private asset management companies (AMCs). The function of an AMC is to manage NPLs transferred from a related financial institution. AMCs will be allowed to borrow (excluding deposit mobilization) and relend funds to existing debtors. They will also be allowed flexibility in setting interest rates, while asset transfers will be free of legal impediments. All taxes and fees incurred in transferring assets will also be exempt.

To finance bank recapitalization, the government will issue up to 300 billion baht of bonds (consisting of 200 billion baht for Tier-1 and 100 billion baht for Tier-2 capital supports). Any additional losses will be fiscalized by issuing more bonds. Initially, the announcement specified 30 June 2000 as the last date for application by financial institutions wishing to participate in the programme. However, the deadline was later amended to 1 November 2000.

Following the announcement of the plan, the cabinet appointed the Financial Restructuring Advisory Committee (FRAC) to oversee the progress of the scheme. The FRAC acts as adviser to the Finance Minister and the BOT governor on admitting financial institutions applying for the capital support facilities and on all relevant details of financial institution recapitalization. The

FRAC commenced operations in August 1998 and will terminate its activities by 31 March 2001.

However, more than one year after the announcement, the effectiveness of the Financial Sector Restructuring Plan is now in doubt. Firstly, NPLs as a percentage of total loans remained high throughout 1998 and 1999. The figure was 36.2 per cent in August 1998, 45 per cent at end 1998, 47 per cent in March 1999, and 47.7 per cent in May 1999, before moderating to 47.5 per cent in June and 45.3 per cent in September 1999. The high level of NPLs reflects the fact that the economy has not recovered sufficiently to alleviate debtors' liquidity problems and that the debt restructuring process has not been efficiently implemented.

Secondly, financial institutions' participation in the capital support facilities is not compulsory. Financial institutions are allowed to find ways to recapitalize by themselves until the end of the application period (November 2000). As the government sets stringent conditions for them to participate in Tier-1 capital support facilities, financial institutions have so far avoided participating in the programme. By end August 1999, one year after the plan's announcement, financial institutions had applied for only 35.5 billion baht Tier-1 and 2.7 billion baht Tier-2 capital supports, against the 200 billion baht and 100 billion baht targets set by the government, respectively. Most financial institutions thus tried to recapitalize by themselves and regarded participation in the programme as a last resort.

Thirdly, as a result of the slow pace of recapitalization and debt restructuring, financial institutions are unwilling to extend loans to businesses for fear of mounting NPLs, which would further weaken their capital bases. The total amount of financial system lending in the first eight months of 1999 fell by 13.4 per cent as against the same period in 1998, while credit outstanding for the business and service sectors amounted to 6.35 trillion baht, down by 622 billion baht from the same period in 1998.

Fourthly, with NPLs as large as 47 per cent of lending portfolios, commercial banks incurred large losses of 171.9 billion baht during the first half of 1999, a much higher amount than the 110 billion to 150 billion baht projected by the authorities. To compensate for such large losses, commercial banks retain very large interest rate margins of 4 to 5 per cent that penalize depositors and "good" debtors.

Fifthly, the takeover of troubled financial institutions by the authorities proved ineffective in solving problems in those institutions. Non-performing loans in state-owned banks was 50.3 per cent of total loans in August 1998, rising to 62.5 per cent by end 1998, and 70.6 per cent in June 1999.

Thus, one year after the announcement, the restructuring plan appeared to be a failure. The major causes were the slow pace of debt restructuring and economic recovery, which resulted in rising NPLs, and the voluntary nature of the plan, which allowed financial institutions to delay participation.

Economic Stimulus Package

To prevent a further recession in 1999, the government employed a stimulative fiscal policy. The government's seventh letter of intent (LOI) approved by the International Monetary Fund (IMF) on 7 April 1999 allows for a fiscal deficit of 6 per cent of the gross domestic product (GDP) for fiscal year 1999, up from 5 per cent in the sixth LOI. The additional deficit of 1 per cent of GDP consists of a 53 billion baht expenditure package announced by the MOF on 30 March 1999. The package, comprising three parts — namely additional public expenditure measures for the 1999 fiscal year, tax alleviation, and energy price reduction — concentrated on increasing government spending to promote employment, stimulate consumption, and lower production costs for businesses.

Additional public expenditure measures for fiscal year 1999 amounted to 53.4 billion baht, to be spent on six programme categories ranging from investment for job creation, improvement in competitiveness for manufacturing and export sectors, to improvement in infrastructure and enhancing the effectiveness of public administration. The funds were financed by the Overseas Economic Cooperation Fund (OECF), the Japanese Export-Import Bank, and the International Bank for Reconstruction and Development (IBRD).

Tax alleviation measures consisted of personal income tax exemption and value-added tax (VAT) rate reduction. From 1 January 1999, the first 50,000 baht of net income would be exempted from personal income tax, whereas previously the first 100,000 baht of net income was subject to 5 per cent personal income tax. The VAT rate, which was raised from 7 to 10 per cent from 16 August 1997, would be lowered back to 7 per cent on a temporary basis for two years, effective 1 April 1999. The personal income tax exemption would result in an annual government revenue loss of 7.9 billion baht, or 5.2 billion baht for the remainder of the fiscal year, while the VAT rate reduction would cause a revenue loss of 46.3 billion baht annually, or 26.2 billion baht for the remainder of the fiscal year. Moreover, the 1.5 per cent VAT on small enterprises with gross revenues between 600,000 and 1,200,000 baht was eliminated, effective 1 April 1999, resulting in an annual revenue loss of 470 million baht, or 200 million baht for the remainder of the fiscal year.

Energy price reduction was aimed at raising consumers' purchasing power and reducing industries' production costs. The electricity price came down to 0.3261 baht per unit, from 0.5071 baht per unit for the period from April to June 1999. The decrease was brought about by a reduction in excise taxes on fuel oil, the strengthening of the baht, a decline in world oil prices, and other miscellaneous factors. These reductions, coupled with the lower VAT from 10 to 7 per cent, resulted in lower average electricity prices by 0.2587 baht per unit, or lower total electricity expenditures of 19.2 billion baht.

The government also reduced wholesale prices of liquefied petroleum gas (LPG) by 0.9091 baht per kilogram from 30 March 1999. Together with the VAT reduction, LPG prices were lower by 11 per cent. Moreover, the excise tax rate on fuel oil was lowered from 17.5 to 5 per cent, thereby reducing the wholesale price of fuel oil by 11 per cent, or 0.52 baht per litre. The lower fuel oil price would lower costs for industry and electricity generation by 1.9 billion baht for the remainder of the fiscal year, and 2.6 billion baht for fiscal year 2000.

All these measures would result in an injection of 132 billion baht into the economy. The heart of the package was to halt the sharp contraction in consumption spending since the start of the crisis in mid-1997.

These measures have certainly helped boost households' purchasing power and stimulate consumption. However, the increase in consumption seemed to be temporary because household income is still depressed in the aftermath of the severe recession of 1998. It is evident that consumer confidence has not fully returned. Moreover, the household sector is still burdened by large-scale unemployment. The latest unemployment figures range between 1 million to 2 million. Such large-scale unemployment simply depresses the much-hoped-for recovery in household income and consumer confidence. Lastly, the increase in government expenditure has to be channelled through an intricate and inefficient bureaucracy, thereby delaying its stimulating effect. By the end of August 1999, government spending was still reportedly less than 50 per cent of the target amount.

In short, the economic stimulus package is likely to be successful on a moderate scale. The gain in improved consumption spending is likely to be temporary if the measures are not supported by strong economic recovery and improving consumer confidence.

Measures to Encourage Private Investment

The package of measures to encourage private investment, announced on 10 August 1999, consists of tax and tariff reduction, new equity investment, real estate sector recovery measures, and financial restructuring for small and medium-size enterprises (SMEs).

The tax and tariff reduction measure involves reducing import duties on 326 capital goods items and raw materials for producing a wide range of products such as animal feed, cosmetics, pharmaceuticals, chemicals, fertilizers, plastics, cotton products, Tin Mill Black Plate (TMBP) iron, hi-carbon iron, and copper cathode. The measure also removes the 10 per cent surcharge on commodities that were subject to higher than the 5 per cent tariff rate. In addition, the measure allows accelerated depreciation with the double declining balance method, which is twice faster than the straight-line depreciation method.

The equity investment measure will establish three equity funds to invest in Thai corporations — the Equity Fund of US$500 million (to be increased to US$1,000 million), intended to inject fresh funds into large corporations in strategic industries; the Thailand Recovery Fund of US$100 million established by the Asian Development Bank (ADB) to invest in medium-sized enterprises with strong competitive potential; and the Fund for Venture Capital, a ten-year closed-end mutual fund of 1,000 million baht, to be established by the MOF to invest in SMEs with strong business potential.

The real estate sector recovery measure will provide fixed-rate housing loans with thirty-year maturities. The funds will be mobilized through 46 billion baht worth of bonds issued by the Government Housing Bank (GHB), of which 21 billion baht will be extended to the GHB's retail clients and the remaining 25 billion extended through commercial banks. In addition, Secondary Mortgage Corporation will purchase 4 billion baht housing loans from financial institutions through bond issues of the same amount. Moreover, the National Housing Authorities (NHA) will purchase a total of 15 billion baht of unfinished real estate development projects from creditors or owners. It will then complete and sell these projects to retail clients. Finally, real estate transfer fees were reduced from 2 to 0.01 per cent of the sales value until end 2000.

The last measure, the financial restructuring of SMEs, involves the restructuring of Small Industry Credit Guarantee Corporation (SICGC) by increasing its capital from 400 million baht to 4,400 million baht in 1999 and to 8,400 million baht in 2003. The maximum fixed-asset size of 50 million baht for SMEs is increased to 100 million baht, while the 10 million baht credit guarantee maximum is raised to 20 million baht. Moreover, the fee of 2 to 2.75 per cent is reduced to 1.75 per cent. The Small Industry Finance Corporation (SIFC) will also be restructured by increasing its capital from 300 million to 2,800 million baht in 1999 and to 7,800 million baht in 2003. The maximum fixed-asset size of 50 million baht is increased to 100 million baht, while the 25 million baht maximum loan amount is raised to 50 million baht. Finally, the Financial Advisory Centres for SMEs will be established with 100 million baht financial support from the government to provide financial restructuring advice to SMEs.

The tax and tariff reduction measure as envisaged in the package should be welcome as another positive step towards greater competitiveness for local industries. The equity investment measure, however, lacks crucial details to inspire investor confidence. Firstly, the definition of "strategic industries" remains to be specified, and it is unclear who will be empowered to do the defining. Secondly, the sources of funds are still largely uncertain, while the target amount of US$1,000 million for the Equity Fund is simply too little for strategic industries, which mostly consist of large firms. The remaining two equity funds, namely, Thailand Recovery Fund and the Fund for Venture Capital, have even less details, without specified fund sources. Thirdly, while the provision of new housing loans by the GHB is beneficial for the recovery of the real estate sector, the NHA's purchase of unfinished property development projects will take six months to a year to materialize because the agency has to evaluate applications carefully to safeguard against approved projects becoming bad assets for the NHA.

It remains to be seen whether more details of the above-mentioned measures will be provided as the schemes become fully operational. The establishment of various equity funds will take at least six months to a year. Thus, the effect of these measures will be long term and will require a certain time period before any definite evaluation can be done.

Other Reform Attempts

During 1998–99, seven economic reform bills were promulgated. The Social Security Act BE 2541 (1998) became effective on 31 December 1998. The Act extends the social security system to cover retirement plans and thus lays the foundation for a more developed and comprehensive social safety net for Thai citizens.

Next, the bankruptcy procedure in Thailand has been completely reformed and raised to international standards with the passing of the Bankruptcy Court Establishment and Procedure Act BE 2542 (1999) on 3 March 1999, followed by the Bankruptcy Act BE 2542 (1999), and three more Acts amending the Civil and Commercial Code on 17 March 1999. According to the old bankruptcy system, the debtor had considerable leeway to delay court procedure while the creditor had no other option than to file a bankruptcy case once the debtor defaulted on loans. Moreover, a typical bankruptcy case might take up to ten years to complete because the case had to go through the ordinary, snail-pace civil court and the long-drawn foreclosure procedure. The new Bills provide alternatives to debtors and creditors, such as renegotiation and debt and corporate restructuring. They also establish a separate court specializing in bankruptcy cases, with its own more efficient court and foreclosure procedures.

The State Enterprise Capital Act BE 2542 (1999) was passed by parliament on 10 March 1999, providing the legal basis for state enterprise privatization. Government capital in state enterprises can now be converted into common shares offered to the public so that state enterprises can be transformed into public companies. This will lead to the liberalization of relevant industries and encourage competition from other players. The Condominium Act BE 2542 (1999) was also passed by parliament on 17 March 1999, allowing 100 per cent foreign ownership in condominiums in Thailand.

However, the most important reform Bill in the pipeline is the Alien Business Law, to replace the obsolete Revolutionary Order No. 281, which prohibited or restricted foreign participation in a number of professions and business sectors. The new law will liberalize and allow more foreign participation in many sectors, except those concerning state and economic security. The draft has been strongly opposed by diverse interest groups, including certain elements in the Senate, which have managed to delay the reading process in parliament. Despite foot-dragging and political lobbying, such a reform Bill is necessary and will be promulgated sooner or later, as the government has shown its determination to push through the reform before the next general election, to be held in the second half of 2000.

Critical Reform Issues

One long-term structural problem is the growing fiscal deficit. The overall budget deficit for fiscal year 1999 amounted to 112.7 billion baht, the third consecutive year that the government has had budget deficits. The fiscal deficit is expected to continue for another three years. The total value of public debt at the end of June 1999 amounted to 1,710 billion baht, or 41.1 per cent higher than the total outstanding at the end of September 1998. Domestic debt accounted for 55.9 per cent of total public debt, while the remaining 44.1 per cent was external debt. Public debt has been rising sharply because the government has to finance several social investment and economic stimulus programmes and structural adjustments. The MOF, NESDB, and BOT estimate that total public debt in fiscal year 2000 will amount to 1,244 billion baht, or 24.3 per cent of GDP. The large size of the public debt could be one factor delaying economic recovery, as the government has to raise increasingly large funds to finance its debt, thereby putting pressure on the financial market and interest rates. The management of such a huge public debt will be a crucial factor for sustainable growth.

Thailand has invested around 2,991 billion baht in infrastructure development over the last thirty years. Utilities such as water and electricity are now available in all urban and suburban centres and almost all rural villages, and there are around 154,000 kilometres of road networks throughout the country. Thailand also has a total of 7.3 million telephones, or 12.18 telephones per 100 people. Several infrastructure construction projects are already under way or in the pipeline, such as an underground railway system in Bangkok, two more deep-water ports in the eastern seaboard area, a new international airport to the east of Bangkok, a new international telephone gateway, the installation of an additional 800,000 telephone lines, and two more optical fibre networks, the expansion of electricity and water distribution systems, several water treatment projects in Bangkok and the surrounding provinces, and so forth.

Nevertheless, there is still room for infrastructure improvement. Private participation in public infrastructure development and service provision is now an urgent task in Thailand in order to relieve the government of the fast rising fiscal burden and to increase the efficiency and quality of service. The promulgation of the State Enterprise Capital Act BE 2542 (1999), which provides the legal framework and procedure for privatization, is the first critical step. What is needed now is the determination to proceed with the privatization plan despite strong opposition from various interest groups. Unfortunately, the prospect for rapid advancement is remote because the year 2000 will see a new general election and a new government. Thus, the existing government is likely to slow down the plan while the new government may not commit itself to private participation.

One of the most important long-term factors contributing to the collapse of the Thai economy in 1997 was the loss of competitive advantage in Thai industries. This drawback was pointed out by overseas investors even before the crisis and had been much discussed among Thai policy-makers since 1997. A study by the Thailand Development Research Institute (TDRI) shows that rising productivity (in technical terms, total factor productivity growth, TFPG) accounted for only 15.8 per cent of economic growth during 1978–90 and only 3.5 per cent during 1991–95. In other words, Thailand's economic growth was boosted mainly by exploiting additional resources rather than by using existing resources more efficiently. Even the high export growth of the second half of 1999 was actually a result of economic recovery in Japan and Southeast Asia rather than the improving competitiveness of Thai exports.

Thus, industrial restructuring and more investment in research and development are two indicators as to whether the upcoming economic recovery and growth will be sustainable. Unfortunately, there have been few policy actions on this front. The most visible ones were the special loan programme by the Export-Import Bank of Thailand for the textile industry to acquire new machinery and the adjustment of the industrial promotion policy by the Board of Investment in 1998. Even the Measures to Encourage Private Investment, which were aimed at the recapitalization of viable enterprises in the real sector, came out only in August 1999, more than two years after the crisis. Therefore, the prospect of serious industrial restructuring in Thailand is remote. This is the main argument for the view that economic recovery in 2000 may only be a technical rebound and will not be sustainable. This also justifies the criticism that the Chuan government and its Finance Minister have so far paid greater attention to financial sector reform but have little understanding of industrial restructuring policy.

Another issue for sustainable growth is the reform of the bureaucracy. It is well known that bloated manpower, inefficiency, and corrupt practices are prevalent at every level of the Thai bureaucracy. The government has implemented a manpower reduction plan for almost a decade, with only moderate success. However, there has been no significant attempt to reduce corruption. Among the causes are deep-rooted cultural factors which encourage corruption at every level of society and make corrupt practices a part of Thai daily life. Every Thai government so far has lacked the political will to stamp out corruption because political parties and politicians themselves are corrupt. Money politics, an inefficient bureaucracy, and corruption will remain, casting doubt on a sustainable recovery despite a new constitution which established an independent anti-graft commission.

NOTES

1. In order to upgrade a doubtful or loss loan to a substandard loan, a client has to adhere to a new payment schedule for three consecutive months or payment periods, whichever is longer. Such a reclassification would allow financial institutions to book interest as income.

2. Again, conditions apply. The utilization of the new loan must not be linked to or used to repay the old debt; close monitoring and control must be exercised over the use of the new loan; and careful credit and cash flow analysis must be conducted to ensure that the borrower has the ability to repay the loan according to a repayment schedule.

3. These taxes include the 3.3 per cent specific tax, the 10 per cent value-added tax, the 30 per cent corporate income tax and all withholding taxes and stamp duties.

4. The incentives are as follows: From 25 November 1998, commercial banks are allowed to adopt market interest rates in calculating the net present value (NPV) of NPLs. This would help reduce the damage incurred by banks from debt restructuring because market interest rates are generally lower than the contract interest rates. Commercial banks, finance companies, and credit foncier companies are allowed to hold in excess of the current 10 per cent limit of a limited company's shares if it is their restructured debtor company. The total portfolio investment is also allowed to exceed the current limit of 20 per cent of the bank's and the credit foncier company's capital fund, and 60 per cent of the finance company's capital fund. However, the excess portion must come from debt restructuring only. These relaxations will be in place for two years from 26 November 1998. Such shares can be held for three years, after which the bank, finance company, or credit foncier company must reduce its holdings in such companies to the 10 per cent limit.

5. This amount consisted of 88 per cent held by Thai commercial banks, 7 per cent by foreign banks, and 5 per cent by finance companies and credit fonciers.

6. For Tier-1 capital, the financial institutions must provide full provisions for NPLs immediately, write off all losses due to existing NPLs with the burden fully on existing shareholders, and propose a viable restructuring plan with the approval of the BOT. For Tier-2 capital, the financial institutions must sign a legally binding debt restructuring agreement with the debtor, and be able to demonstrate to the BOT that the debtor has been able to service the loan according to BOT regulations on corporate debt restructuring.

VIETNAM

VIETNAM
The Politics of Immobilism Revisited

Carlyle A. Thayer

Reform Immobilism

In an article written in 1996, Brantly Womack described Vietnam's slow pace of policy change and lack of decisive political leadership as "reform immobilism".[1] Womack argued that there were three countervailing factors that explained why "reform immobilism" became the consensus view within the Vietnam Communist Party (VCP). First, Vietnam's policy of renovation had proven to be the most successful economic policy ever adopted by the VCP. Further success, he argued, was dependent on "decentralization, decontrol, and internationalization". Second, the success of renovation led to the emergence of "negative phenomena" which required "political regulation rather than more market forces". Third, the success of reform efforts, coupled with a peaceful international environment, dissipated the sense of national crisis, which spurred renovation in the first place. As a result, the "conservatives have no alternative to reform, the reformers cannot deny the importance of order and redistributive measures".

Womack also acknowledged that a number of other forces, such as centre-provincial tensions and differing generational views, also contributed to policy caution. In Womack's view, immobilism "implies a middle course of muddling through and policies that are conflicting in their effects … The central leadership is in gridlock but the traffic creeps around". He concluded that "the structural weakness of immobilism is that it is permanently behind the curve of societal developments". This chapter reviews domestic and foreign policy developments in Vietnam during 1999 with this framework. It notes that the same three key factors — support for reforms, the need for political control and a non-crisis atmosphere — still operate to constrain the pace of reform.

The Economy

During 1997–98 Vietnam was affected by "four typhoons" — declining growth rates, peasant unrest in Thai Binh province, a devastating typhoon which struck

CARLYLE A. THAYER is Professor of Southeast Asian Security Studies at the Asia-Pacific Center for Security Studies in Honolulu, currently on leave of absence from University College, the University of New South Wales.

in late 1997, and the aftershocks of the Asian financial crisis. As early as late 1996 Vietnam first began to experience a decline in foreign direct investment and a drop in external trade.[2] This was the first time since *doi moi* was adopted that economic growth rates had declined. Vietnamese leaders did not, however, perceive these developments as crisis-like or necessitating a marked step-up in the pace of reforms.

Vietnam's economic downturn had many internal causes such as a poor investment climate resulting from excessive bureaucratic red tape, a Byzantine system of rules and regulations, and pervasive corruption. But the root causes were more fundamental. These included government favouritism for 6,000 inefficient and debt-ridden state-owned enterprises (SOEs) and a weak and corrupted financial and banking system. The decline in Vietnam's economic growth rates sparked repeated calls by officials from donor countries and international financial institutions, as well as Vietnamese and foreign economists, for Vietnam to step up the pace and expand the scope of its economic reform efforts. Yet during 1997–98 Vietnam's leaders chose to "batten down the hatches" and ride out the regional economic storm.

According to a World Bank memorandum on Vietnam issued in late 1998, the external shock of the Asian financial crisis amounted to a "kick in the stomach", which it estimated was equivalent to the loss of US$3 billion or 12 per cent of Vietnam's gross domestic product (GDP). The World Bank further stated:

> The economic situation is quite serious for Vietnam — threatening to undermine and reverse the remarkable progress … that was achieved over the past decade. Vietnam can still avoid a worsening situation, but this will require stepped-up reform of both policies and programs, and change in the pattern of support from the international community.

For the first time, the World Bank signalled that certain types of financial assistance would be contingent on Vietnamese reform efforts. Meanwhile, the International Monetary Fund (IMF) in 1996 ceased providing assistance to Vietnam until appropriate reform measures were adopted.

Conditionality on aid was endorsed by the sixth meeting of the international donor community that met in Paris in December 1998. The donor community agreed to provide US$2.2 billion in development assistance. An additional US$500 million was made contingent on Vietnam's adoption of an "accelerated *doi moi* programme". The donor meeting obtained Vietnam's endorsement of a three-point programme to accelerate structural and sectoral reforms in 1999: (a) comprehensive state enterprise reform programme with timetables and targets for SOEs to be restructured, merged, equalized, divested, and liquidated; (b) a restructuring plan for the whole banking sector, including comprehensive restructuring of the four state-owned commercial banks; (c) and a comprehensive three-year trade reform programme, with key milestones for each year.

Although Vietnam agreed to the three-point reform programme in late 1998, it undertook no steps in 1999 to carry out this commitment. Indeed, the international donors' meeting that met in Hanoi in December 1999 appeared to be a re-run of the 1998 meeting. Donors pledged US$2.2 billion in highly concessional loans and grants. And once again they pledged an additional amount — US$700 million — in concessional aid. The concessional aid package was specifically targeted to cover the costs of debt restructuring in SOEs, re-financing the banking system, and retraining the unemployed. But, according to Minister of Planning and Investment, Tran Xuan Gia, "you cannot buy reforms with money ... no one is going to bombard Vietnam into acting".[3]

New aid pledges in 1999 brought the total pledged to Vietnam since 1993 to US$13 billion, but only US$6.4 billion has been disbursed.[4] The World Bank praised Vietnam for its efforts in reducing the incidence of poverty in 1999 but warned that these gains were fragile and could be reversed if further reforms were not carried out.[5] The international meeting of donors underscored once again that Vietnam risked being left behind by other states if it did not accelerate the pace and scope of reforms. According to a statement released by the donors meeting:

> Delegates commended the Vietnamese Government for remarkable progress in reducing poverty, but this was tempered with concern that the slow pace of reforms might leave Vietnam trailing behind, as the rest of the region recovers from economic crisis. This in turn would leave Vietnam unable to sustain reductions in poverty in the future.[6]

Vietnam is known to be drawing up a three-year reform package based on inputs from several ministries; but officials with responsibility for the plan repeatedly refuse to commit themselves to a deadline for implementation.[7]

Officially, Vietnam's economy grew by 4.8 per cent in 1999; independent assessments place GDP growth rates at 4 per cent or less.[8] The World Bank estimates that GDP growth rates will decline to 3.5 per cent in 2000 and then to 3 per cent in 2001. At the same time, Vietnam's population is expected to keep increasing. The future appears bleak, economic stagnation at best, economic crisis at worst.[9] In these circumstances the World Bank, the IMF, and the international donor community are in agreement that Vietnam must restructure its economy, liberalize trade, and carry out urgent reforms in the financial and banking sectors.

The above analysis confirms that the three countervailing factors identified by Womack as contributing to "reform immobilism" continue to operate and stall reform efforts. Economic reforms continue to have widespread support in Vietnam. Senior government officials continue to express their support for continued renovation. Minister of Planning and Investment Tran Xuan Gia has stated, for example: "We agree that without accelerated reforms we cannot grow rapidly and therefore the question is how best to accelerate the *doi moi* process."[10] Vietnam is seeking IMF and World Bank policy advice as it draws up its next five-year plan (2001–5).

Support for reforms, however, is tempered by concern to maintain political control. Vietnam's ideological conservatives argue that World Bank conditionality on aid is tantamount to a breach of national sovereignty. They do not believe Vietnam is in crisis or is about to enter a period of crisis. This was clearly evident in the government's economic report delivered to the fifth session of the National Assembly (tenth legislature) in early May 1999. According to Deputy Prime Minister Nguyen Tan Dung, Vietnam had achieved many positive results — a positive growth rate of about 4 per cent and the maintenance of political security and social order. "It is also clear proof," he argued, "that our party's and state's lines and policies on the renovation process are correct." Dung mentioned a number of weaknesses and shortcomings and forecast that these would result in lower growth rates in the future. On the crucial matter of SOE reform, Dung failed to spell out a comprehensive reform programme along the lines advocated by the World Bank and international donor countries. The end result has been excessive caution and gradualism. Some aspects of the donor community's reform programme have been adopted. The sixth session of the National Assembly, for example, adopted the Enterprise Law and revised Law on Domestic Investment.

Domestic Developments: The Party

During the eighteen-month period from the onset of the Asian financial crisis to late 1998, the VCP's Central Committee met three times (December 1997, July 1998, and October 1998). It was only at the October meeting, the sixth plenum (first session), that economic issues were discussed in detail. The plenum's final communiqué declared Vietnam had achieved a "big success" because it had maintained political stability and a 6 per cent GDP growth rate. Priority was placed on agriculture and rural development.

The October 1998 sixth plenary meeting was a split session. This is highly unusual, if not unprecedented. In addition, the second session was postponed five times due to divisions in the Politburo over consolidating government ministries and leadership changes. The sixth plenum (second session) was held under the shadow of several important developments. Firstly, the VCP was faced with a new round of internal party dissent spearheaded by very senior retired officials. Foremost among them was General Tran Do, former head of the party's Ideology and Culture Commission. General Do has been continually vocal since peasant unrest in his native province of Thai Binh turned violent in late 1997. General Do was expelled from the party. This provoked a renewed round of protests and even one resignation by a former high-level military historian. Secondly, the sixth plenum (second session) was held amidst speculation of major changes in party and state leadership sparked by the death of Politburo member, and former Minister of National Defense, Doan Khue.

The sixth plenum (second session) was the first of three Central Committee meetings to be held in 1999. This too is unusual, but not unprecedented, as the party statutes require only one meeting every six months. The sixth plenum (second session) met from 25 January to 2 February 1999. The meeting discussed "fundamental and urgent issues" concerning party-building. In other words, the meeting focused on ways and means to improve the efficiency and administrative performance of the VCP in implementing Vietnam's reform programme but not on economic policy *per se*. The sixth plenum (second session) focused its attention on ways to counter the degradation in the party's ranks caused by corruption, excessive bureaucracy, individualism, and internal disunity. No decision was taken to fill the Politburo seat left vacant by the death of Doan Khue, nor were any other leadership changes announced. Indeed, party spokesmen went out of their way to ridicule the foreign media for its pre-plenum speculation on leadership changes.

The sixth plenum (second session) resolved to launch a three-year criticism and self-criticism campaign designed to rid the party of its degenerate members and restore party unity. In the mean time, party officials were tasked with drawing up guidelines on the question of the extent to which a party member and his/her family members can participate in private economic activities. The sixth plenum (second session) also postponed the question of leadership changes until a later date. It set up a task force to draw up a plan to slash the party and state bureaucracies to be presented to the next Central Committee meeting.

The Central Committee held its seventh plenum from 9 to 16 August. The main agenda item was on

> issues relating to the organization and apparatus of the political system, wages and social allowances funded by the state budget, and preparations for the upcoming ninth national party congress.

The plenum considered the report on reforming the party and state bureaucracies and resolved to lay off about 15 per cent of personnel. The last plenum of the year, the eighth, met from 4 to 11 November. It was concerned with four main issues: attaining the goals set in the socio-economic plans up to the year 2000, assessing the results of the criticism–self-criticism campaign, leadership change, and preparatory work for the ninth national party congress scheduled for the first quarter of 2001. This plenum was overshadowed by severe flooding in central Vietnam which extended over a six-week period from early November and left over 700 persons dead.

Immediately after the plenum a number of leadership changes were announced. These fall into three categories: disciplinary cases, a government reshuffle and reassignment of party officials. On 11 November it was announced that Central Committee members Ngo Xuan Loc and Cao Sy Kiem had received party disciplinary warnings. Loc was dismissed as deputy prime minister for his involvement in a scandal surrounding the Thanh Long water park in Hanoi and for his role in encouraging speculation in the cement market in

1995. Cao Sy Kiem was dismissed as governor of the State Bank for misman-aging loans that resulted in an explosion of bad debts. Former customs direc-tor Phan Van Dinh was charged with corruption while in office. In December the National Assembly removed two deputies, one for being implicated in the Thanh Long scandal and the other for negligence. Also in December it was reported that Nguyen Thai Nguyen, deputy head of the Government Office and aide to Prime Minister Phan Van Khai, was being investigated for unspeci-fied violations of the law. The foreign press reported rumours that Nguyen had passed sensitive economic and military information to a foreign country, presumably China.

The National Assembly also carried out a reshuffle in government posts designed in part to reduce the workload of senior government officials. For example, Politburo member and Deputy Prime Minister Nguyen Tan Dung, relinquished his position as Governor of the State Bank to Deputy Governor Le Duc Thuy. Dung was given responsibility for the State Bank while Cao Sy Kiem was under investigation. Early in the new year the National Assembly Standing Committee announced that Foreign Minister Nguyen Manh Cam would give up his portfolio to concentrate on his duties as deputy prime minster. He was replaced by his most senior deputy, Nguyen Dy Nien. At the same time, another deputy foreign minister, Vu Khoan, replaced Truong Dinh Tuyen as minister of the ailing Trade Ministry.

The final round of leadership changes involved the reassignment of senior party officials. On 13 January 2000 it was announced that Politburo member Truong Tan Sang, secretary of the Ho Chi Minh City Party Committee, was being brought to Hanoi to head the Central Committee's Economics Depart-ment replacing Phan Dien. Phan Dien, in turn, replaced Truong Quang Duoc as secretary of the Danang City Party Committee. Politburo member Nguyen Manh Triet was appointed secretary of the Ho Chi Minh City Party Commit-tee, vacating his post as head of the Central Committee's Mass Mobilization Department. This position was taken by Truong Quang Duoc. Central Com-mittee member To Huy Rua, a former deputy director of Ho Chi Minh Na-tional Political Academy, was appointed secretary of the Haiphong City Party Committee. Party leadership changes were rounded out in March 2000 when it was announced that Le Xuan Tung, secretary of the Hanoi Party Committee, and Nguyen Phu Trong, chief of ideological, cultural, scientific, and educa-tional affairs at the Central Committee, would swap positions.

Foreign Relations

United States–Vietnam Relations

In February 1999 President Clinton affirmed that Vietnam was "fully co-operating in good faith" in all areas where the United States sought progress in identifying and repatriating the remains of U.S. service personnel who were listed as missing-in-action during the Vietnam War. Vietnam's positive action on immigration matters enabled President Clinton in June to extend the waiver on the Jackson-Vanick amendment to the 1974 Trade Act. The Trade Act prohibits certain types of funding to countries that restrict emigration. President Clinton first waived the amendment in March 1998. As a result of the second waiver, U.S. export promotion and investment support programmes offered by the Export-Import Bank, Overseas Private Investment Corporation, Department of Agriculture and Trade and Development Agency were permitted to continue their activities.

In 1999 Vietnam and the United States made substantial progress in their negotiations on a Bilateral Trade Agreement (BTA) which had begun in September 1996. Major progress was achieved at the eighth round of negotiations held from 14 to 18 June. The ninth round was held in July. During these negotiations Vietnam was extremely reluctant to grant the United States access to certain protected sectors of its economy such as telecommunications. The chief sticking points concerned non-tariff barriers and tariff reduction schedules. Vietnam sought an eight-year time frame; the United States insisted on four years. On several occasions, when an impasse developed, the United States successfully sought the intervention of Deputy Prime Minister and Politburo member Nguyen Tan Dung.

On 25 July, it was announced that a major breakthrough had been reached and the United States and Vietnam had agreed in principle on the text of a trade agreement. The final product reportedly ran to nearly one hundred pages of text and was considered to be the most complex trade agreement in U.S. history. The BTA reportedly contains four major chapters including services (accounting, banking, insurance, and telecommunications), intellectual property rights, trade and goods (tariffs and quotas), and investment (equal footing for American investors). Under the terms of the draft BTA, Vietnamese goods would have access to the American market on a "normal trade relations" basis. As a result, according to estimates by the World Bank, Vietnamese exports to the United States would double in the first year from US$470 to nearly US$1 billion. The BTA would also lay the foundations for Vietnam's membership in the World Trade Organization (WTO).

In return for these benefits, Vietnam would open its market to U.S. companies in areas that have been heavily protected. But, because of presently existing corruption and heavy-handed bureaucracy, analysts do not expect a marked inflow of U.S. investment immediately after the trade agreement takes effects. In addition, U.S. investors will be able to exercise sole ownership over certain enterprises. In the long run Vietnam will be exposed to stiff competition and the world's best practices. It is likely that its state-run sector will be hit badly as inefficient companies go bankrupt. Unemployment is likely to rise.

A further round of technical negotiations was held from 25 August to 2 September at which the final text was reportedly hammered out. All that was left was Hanoi's approval. U.S. officials indicated that a signing ceremony could take place during the summit of the Asia-Pacific Economic Co-operation

(APEC) in New Zealand on 13 September between Premier Phan Van Khai and President Bill Clinton. Progress was abruptly derailed on 11 September when Vietnam informed the United States it was not prepared to sign the agreement as scheduled.

What accounted for this turnaround? Vietnamese sources point to the visit of U.S. Secretary of State Madeleine Albright earlier that month. According to one account:

> she sidestepped items on the agenda — human rights and the trade agreement — and asked about Vietnam's plans to implement true democracy and multiparty politics [of which it has none].[11]

Secretary-General Le Kha Phieu "was surprised and peeved to be receiving more advice from another American about how to run Vietnam". It was more likely that Secretary Albright's visit only added fuel to the fire. Her visit coincided with circulation of the Vietnamese translation of the draft text of the BTA for the first time. This set off a firestorm of protest by those whose interests were most affected. They effectively lobbied Politburo adviser Do Muoi, the former VCP secretary, to intervene. Do Muoi did so and on 7 October the party Politburo reaffirmed its decision to postpone agreement with the United States (further discussion appears below in the section on Sino-Vietnamese relations).

On 30 October, key aides to republican leaders on the House Ways and Means Committee and Senate Finance Committee stated that a trade agreement could be reached in early 2000 if Hanoi assented before January when Congress was scheduled to resume. According to one aide: "There's a lot of good will, and I think we've got enough support to move this, if and when the package becomes final." The draft U.S.-Vietnam trade agreement was formally considered by the party Central Committee's eighth plenum that met in Hanoi from 4 to 11 November. At this meeting it was clear that Vietnam's leadership was still divided on this issue. Immediately after the plenum, Dao Duy Quat, deputy chief in charge of the party's Ideology and Culture Commission, stated: "There are a number of provisions with which we need further negotiations to be undertaken with the U.S. side." Quat revealed that the provision for annual review of normal trade status was "inequitable for Vietnam".[12] Quat declined to go further into the matter other than to indicate there were problems with the wording of the preface.

Vietnam then conducted an in-house review of the draft and the details of the U.S.-China trade agreement reached on 15 November. This review proved inconclusive. Party reformers and conservatives remained deadlocked. On 10 January 2000, Prime Minister Phan Van Khai revealed as much when he told *Thoi Bao Kinh Te* newspaper:

> This is an important issue ... The Government has reported the issue to the Party Central Committee Political Bureau and is waiting for further instruction from the party. If the Party Central Committee Political

> Bureau agrees that the government should conduct further negotiations with the U.S. side on some issues, the Government will continue to work with the United States to modify the draft and will sign the agreement eventually.

Dao Duy Quat echoed these remarks a few days later. He once again focused on the provision for annual renewal of Vietnam's normal trade status and argued that Vietnam should be given special consideration because of its low level of development. U.S. officials, on the other hand, absolutely refused to reopen negotiations but stated they were willing to make "points of clarification".[13] This position was reiterated in February during the visit to Hanoi by Congressman Bill Archer, chairman of the House Ways and Means Committee. Archer met with newly appointed Trade Minister Vu Khoan, who stated that Vietnam wanted further discussions and clarifications. Archer replied that "it was not possible to renegotiate" but that further discussion could be held. Reporters travelling with Archer were informed that Vietnam was in the process of drafting a letter to the Office of the U.S. Trade Representative in Washington outlining its views and listing topics for discussion.

Meanwhile, U.S. officials have expressed doubts that the trade agreement can be signed and ratified by Congress before the end of the Clinton administration. U.S. Ambassador to Vietnam Pete Peterson publicly warned the Vietnamese side that he was

> not absolutely certain that we'd get it [approved by Congress] this year. The other reality is that if [the congressional approval process] goes beyond this year it's not likely that it's this trade agreement we would be willing to sign.[14]

Despite this set-back, U.S.-Vietnam relations hit a high note in March 2000 when William Cohen became the first U.S. Secretary of Defense to visit Vietnam since the end of the Vietnam War in 1975. Cohen's visit had been twice postponed. His purpose was to advance practical forms of military-to-military co-operation within the broader framework of U.S.-Vietnam relations, including priority for a full accounting of U.S. servicemen still listed as missing-in-action. In his discussions with his Vietnamese counterpart, Minister Pham Van Tra, Cohen suggested a package of modest proposals including U.S. assistance in disaster management, mine clearance, search and rescue, tropical disease research and archival assistance in locating the remains of Vietnamese soldiers killed during the war. Secretary Cohen made clear, however, that bilateral military relations must be conducted in a "transparent manner" so that there would be "no misunderstanding or miscalculation" by other countries in the region. In an address to Vietnam's National Defense University, however, he stressed the collective muscle of the Association of Southeast Asian Nations (ASEAN) in dealing with China on the issue of conflicting territorial claims in the South China Sea:

One of the very important and beneficial aspects of ASEAN is that you have collective interests, and those collective interests can, in fact, if you act in concert, give considerable leverage in dealing with China in the future on a peaceful and cooperative basis.[15]

Sino-Vietnamese Relations

During 1999, China and Vietnam worked out a so-called "new mechanism" to govern their bilateral relationship in the next century. Agreement was reached during the visit to China by Le Kha Phieu, secretary-general of the VCP in February to March. China and Vietnam reiterated their commitment to set-tling land border and territorial disputes in the Gulf of Tonkin before the end of the year 2000. Bilateral ties were further reinforced in May when Deputy Prime Minister and Politburo member Nguyen Tan Dung journeyed to China to study the applicability of its reform process particularly in the state-owned sector. Dung held talks with his counterpart Vice-Premier Wu Bangguo.

Cross-border relations continue to develop positively despite unconfirmed reports of a small-scale Chinese military incursion in May. The China-Vietnam joint working group on the land border held its fifteenth meeting in Hanoi over a period of four weeks from 22 June to 22 July. Both sides worked hard to reach agreement on seventy-six disputed areas before the end of year dead-line set by their party leaders. China completed its de-mining efforts along the border and postal services between Lang Son province and Guangxi were restored. A border trade fair was successfully held in Guangxi in September, while construction on a bridge across the Nam Thi River between Lao Cai and Kehou commenced. During the third-quarter of the year Vietnam sent delega-tions to China representing the National Assembly, Ho Chi Minh Communist Youth Union, Vietnam Union of Friendship Organizations, and the Vietnam Journalists Association. China, for its part, sent to Vietnam delegations repre-senting the Chinese Communist Party Central Commission for Document Edition and Research and the Chinese People's Political Consultative Confer-ence which attended the fifth congress of the Vietnam Fatherland Front. During September, Vietnam sponsored a number of effusive public ceremonies to mark the fiftieth anniversary of the founding of the People's Republic of China.

Despite the public veneer of increasingly close political relations, underly-ing tensions remained nonetheless. These surfaced later in the year when China reached a trade agreement with the United States. According to one report, the May border incident so angered VCP secretary-general Le Kha Phieu that he argued before a Politburo meeting on 10–11 June that now was the time to make concessions to the United States and reach a final trade agreement. Phieu won over a majority. The Politburo's views were quickly translated into concrete results at the successful eighth round of discussions held in Washington a week later and the breakthrough ninth round of talks in Hanoi the following month.

Yet in September Vietnam balked at signing a bilateral trade agreement with the United States at the eleventh hour. This came amid speculation that Vietnam, which already had serious reservations about the trade agreement's impact on the domestic economy, was waiting for China to reach an accord with the United States first. On 7 October the VCP Politburo reaffirmed its decision to postpone the trade agreement with the United States. Immediately after the meeting, trouble-shooter Pham The Duyet, a member of the Politburo Standing Board, was dispatched to Bejing for discussions with key Chinese officials, Hu Jintao and Li Ruihuan. Both were members of the Chinese Communist Party's Politburo Standing Board. There he learned about Chinese concerns over the proposed text of their draft agreement with the United States which was still in the process of being negotiated. On his return, Duyet reported Chinese reservations to fellow members of the Politburo. This only confirmed their decision to postpone the matter. According to Robert Templer, former Hanoi correspondent for Agence France-Presse:

> If [Vietnam] got a trade agreement with the U.S., they would see that as upstaging China. It's not that China told them not to sign it. It's just that they didn't want to upset China. Vietnam felt it was better to wait until China got its own WTO agreement first.[16]

The draft BTA was the subject to a full review at the Central Committee's eight plenum held in November. This meeting resolved to press the United States to discuss various Vietnamese concerns. Vietnamese leaders were therefore unpleasantly surprised when on 15 November, four days after the meeting adjourned, China and the United States announced agreement on their trade deal. President Tran Duc Luong stated that Hanoi would study the U.S.-China deal. Other Vietnamese officials grumbled about being misled by the Chinese. One source was quoted as stating that Chinese advice could not be trusted again. This set the stage for Premier Zhu Rongji's official visit to Hanoi from 1 to 4 December.

Premier Zhu's visit to Vietnam was the last stop in a four-nation swing which took him to Malaysia, the Philippines, and Singapore. Prior to his arrival in Hanoi, Zhu was explicit in his view that China's entry into the WTO would benefit all of Southeast Asia including Vietnam. Zhu visited Ho Chi Minh City first where he encouraged economic relations with China's southern provinces and cities.

In Hanoi, Zhu had to contend with Vietnamese anxieties about the implications of the U.S.-China trade agreement. Zhu was hosted by his counterpart, Prime Minister Phan Van Khai. After closed-door talks, it was announced that the two leaders had exchanged views on "comprehensive co-operation" in the fields of economics, trade, science and technology, tourism, and culture and education. Zhu promised to promote Chinese investment Vietnam. It was also disclosed that Vietnam's negotiations with the United States on accession to the WTO had been discussed. When asked by reporters for his views, Zhu was rather non-committal. In essence, it was up to the Vietnamese to decide where their best interests lay. Zhu also held substantive discussions with party Secretary-General Le Kha Phieu and former party Secretary-General Do Muoi.

In a major development, both Khai and Zhu announced that negotiators had reached an "important consensus" on a formal land border treaty. They further pledged to conclude their talks on the delineation of the Gulf of Tonkin during the year 2000. On 30 December Chinese Foreign Minister Tang Jiaxuan and Vietnamese Foreign Minister Nguyen Manh Cam signed an historic treaty on the land border in Hanoi.

Other External Relations
This section provides a brief overview of Vietnam's relations with ASEAN members, Japan, Korea, Australia, South Asia, Europe, Cuba, and Latin America.

In December 1998, Vietnam hosted the sixth ASEAN summit in Hanoi. Foreign Minister Nguyen Manh Cam used this opportunity to lobby strongly for Cambodia's admission into ASEAN. ASEAN leaders, however, agreed to admit Cambodia at a later date. On 30 April a ceremony was held in Hanoi to formally welcome Cambodia as ASEAN's tenth member. Immediately after the ASEAN summit, Vietnam received the President of the Philippines, Joseph Estrada, on a two-day official visit. The former President of the Philippines, Fidel Ramos, visited Hanoi in March. The Foreign Minister of Brunei and the Philippine Defense Minister both visited Hanoi in April. In mid-year Thailand and Vietnam held the sixth session of their Joint Commission for Economic Co-operation at ministerial level. On 19 July the commanders of the Thai and Vietnamese navies signed a memorandum of understanding on joint sea patrol in the Gulf of Thailand. Vietnam received an Indonesian parliamentary delegation that same month.

In December 1998 Japan pledged a 102.3 billion yen aid package to Vietnam to assist in developing its infrastructure. Prime Minister Phan Van Khai visited Japan from 28 to 30 March 1999. In discussions Japan pledged more than 10 billion yen in tied loans. Each party extended most-favoured-nation status to the other. In April, in response to a written request from Prime Minister Khai, Japan informed Southeast Asian finance ministers that it would include Vietnam in the US$30 billion Miyazawa Plan. Vietnam was allocated US$160 million in concessional loans under this plan. In January 1999 the Republic of Korea announced that it would provide Vietnam with US$5.3 million in non-refundable development aid that year. In April, South Korea and Vietnam held the fourth meeting of their Joint Economic Co-operation Committee in Hanoi. South Korea is Vietnam's fourth largest foreign investor with 242 projects capitalized at US$3.2 billion. In July, Foreign Affairs and Trade Minister Hong Soon-Young visited Hanoi for discussion on ways to expand bilateral economic ties.

In late January 1999 Deputy Prime Minister and Foreign Minister Nguyen Manh Cam paid an official visit to India to attend the ninth session of the

Intergovernmental Committee for Economic, Cultural, Scientific, and Technical Co-operation. On the eve of his visit it was announced that India and Vietnam had reached agreement on co-operation in nuclear energy. In May, Vietnam received the Foreign Ministers of Bangladesh and Sri Lanka.

In February 1999 Australia and Vietnam held the fifth meeting of their Joint Trade and Economic Co-operation Committee at ministerial level. Vietnam agreed to lift duties that discriminated against Australian dairy exports to Vietnam. Bilateral trade, which grew 39 per cent in 1998, reached US$1 billion for the first time. Prime Minister Phan Van Khai paid an official visit to Australia from 31 March to 3 April. At this time Australia announced it would increase its official development assistance to Vietnam to A$236 million for the 1998–2001 period. A separate agreement on co-operation in education and training was also signed. Prime Minister Khai offered to support Australia's integration in the region.

In January 1999 Germany agreed to swap Vietnam's debt of US$21.6 million for help in providing environmental protection measures. This agreement is a continuation of the Debt for Nature Swap signed in August 1994. In April Foreign Minister Nguyen Manh Cam paid a nine-day working visit to Germany. In June, Germany pledged continued support for a programme to assist Vietnamese people returning home from Germany. In February, the Foreign Minister of Denmark, Niels Helvag Peterson, visited Vietnam and announced his government's contribution of US$111 million for land-mine clearance. A soft loan agreement of US$40 million for the 1999–2000 period was also signed. In March, Britain's Prince Andrew paid a five-day friendship visit to Vietnam to promote trade. Shortly after, a high-ranking Vatican official visited Hanoi to discuss diplomatic relations. In July, France agreed to provide 3.6 million francs as support for the second phase of an aviation security programme. In September Prime Minister Phan Van Khai paid official visits to Sweden, Finland, Norway, and Denmark, where he signed a number of aid agreements.

In February 1999 Vietnam received the Cuban Foreign Minister, and in July Secretary-General Le Kha Phieu and a large party delegation visited Cuba to reaffirm traditional ties. Vietnam and Cuba signed a memorandum of understanding covering Vietnamese rice sales to Cuba for the period 2000–3. The visit was also important for the display of solidarity between the two Third World socialist states.

In January 1999 the President of Tajikistan visited Vietnam and signed five agreements covering investments, and scientific, technical, and economic co-operation. In March, Poland's President Aleksander Kwansniewski ended a ten-year hiatus in relations, with a visit to Hanoi. Two-way trade between these countries was estimated at between US$80 million and US$100 million in 1998. In May, Romania's Foreign Minister visited Hanoi briefly. In June, Vietnam and Belarus held the second meeting of their Intergovernmental Commission for Trade, Economic, Scientific, and Technical Co-operation. Two-way trade is extremely modest, amounting to US$24.3 million in 1998. In July

Vietnamese Defence Minister Pham Van Tra visited Minsk for closed-door discussions on "military-technical co-operation".

In 1999, in a new development, Vietnam dispatched its Deputy Prime Minister and Foreign Minister Nguyen Manh Cam, and Deputy Trade Minister Le Danh Tinh, on a whirlwind tour of South America. During the period 14 to 19 September, Cam visited Argentina, Chile, and Peru to discuss trade and investment opportunities and to study the workings of the Common Market of the South (MERCOSUR). Cam was also interested in exchanging information with Chile and Peru, both APEC members, about oceanography, deep-sea fishing, seafood processing, and the construction of fishing vessels.

Conclusion

Domestic and regional developments in the late 1990s have presented Vietnam with its most difficult set of challenges since the mid-1980s when it embarked on a domestic reform programme known as *doi moi* and an external policy of diversifying and multilateralizing foreign relations. Domestically, Vietnam's leaders are confronted with the difficult choice of determining the pace and scope of reform efforts at a time of great uncertainty caused by the Asian economic crisis. Vietnam's recovery and future development prospects also depend on encouraging foreign direct investment and seeking new markets. Europe and North America have been targeted. The U.S.-Vietnam bilateral trade agreement holds the potential to really open up Vietnam's market and speed not only its membership in the WTO but its economic integration into the global economy.

Vietnam is unable to move decisively forward due to immobilism in its political system. Three countervailing factors have led to policy stalemate — a sincere desire to continue with reform, fear that economic reform will be destabilizing and a perception that Vietnam has weathered the worst of the Asian financial crisis and can continue on its present course.

Vietnamese party conservatives compare calls for *doi moi* II with the "big bang" approach to the reform of socialist economies in Eastern Europe and the Soviet Union. They argue that such policies would only result in internal chaos. Indeed, they argue, especially in light of NATO (North Atlantic Treaty Organization) intervention in Kosovo and the mistaken bombing of the Chinese embassy in Belgrade, that imperialist forces still maintained the objective of overthrowing communist regimes and rolling back socialism. Party conservatives are also extremely reluctant to quickly equitize SOEs for fear of generating unemployment and discontent among their support base. There are considerable vested interests in the present system of SOEs that involve party members at national, provincial, and local levels. Perhaps more importantly, party conservatives are not intellectually or emotionally committed to the development of a free market and the dominance of the private sector. Such reforms would undermine the basis of their power in their view. They seek instead to maintain state control over the economy.

Vietnam's current party leaders see a *doi moi* II as more threatening than the status quo. In fact, they argue that Vietnam has achieved success in maintaining social and political stability and positive growth rates. In their perspective Vietnam's limited integration with the global economy is a blessing in disguise. Because of a weak financial market, the lack of a stock exchange, and the non-convertibility of the *dong*, they argue, Vietnam was spared the worst effects of the regional economic crisis. In brief, the adoption of *doi moi* II would undermine the basis of one-party rule, while the preservation of the status quo offers the possibility of prolonging the party's hegemonic position.

Vietnam's leaders face a difficult choice. They can place a premium on political stability at the expense of urgent economic reforms. This choice may undermine the performance legitimacy of the regime because unaddressed economic reforms will only handicap Vietnam in the future. Or, Vietnam's leaders can embark on fundamental economic reforms, which entail a degree of risk, to ensure that they do not fall further behind as regional states resume economic growth.

Externally, Vietnam faces an ASEAN in considerable disarray due to its untimely enlargement. Politically, ASEAN is divided between its politically open and politically closed states.[17] Economically, the Asian economic crisis has slowed the pace of regional integration and put in doubt the timetable for tariff reductions under the ASEAN Free Trade Agreement (AFTA). Vietnam is formally committed to developing a market-orientated economy albeit under state control, opening up its economy, and integration with the regional and global economy. The Asian financial crisis has raised serious doubts in the minds of some party leaders and they have deliberately slowed the pace and scope of this process. The current picture is a very mixed one as Vietnam tries to insulate itself from the adverse effects of globalization, preserve its national identity, and integrate with a region of great economic and political diversity.

The above developments suggest that the VCP will be preoccupied with internal matters in the buildup to the ninth party congress scheduled for the first quarter of 2001. During this process, party conservatives are likely to be highly sensitive to any loss of control. Not only is there residual distrust of Vietnam's former adversary, the United States, but Vietnam's ideologues are viscerally opposed to the intrusive forces of global capitalism. Party Secretary-General Le Kha Phieu will face mounting pressure from all sides to take action against corrupt high-ranking officials and internal party dissenters. The pace of decision-making is likely to slow. In this climate Vietnam is not expected to embark on any new bold efforts to kick-start a process of *doi moi* II. By maintaining the status quo, however, Vietnam risks being left behind other regional economies as they recover from the Asian economic crisis. Without renewed reform Vietnam's economy could slide into deep recession putting social and political stability at risk.

NOTES

The views expressed in this chapter are the author's and do not reflect the policy or position of the Asia-Pacific Center for Security Studies, the Department of Defense, or the U.S. government.

1. Brantly Womack, "Vietnam in 1996: Reform Immobilism", *Asian Survey* 37, no. 1 (January 1997): 79–87.
2. See remarks by Gerrit Thisses, ABN-AMBRO country manager for Vietnam quoted in Duong Phong, "Growing Need for Doi Moi, Phase Two", *Vietnam Investment Review*, no. 30 (10–16 January 2000), p. 10.
3. Agence France Presse, 15 December 1999.
4. Associated Press, 15 December 1999.
5. Quoted by Agence France Presse, 15 December 1999.
6. Agence France Presse, 15 December 1999.
7. See remarks by Tran Xuan Gia, Minister for Planning and Investment, that "more discussions were needed", quoted by Reuters, 15 December 1999; see also Catherine McKinley, "International Donors Renew Aid to Vietnam, Pledge $2.1 Billion", *Asian Wall Street Journal*, 16 December 1999.
8. "Economic Outlook: Vietnam", Economist Intelligence Unit, 10 January 2000; Deutsche Presse-Agentur, 15 December 1999.
9. David Dapice, "Point of No Return", *Vietnam Business Journal*, February 2000, internet edition, argues: "The two [decline in export-orientated foreign direct investment and official development assistance] contracting together could have a strong and interacting effect, effectively creating an economic crisis."
10. Deutsche Presse-Agentur, 15 December 1999.
11. David Lamb, "Delay Rattles Certainty of U.S.-Vietnam Trade Accord", *Los Angeles Times*, 1 November 1999.
12. Reuters, 11 November 1999.
13. Mark McDonald, "U.S.-Vietnam Trade Deal Could Be Derailed", *San Jose Mercury News*, 28 January 2000.
14. Reuters, 9 March 2000.
15. Quoted in Michael Richardson, "Cohen Urges Hanoi to Help Settle China Sea Dispute", *International Herald Tribune*, 15 March 2000.
16. Sherri Prasso, "Behind Vietnam's Surprise Veto of a U.S. Trade Deal", *Business Week Online*, 15 November 1999.
17. Carlyle A. Thayer, "Reinventing ASEAN: From Constructive Engagement to Flexible Intervention", *Harvard Asia Pacific Review* 3, no. 2 (Spring 1999): 67–70; Thayer, "New Fault Lines in ASEAN?" *Asia-Pacific Defence Reporter* 26, no. 9 (February/March 2000): 26–27; Thayer, "ASEAN Disunity Affects Regional Security", *Asia-Pacific Defence Reporter 1999 Annual Reference Edition* 25, no. 1 (January–February 1999): 11–12.

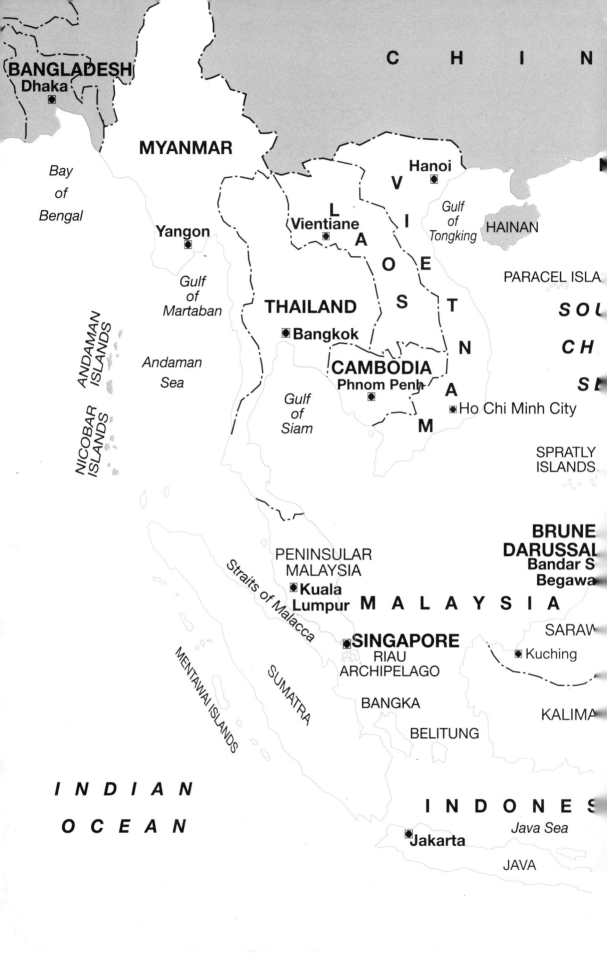